FLEET STREET RADICAL

FLEET STREET RADICAL

A. G. Gardiner and the *Daily News*

STEPHEN KOSS

ARCHON BOOKS
1973

Library of Congress Cataloging in Publication Data

Koss, Stephen E
    Fleet Street radical.

    Bibliography: p.
    1. Gardiner, Alfred George, 1865–1946. 2. The Daily news,
London. I. Title.
PN5123.G28K6   070.5'092'4   72-12884
ISBN 0-208-01312-1

Printed in Great Britain

For Lionel Robbins

Contents

Acknowledgements

It is no exaggeration, however much a commonplace among authors, to say that this book could not have been written without the counsel and cooperation of many individuals.

Acknowledgement is due, and gladly made to the following copyright holders: Sir Richard Acland; Viscount Addison; the Earl Beauchamp; the First Beaverbrook Foundation and the National Library of Wales (Lloyd George papers); Mrs Dorothy Cheston Bennett; Mr Mark Bonham Carter; the British Library of Political and Economic Science (Passfield and Courtney papers); Mr L. J. Cadbury; Dame Sybil Thorndike Casson; Miss D. Collins (G. K. Chesterton papers); Mr Basil Cozens-Hardy; the Earl of Derby; Baron Greenwood of Rossendale; Professor N. G. L. Hammond; Viscount Harcourt; Sir Geoffrey Keynes; Professor Ann K. S. Lambton (Cecil of Chelwood papers); Mr Malcolm MacDonald; Mr David McKenna; Mr A. D. Maclean; Mrs Lucy Masterman; Mr A. M. Pollen; Lord Primrose and the trustees of the National Library of Scotland (Rosebery papers); Professor Joan Robinson (Major-General Sir Frederick Maurice papers); Mr B. Philip Rowntree; Viscount Runciman of Doxford; Mr L. P. Scott; Viscount Simon; the Society of Authors and the Shaw Estate (Bernard Shaw papers); Mr Frank Swinnerton; Viscount Thurso of Ulbster; Dr Arnold Toynbee (Gilbert Murray papers); Sir George Trevelyan; the University of Illinois Library and the Wells Estate (H. G. Wells papers); Mrs P. J. Wheeler (Robert Lynd papers); Mrs R. Wilson Walker (Vivian Phillipps papers); and the Yale University Library (Edward M. House papers). I offer my sincere apologies to anyone whom I was unable either to trace or contact.

The unpublished journals of Arnold Bennett were consulted by permission of the Henry W. and Albert A. Berg Collection, the New York Public Library, Astor, Lenox and Tilden Foundations. Gardiner's correspondence with Mr Frank Swinnerton was obtained by arrangement with Professor Blair Rouse and the University of Arkansas Library.

I enjoyed a long and stimulating conversation, appropriately enough in the smoking room at the Reform Club, with Mr Swinnerton, who afterwards answered many trans-Atlantic queries. I am also grateful for the information and assistance which I have received from Miss Margaret

Ratcliffe, Lord Salter, Mr L. J. Cadbury, Mr John Lehmann, and Mr Arthur Krock.

Mr David Ayerst provided me with materials from the archives of the *Guardian*, of which he is the accomplished 'biographer'. Dr Alan O'Day sent me copies of Gardiner letters among the Runciman papers, which he was then helping to catalogue for the university library at Newcastle upon Tyne. I was assisted in my attempts to track down manuscript collections and copyright holders by Mr Denis Duncan, the former editor of the *British Weekly*, Mr C. A. Seaton, librarian of the *Spectator*, and Mrs Frances Trueman of Messrs A. P. Watt and Son, London. Among the other librarians and archivists who facilitated my research, I should like to make special mention of the following: Miss Judith Schiff of the Yale University Library; Mr George Awdry of the National Liberal Club; Mr D. S. Porter of the Bodleian Library, Oxford; Miss D. Tindall, formerly of the Reform Club; and the staff of the British Museum Newspaper Library at Colindale.

Various friends and colleagues (by no means mutually exclusive categories) read and criticized chapters or groups of chapters: Dr Peter Clarke; Professor Alfred Havighurst; Professor F. M. Leventhal; Professor Robert McCaughey; Dr A. J. A. Morris; and, with characteristic piquancy, Mr A. J. P. Taylor. The entire manuscript was read by Professor Peter Stansky and Mr A. F. Thompson, each of whom made valuable suggestions about content and conception.

The American Philosophic Society supported the project with a grant from its Penrose Fund. Supplementary assistance was received from the Barnard College faculty research fund.

I owe a particular debt of gratitude to the members of the Gardiner family, who placed at my disposal the treasures of their attics and their memories, who urged me to give free expression to my opinions, and who have given me the reward of their friendship. I recall with particular fondness a summer day at Whiteleaf in Buckinghamshire with three of A.G.G.'s daughters – Miss Gwen Gardiner, Miss Phyllis Gardiner, and Mrs Stella Mallon – and a son, Mr Gilbert Gardiner. A fourth daughter, Lady Robbins, and her husband (who is A.G.G.'s surviving literary executor) offered unstinted help and indispensable encouragement. Lord Robbins read successive drafts of the manuscript, rescuing me from several errors of fact while allowing me complete freedom to commit possible errors of judgment. And I must thank Mr Patrick Gardiner, custodian of his grandfather's papers, and his wife, Susan, for their many kindnesses. I hope that the finished product will justify their confidence.

Lastly, I wish to record my deep gratitude to my wife and children, who shared the pleasures, but also the difficulties, of the years in which this book was in preparation. Their collaboration was close and constant, and I thank them for it.

Introduction

Badgered by his friend and publisher, Hugh Dent, A. G. Gardiner, then seventy years old, toyed with the notion of writing his auto-biography. 'But, lord,' he exclaimed in benign exasperation,

the idea of work makes me all of a tremble. I grow lazier & lazier & more content to just sit on the bank & watch the stream of this silly, amusing, fantastic & insane world go by. And to think that there was a time when I used to fancy I was ordained by heaven to keep it in bounds & prevent it from slopping over. Nothing like being an editor for getting [a] swollen head – except sitting on the Treasury bench which is equally fatal to one's sense of proportion.

Three years later, he made another start, and spent a June evening 'burrowing among old papers, letters, articles, &c. that I had not seen for twenty years or more'. By the early hours of the morning, he had 'just surrendered myself to the pleasure of living that old forgotten life over again', and the tome remained unwritten. Finally, in 1941, to appease his Reform Club friends who insisted 'that I had a duty to society to write my reminiscences', he made a last attempt, again un-successful. '. . . I lack the conviction, the assurance & the industry', he apologized. 'But I am making a few notes that may be serviceable to someone else when I have quitted the stage.'[1]

Not that biography was, strictly speaking, any substitute for auto-biography: on that score, Gardiner, who preferred to write the former and read the latter, was most emphatic. At its best, biography was a wholly different genre, with its own perspectives, intentions, and limitations; at its worst, it could be either a wearisome recitation of facts or a precious catalogue of anecdotes. To a greater extent than autobiography, its story ought to transcend the life with which it was immediately concerned. It could not pretend to speak for its subject

1. Gardiner to Frank Swinnerton, 4 September 1936, 6 June 1939, and 16 November 1941, Swinnerton Papers (University of Arkansas Library).

I

or to reveal his innermost feelings. Yet it might manage, as the primary source seldom can, to place its subject objectively in the context of historical events and, in the process, to comment upon those events. 'There are few more agreeable forms of impertinence than to sit in judgment upon other people,' Gardiner reflected. He had learned from his own experience that the most that a biographer can offer his readers is a calculated guess, 'however honest, which is founded upon a few factors in an infinite sum'. And yet such a guess is, in itself, 'a conspicuous public service', for unless it is hazarded, 'we can have no estimate of the values of men', and therefore 'cannot hope to weigh and measure the forces that are shaping events'.[1]

In 1923 Gardiner debated 'The art of biography' at the London School of Economics with Philip Guedalla, who made his reputation with books on Wellington, Palmerston, and Napoleon III. The meeting was chaired by H. H. Asquith, an autobiographer, whose volumes of memoirs were twice as many, twice as heavy, and not half so popular as his wife's. Gardiner gave generously of his advice to any prospective biographers in the audience: Boswell and Carlyle had achieved immortal successes because each of them had been 'friendly' and at all times 'anxious to do his best for his subject'; Lytton Strachey, by contrast, was too concerned with parading his wit and, consequently, never rose above caricature. 'Every biography,' he insisted, 'like every good picture, was a portrait of two persons – the writer and its subject', and in the vast majority of cases, 'it was wise for the . . . biographer to appear as little as possible, definitely and specifically, in person'.[2]

What would Gardiner have expected of his own biographer? Sympathy not so much for himself as for the principles he defended in an age when principles were increasingly a professional liability. There can be no doubt that he would have scorned reverence. As one who fought his own battles, which were contemporary ones, he did not look to posterity for vindication. And as one who welcomed a good argument, even if it rarely changed his mind, he would not have wished to shrink from controversy. Least of all would he have expected to agree with all of his biographer's observations and conclusions. After all, how many subjects find satisfaction with their portraits either on canvas or in print? He kept a collection of letters from

1. *Nation*, 12 November 1921.   2. *Morning Post*, 6 June 1923.

eminent persons who, in fact, complained that they could not see their reflections in the glass he held up to them. 'I am very pleased to be written about by you,' H. G. Wells told him, 'but I confess I don't recognize the portrait; a simple sluggish rather melancholy and timid man is what I am & God knows it anyhow. This Cracker: it isn't me.'[1] Thomas Hardy, 'flattered by the good things you said', nonetheless felt obliged to report that 'friends of mine are protesting against this estimate as preposterous & an utter misrepresentation of character'.[2] And Margot Asquith, who praised his sketches of famous men ('*No* one cd. have written the Baldwin or A. Balfour as you have done'), thought him less successful in his treatment of women, particularly herself: 'Your "Margot" as you call her is a vulgar noisy female . . . who wd. tire the most vital of us & bore the others. . . . I am not the egotistical, noisy, scattered creature you imagine.'[3]

It is to his panoply of character sketches, most of which first appeared in the *Daily News*, that one must look for Gardiner's approach to biography. The three full-scale lives he wrote – George Cadbury, Sir William Harcourt, and John Benn – were commissioned by the respective families who, to one extent or another, exercised an editorial jurisdiction over the finished product. But as the author of his capsule portraits, he was the master of his own pen, penetrating in his insights and bold in his pronouncements. Although the majority of these pieces were unrepentantly partisan, they did not hesitate to record either a noble trait in an adversary or a weakness in an ally. Didactic without being dull, his intention was frankly to instruct, often his subject as well as his readers. By far his most successful efforts were studies of men with whom he enjoyed contact or at least had seen at close range. As time passed, he lost the intimacy with policy-makers upon which his style depended and, if not a keen interest in events, then certainly a sympathy for them. But in the first

1. [September 1912], Gardiner Papers (hereafter cited as G.P.)
2. 17 March 1908 (copy), G.P.
3. 10 and 14 May 1925, G.P. Other ladies were less difficult to please. 'Your article on me last Saturday was so wonderful', Sybil Thorndike wrote (12 February 1926). 'You seemed to understand exactly the sort of technical difficulties I've had in work . . . and it is such a help and encouragement to have a word of real cheer from one whom we admire so much.' And Beatrice Webb was always 'gratified' to reread Gardiner's 'amusing sketch [in the *Daily News*, 25 May 1912] of the old Webbs, before they had reached old age' (15 November 1935).

3

quarter of the century, when he occupied a commanding position, there were few who could equal and none who could surpass him as a judge of public men, their ambitions, their disabilities, and the predicaments that history had assigned to them.

Although he specialized in analysis of character and motive, Gardiner made no pretence to a mastery of psychological theory, about which he did not suppress a mild scepticism. Rather, like William Hazlitt, his assessments were based on 'looks, words, actions'. To a considerable extent, they were also based on his own initial reactions. 'First impressions are often the truest,' Hazlitt had declaimed, 'as we find (not infrequently) to our cost, when we have been wheedled out of them by plausible professions or studied actions.' Gardiner's procedure was first to deliver a verdict and then to proceed to gather the evidence to support it. More remarkable than the alacrity with which he made up his mind was the near inevitability with which time corroborated his views. Rarely was he surprised by the appearance of a virtue for which he had not given credit, and rarer still was he disappointed by the discovery of a serious fault he had not suspected. In the few cases that he was proved grievously mistaken, he reproached himself no less bitterly than he chastised the individual who had betrayed his powers of perception. A man who entered reservedly into friendships, most relaxed in the circle of his own family, he stood somewhat at a distance from his contemporaries, the better to observe their behaviour. It was his ability to recognize and delineate character that brought his greatest success as an editor, a literary critic, a political analyst, and, needless to say, as a biographer. Much of his journalistic output, by its very nature, lost its value with the passing moment; but his celebrated portrait gallery survives as a spendid introduction to the personalities and problems of early twentieth-century English society.

In what substantive ways would this book have differed had Gardiner written it himself? For one thing, it would have provided more extensive discussion of his early years, about which little remains known. The 'few notes' that he bequeathed to his biographer, whoever he might be, recount the same half-dozen anecdotes that he repeated to his children, his friends, and, in semi-fictionalized form, to the readers of his 'Alpha of the Plough' columns in the *Star*. In addition, he presumably would have had more to say about the later decades of his life, about which material is nearly as scarce. After his departure from the *Daily News*, which he had edited for nearly eighteen years, he wrote a regular feature for an American syndicate, and contributed to the *Atlantic Monthly*, the *Nation*, the *Passing Show*, and, weekly for twenty-three years, to *John Bull*. But there is not much else to be said of this coda to his Fleet Street career, when his journalistic activity was largely confined to his study or to the committee room on the Reform Club mezzanine, where he and Hilaire Belloc would scramble for possession of a particular table from which they both drew inspiration.

It is probable that Gardiner, too, would have conceived of the project essentially as an account of his working life, with special emphasis on his connection with the *Daily News* from 1902 to 1921. Not necessarily his happiest years, these were the ones when he had been most actively and meaningfully engaged. The bulk of the material he accumulated, obviously with a view to writing his memoirs, pertains to this period. But even for these years, the records he kept are far from self-sufficient. Like most journalists, he was a poor letter-writer who, if he had something to say, put it directly into print. As one who found it easier to declare himself publicly, he was, by his own admission, 'not a very good hand' at expressing his personal emotions, 'especially when they are the things I most deeply feel'.[1] Relatively few of his letters survive, and these betray the haste with which they were written: succinct to the point of abruptness, they lapse at intervals into an idiosyncratic shorthand. 'I never write a letter of more than four pages (this is one of the few principles I still cling to in a reeling world)', he boasted to his daughter Gwen, who was away at school.[2] But he seldom found occasion to write letters of even this modest length – a page counted as a quarter of a small folded sheet – to his children, who stayed close to home, to his colleagues, whom he saw at the office six days a week, or to his literary and political cronies, with whom he lunched at the Reform Club and gathered afterwards in the 'red corner' of the smoking room. In later years, when he was no longer in circulation, he had ample time to enter into correspondence, but less to say and fewer people to whom he cared to say it. No one amused him more than his friend and

1. Gardiner to his wife, 25 March 1936 (courtesy of Miss Phyllis Gardiner).
2. 21 January 1918 (courtesy of Miss Gwen Gardiner).

neighbour, S. K. Ratcliffe, whose private communications from America were ten times the length of his published dispatches. Gardiner, who had no more patience to read letters than to write them, was glad to welcome Ratcliffe home 'for several reasons, among them that we shall have fewer letters to leave unread'. [1]

Had this been a work of autobiography, memory might well have compensated for the paucity of personal correspondence. But memory is not always a reliable servant, and there are indications that, under the influence of subsequent developments, Gardiner found certain episodes difficult or inconvenient to recall: the disillusionment he suffered during the First World War made him reluctant to publicize his earlier 'pro-German' activities, not that they had been the least indefensible in the circumstances; the furious detestation of Lloyd George with which he emerged from that ordeal was allowed to obscure the intimacy of their earlier collaboration; the ardour of his commitment to Asquith and Grey in the 'twenties induced him to glorify prewar policies of which he had been an outspoken critic; and, at the end of the 'thirties, his hostility to fascism blinded him to the truth that, in his eloquent attacks on the Versailles Treaty, he had helped to foster the spirit of appeasement that he eventually condemned. None of these examples should be taken to imply either disingenuousness or self-delusion. First and foremost a journalist, his primary commitment was always to issues immediately at hand, and he looked on the past as a prelude to the present. Theoretically, at any rate, a historian is equipped to take a longer view and to interpret material in a calmer atmosphere and a better focused light.

Few historians would dispute Gardiner's conviction that an account of his working life deserved to be written, however much they might disagree with his idea of the conclusions to be drawn. Trevor Wilson has cited the press as 'the great untapped source for the writing of recent British political history', [2] and, more recently, his edition of *The Political Diaries of C. P. Scott* (1970) has contributed significantly to our understanding of the men who wielded editorial power. A. M. Gollin has demonstrated what can be done – and, indeed, what remains to be done – by his excellent study of *The Observer and J. L Garvin* (1960). We have biographies, mostly of a depressing quality,

1. Gardiner to Swinnerton, 7 October 1942, Swinnerton Papers.
2. *The Downfall of the Liberal Party, 1914–1935*, preface.

of a variety of Fleet Street figures, as well as an array of memoirs in which gossip crowds out analysis.[1] Although we have become more conscious of the role played by newspapermen in the policy-making process, with few exceptions their personalities remain shadowy, their motives obscure, and their methods of operation a mystery. These men, who acted as the consciences, the partners, and the antagonists of the politicians, who guided public opinion and articulated it, surely have much to tell us about the dominant themes of a crucial period. And yet, as Max Beloff has concluded, 'the documentation of journalists and publicists is . . . very uneven, and only now beginning to be explored'.[2]

The era to which Professor Beloff made specific reference spanned the years from the Diamond Jubilee of 1897, when British self-confidence stood at its zenith, to the Imperial Conference of 1921, an occasion for profound national reappraisal. It was precisely in these years, against a background of cataclysmic change, that A. G. Gardiner attained prominence and enjoyed his greatest popularity. A graduate of the provincial press, he came to London in 1902 to edit with courage and sensitivity the *Daily News*, the best-selling Liberal newspaper and, by contemporary standards, the most fearless. From the autumn of 1919 until the early spring of 1921, he continued his celebrated column for the *Daily News*, after having been made to exchange his editor's chair for a back seat on the board of directors. Beginning in 1915, he also wrote a weekly feature for the *Star* under the pseudonym of 'Alpha of the Plough' (his identity soon became an open secret) in which he mused about the delights of cricket, the perils of bee-keeping, and the majesty of the London sky on a clear winter night. In subtle ways, 'Alpha', too, was a critic of his times, but it was neither his nature nor his purpose to be as emphatic as his alter-ego, 'A.G.G.'

To measure an editor's influence on contemporary opinion and events is never an easy matter. Even where we have reliable circulation

1. A recent exception is A. J. P. Taylor's *Beaverbrook* (1972) which makes clear that, occasional appearances to the contrary notwithstanding, its subject's influence owed surprisingly little to his press connections.
2. *Imperial Sunset*, i, 52. Beloff has assessed one journalist's 'contribution to the formation of the public mind' in his essay, 'Lucien Wolf and the Anglo-Russian Entente 1907–1914', in *The Intellectual in Politics*, pp. 111–42.

figures, we cannot tell how many people read each copy of a news-paper, how carefully, and to what degree they imbibed its message. More often than not, an editor has preached to the converted, only to take or receive credit for the souls he has saved. That Gardiner's pronouncements carried weight is not always as clear as the fact that they were presumed to carry weight by the public figures who peti-tioned for his support and by others who resentfully replied to his criticisms, not daring to allow them to go unanswered. Is there any better index to editorial success?

Always an alert observer of the domestic and diplomatic scene, Gardiner was, in his prime, often a participant and sometimes a catalyst in the events he described. At the beginning of the Second World War, the editor of *John Bull* commended him as 'the man who has always been right', and embarrassingly affixed this label to his by-line. It would, however, be safer to say of him as he said of John Ruskin: 'He was sometimes on the wrong side but he was never on the side of wrong.' His career provides information about the ethics and organization of an industry, secretive by tradition and readier to train its spotlight elsewhere than upon itself. It reveals the participa-tion of the press in the early twentieth-century conflicts between the parties, among party leaders, and, no less frequently, between front-bench policy and back-bench sentiment. It demonstrates in operation the forces that shaped public opinion and then brought it to bear upon governing authorities. It testifies to the Byzantine network of relationships that existed between editors and proprietors, on the one hand, and between them and politicians, on the other. Perhaps most significantly, his experiences help to document the divisions that afflicted the Liberal Party before the war and that soon engulfed it. It was by no means accidental that an editorial career that reflected so faithfully the vicissitudes of Liberalism should be counted among the fatalities of the Liberal collapse.

Gardiner belonged to what has often been designated as a 'golden age' of newspaper editors, probably the last, when the leading dailies were entrusted to men who knew their minds and spoke them with forcefulness and effect. Like the principal members of their staffs, they were sufficiently familiar to their readers to require as identifica-tion only a set of initials, usually three, at the foot of a column. With the possible exception of J. A. Spender of the *Westminster Gazette*, whose clientele was small but select, Gardiner was the most prominent on the Liberal side. C. P. Scott, although indisputably of their rank, was based in Manchester and, in any case, did not appeal in his own name in the manner of the other two. Spender's independence was compromised, at least in Radical eyes, by his intimacy with Asquith and Grey, with whom he shared the Balliol tradition and for whom he was usually an apologist. His writing was less pungent than Gardiner's and, even when his arguments were more logical, they somehow tended to carry less conviction. As a biographer, too, he was less successful, although a good deal more prolific: whereas Gardiner's two-volume life of Sir William Harcourt remains a standard work of its type, Spender's books have either been superseded or largely forgotten. Despite his sharp disagreements with Spender, principally over Liberal foreign policy, Gardiner always respected his integrity and admired his professionalism. In later decades, the two men engaged in a mutual commiseration that brought them closer than they had ever been in happier days, when their party had enjoyed office and they their editorships.

Other important Liberal editors of this period included H. W. Massingham of the weekly *Nation*, Robert Donald of the *Daily Chronicle*, Ernest Parke of the *Star*, and F. W. Hirst of the *Economist*. But the Liberals could claim no monopoly upon editorial talent. The *Observer* and also for a time the *Pall Mall Gazette* provided a platform for J. L. Garvin, who spoke with enormous authority in Tory councils. The *Spectator* was stamped with the personality of John St Loe Strachey; and each to a lesser extent, the *Morning Post* and the *Daily Express* were dominated by H. A. Gwynne and R. D. Blumenfeld respectively. Further down the list, the *National Review* gave vent to the obsessions of its owner–editor, L. J. Maxse, while *John Bull* serviced the ego of Horatio Bottomley. Predictably, *The Times* held aloof from the general trend: its editors, strong personalities in their own right, tended to be governed by the conventions of Printing House Square and, in Lord Northcliffe's time, eclipsed by their proprietor.

The day of the great editors was, almost from its dawn, doomed by 'the inexorable operation of material facts'.[1] Social and political

1. Except where otherwise noted, these paragraphs are based on the following Gardiner writings: 'From the old order to the new', the *Graphic*, 4 October 1919;

factors also combined against it. The franchise and educational reforms of the previous century, following the repeal of stamp duties,
had created a tremendously enlarged reading public, better able to
afford the reduced price of a daily newspaper. But this situation,
which first elevated the status of editors, soon made them pawns in a
fierce competition for sales and advertising revenues. The 'merchant
of ideas', as Gardiner thought of himself, who had formerly served
those principles that he shared with his limited readership, was now
required to appeal more broadly and to satisfy advertisers, who
threatened to transfer their accounts if the circulation dipped or an
editorial grated.

Proprietors, too, changed in spirit and in relation to their editors.
Once silent partners, prepared to sustain financial losses out of
devotion to an ideal, they now aspired to profits, honours, and
authority. Gardiner ascribed this new attitude to the advent of Alfred
Harmsworth, Lord Northcliffe, whose success with the *Daily Mail*
inspired envy and imitation. A friend of Gardiner's, 'one of the most
distinguished of living journalists', reproached Northcliffe for 'taking
the wrong line', and Northcliffe's reply was 'to call for his circulation
ledgers and to show the favourable effect that his policy had had
upon the sale of his journals'. But not even Northcliffe was appeased
by mere financial reward: 'I see my way to getting large circulation,'
he accosted E. T. Cook, 'but how am I to get influence? Tell me that.' [1]

Gardiner was often too quick to blame Northcliffe ('with his eager
interest in the moment, his passion for sensation, his indifference to
ideas, his waywardness, and his dislike of abstract thought') for a
revolution in Fleet Street that was in many ways inevitable. 'English
journalism', as he himself acknowledged,

had, at the end of the nineteenth century, reached a stage in which some
sweeping change was imminent. It had remained essentially what it had
been for more than a century – the vehicle of the thought, the interests and
temper of the leisured and educated middle class, relatively small in numbers but great in influence. Its appeal was sober and restrained, its methods

---

'Two journalists', the *Nineteenth Century and After*, cxi (1932), 247–56; his various
published essays on Lords Northcliffe, Beaverbrook, and Rothermere; and his
letter to H. Cozens-Hardy, 1928?, cited in Pope and others, *The Story of the Star*,
pp. 22–3.
 1. Cited in Gollin, *The Observer and J. L. Garvin*, p. 2.

grave and unadventurous, its spirit dignified even to dulness. The great change that had come over the face of English society in the preceding quarter of a century found little reflection in its character or appeal. . . . The democracy had taken possession of the seats of the mighty, but the journalists seemed unaware of the fact.

It was therefore not the idea of change, but the forms it took that Gardiner deplored. He might have considered that Northcliffe was as much the product as the agent of the new order, that while his success was unprecedented and unparalleled, his most reprehensible qualities were characteristic of a breed that conceived of journalism more as a trade than as a profession. And, as a student of Hazlitt, Gardiner should have known that Northcliffe was not the first proprietor of *The Times* whom one could accuse of invariably enlisting 'on the side of the big battalions'.

Neither his pride nor his sense of propriety would permit Gardiner to acknowledge a modicum of good on the part of the press lords, who run their empires 'with the same material outlook as that with which a brewer runs a brewery', who coerced small independent-minded journals into syndicates with 'multitudinous voices echoing one masterful will', and who, most unpardonably, disrupted parties and toppled governments by their irresponsible intrusions. Although Lord Beaverbrook professed that his object was to free the journalist from an unholy dependence on the politician for 'scraps of information',[1] Gardiner suspected Beaverbrook, as he did Northcliffe and Rothermere, of sinister designs 'to reduce Downing Street to the position of an annexe of Fleet Street'. To his despair, the politicians, insecure and unscrupulous, proved no less eager to barter titles and preferments than proprietors to auction off their support.

Gardiner preferred to identify himself with the older tradition of Delane and Barnes, Morley and Greenwood, and the second John Walter, of whom Lord Melbourne complained, 'the trouble is that the damned fellow wants nothing'. He could recall the days when an editor, who still stood for something, 'was . . . the crown and summit of things – tottering visibly, but still there', when 'the news pages bore the stamp of his mind and went "to bed" like good children before the head of the household sent his Sinaitic page to the foundry'. Before the time had run out on his own editorship, it was already

1. Beaverbrook, *Politicians and the Press*, pp. 9–10.

customary along Fleet Street for editors, after dutifully reciting the proprietor's instructions to their staffs, to head for home 'before the serious business of preparing the headlines begins'. How different things were under Scott, Massingham, Spender, and Parke, 'men . . . in the line of the great founders of journalism, who conceived their calling to be a public trust in the first place, and a commercial enterprise only in the second'. These were men, among whom Gardiner counted himself, who

regarded themselves as the guardians of the public interest against the ambitions of politicians on one side and the hysteria of the mob on the other. Their aim was not to transfer power from Westminster to Fleet Street, nor to make Government subservient to a Press-inspired dementia, but to make Parliament the vehicle of an enlightened and instructed public opinion.

Not surprisingly, the editors who commanded Gardiner's abiding respect sooner or later fell victim to the same forces that evicted him from the *Daily News*. It was H. W. Nevinson's contention that 'all the very best editors' of his lifetime were 'deposed on account of their excellence', and he reckoned that he had served no fewer than seven, Gardiner included, who shared that fate: Parke was encouraged to resign from the *Star* in 1918; Donald was summarily dismissed from the *Daily Chronicle* the following year; Spender left the *Westminster Gazette* in 1922, when it was converted to a morning paper in a last, desperate bid for sales; Massingham was deposed at the *Nation* months before his death in 1924; and H. N. Brailsford was ejected from the *New Leader* two years later. Even the mighty Garvin, whose marathon reign at the *Observer* lasted until 1942, eventually lost the confidence of his proprietor and was turned out to pasture. A controversialist at the helm, once the *sine qua non* of any paper that hoped to make its mark, came to be looked upon as a threat to a paper's reputation and solvency. All the while, rising production costs and increased prices for newsprint brought a wave of mergers and bankruptcies that took a disproportionately heavy toll on Liberal journals, always short of capital and further weakened by their party's decline.

In most cases, these editors were still young, with considerable reserves of talent and fight left in them, when they lost their chairs. Some found places on the weekly journals of political opinion, which have since proved a refuge for the individualists of the profession. Most filled their remaining years with freelance work, which was profitable, but seldom satisfying. Nearly all of them wrote articles, books and memoirs in which they pondered the changes that had overtaken them and the world they had known. Gardiner, who had been unusually young when he first took command at the *Daily News*, was only fifty-four when he surrendered it. But already he could look back on a career as rich and exciting as any about which he himself had written.

1. The making of a journalist

For the benefit of his old friend Frank Swinnerton, who was writing a novel in which the hero was an ambitious young journalist,[1] A. G. Gardiner penned a brief sketch of Fleet Street as he had found it near half a century earlier. His story, a hasty blend of fact and fantasy, was loosely patterned on his own experiences and those of his older brothers. It told of 'Young Nibs', who serves an impatient apprenticeship first in the provinces and then in the London suburbs, both equally removed in spirit from 'the heavens' about which he constantly daydreams. Nibs had made adolescent pilgrimages to the shrines along Bouverie and Tudor streets, which he could recognize at sight from the books he had read, and had visited the Institute of Journalists, of which Gardiner was twice president. In the editorial room of the *Puddleton Herald*, where Nibs was first employed, he had pored over the pages of *Sells Directory*, 'and he could have passed an examination on the population of towns, and the morning, evening, and weekly papers' in each of them. The citadel of the British press, he knows, 'can't be stormed out of hand'; and so he dutifully practises his craft and waits for opportunity to strike. With perseverance, diligence, and a bit of luck, the big moment finally arrives. (Swinnerton was given his choice of two alternative routes up the ladder, 'according to your conception of Young Nibs'.) An article he has written on a local event comes to the attention of the proprietor of the *Daily Spark*, one of 'the Napoleons of Fleet Street', who summons him for an interview the next morning. A top hat perched uneasily upon his head ('top hats survived in 1904') our hero passes muster

1. According to Mr Swinnerton, Gardiner's essay (which exists undated among the Swinnerton Papers) was intended to provide background for the novel *Master Jim Probity* (1952), retitled 'quite inappropriately' by its American publishers *An Affair of Love*. 'The hero of that book was a young journalist,' Mr Swinnerton has recalled. 'I have glanced through it, without discovering what use, if any, I made of A.G.G.'s notes', Swinnerton to the author 20 June 1970.

14

and gets the 'Big job'. By this time, Gardiner reminded Swinnerton, 'the great Northcliffe revolution' had already begun to corrupt the soul of the profession: 'old respectables [were] going to [the] dogs & the era of smart young journalists [had] set in.' But the air of Fleet Street remained bracing, an immense amount of important work was still to be done, and Young Nibs had won the place to which he had long aspired 'among the Olympians'.

The saga was one that Gardiner knew by heart. He had met countless young hopefuls, a few of whom had inspired him by their example, to some of whom he had given assistance and encouragement, and most of whom had waited in vain for recognition and reward. One of them was his brother Arthur, the envy of his youth, whom he eventually outdistanced. Another was himself. There had also been his young colleagues against whom he had raced to file his 'scoops' at Chelmsford or Bournemouth or Blackburn. And a bit later there were those who had been lucky enough to find places on the staffs of the London dailies, some no longer young, but still waiting for the satisfaction of seeing their initials in print. Gardiner could reflect that he had been supremely fortunate: his rise came quickly and it had taken him directly to the top.

In a field dominated by selfmade men, he was more genuinely selfmade than most. But although his greatest admiration was reserved for those who had come up through the ranks, he was jealous neither of youth nor of those who enjoyed advantages that he had been denied. Forced to leave school at fourteen, he lacked a formal education; nonetheless, he managed to acquire a learning rare among the leading Fleet Street figures of his day. 'Show me a man's books and I will tell you his character,' he boasted,[1] and by his own test he qualified as an honorary freeman of the eighteenth century. But his interests were wide, and he read as much for edification as for information. At intervals that became shorter with the passing years, he returned to old favourites to see how well they stood the test of comparison. His pronouncements on literature and history were as authoritative as those on world affairs; and his grasp of political issues was matched by an intricate knowledge of Bach.

In bearing he was distinctly patrician, standing to the full height of his five-feet nine-and-a-half inches, with fine features and a full crop

1. 'Sir Edward Grey', in *Prophets, Priests and Kings*, p. 75.

of hair that began to whiten at an early age. Thomas ('Tom') Jones, introduced to him at the Reform Club in 1916, presumed that Gardiner 'might have some good aristocratic blood in him'.[1] He could not have been more wrong. It was the blue of Gardiner's editorial pencil and not of his blood that was responsible for his confidence, always more professional than personal. To him, journalism was much moιe a public service than a career, Liberalism much more a mission than a party affiliation. He never doubted the righteousness of either his calling or his cause, and what some misjudged as haughtiness or conceit was in fact a reflection of his self-conscious fidelity to a tradition which, he only hoped, he was worthy to defend.

About his early life there is little known and still less that bears retelling. The fly-leaf of a family Bible records the marriage of his parents, both twenty-two years of age, in 1848, and the birth of their eight children over the next seventeen years. Alfred George, born on 2 June 1865, was the youngest. His father, Henry James Gardiner, was a cabinet maker who suffered from unsteady employment and, according to various sources, from frequent recourse to the bottle. His mother, née Susannah Taylor, was the mainstay of the family. A sister died of scarlet fever during an epidemic which her youngest brother, for a time, was not expected to survive. Although he was still writing a weekly column in his eighty-first year, he was at twenty diagnosed for a heart ailment and again told that he had not long to live. Two of his brothers emigrated to the United States. Differences of age and interest, as well as the necessity to take early employment, caused the children gradually to drift apart; by the time his parents died, A.G.G. kept little direct contact with several of them.

When times were particularly bad, Alfred was sent round to the local baker, who hadn't the heart to refuse further credit to so small a boy. He recalled such occasions without shame or resentment, but rather with a certain fondness. The legacy of those years was a life-long aversion to taxicab travel, which he thought a useless extravagance, and a professed devotion to simple ways, at least where his personal comfort was concerned. It was 'the penury of my spirit', and not of his pocketbook, that inspired his thrift, and he facetiously

1. Entry for 7 December 1916, Thomas Jones, *Whitehall Diary*, i, 8. Jones was an academic and civil servant – also a Welshman – whom Lloyd George appointed as deputy secretary to the War Cabinet.

marvelled how Frank Swinnerton, 'a fellow who scratches his living as I do, out of his pen', could indulge himself in 'jolly joy rides' on the Continent. 'I count the twopences that flow from me like gouts of blood', he jested, calculating that each word he wrote was worth two-pence on the market, and that a Riviera holiday would cost so many million words.[1] Yet, as Swinnerton knew as well as anyone, Gardiner was a generous friend, husband, and father, who provided his four daughters as well as his two sons with the best possible education, regardless of expense.

Despite whatever deprivation he may have suffered, his reminis-cences of youth were happy ones. The family house at Chelmsford bustled with activity, and 'on moonless nights when the sky put on a coverlet of high clouds', he could stand in the garden and watch the 'ruddy glow' of London in the distance.[2] His attendance at cricket matches began at a tender age with the discovery that, 'by lying flat on [his] stomach and keeping [his] head very low', he could 'see under the canvas and get a view of the wicket'.[3] So did his passion for books, around which he spun elaborate romances. In his seventy-sixth year, he continued to enjoy vivid memories of

a far-off moment in my own childhood (I suppose at about the age of eight) when under the emotion aroused by a book called *The Story of the Hundred Days*, I decided straightaway to go & enlist in the Black Watch (oh, that glorious name), packed a little bag with a nightshirt & started down the road to the station. On the way it occurred to me that at the station I should have to take a ticket & that a ticket required money which I hadn't got. So I turned back, explained to my mother my intention & asked for the, to me, enormous sum of half a crown for a ticket to Scotland. She was unsympathetic & that adventure ended in tears.[4]

Under the influence of the same swashbuckling story, he fell rap-turously in love with a soldier's daughter, 'frightfully plain, but then, – well, she had come from India'.[5] Six years later, on his fourteenth birthday, he met Ada Claydon, whom he was to marry when he was twenty-two.

1. Gardiner to Swinnerton, 7 February 1926, Swinnerton Papers.
2. 'The future of London', *Daily News*, 1 January 1914.
3. 'W.G.', in *Pebbles on the Shore*, pp. 24–5.
4. Gardiner to Swinnerton, 25 May 1941, Swinnerton Papers.
5. 'On falling in love', in *Pebbles*, pp. 82–3.

At school, he excelled at geometry, for which he was awarded a prize in 1877, and at 'freehand and model drawing'. All his life he practised this latter art in the margins of memoranda, on the backs of envelopes, in the sketches of foreign scenes that illustrated his letters home, and in the portraits that adorned the notes and poems he wrote to his children, especially on their birthdays. But it was another talent that he took more seriously. From the time he had learned to read, he was determined to write: stories, poetry, and articles. Here he had his older brothers to inspire and instruct him. Three, and possibly all four of them, had preceded him to jobs on the *Chelmsford Chronicle*, which became in 1884 the *Essex County Chronicle*, and his earliest ambition was to follow in their footsteps. His brother Arthur took the keenest interest in his development, and A.G.G. recalled him as a formative influence:

> I stood in awe of him not only on account of his years – he was five years my senior – but still more because of the greater exactitude of his mind, his superior will power & a physical courage which I did not share. Our relative qualities in this respect were defined by the nicknames conferred on us at school. He was 'Pug Gardiner': I was 'Pug's brother'. He did the heroic things in the playground, on the river, in the cricket field. I looked on, not I think in envy, but with a sort of reverent admiration. . . . I owed much to him for he led me into the world of books and by his own tastes gave me a sense of the things of the mind. But he was a hard taskmaster. It was his lot to supervise my practice work in journalism & I withered as his scornful pencil scored my 'copy' and reshaped my sentences. Occasionally I broke down under his lash.

When he had had too much and melted into tears, Gardiner remembered with belated gratitude, his brother would scold him ('Don't be an ass!') and they would get on with their work. Arthur won respect not only by the 'severity' with which he 'exercised the authority of an elder brother', but also by the enviable success he enjoyed. One morning, a column from the leader page was cut from the copy of the *Standard* at the family breakfast table, and Alfred, who had suspicions, bought another copy and discovered that the piece in question had been written by his brother, who was too modest to share his fame with the others. A.G.G. described the incident in one of his 'Alpha' columns, disguising the two principals as Jonathan and Geoffrey, and related how the younger, eager 'for adventure of his own', followed the elder's example and 'began to retire to his bedroom early and write long and late'. Finally, he too achieved success, when an essay 'that had grown worn and crumpled by many transits through the post' was accepted by a London editor. [1]

Like Arthur, Alfred compiled a 'quotation book' in which he inscribed passages from his favourite authors (Virgil, Dr Johnson and Robert Louis Stevenson appear most frequently), epigrams, snatches from political speeches, and literary and historical anecdotes. Long afterwards, he continued to make entries and to borrow from its crammed pages for articles. His notebook, gradually expanded into a second and a third, became a quarry of useful material, and he often tapped the same vein more than once, gradually adding his own cuttings to his selections from more eminent sources. His reading, too, was chosen with Arthur's assistance to expand his knowledge and improve his style. He devoured the works of Hazlitt, whose form and temper he strove to emulate, and those of Macaulay, from whom he imbibed a view of history as well as a rhythm of language.

At seventeen years of age and with his father's agreement, Alfred was apprenticed to Frederic Henry Meggy of Chelmsford, who was to instruct him in 'the art of shorthand writing and reporting'. His payment, according to the terms of his indenture contract, appears to have been significantly higher than usual, perhaps because of Meggy's previous experience with Alfred's brothers. In his first year, the boy was to receive weekly wages of ten shillings, which would rise to twelve shillings in the second year and fifteen in the third. Alfred promised in return, among other things, that

he shall not waste the goods of his said Master nor lend them unlawfully to any; [that] he shall not contract matrimony within the said term; [that] he shall not play at unlawful games whereby his said Master may have any loss . . .; [and that] he shall not haunt Taverns or Playhouses nor absent himself from his said Master's service day or night unlawfully. [2]

Meggy's connection with the *Chelmsford Chronicle* is not clear, but his apprentice moved directly to a place on that journal.

1. Autobiographical notes, G.P.; 'A tale of Fleet Street', in *Many Furrows*, pp. 80–3.
2. Agreement dated 26 June 1882, G.P.

Gardiner was still young in years and small in stature when he got his first job. His legs dangling from the tall stool on which he was seated, he submitted to the ordeal of an interview by two heavily bearded gentlemen, the first of whom gravely observed 'He's very small,' to which the second thoughtfully replied 'Yes. He is. . . . But he'll grow.'[1] As a junior reporter, he was out of the office more than in, racing through 'the wilds of Essex' by dog-cart to gather news: 'a petty session at Southminster, a prize giving at Felsted school, a regatta at Maldon, a church festival at Rothings.' It was necessary to obtain the cart hitched to the fastest pony if he was to return first with the story, and his anxiety about outpacing his rivals was exceeded only by his fear of horses. Happily, his command of shorthand allowed him to save precious minutes. He never forgot the perils of the East Anglian country lanes, especially on the night of Guy Fawkes celebrations: it was a world, soon to perish, in which 'travel in the English countryside was much the same as it [had been] in the days of Jane Austen or, for that matter, of the Norman Conquest'.[2]

With little promise of significant advancement at Chelmsford, where he stood perpetually in Arthur's long shadow, he took a similar job with the bi-weekly *Bournemouth Directory*. His lodgings were at a house which also accommodated visitors to the seaside resort. There he met a young lady on holiday with her family who, impressed with his conversation and his scrapbook of cuttings, encouraged him to try for a position on an evening paper that was being set up in her native Blackburn. 'As an experienced & thoroughly qualified reporter, I beg to apply for one of the situations vacant on your staff', he began his letter to T. P. Ritzema, the proprietor of the *Northern Daily Telegraph*:

For five years I was engaged in the literary department of the 'Essex County Chronicle', first as junior reporter and subsequently as assistant sub-editor & reporter. In those capacities I became acquainted with every branch of a journalist's work, and the testimonial which I received from the proprietors of the 'Chronicle', and a copy of which I enclose, will testify to the satisfaction which my services gave them. Since leaving the

1. Frank Swinnerton, *Autobiography*, pp. 309 ff.
2. Autobiographical notes, G.P.

'Chronicle', I have been engaged by Messrs. Mate & Sons as chief reporter for Bournemouth & the surrounding district.

I take a verbatim note, transcribe with rapidity, & condense with discretion. I have had large experience in descriptive writing, and, while on the 'Essex Chronicle', regularly contributed leader notes.

I am twenty-two years of age, unmarried, & a total abstainer. The salary I should imagine would be £2-5 a week. [1]

Ritzema replied affirmatively, apparently not requiring a personal interview, and, early in 1887, Gardiner left Bournemouth after less than a year.

The *Northern Daily Telegraph* was to be his proving ground. He remained a member of its staff for fifteen years, and became the editor of its weekly edition in 1899. Selling for a halfpenny, it had begun publication the October before Gardiner's arrival, boasting in its first issue that its 'politics . . . will be distinctly and thoroughly Liberal. That is a fact which needs no concealment or apology, but must be in itself a recommendation to intelligent readers.' There was at the time no daily newspaper in Lancashire north of Manchester, and none in the area that effectively promoted Liberal interests: Blackburn itself had only weeklies (the *Evening Express* was founded in 1887); at Preston, the *Lancashire Evening Post* got started a few weeks later. 'No pains will be spared', the readers of the *Telegraph* were assured, to make the organ 'a faithful mirror' of national life; and, with a pointed reference to Lord Randolph Churchill's speeches on Tory democracy that week at Bradford, it was specified that these were no 'mere Randolphian promises'.

The founding of the *Telegraph* was the outcome of a bitter conflict among Lancashire Liberals, who were prey to the disputes that had brought down Gladstone's third Government and had divided their party. The new paper was intended to provide a voice for the radical faction, loyal to Gladstone and gathering strength at the expense of Whig traditionalists. It was fervent in its devotion to social reform and to Irish Home Rule, which the presence of great numbers of Irish immigrants made a burning issue in the area. Its appearance touched off a press war not so much with its Tory competitors, who welcomed dissension in the Opposition camp, as with the organs of

1. Gardiner to [Ritzema], 12 September 1886 (copy), G.P.

21

other varieties of Liberalism, who could not forgive its challenge to their monopoly. On 17 December 1887 the owners of the *Telegraph*, calculating that their sale was three times that of the *Evening Post* 'and at least six times that of the local Tory evening sheet', denounced 'the milk-and-water character' of pre-existing Liberal journals, whose failure to service northern Lancashire had allowed populous towns like Preston and Blackburn to become 'bigoted Tory strongholds'.[1]

Gardiner's promotion came as rapidly as the *Telegraph*'s success. Still in his twenties, he became first assistant editor and then chief leader-writer. Without a by-line, he contributed a 'Cyclist's Sketch-book', and, as 'Argus', he wrote numerous travel articles. His news accounts were published anonymously or, simply, 'by a Correspondent'. As 'The Tatler', he wrote literary and art reviews, as well as his first series of biographical sketches. Extended pieces, especially those expressing controversial opinions, occasionally appeared over his own name. And it soon became his regular task to review the year's events in a full-page article each December.

At first glance, one would hardly have expected a young man from the south-east, raised in a background of working-class Toryism and an Anglican to boot, to move comfortably among north country non-conformists. It was, however, in such a milieu that Gardiner found himself at the *Telegraph* in Blackburn and, to no less an extent, at the *Daily News* in London. Ritzema, whom he served in both places, was a Primitive Methodist who, the story was told, tried to drum up sales with the slogan 'Get right with God and read the *Daily News*'.[2] Gardiner, so far as he practised any faith, did so more quietly. It was his custom to pay an annual visit to the local church at Christmas, when he found services an aesthetic experience and an occasion for family gathering. Yet his puritan instincts blended naturally with the evangelical concerns of his employers and colleagues. An enemy of privilege and monopoly, he was as opposed as any nonconformist to the iniquities of an established church; and despite his later fondness

---

1. This view of the Liberal press in the northwest has received support from P. F. Clarke in his masterly study of *Lancashire and the New Liberalism*, where George Toulmin's *Lancashire Evening Post*, the *Telegraph*'s most belligerent rival, is described as having 'preached a rather staid Liberalism of a distinctly Imperialist hue' (pp. 130–1).
2. Wilson Harris, *Life So Far*, p. 81.

for a good glass of wine with a club lunch, his father's negative example left him a confirmed temperance reformer. At Blackburn, where it was estimated that 'one in every thirty-three houses . . . is a public house',[1] he saw an inextricable link between drunkenness, squalor, and Conservatism. 'Slumdom to a man and to a woman is on the side of drink', he wrote in the *Blackburn Weekly Telegraph* on 6 October 1900, 'and therefore on the side of Toryism'. He held himself and, as much as possible, those around him to the highest moral standards, detesting vulgarity and despising corruption. As much as any Methodist, Quaker, or Unitarian, he defined godliness in terms of good works, and might best be described as he described George Jacob Holyoake, an unrepentant atheist, as 'an advocate of the Religion of Usefulness'.

It was common enough, though not entirely fair, for late Victorians to equate Toryism and drink. Conservative politicians, presumably with the brewers in their pockets, showed greater leniency with regard to licensing laws. This was obviously the prime factor in Gardiner's becoming a Liberal, and one of Radical complexion. It is noteworthy that in later life one of his closest friends was Leif Jones, an ardent temperance reformer. There is no evidence that his brothers shared either his politics or his youthful teetotalism. Perhaps, being older, they were less impressed by their father's drinking. Nor was his Liberalism reinforced by his early newspaper connections: the *Chelmsford Chronicle* professed to take an 'independent' line, while the *Bournemouth Directory* described itself as 'neutral'.

A few months short of his twenty-third birthday, Gardiner was sufficiently secure in his position to marry his childhood sweetheart, Ada Claydon. She was the daughter of a gardener, and already twenty-three. Four of their six children were born at Blackburn, where they made a loving home. Shortly before the end of the century, Gardiner assumed the editorship of the *Weekly Telegraph*, continuing to contribute to the daily edition when the subject warranted. Proud of his efforts, he sent a copy of the first number to a former colleague at Chelmsford, who praised the quality of its features, the size and clarity of its type, and its young editor for 'displaying so much energy and ability'.[2] Again, his pieces rarely bore his name and were usually

1. The Bishop of Manchester in 1879, quoted in Clarke, *Lancashire*, p. 34.
2. (?) to Gardiner, 8 October 1899, G.P.

signed 'The Tatler'. With greater frequency, he provided biographical portraits of Blackburn personalities: members of Parliament, aldermen, physicians (including Dr E. S. Morley, John's brother), industrialists, religious leaders, and cricketers. His writing in this period was flavoured with a heavy dose of literary allusions, later reduced to a *soupçon*, and with quotations that were often obtrusive from sources of various as Shakespeare, Molière, and *The Mikado*. The precursors of the superb *Daily News* sketches that he later collected into popular volumes, these early essays in miniature biography were far less successful, perhaps because the local dignitaries about whom he wrote could not sustain either the phrases he lavished upon them or the significance that he perceived in them.

If his *Telegraph* articles failed to meet the high standard that he set for himself in the next century, they nonetheless revealed a considerable talent and pointed to the directions in which it would develop. The essential problem was that he had yet to separate his 'A.G.G.' style, declaratory and combative, from his 'Alpha' style, gentle and discursive. As a result, his descriptive pieces tended to lack spontaneity, his factual accounts to be encumbered with unwieldy metaphors and paeans to nature. Here he exhibited a characteristic that he was quick to perceive in other members of his literary circle: Chesterton, Shaw, and Wells, all of whom prefaced their surnames with a pair of initials, combined antithetical qualities that Gardiner ascribed to each of their respective Christian names. Arnold Bennett, he was fond of recalling, was christened Enoch Arnold Bennett, and Enoch – shy, sensitive, and generous – was 'the sleeping partner in the concern of which his junior, Mr Arnold Bennett, is the brilliant and spectacular head'.[1] So might his friends have observed of him. Not that Alfred and George warred incessantly within his breast, but he alternated periods of serenity, in which he gloried in the continuity of English history and the integrity of English character, with moments of almost morbid apprehension, in which he decried the folly of mankind in general and politicians in particular. This duality manifested itself in two writing styles, each of which detracted from the other and neither of which would realize its potential until it had been distilled.

As always, Gardiner was too concerned with the fate of great issues

1. Certain People of Importance, p. 81.

to engage in idle introspection. His arrival at Blackburn was co-incident with the disruption of the Liberal Party over the Irish question, and the years that followed witnessed a steady deterioration of the Liberal position. The retirement of Gladstone in 1894, al-though long in coming, reduced the party's hopes of recovery and virtually destroyed the chances of legislating Home Rule. It brought to the surface a fissure, which had its origins in the previous decade, between the imperialist wing of the party and the advocates of re-trenchment, fiscal and territorial. Subjected to the strains of prolonged opposition, the Liberals were hopelessly divided over tactics and policy. The breach was widened by the successive imperial controver-sies of the 'nineties, culminating in the Boer War, in which Lord Salisbury's Government enjoyed a large measure of support from the Liberal Imperialists.

Gardiner, who stood firm among the so-called 'Little Englanders' of the party, regarded the nation's imperial escapades as a senseless distraction from domestic needs and an affront to international morality. He was distressed by popular enthusiasm for acts of jingo rapacity, and, still more, by the inability of the Liberal Party, either locally or in Parliament, to mount a counteroffensive. Like most early twentieth-century Liberals, particularly journalists,[1] his allegiances originated in the dark days of the Boer War, when the issues were clear and alignments fast: this fact goes far to explain his reverence for Morley and Harcourt, his inveterate distrust of Asquith and Grey before 1914, and the remorselessness with which he later turned against Lloyd George, his fellow 'pro-Boer' who betrayed the prin-ciples of their common struggle.

Blackburn, although it proudly counted John Morley among its native sons, had a history of dogged resistance to the Liberal cause; indeed, its voters had rejected Morley himself in 1868. In the face of certain defeat, the party did not field candidates for the two Black-burn seats in the 'khaki' election of 1900, when Joseph Chamberlain mischievously taunted that 'a seat lost to the Government is a seat gained (or sold) to the Boers'. Yet the contest did not pass without excitement. The challenge to the Tory ascendancy came from Philip Snowden, a newcomer, who stood as a socialist and, notwithstanding,

1. Trevor Wilson makes this point about C. P. Scott: *The Political Diaries of C. P. Scott*, pp. 28–9.

received Gardiner's warm endorsement. Such a candidacy was as yet a rare occurrence, for which enthusiastic Liberal support was unusual. In this respect, Gardiner anticipated the policy of Lib–Lab accommodation that his party's national executive was to adopt three years later. [1] There was never any hope that Snowden, in 1900, would amass sufficient votes to unseat either of the Tory incumbents, but his poll was incomparably better than any Liberal candidate could have managed and (owing partly to the fact that Blackburn was a double member constituency) larger than any hitherto achieved elsewhere by an independent Labour candidate. Snowden's candidacy revived political opposition in the constituency, paved the way for his victory in 1906, and launched an impressive career. Gardiner, his pen ignited, distinguished himself as a doughty fighter and a brilliant polemicist. [2]

From the first, Gardiner was resigned to the fact that Blackburn, true to its colours, would chose 'the mild aperient of Toryism'. Nor, as Snowden's ministerial performances of the 'twenties were to show, was he at all mistaken in his appraisal of the candidate, whom he regarded as more the champion of an abused Radicalism than the exponent of an abstract socialism. He admired Snowden's moral fervour and celebrated the 1900 campaign as 'one of the most memorable events in the history of Blackburn. I can compare it to nothing but those tides of spiritual revivalism that periodically sweep over the land', he told his readers:

> He [Snowden] came without friends, without money, without prestige, without organisation. In a word, he had no stock-in-trade but himself. . . . At a time when official Liberalism had thrown in the sponge . . ., when 'khaki' was in full blood – at such a time it seemed nothing short of impertinence for a stranger from Keighley, young, poor, unsupported by wealth or influence, to fling himself into the arena, and challenge the inevitable. [3]

1. See Bealey and Pelling, *Labour and Politics*, pp. 298–9.
2. Snowden's biographer acknowledges the valuable support received from Gardiner, 'a journalist of genius': Colin Cross, *Philip Snowden*, pp. 51–2; see also P. F. Clarke, 'British politics and Blackburn politics, 1900–1910', *The Historical Journal*, xii (1969), 302–27.
3. See particularly Gardiner's columns (as 'The Tatler') in the *Northern Daily Telegraph*, 15, 29 September and 5 October 1900.

With good reason, political events were accorded special promin- ence when Gardiner came to publish his diary for 1900, a year 'as full of movement and incident as a dime novel'. Snowden, and the issues he had raised, had left the people of Blackburn

wiser and a good deal sadder. . . . We do not want to sing Jingo ballads. . . . We have begun to realise the cost of our picnic to Pretoria – that picnic which was to end with a display of fireworks by Christmas, 1899, and which is still in progress; which was to be accomplished by 50,000 men, and is still employing a quarter of a million; which was to cost ten millions of money, and has already cost a hundred millions; which was to settle every- thing, and has settled nothing, but has raised up for us an 'Ireland over the sea'.

Although this feature was his annual assignment, never before had he composed it with such pungency or managed so well to identify local developments with national trends. Pointing to cutbacks in cotton manufacture and the loss of wages the previous January, when a holiday had been declared to commemorate the departure of local volunteers, he concluded that 'the district has contributed its share in blood and treasure' to the South African 'tragedy'. His review of the next twelve months was even more bleak: 1901 had brought the 'sorrow' of Queen Victoria's death, but no relief from the misfortunes of the Boer War. The census had revealed a drop in Blackburn's population, the Blakewater had overflowed its banks into the town, and the decline of the cotton industry had remained unchecked. 'Taxa- tion has enormously increased, while, on the other hand, the trade returns of the year have been distinctly on the down grade, and the United States have suddenly revealed their stupendous possibilities as commercial rivals.' The future belonged to those nations that invested in education, not to those that dissipated their resources upon farflung adventures.

Always inclined to see problems in a political light, Gardiner ascribed Britain's plight at the turn of the century to a Tory Parlia- ment, dominated by agents of 'wealth and privilege' and insensitive to enlightened opinion. On 18 January 1902, in one of his last leaders before leaving Blackburn for London, he attempted to awake the electors of Lancashire to their true interests:

When the weavers of Blackburn are called upon to elect representatives they send two cotton manufacturers to plead the cause of the operative. When the weavers and iron-workers of Accrington want a member to explain their needs they send a lawyer. When the operatives of Darwen seek a spokesman they choose a brewer. The weavers of Preston elect a coalowner and an offspring of a great brewing-house; those of Nelson and Clitheroe, a landowner; those of Chorley, the son of a peer; and so on. . . . Why, in short, should Parliament be the perquisite of money and not of men, of property and not of poverty?

The payment of salaries to members would allow men of modest means to sit in Parliament, and thereby render that body more truly representative of the nation. But what was needed was nothing less than a greater self-consciousness on the part of voters, who too often continued to defer to their social superiors, a greater spirit of service and sacrifice on the part of MPs, who too often appealed to the worst in national instincts, and a greater vigilance on the part of an independent and responsible press. To these ends, he dedicated his career.

Gardiner was justly confident that his efforts at Blackburn were not in vain. Although the constituency's two seats remained in Tory hands, the Liberals had registered encouraging gains in recent municipal elections. And there was comforting evidence that a reaction had set in, especially among church and labour groups, against the Government's South African policies. His young family gave him inestimable pleasure, and he enjoyed the company of colleagues and neighbours. As time passed he assumed an active role in the cultural as well as the political life of the community. To the Blackburn Literary Club, he lectured on 'Contrasts in English prose', choosing his examples from an assortment of his favourites: Bacon, Addison, Johnson, Ruskin, Carlyle, Stevenson, and 'one of Blackburn's most distinguished sons – Mr John Morley'. To a similar group at nearby Darwen, he delivered a talk on 'Jack Falstaff'. The first of several portraits he wrote of Thomas Hardy, with whom he shared 2 June as a birthday, initiated a long and affectionate correspondence between them.

In short, he had put down roots in Lancashire by the time he was called to London to fill the vacancy at the *Daily News*. Of course, like every self-respecting provincial editor, he had pictured himself seated behind a Fleet Street desk, but at thirty-six, he was too young to have anticipated the prize that fell to him. There is no evidence that, at this juncture, he was seeking either a wider audience or a more prominent platform. Yet the cause he served had too desperate a need for his talents to allow him to continue on the sidelines.

Young Nibs had arrived among the Olympians.

2. The *Daily News* changes hands

The events that brought A. G. Gardiner to London were the product of new forces, as yet barely perceptible to contemporaries, in the world of journalism and public affairs. An index to the state of political parties and popular opinion, the palace revolution that occurred at the *Daily News* office in Bouverie Street made a significant contribution to the Liberal recovery of which it was itself a portent.

Party organizations, the feuding factions within them, and often individual leaders, placed great store – and rightly so – on having at their disposal a London daily to propagate their views in the country and to bring more subtle pressures to bear on colleagues and opponents at Westminster. The time had passed, however, when a new metropolitan newspaper, particularly one propounding Radical or progressive views, could muster sufficient capital, confidence, and sales to compete in an arena where, for reasons of prestige no less than economy, space was limited and rivalry intense. Not, in fact, since 1888, when T. P. O'Connor recruited capital of £48,000 to launch the *Star*, had a Radical paper made a successful debut, achieving for itself both an identity and a healthy circulation. True, eight years later the future Lord Northcliffe founded his phenomenally successful *Daily Mail* with a mere £15,000, but the *Mail* was designed to yield dividends, not influence, and its proprietor had to acquire other established properties to exercise the 'public power' that he craved. [1] By the turn of the century, the price of creating a new political organ was, by most standards, prohibitive; and, in any event, it was better tactics to capture control of an existing newspaper that came equipped with a functioning plant and staff, an element of tradition, and, it was hoped, a loyal readership.

No less fierce than the competition among newspapers, even those professing allegiance to the same party, was the competition that invariably arose for control of editorial policy. It was a struggle that

1. Gollin, *The Observer and J. L. Garvin*, p. 8.

had profoundly unsettling effects in Fleet Street, persisting throughout the time of Gardiner's *Daily News* tenure and ending only after the First World War, with the wholesale amalgamation of newspapers and the consequent growth of syndicates. Reflecting the political turmoil and acrimonies of the period, there was a feverish scramble for investors, a more vigorous assertion of proprietary rights, and frequent exchanges of editorial chairs. Economic and personal factors certainly played a part, but the underlying cause of the situation was a new relationship between politicians and the press, more intimate and farreaching in the early decades of the twentieth century than at any time before or since. These were the conditions under which Gardiner arrived at the *Daily News* in 1902, under which he laboured for seventeen years, and, finally, under which he was eventually relieved of his command.

The Boer War, which intensified the distress of the post-Gladstonian Liberal Party, completed the process of solidifying the Unionist alliance first forged in 1886. Popular opinion, at least as measured by its more vocal elements, gave eager support to Lord Salisbury's Government and to its military operations in South Africa. Sir Henry Campbell-Bannerman, his leadership of the Opposition accepted grudgingly, if at all, by some of the most prominent names in his own party, could derive scant satisfaction from the London press. Nor for that matter could the majority of Liberal backbenchers, his followers, who opposed the war on moral, economic, and diverse other grounds. The party savagely divided, the newspapers on which it had customarily relied tended to throw in their lot with the Liberal Imperialist dissidents, more critical of Campbell-Bannerman than of Unionist policy. Anti-jingo, let alone 'pro-Boer' views, were as under-represented in the press as in the House of Commons. Unionist journals, as one might expect, stood firm in support of the Government and the war, with even the *Spectator*, the highminded weekly that so often diverged from the official path, assuming an orthodox position. The most that Liberal editors seemed disposed to attempt was a cautious disapproval of the conduct of the war; they did not dare to question its origins or condemn its nature for fear that they might cast doubts on their patriotism and their party's fitness to govern an empire.

Newspaper proprietors, with a natural regard for sales and

advertising revenues, took a more timid approach than editors. In 1899 H. W. Massingham quit the editorship of the *Daily Chronicle*, taking with him Harold Spender and Vaughan Nash, sooner than obey instructions to desist in his 'pro-Boer' pronouncements; the three were eventually to find places with Gardiner on the *Daily News*. But at this juncture the *Daily News* was hardly a haven for critics of the Government or the war. Edited by E. T. (later Sir Edward) Cook, who, until 1896, had taken charge of the *Westminster Gazette*, it identified the war as a crusade for fundamentally Liberal principles and tactlessly reminded its readers that Sir Alfred (later Viscount) Milner, high commissioner in South Africa and the *bête-noire* of the 'pro-Boers', had Liberal credentials.

Under these circumstances, the *Westminster Gazette* was not much help. It had been founded in 1893 by Sir Frank Newnes, whose properties included the vastly more popular *Tit-Bits*, and whose *Daily Courier*, started in 1896 as a further service to the Liberal party, proved a quick failure. The *Westminister*, intended by its sponsors to fill the void among evening newspapers left by the defection of the *Pall Mall Gazette* from the Liberal camp, was distinguished by its effective use of photographs and cartoons, the high tone of its editorial comment and literary criticism, and, not least, by the green stock (Gladstone had personally approved the colour) on which it was printed. *Punch* good-naturedly christened it 'the pea-green incorruptible'. With Cook's departure, the *Westminster* passed to the mild and thoughtful J. A. Spender, Harold's better-known brother, who, working intently for a restoration of Liberal unity, thought it prudent to say as little as possible about the imperial issues that racked the party. Besides, Spender's close affiliation with members of the Liberal Imperialist circle precluded any strong criticism of the war on his part. Despite the esteem in which it was held, the *Westminster Gazette* never built its circulation beyond 27,000 copies and, by Spender's calculation, its successive proprietors sustained losses totalling more than half a million sterling. As one historian of the British press has remarked, 'in the age of Northcliffe there were not many to be found to buy a paper which offered prizes for Greek and Latin verse'. [1]

The *Daily News*, the *Daily Chronicle*, and the *Westminster Gazette*,

1. Kurt von Stutterheim, *The Press in England*, p. 99.

not a money-maker among them and each in its way deficient as an opposition organ, virtually held the field to themselves. The *Morning Leader* (which was to merge with the *Daily News* in 1912) and the *Star* were both loyal to Campbell-Bannerman, but they carried little weight in party councils and less beyond. The *Speaker*, a weekly forum for Radical opinion that was founded in 1890, had remained true to its colours, but its circulation had always been pitiably small and its financial losses staggering. In 1899, with the retirement of Sir Wemyss Reid, its original editor, Sir John Brunner, its proprietor, was relieved to hand its modest resources over to a group of younger Liberals, J. L. Hammond chief among them. But the *Speaker* did not survive long into the new century and in 1907 it was refloated as the *Nation* under Massingham's editorship. Finally, there was the *Manchester Guardian*, which was never to be discounted. Edited by the redoubtable C. P. Scott, it made 'righteousness readable', as Lord Robert Cecil nicely put it, and maintained an implacable opposition to the war. Pre-eminent among provincial newspapers, it was by base and focus provincial nonetheless.

The *Daily News*, its editorial vagaries notwithstanding, was regarded as the chief organ of the Liberal Party. Indeed, it advertised itself as the largest selling Liberal newspaper in the world, a sad commentary on Liberal fortunes. Its first issue had appeared in January 1846, ten years after the stamp tax on newspapers was reduced from fourpence to a penny and eleven years before this controversial surcharge was entirely abolished. The new publication and its friends led the campaign to repeal this 'tax on knowledge': 'So long as this penny lasts,' Richard Cobden declared in 1850, 'there can be no daily Press for the middle or working classes; who below the rank of a merchant or a wholesale dealer can afford to take in a daily paper at fivepence [then the price of the *Daily News*]?'[1] Dedicated to Cobdenite principles of Free Trade and social justice, the *Daily News* was concerned from the start with reaching the widest possible audience, not to increase its profits, but to disseminate its message.

As no subsequent editor was ever permitted to forget, the first occupant of the big chair at the *Daily News* was Charles Dickens, who remained barely long enough to enunciate the paper's creed:

1. Quoted in Kennedy Jones, *Fleet Street and Downing Street*, p. 89.

'The Principles of the *Daily News*', he proclaimed on the first day of publication, 'will be Principles of Progress and Improvement; of Education, Civil and Religious Liberty, and Equal Legislation. . . . It will be no part of our function to widen any breach between Employers and Employed; but it will rather be our effort to show . . . their mutual dependence.' After twenty-six days and seventeen issues, Dickens abruptly terminated his editorship, which he looked back upon as a 'brief mistake' he had made. Yet his successors dutifully invoked his memory and drew inspiration from him, much as writers for the *Pall Mall Gazette* were flattered to contemplate their Thackerayan tradition. Gardiner felt a particular affinity for Dickens in matters of social conscience and literary taste, and the stenographic skills that they shared.

At the time of its first appearance, the *Daily News* provided stiff competition for the established London dailies. By 1854 it ranked third in sales, although its circulation of 53,000 was a tenth that of *The Times*, against which it bravely pitted itself. Within a year it was also eclipsed by the *Daily Telegraph*, reinvigorated by the ownership of Jacob Moses Levy. Dickens had been succeeded as editor by John Forster, his friend and biographer, but the editor most responsible for the paper's early success was Frederick Knight Hunt, who combined political courage and an ability to recruit talent. It was during Hunt's brief tenure, which ended in 1855 with his premature death, that Harriet Martineau began her long and productive affiliation with the *Daily News*. Gardiner proudly reckoned that she had contributed some 1600 pieces, of which a good number had been attacks upon 'that rotten oracle', *The Times*.

Throughout the second half of the century, the *Daily News* consistently distinguished itself by its adherence to the principles of an advanced Liberalism. Without deference to vested interests, it championed such causes as Italian unification, the anti-slave side in the American civil war, the crusade against the 'unspeakable Turk', and the campaign against privilege and monopoly at home. In 1868 its price was reduced to a penny, and, under Sir John Robinson's expert stewardship, its circulation trebled to 150,000. Archibald Forbes's dispatches from the battlefields of the Franco–Prussian war followed in the tradition of Russell's from the Crimea. In the 1870s the paper was stamped with the personality of its editor, Frank Hill, to whom T. P. O'Connor paid tribute as 'a very brilliant and very cynical and rather saturnine figure' who was, most of all, a devoted Gladstonian.[1] There were even occasions when the *Daily News*, under Hill's direction, went so far as to upbraid Gladstone for backsliding in a Whiggish direction and for paying insufficient regard to Gladstonian ideals. After Gladstone resigned in 1874, he complained to his brother that a 'popular class of independent Liberals, who have been represented by the *Daily News*', had been 'one main cause of the weakness' of his late Government: 'We have never recovered from the blow which they helped to strike on the Irish Education Bill.'[2] The *Daily News* therefore boasted a tradition, of which Gardiner was acutely conscious, of stopping at nothing to return errant Liberals to the cardinal tenets of their faith.

The paper was celebrating its jubilee in 1896, when E. T. Cook accepted the proprietors' invitation to transfer his services from the *Westminster Gazette*.[3] He considered the move 'professionally a promotion', and was especially grateful for the opportunity to give freer expression to his personal views. Among the directors, Arnold Morley, a former Liberal chief whip, was said to have been intrumental in securing Cook's appointment. Under new management, the paper quickly attuned itself to the imperial ideas that were gaining currency in the country and that were advanced within the party by Lord Rosebery, who had briefly succeeded Gladstone in the premiership and who, until the autumn of 1896, led the Liberals in opposition. Although Cook successfully recharted the paper's basic policies, he was not sufficiently strong to effect a purge of the staff he had inherited, and had to tolerate as his leader-writer Herbert Paul, an intrepid Little Englander whom he regarded as a 'thorn in the side' and with whom he inevitably disagreed on the crucial issues of the day. The editorial office in Bouverie Street had become a microcosm of the Liberal Party, experiencing a temporary triumph of imperialist doctrines in the face of bitter resistance from entrenched traditionalists.

Cook's advent had no obvious effect on the paper's circulation

1. *Memoirs of an Old Parliamentarian*, i, 51.
2. Gladstone to Robertson Gladstone, 6 February 1874, quoted in Morley, *Life of Gladstone*, ii, 495.
3. J. Saxon Mills, *Sir Edward Cook*, pp. 157 ff.

figures, which declined continuously during the 1890s and reached the low point of 55,969 in 1899. Cook's admirers assigned him credit for the fact that the trend was modestly reversed in 1900, when the *Daily News*, outspokenly imperialist, achieved sales of 61,000. In point of fact, there was no dramatic rise until 1904, when a reduction in price to a halfpenny rendered the *News*, like the *Daily Chronicle*, more competitive with the *Daily Mail*. Nor is Cook entitled to the encomiums he received from some quarters for keeping 'the party from becoming a "Kruger clique"'. It is more than doubtful that he changed the minds of many who thought the cause of the Transvaal president more noble than that of the British colonial secretary. On the contrary, Cook exacerbated tensions and widened the breach between the wings of the Liberal Party by his exculpation of Chamberlain, his professions of brotherhood with the Uitlanders, and his extravagant tributes to Milner and Kitchener. Most conspicuously, he contributed to the atmosphere of suspicion and intrigue by maintaining an allegiance to Lord Rosebery, whose band of followers refused to accept as final his formal renunciation of the Liberal leadership. Sir William Harcourt, Rosebery's longtime rival and the *de facto* heir to his unenviable legacy, dubbed the editor of the *Daily News* 'Cook of Berkeley Square', a reference to Rosebery's London address, where Liberal Imperialists allegedly caballed. Campbell-Bannerman, whom the members of the parliamentary Liberal party elected to succeed Harcourt in 1899, when the latter had had enough of a thankless task, was known to harbour similar sentiments.

For the party's official leadership, which was attempting to negotiate a course between the two extremist positions, the shabby treatment it received in its own press was not only embarrassing but also debilitating. Harold Spender, who was biding his time on the *Manchester Guardian*, found the situation 'pretty desperate'.[1] Others, better placed within the party, shared his concern and took particular offence at the way that Liberal editors slanted their comment and coverage in Lord Rosebery's favour. Typical was the treatment accorded a conciliatory speech that Campbell-Bannerman delivered at Dundee in November 1900. 'Your statement as regards Lord R. was perfectly reasonable and candid', J. Emmott Barlow, Liberal M.P. for Frome, assured his chief. 'What is to be done with the Daily News!

1. *The Fire of Life*, p. 107.

We cannot go on with such a paper as our official organ. It does a great deal more harm than good.'[1] Campbell-Bannerman, who took press abuse in his stride, was soon moved to admit confidentially to J. A. Spender that 'the tone of the Times and other papers' had done the party no good: 'I am not very thin-skinned, & I confess it is rather contempt than resentment that their silly facetiousness excites in me.'[2]

Many were convinced, some with heavy hearts, that the solution to the party's problems was to be found in Lord Rosebery's return to the leadership. Leicester Harmsworth, who sat for Caithness as a Liberal, pulled no punches when he called on Campbell-Bannerman on 22 November 1900. He implored Sir Henry to step aside for Rosebery, and tellingly argued that when he had urged his brother Alfred, proprietor of the *Daily Mail*, 'to join the Liberal Party & carry his paper (1,400,000 circulation) with him', the elder Harmsworth had asked 'how could he, to a disunited party?'[3] Campbell-Bannerman, never easily intimidated, counted among his loyal supporters men with ample means to effect more acceptable remedies.

The Liberal Party, its ranks thinned of wealthy landowners by the Whig exodus of the 1880s, was nonetheless well stocked with men of commerce and industry who might, collectively if not singlehandedly, subscribe the capital to launch a new party newspaper. The overriding difficulty was that these plutocrats, even those who agreed in their opposition to the war, were diverse in their backgrounds and often idiosyncratic in the causes they chose to embrace: Irish Home Rule, disestablishment, temperance reform, abolition of the House of Lords, the eight-hour day, to name a few of the most obvious and the most dignified. Each potential contributor demanded assurances that a new journal would back his particular hobbyhorse, which made proceedings difficult. Corrie Grant, who continued his active service to the party after his retirement from the House, was responsible for

1. Barlow to Campbell-Bannerman, 18 November 1900, Campbell-Bannerman Papers, Add. MSS 41,236, fol. 24.

2. Campbell-Bannerman to Spender, 16 May 1901, Spender Papers, Add. MSS 46,388, fol. 6.

3. Memorandum by Campbell-Bannerman, 22 November 1900, Campbell-Bannerman Papers, 2nd ser., Add. MSS 52,517 (provisional). This was a generous estimate of the *Mail's* circulation in 1900, which has been put elsewhere at 989,255: Stutterheim, p. 69.

recruiting support and soon found himself hopelessly entangled in the strings that were attached to the pledges he received. By the end of 1900 it was decided to seek control of an existing newspaper, which would require less capital and consequently fewer benefactors. Even so, the essential problem was not averted.

It was no secret that the *Daily News*, like so many Fleet Street properties, was in difficult financial straits.[1] That was not in itself to imply that the paper stood in danger of closure. Harold Spender traced the predicament as far back as 1873, when Henry Labouchere, the fiery Radical, 'had avenged himself on Mr Gladstone . . . for refusing him office by selling out the whole of his shares in that great paper', leaving it 'starved . . . of capital'. Since that time, proprietors had come and gone, prepared to sustain losses for the sake of the party and never pleasantly surprised to the contrary. They had not minded so long as there had been the compensation of electoral gains and some confidence in the future of Liberalism. Now, in the Boer War period, the sacrifice no longer seemed justified: it was a long time since the party had enjoyed office, longer still since it had commanded a comfortable majority, and the prospects were not remotely encouraging.

It was not so much a matter of the paper's shaky finances, hardly a new situation, as the growing despondency on the part of its owners that precipitated a complete change of control at the end of 1900. At least one of them, Lord Ashton, seriously disputed the editor's imperialist arguments, and saw no reason to continue his support. Others, including Henry Oppenheim, backed Cook but thought the costs disproportionate to the results. Even Arnold Morley, confronted with further opposition from members of his family, lost heart. Ashton's 'violent pro-Boerism made the continuation of present conditions impossible', he notified Cook on 12 December; the *Daily News* was 'losing money and he wanted to be quit of the whole thing'.

1. The most ample account of the purchase of the *Daily News* appears in W. T. Stead's *Review of Reviews*, xxiii (1901), pp. 147–53. Further information can be found in the following: Harold Spender's memoirs, *The Fire of Life*, pp. 107–13; Spender's biography of Lloyd George, *The Prime Minister*, p. 121; J. Saxon Mills's life of *Sir Edward Cook*, pp. 192–6, which quotes extensively from Cook's diary; Archibald Marshall's memoirs, *Out and About*, pp. 74 ff.; and G. K. Chesterton's *Autobiography*, p. 120.

It was David Lloyd George, revealing a genius for tactics that were later to be synonymous with his name, who engineered the takeover. Discerning that the proprietors might be persuaded to divest themselves of a burden over which they were in conflict, he wrote 'two very careful letters' (which he read to Harold Spender over dinner at Gatti's) to George Cadbury and Franklin Thomasson, two rich Liberal businessmen, each of whom agreed to subscribe to the venture. Others provided smaller amounts or, like John Morley, purchased debentures. With adequate capital in hand, negotiations were opened. [1]

Arnold Morley, who never doubted the uses to which the Lloyd George syndicate intended to put the *Daily News*, described the prospective owners to Cook as 'men with whom you will not be able to work'. From another sympathetic proprietor Cook heard that the bidders were 'extreme men', who had announced that they would retain Herbert Paul but appoint a new editor. By the last day of the year, the deal had gone through, and Lloyd George declared that henceforth the *Daily News* would 'take a neutral line on the war'. Cook, whom no one could expect to swallow such medicine, wrote in his diary that he 'could not on any account do [the] trimming' for men whom he considered the agents of all that was most mischievous. He went down fighting, declaring in his farewell leader on 10 January that the 'object' of the *Daily News* under his editorship had been 'to keep steadily in view the larger interests and duties of the country as an Imperial power, and to sink, in some measure, mere party considerations in the face of national emergencies'. The leading Liberal Imperialists sent him letters of mutual commiseration, and Rosebery, writing to another lieutenant, admitted that 'the cause has received a great blow. . . . We shall now have a Liberalism preached from the

---

1. According to Harold Spender, whose account suffers from various inaccuracies, Cadbury and Thomasson each put up £25,000. Cadbury, however, told C. P. Scott that the sum was £20,000 each, with £35,000 from other proprietors and £40,000 raised by the sale of debentures. Cadbury to Scott, 1 January 1902 (copy), *Guardian* Archives. R. C. Lehmann, among the new proprietors, wrote to his wife on 8 January 1901: 'Yesterday we met at the office of the D.N. solicitor and agreed with the other side on a price for the goodwill of the D.N. They asked £50,000; we offered £40,000 – and eventually the difference was split at £45,000, a very good bargain for us I am sure': Lehmann Papers.

old Liberal pulpit which will alienate every sane man in the country.'[1] The other side was correspondingly jubilant. F. W. Hirst, a young Radical journalist who was then assisting John Morley in writing his three-volume *Life of Gladstone*, learned from a friend that Cook was slighted by Morley's failure to convey a message of condolence. 'J.M. does not shed crocodiles' tears,' Hirst tartly replied.[2]

The new management of the *Daily News*, while critical of the war in general, was by no means as militantly pro-Boer as its antagonists alleged. For a few weeks, imperial topics, which were acknowledged to be those that divided the party most, disappeared from the leader page, which was filled instead with commentary on social issues, local election campaigns, foreign developments, and 'a mysterious epidemic of neuralgia' that had been reported. J. Saxon Mills, a staff member of imperialist sympathies who briefly survived Cook's departure and later wrote a highly complimentary biography of him, was symptomatically required to expunge from an article on King's College, London, any mention of Alfred Milner, perhaps its most celebrated living graduate. The newly installed board of directors, of which Cadbury was chairman and Lloyd George a member, regarded the war as only one aspect of the national crisis, which was fundamentally a moral one. In keeping with this view, they dedicated the paper to the struggle against those attitudes and conditions that fostered a spirit of jingoism. Cadbury, a cocoa manufacturer and a devout Quaker, decreed that the paper would carry no advertisements for alcoholic beverages, and later proscribed all racing and betting features. At his own expense and initiative, complimentary copies were sent to every nonconformist minister in the country and to every religious journal in the English-speaking world. Any profit made by the paper was to be applied to 'better housing for the people', a cause with which the Cadbury family had achieved notable success among its workers at Bournville, outside of Birmingham. As the weeks passed, the *Daily News* asserted itself more and more boldly against the war, providing a daily count of the Boer civilians who had died in British concentration camps. Sales suffered, and there were recurrent fears of mob attacks upon Bouverie Street. From Cape Town,

1. Rosebery to R. W. Perks, 6 January 1901 (letterbook) Rosebery Papers. (I am grateful to Dr Peter Jacobson for this citation.)
2. Hirst, *In the Golden Days*, p. 214.

Mills wrote a letter to *The Times* (6 July 1901) in which he claimed to know on good authority that General Botha, the Boer commander, was an avid reader of the *Daily News* and much encouraged by it. The War Office inflicted a heavy blow by barring the paper's correspondent from South Africa. Cadbury, who interpreted each threat or attempt at harrassment as a measure of success, confided to Harold Spender that the early months of his chairmanship had cost him £10,000. When Spender consoled him with the thought that his efforts had probably 'saved ten thousand lives, . . . his face brightened with a beautiful smile. "Ah! in that case," he said, "I will willingly bear the loss." '

Although Gardiner's name is intimately linked with the *Daily News* in its Cadbury era, it was not in fact until a year had passed that he began his historic connection with the paper. Cook's immediate replacement was P. W. Clayden, a seventy-three-year-old veteran, who was swiftly followed by R. C. ('Rudie') Lehmann. Recommended for the post by John Morley,[1] whose election to Parliament had been preceded by a brilliant editorial career, Lehmann had invested in the paper to the sum of £10,000. As editor he relinquished the seat on the board to which his shares entitled him. Personal assessments agree to his high qualities of intellect and character, but differ with regard to his journalistic ability. His secretary, Archibald Marshall, whom he subsequently appointed as literary editor, contended that Lehmann would have succeeded admirably had he not been plagued by wartime conditions and rivalries among his colleagues. But Harold Spender argued that Lehmann, 'not by nature a daily journalist', lacked 'a proper "flair" for daily news'. The brevity of Lehmann's earlier stint at the bar, his unimpressive record as a member of Parliament from 1906 to 1911, and especially the rapid succession of his editorial affiliations, have been taken to suggest limited powers of application and endurance. Yet one cannot deny his talent for assembling personnel. Herbert Paul remained as chief leader-writer; Harold Spender was brought from the *Manchester Guardian*, reportedly at a

1. According to W. T. Stead, it was initially proposed that Morley should himself assume the editorship, with H. W. Massingham as 'acting editor' under him. *Review of Reviews*, xxiii (1901), 153. Morley's letter of congratulation to Lehmann (31 December 1900) testifies to his influence in obtaining Lehmann's appointment: Lehmann Papers.

reduced fee; H. W. Massingham became parliamentary correspondent, replacing H.W. (later Sir Henry) Lucy, better known to *Punch* readers as 'Toby, M.P.', who, Lehmann complained, afforded the *Daily News* only 'the rinsings of his blotting pad'; and he hired P. W. Wilson, Hilaire Belloc, E. C. Bentley, and G. K. Chesterton, who were to form the nucleus of Gardiner's staff. On 18 July, only seven months after his appointment, Lehmann tendered his resignation. It was formally accepted by Cadbury, on behalf of the directors, who denied him their support in his recurrent disputes with David Edwards, the paper's manager. Morley consoled his protégé that the directors had 'made your position one that you could not hold with a shred of self-respect'.[1] Paul, who agreed that Lehmann had 'been abominably treated', nonetheless begged him to reconsider for the sake of the *Daily News*, which 'cannot stand these constant changes. It will smash, and the chief organ of Liberalism in England will be extinguished.'[2] But Lehmann had had enough, and Edwards, an acquaintance of Lloyd George from Caernarvon, took over from him.

In the months following the 'khaki' election of 1900, when Liberal fortunes were at their nadir, the movement towards Lord Rosebery accelerated. In the *Westminster Gazette*, J. A. Spender increased his pressure on Campbell-Bannerman to achieve a formula for accommodation, and his campaign received private encouragement from Herbert (later Viscount) Gladstone, the chief whip.[3] John Morley and other outspoken 'pro-Boers' wrote off Spender as 'a thorough Roseberyite', and dreaded his undoubted influence.[4] Gladstone also sought to enlist the *Daily News* in his attempt to bring a rapprochement between Campbell-Bannerman and Rosebery, and thereby brought to the surface the divisions among the new proprietors of that paper. As the time approached to celebrate the *Daily News*'s first anniversary under 'pro-Boer' control, there were already serious disputes between Cadbury and J. P. Thomasson, Franklin's father and the custodian of the family purse. The elder Thomasson served notice 'that I don't feel disposed to put more money' into a paper whose cir-

1. Morley to Lehmann, 22 July 1901. Lehmann Papers.
2. Paul to Lehmann, 19 July 1901, Lehmann Papers.
3. Spender to Gladstone, 17 December 1901, Viscount Gladstone Papers, Add MSS 46,042, fols 1–2.
4. Hirst's diary for 15 July 1901, quoted in *In the Golden Days*, p. 226.

culation had failed to rise sufficiently and that took a more 'socialistic' line than he could support: 'I don't for instance think the State has anything to do with Old Age Pensions or Housing the people. . . . Politicians nowadays seem to think the State should be *generous* whereas I think its business is simply to be just.'[1] Cadbury, a Radical of another persuasion, advocated increased taxation on land values and liquor licences to pay for old age pensions, and his support of public housing was well known. 'Is it possible,' he asked C. P. Scott, to whom he sent a confidential copy of Thomasson's letter, 'however harmoniously we may desire to work together, that there can be consecutive policy, or that the responsible parties can take any very definite line, or feel the confidence in the Board which they ought to do?'[2]

These conflicts of opinion among the proprietors, which would have surfaced sooner or later, might have been kept subordinate to the primary objective of opposing the war had political controversy not complicated matters. Edwards, with whose editorial services Cadbury and the Thomassons were equally displeased, dismissed with unconcealed contempt an attempt by Rosebery to paper over party differences. Three of the directors on the board of five took Edwards's part against Cadbury, who confessed that he had been 'delighted' with Rosebery's Chesterfield speech 'as he went much further than I should have expected him to go, and even though I entirely differ with him on many points'.[3] Cadbury immediately fired off a letter to Lloyd George, who had just risked life and limb by carrying the antiwar banner to Birmingham Town Hall in the heart of Chamberlain country: 'I think the "Daily News" is making a great mistake in not accepting the conciliatory lines laid down by Lord Rosebery. If you see [Harold] Spender or Edwards, you might say that I am very much disappointed with their attitude towards Rosebery, & I think that Edwards will have a bad time of it when the Directors meet unless they change their attitude.'[4]

1. Thomasson to Cadbury, 19 December 1901, copy enclosed in Cadbury to Scott, 20 December 1901, *Guardian* Archives.
2. Cadbury to Scott, 20 December 1901 (copy), *Guardian* Archives.
3. *Ibid.*
4. Cadbury to Gladstone, 19 December 1901, and Cadbury to Lloyd George, 19 December 1901 (copy), Viscount Gladstone Papers, Add. MSS 46,059, fols 102–3.

Cadbury and the Thomassons, who between then controlled more than half the shares, were convinced that under existing arrangements there was little that could be done. Of the many difficulties that they faced, 'perhaps the greatest is that Mr Edwards by the agreement first made is upon our backs for five years like the old man of the sea.' The removal of Edwards would require nothing less than the reconstitution of the board, which Cadbury accepted as the only solution. But who was to buy out whom? 'Of course,' he wrote to Scott, 'my personal comfort would be served by selling out my shares and getting out of the concern for which as far as I can see as a man of business there is little or no chance of success.'[1] Yet he dreaded the possibility that a controlling interest in the paper would be acquired by the imperialists. A final decision would have to await a board meeting on 9 January, 1902, but as early as 20 December, Cadbury contemplated the prospect of obtaining an exclusive proprietorship. He contacted T. P. Ritzema, owner-manager of the highly successful *Daily Telegraph* at Blackburn, who had recently helped to establish the *Daily Argus* at Birmingham and who provisionally agreed to superintend the business side of the *Daily News* in the event that Cadbury took over. At the same time, he appealed for advice from Scott, with whom he and Ritzema conferred at Manchester on 2 January.

By the time he met Scott, Cadbury had accepted as his 'duty' the 'tremendous responsibility' to continue the *Daily News* as a 'power for peace'. It was not personal influence that he sought:

My sole desire in taking up so great a responsibility would be that whoever was in command might feel that I should always support him in helping forward any movement that would promote the welfare of the masses of this country, and to carry on a paper that every true Christian patriot of every denomination and of none could take up with a certainty that it would plead for righteousness.[2]

He did not seek financial reward. J. E. Taylor, who as proprietor of the *Manchester Guardian* applauded Cadbury's 'altogether incalculable assistance and support to the party', heard from a reliable source that 'in private conclave, . . . when some of the proprietors expressed the fear of not getting any dividends, . . . Mr Cadbury said that he

1. Cadbury to Scott, 20 December 1901 (copy), *Guardian* Archives.
2. Cadbury to Scott, 28 December 1901 (copy), *Guardian* Archives.

for one should be well satisfied to go without profit in such an enterprise'.[1]

Much would depend on the choice of an editor, and Cadbury expressed strong interest in L. T. Hobhouse of the *Guardian* staff. Like Taylor, who had recently cited 'the wisdom of trying to establish . . . a friendly alliance with the regenerated *Daily News*',[2] Scott was alert to the mutual advantage of an informal collaboration. Dismissing Cadbury's suggestion that he might exercise a vague editorial jurisdiction from Manchester, Scott volunteered to help in the selection of a full-fledged editor and, on this basis, advanced Hobhouse's candidacy: 'I would gladly advise with your Editor on any question of policy on which he cared to consult me and if he were a friend of mine that would be easy.'[3] Cadbury was confident that 'men like Messrs Massingham, Paul, etc.', whom he did not consider suitable for the appointment, 'would be willing for their services to be retained while kept in hand by the Editor', provided Scott was known to be a party to the arrangement. Meanwhile, Ritzema recommended as business manager H. C. Derwent of the *Bradford Daily Telegraph*, whom he had trained at Blackburn and whom Cadbury knew to be 'a devoted Christian worker, superintendent of a Sunday School, etc., a combination rather difficult to meet with in a first-class man of business'.[4]

As Cadbury expected, the decision was reached on 9 January 'to wind up the Company and make it into a private concern': on this matter he had the support of Franklin Thomasson and Lehmann. But it was not yet known which of the two dominant partners would provide the capital to assume possession. Each professed a willingness to step aside in favour of the other, and nearly a month had passed before J. P. Thomasson, who was on holiday in the south of France, decided that Cadbury was better suited to shoulder this particular burden. It was not economy that prompted the Thomassons' withdrawal: five years later Franklin sustained losses on the shortlived *Tribune* rumoured to be as high as three-quarters of a million pounds. The transfer of power at the *Daily News* thereupon proceeded as quietly as possible

1. Taylor to Scott, 31 December 1901 (copy), *Guardian* Archives.
2. Taylor to Scott, 7 January 1901 (copy), *Guardian* Archives.
3. Scott to Cadbury, 12 January 1902 (copy), *Guardian* Archives.
4. Cadbury to Scott, 3 January 1902 (copy), *Guardian* Archives.

out of consideration for the new proprietor, who feared that the paper's 'influence for good would be greatly lessened' if it were known to be in the pocket of a single individual.

Edwards surrendered his editorial and managerial duties, presumably for a financial settlement, and after an extended convalescence became managing director of the *Daily Express and Evening News* at Nottingham. His removal from the *Daily News* had been dictated by the complexities of Liberal politics, with which few could cope, by deteriorating relations with the trade unions, and especially by the fundamental inability of his employers to agree among themselves. Few realized how close to disaster the paper had come: at very least it might have fallen to the imperialists of either party who had discreetly tendered offers or, like a variety of recent properties on the market, to the house of Harmsworth; at worst, it might have disappeared. According to a report of the Press Association, it had cost Cadbury a further £135,000 to retrieve the situation. Now, for the first time in many years, the *Daily News* was equipped to speak with force and clarity in party and national affairs. But with whose voice was it to speak?

3. The street of adventures

On the morning of Monday, 3 March 1902, yet another 'new' *Daily News* was born. Bemused readers, to whom the event must have seemed a ritual, probably greeted the announcement with a degree of scepticism. Cynics were already calculating the sums that George Cadbury would lose. Among the better informed, there was particular curiosity about the unknown young man from the provinces who, at only thirty-six years of age, presumed to occupy the chair of the mighty Dickens. It would have been impossible to perceive the distinction that he would bring to that place, let alone the political and social cataclysms that would attend his long editorship.

A. G. Gardiner owed his unlikely appointment to a combination of circumstances. L. T. Hobhouse, whom C. P. Scott had nominated for the position, was more attracted by the prospect of returning full-time to his philosophic pursuits; within a few months he resigned as leader-writer for the *Manchester Guardian*, although he retained a lifelong connection with that paper and the intimate confidence of its editor. It was undoubtedly all to the best that Hobhouse proved unavailable, for neither in style nor temperament was he well suited to the requirements of the *Daily News*. With little time to spare, Cadbury deferred to the experience of T. P. Ritzema, his general manager, who had lobbied from the start for Gardiner. 'Mr Ritzema told me that he did not feel it would be wise at first to make many changes in the staff,' he wrote to Scott on 15 February, 'except that he is putting a man of his own training to take the place of Edwards who was manager *and* editor of the "Daily News", but I quite hope in time we shall make use of your suggestion to obtain some help from Mr Hobhouse.'[1] Perhaps Cadbury exaggerated his disappointment and belittled Gardiner's significance in an attempt to mollify Scott, but any misgivings on his part would have been understandable. Recent experience attested to the imperative need for a strong editor, and he

1. Cadbury to Scott, 15 February 1902 (copy), *Guardian* Archives.

47

had only Ritzema's word that Gardiner was equal to the task. Yet, a man of intense faith, he was more prepared than others to take a risk. J. E. Taylor, to whom Scott communicated news of the appointment, regretted that the *Daily News* had not obtained someone of greater stature: 'I am afraid Cadbury is not going the right way to make the *D.N.* a success. He needs a very able and experienced Pressman to advise and guide him.'[1]

As Cadbury soon came to realize, however, the fact that Gardiner was relatively an unknown quantity carried certain advantages. At a time when Liberal journalists tended to be identified with one faction or another, the editor of the *Daily News*, whatever his commitments, was not compromised by previous associations. This made considerably easier the paper's efforts to 'consolidate' the Opposition 'so that Liberal Imperialists and Independent Labour men may work together to save their country'. Indeed, as Cadbury soon boasted to Herbert Gladstone, 'our chief Editor, Mr Gardiner, is fortunately for the paper a very retiring man who does not go into Society and who will therefore I think be able to retain his independence'.[2]

But Gardiner had not left Blackburn, where his place was comfortable and secure, to become either a stopgap or a dummy editor at the *Daily News*. His views about the management of a paper were at least as definite as those about the national political situation. He carried with him the benedictions of dozens of northern journalists, all of whom envied his opportunity and many of whom applied for places on his staff. Among the most touching was one from an old-timer, who had given him his first significant boost, and who professed to have known that 'this would be the next step' the moment he had heard of Ritzema's connection with the *Daily News*:

I think your success vindicates my own judgment & foresight, when I brought you out of the obscurity of a District Reportership at Burnley to the head office of the *Telegraph* at Blackburn, now, I suppose, some fifteen years ago. I recognized, at that time, the literary 'flavour' of your Notes, & said that you would go higher & make a mark in journalism.[3]

The Liberal association at Blackburn, while lamenting the loss 'of a

1. Taylor to Scott, 27 February 1902 (copy), *Guardian* Archives.
2. Cadbury to Gladstone, 9 June 1902, Viscount Gladstone Papers, Add. MSS 46,059, fol. 218.
3. J. Quarl (?) to Gardiner, 13 February 1902, G.P.

journalist of rare literary culture and wide intelligence', passed a resolution offering 'felicitations to Mr Gardiner with the hope and expectation that he may have a successful career in the distinguished position to which he has been called'.[1] Philip Snowden, whose candidacy Gardiner had eloquently championed in the last general election, was 'as pleased with your success as if it were my own because it is deserved'.[2] And his family at Chelmsford, without suppressing their continued disapproval of his politics, gloried in his good fortune: 'Never mind about the liberal paper,' his mother consoled him, trusting that he would not be contaminated by the company he kept; and his sister Alice graciously added: 'We forgive you.'[3]

Gardiner preceded his wife and children to London, where he put up at the Victoria Hotel in Northumberland Avenue. He spent the better part of a fortnight consulting his new colleagues, calling upon estate agents, and exploring the byways of the metropolis. 'I am feeling most anxious about you,' his wife wrote from Blackburn. 'I hope you are feeling as well as it's possible to be – with so much to do & think about. I should get some disinfectant to have on you as influenza is so bad in London.' For both of them, the pain of separation was acute. 'We feel dreadfully dull during the evenings. I shall be glad to get there as soon as possible.' Better equipped than her husband to manage practical affairs, she took charge of getting their possessions 'ready for removery' to the house he had taken in Finchley Road, Hampstead. They would require a new and larger dining table, and the prices in the shops (some as high as six pounds) filled her with alarm. Concerned lest he neglect the sartorial demands of his new station, she packed him a new stud – which she hoped he wouldn't lose – and dress shirt 'if you should want to wear your evening things'.[4]

In the weeks that followed his arrival, Gardiner had little time for social pleasures, even had he the inclination. To a greater extent than either Cadbury or Ritzema had anticipated, he was devising changes in the content and format of the *Daily News*. His first issue, while taking care not to disfigure the paper's 'good old face', introduced an

1. *Northern Daily Telegraph*, 17 February 1902.
2. Snowden to Gardiner, 13 February 1902, G.P.
3. 11 February 1902, G.P.
4. 2 March 1902, G.P.

array of new features, a bolder typography, and an expanded literary section. There was the promise of an increase in the number of pages as further ingredients were added. Gardiner's Blackburn experience served him to obvious advantage, and he continued the column of 'Table Talk' that had won him a following in the north. Other regular features were conceived with the aims and readership of the *Daily News* specifically in mind: 'News from the Provinces', 'The Metropolis', and 'Life and Labour', described as 'a daily record from field, factory, and workshop'. Cadbury, who took legitimate pride in his own industrial relations, was gratified to offer 'service' in this way 'to the cause of Labour'.[1] A generous benefactor of the I.L.P., he was no less pleased by the paper's efforts to forge an alliance between the political forces of Liberalism and Labour, even if this meant supporting an L.R.C. candidate against a Liberal, as in the celebrated 1903 by-election at Barnard Castle.

The new regime at the *Daily News*, as Elie Halévy recognized, 'was Puritan as well as Radical'.[2] Not only were betting advertisements and 'tips' rigorously excluded, but also any form of racing news. 'Betting is indubitably a serious national evil,' proclaimed the March leader that heralded this policy, 'which is slowly spreading a rot through all the most valuable classes in our community.' The decision brought letters of congratulation from nonconformist clergymen, as well as a flurry of protests from readers, many of whom threatened to cancel their subscriptions. Gardiner replied on 5 March with polite assurances that 'so far from our circulation having been "injuriously affected" by the exclusion of betting, it has greatly increased since the "new departure" was made'. Years later, however, he admitted that the experiment had been 'well-intentioned but mistaken': the *Daily News* had not inspired its rivals by its example and, at the same time, its revenue and news coverage had suffered. What some had 'welcomed . . . as a courageous protest against a great national evil', had been 'resented' by countless others 'as an unwarrantable censorship of public morals'.[3]

It took a while for the paper's features to fall into place and for

1. Cadbury to John Burns, 15 December 1902, Burns Papers, Add. MSS 46,298, fol. 103.
2. *The History of the English People in the Nineteenth Century, Epilogue*, i, 108.
3. *Life of George Cadbury*, p. 221.

eyes to grow accustomed to them. Ritzema, who waited a full week before 'jotting down one or two of my mental comments' for Gardiner's benefit, confessed that his initial reaction had been one of doubt:

When I opened the paper last Monday the cumulative effect of the changes was a little startling, & I could not help thinking that some of the alterations had been made without properly balancing the accounts of loss & gain. . . . Since then the appearance of the paper each day has been suggestive of the growth of an idea – a strong, consistent idea – & I think all the little developments that have taken place in the past week have been for the better.

In Ritzema's case, misgivings speedily gave way to a feeling 'that the "Daily News" is going to enjoy a greater influence & a greater prosperity in the future than it has had in the past'.[1] Others were not nearly so sanguine. 'The *Daily News*', J. E. Taylor wrote to Scott on 15 March, 'seems to me not to improve, but to continue lamentably uninteresting'.[2] Fortunately, it was his own proprietor whom Gardiner had to satisfy, not Scott's. Cadbury's confidence was fully rewarded, and by early June he could report to Herbert Gladstone that 'the circulation of the paper is going ahead most satisfactorily, so that one can now feel secure that its permanent existence, which three months ago seemed doubtful, is assured'.[3]

Among the initial difficulties was a long-standing dispute with the paper's compositors, whose powerful trade union made demands that the management considered exorbitant. Ritzema retaliated by secretly recruiting a staff of non-union printers, and by giving orders to turn away the regular crew with severance pay. E. C. Bentley, who deputized for Gardiner as assistant editor, recalled 'the chaos in the composing room' that night, and 'the appalling journalistic nightmare' of relying on printers who were strangers to each other and to the equipment. Cadbury was forced to call upon his old friend, John Burns, to arrange a hasty settlement by which the new compositors departed with a month's salary and the original staff was welcomed back at terms that 'organized labour' greeted 'with pardonable glee'.[4]

1. 10 March 1902, G.P.
2. 15 March 1902 (copy), *Guardian* Archives.
3. 9 June 1902, Viscount Gladstone Papers, Add. MSS 46,059, fol. 218.
4. Bentley, *Those Days*, p. 240; also Kent, *John Burns: Labour's Lost Leader*, p. 133.

One cannot hold Cadbury responsible for Ritzema's foolhardy assault on the unions, which resulted in a further drain on his pocket. 'His object', Gardiner explained, 'was to secure the advocacy of the *Daily News* for the social policy in which he was interested, and having secured that he left all the business details to the managing director, and the control of policy to the editor.'[1] With regard to the political situation, the leader page remained more outspokenly critical of Lord Rosebery than Cadbury thought advisable. There was no doubt in Gardiner's mind that Liberal Imperialism was a pernicious creed, and that its standard-bearer had neither 'the hard core of character' nor the fidelity to principle required of a Liberal leader: 'He is the Flying Dutchman of politics – a phantom vessel floating about on the wide seas, without an anchor and without a port.'[2] In every respect, Gardiner preferred Campbell-Bannerman, whose detractors found him too unassuming and insufficiently inspiring. 'Sir Henry Campbell-Bannerman would not himself claim to be a Bright or a Gladstone,' he conceded on the third day of his editorship. 'But there have been times when men of simple, straightforward honesty and transparent clearness of purpose have been more necessary to the salvation of the people than any great orator.' Campbell-Bannerman's one rhetorical flourish – his condemnation of British 'methods of barbarism' in South Africa – echoed in the pages of the *Daily News* long after he had come to regret the phrase as a tactical error.

It was a cruel irony that 'the public revenged itself, not on those who were responsible for . . . [the] concentration camps and farm burnings, . . . but on those who opposed [the war], and whose opposition was supposed to be a source of encouragement to the Boers'.[3] The *Daily News*, prominent among the offenders, incurred bitter resentment, frightening away advertisers and bringing sales down as low as 30,000. A clergyman's wife, who described herself as 'a most enthusiastic Gladstonian, & a reader of the Daily News for 30 years', implored its editor to refute the rumour that his salary was subsidized by President Kruger of the Transvaal.[4] Others, who shared

---

1. *Life of George Cadbury*, p. 221.
2. See, for example, 15 February 1902; also *Prophets, Priests and Kings*, pp. 184–5; the *Nation*, 14 July 1923.
3. *Life of George Cadbury*, p. 218.
4. Emily A. Maddy to Gardiner, 28 June 1902, G.P.

the pro-Boer stigma, were too familiar with such imputations to pay them heed. Sir William Harcourt, gratefully declining an invitation from his future biographer to publish a 'message' that might rally the party faithful, sent assurances that

there is no journal with whose editor I would more gladly comply. I feel a sincere appreciation & admiration of the stout and able stand the Daily News has made for the great principles of the Liberal Party and its old watchwords of Peace, Retrenchment & Reform. [1]

Nor was Gardiner successful in enlisting the pen of John Morley, who expressed 'hope that the D.N. prospers. It has a look of life about it such as it has not worn for a long time.' [2]

Gardiner did not, however, have to rely on Liberal elder statesmen, whose testimonials he valued, to fill the columns of his paper. At his disposal was a retinue of impressive talents, who combined to make the *Daily News* one of the most exciting journalistic and literary forums of its day. The excitement was not confined to the printed page, for the offices at Bouverie Street were tenanted by personalities as many-sided as the issues they embraced. As men of letters, they figured prominently in what Frank Swinnerton has described as 'the Georgian literary scene'; as political spokesmen, however, they were without exception quintessentially Edwardian: vaguely nostalgic and, at the same time, impatient for change. Any Fleet Street editor would have been proud to head such a team, but it is doubtful whether anyone else could have maintained a reasonable harmony among so many prima donnas. Unlike certain other prominent editors of his day, who were known to reserve their time and sympathy for senior staff, Gardiner was equally accessible to all his colleagues, whose visits he welcomed to the cramped, cluttered room that he shared with his secretary, G. G. Desmond. By his own admission, Desmond was 'the very worst Editor's Secretary that a great London daily ever saw and secretary to a better Editor than I ever expect to see again'. [3] Far too modest, he functioned admirably, somehow always managing to extract the relevant document from the chaos on his chief's desk. If a caller had confidential business, Desmond would 'wander out

1. 6 June 1902 G.P.
2. 30 September 1903, G.P.
3. Desmond to Gardiner, 12 September 1919, G.P.

discreetly and drop in on someone else down the corridor'.[1] But Gardiner, who did not wait for problems to be brought to him, kept a watchful eye on situations that threatened to disrupt working relationships. Bentley credited him with 'a faculty of getting on good terms with all men, great and small',[2] that was as useful in office politics as in his own writing. Behind the scenes, he functioned as a counsellor to the members of his staff, as an intermediary between them, and, to an extent that few realized, as their agent in disputes with the Cadburys.

Several of A. G. G.'s most illustrious contributors had preceded him to the *Daily News*, but it was he who provided them with full opportunities to achieve distinction. Chief among them was G. K. Chesterton, an extravagant figure in every sense, who, with his 'colossal frame', pince-nez, and 'great waves of hair surg[ing] from under [his] soft, wide-brimmed hat', was undoubtedly 'the most conspicuous figure in the landscape of literary London'.[3] Gardiner loved him dearly – Chesterton was godfather to his youngest child, Gilbert – despite certain painful incidents that punctuated their professional relations. Although his habits could not have been more different, he rejoiced in Chesterton's 'sheer ebullience of spirit', marvelled at his lack of self-consciousness, and celebrated his humanity:

> He is not of our time, but of all times. One imagines him drinking deep draughts from the horn of Skrymir, or exchanging jests with Falstaff at the Boar's Head in Eastcheap, or joining in the intellectual revels at the Mermaid Tavern, or meeting Johnson foot to foot and dealing blow for mighty blow.

Chesterton had been an occasional reviewer and guest columnist on the *Daily News*, but Gardiner installed him upon 'a Saturday pulpit, rather like a Sunday pulpit', but with the guarantee of 'a larger congregation, . . . whatever were the merits of the sermon'. Chesterton took special delight from the fact that he could preach to the non-conformist multitudes 'all about French cafés and Catholic cathedrals; and they loved it, because they had never heard of them before'. Week after week, he would give vent to his boundless energy and engage, with brilliant results, in argument for its own sake. 'You may tap any

1. Harris, *Life So Far*, p. 84.
2. *Those Days*, p. 231.
3. Gardiner, *Prophets, Priests and Kings*, pp. 331–41; also Chesterton, *Autobiography*, pp. 120, 184.

subject you like,' Gardiner wrote of him; 'he will find it a theme on which to hang all the mystery of time and eternity.' His editor, no more than his readers, knew what to expect from Chesterton's pen, and Wilson Harris described the 'turbid agitation' in the office on Friday afternoons, when Chesterton's copy was anxiously awaited:

It arrived in all sorts of shapes and by all sorts of means – occasionally in a taxi accompanied by its author, occasionally in a taxi unescorted, occasionally by post-office messenger. It was written on any kind of paper that might be at hand, once at any rate, when G.K.C. was in the throes of moving house, on a piece of wallpaper. He was completely negligent about money, and frequently without any; when he arrived at the office with his copy in that condition the commissionaire would have to pay the taxi-fare. [1]

H. W. Massingham, another colleague whom Gardiner found awaiting him, made appearances in Bouverie Street that were nearly as few as Chesterton's, although hardly as memorable. Following the example set by his predecessor, Sir Henry Lucy, who stayed at the House 'from the time the Speaker takes the Chair till he leaves it', [2] Massingham spent his working hours patrolling the lobbies and galleries at Westminster, where few secrets escaped his detection. Occasionally, when the House was not sitting, he would share his confidences and dire prognostications with those at the office, and Bentley, who pungently described him as 'a combination of St Francis and Rabelais', was among those who liked to 'listen to his vigorous, humorous, utterly irreverent talk, his stream of curious profanity'. [1] An intense soul, whom few found ingratiating, he enjoyed cordial relations with Gardiner, with whose political and social views he was generally in accord. After 1907, when Massingham left to edit the *Nation*, he joined with Gardiner to promote a variety of common causes – welfare legislation, naval disarmament, friendship with Germany, the League of Nations – and eventually the two men shared a fierce hostility to Lloyd George. In 1922, after Gardiner's eviction from the *Daily News*, Massingham found him a temporary berth at the *Nation*, where his own editorship was to expire a year later.

1. *Life So Far*, p. 85.
2. Quoted in Seymour-Ure, *The Press, Politics and the Public*, p. 199.
3. *Those Days*, p. 229.

Along with Chesterton and Massingham, Gardiner inherited Harold Spender, with whom he was never particularly close, Vaughan Nash, who resigned in 1905 to become Campbell-Bannerman's private secretary, and the acerbic Herbert Paul, whose tenure did not long survive Gardiner's advent. Notwithstanding their 'pro-Boer' reputation, the new management took strong exception to a defamatory obituary notice Paul had written of Cecil Rhodes, and on 1 April 1902 he found a letter on his desk informing him that his services were no longer required. 'I am sure that Gardiner himself had nothing to do with it,' H. W. Nevinson testified, 'but there was a power on that paper behind the editor, as I was myself to discover in 1909.'[1]

Nevinson was one of Gardiner's own appointments, who did not allow Paul's unhappy experience to discourage him from applying for a job on the *Daily News* a few days later. Gardiner was unable to offer him anything at the time, nor the following January, when he promised to send him to cover Balkan events 'if he sent anybody'.[2] It was not until 1908, when Nevinson returned from an assignment in India for the *Manchester Guardian*, that he took up with the *Daily News* as leader-writer. The association lasted only fourteen months, and ended in acrimony when his superiors refused to sanction his strong line against the forced feeding of imprisoned suffragettes. In his own case, unlike Paul's, Nevinson was less inclined to exonerate the editor. Gardiner, in turn, came to look on Nevinson as a vaguely pestilential creature, insufferably self-righteous and self-centred. When Nevinson died in 1941, Gardiner confided that he did not envy St Peter, who

will find him something of a handful, for I can't imagine him [Nevinson] comfortable in heaven with no heroics to indulge in & nothing to do but twang a harp. He was a romantic figure & at his best a fine writer & something of a poet. He sincerely hated injustice, but was his own dauntless hero, mounted on a horse, armed with flashing sword, demanding to be supplied with more dragons to slay & very uncomfortable if he was not boiling with indignation about something or somebody. He was one of the vainest men I have known (John Burns & Chiozza Money ran him neck & neck) & was

1. *Changes and Chances*, p. 315.
2. Nevinson's diaries, entries of 8 April 1902 and 8 January 1903, Bodleian Library, Oxford. The manuscript diaries present a more sympathetic portrait of Gardiner than the autobiographical volumes Nevinson produced from them.

as passionate in his loves as in his hates. I was one of the latter. [J. A.] Spender, of course, but the most intense I think [was] that kindly & selfless soul Graham Wallas, who was at Shrewsbury Sc'l. with him and whose mere contiguity he could not endure. [1]

After Nevinson left the *Daily News* in 1909 he returned to both the *Daily Chronicle* and the *Manchester Guardian* for short stints, but the outbreak of war in 1914 found him back on the *Daily News* as Berlin correspondent.

Many of the most celebrated names in Liberal journalism, Nevinson among them, importuned Gardiner for places on the *Daily News* and had to wait, sometimes for years, for an appropriate slot. The mere rumour of an impending vacancy brought applications from Fleet Street veterans and even from such public figures as Ramsay MacDonald, who, in 1905, as much for reasons of prestige as financial need, unsuccessfully nominated himself to succeed Vaughan Nash. This was partly a tribute to the paper's enhanced stature, and partly the result of chronic underemployment among Liberal journalists, whose papers were too few and too poor to keep them steadily engaged. Gardiner, who admired MacDonald and many of the applicants whom he rejected, chose his colleagues not only for their abilities but also for the way that they promised to fit into the general operations in Bouverie Street. He could not afford to allow the leader page, or, for that matter, the literary department, to be dominated by writers of any particular school or obsession, and it was with profound misgiving that he appointed Nevinson to share leader-writing assignments with the likeminded H. N. Brailsford.

Along with Brailsford and Nevinson, the roster of leader-writers for the *Daily News* included J. L. Hammond, R. C. K. Ensor, and C. F. G. ('Charlie') Masterman, who came to the paper in the capacity of literary editor. But Masterman's 'consuming passion, the alleviation of the condition of the people', soon drew him more topical assignments. A figure of Chesterton's bulk, who exceeded even G. K. C. in personal untidiness, C. G. F. shared with his editor an abiding concern for social reform and a commitment to Radical politics. His subsequent parliamentary and ministerial careers, from which his friends expected so much, subjected him to merciless attacks from the Tory right that made it difficult, and ultimately impossible,

1. Gardiner to Swinnerton, 16 November 1941, Swinnerton Papers.

for him to retain a seat. Gardiner spoke for many in 1927,[1] when he mourned Masterman's early death as 'a tragedy of unfulfilment' that epitomized their party's grief and the debasement of political morality. He fondly recalled the afternoon, nearly twenty-five years earlier, when Masterman had appeared at his door like an apparition for an interview that had been arranged by their mutual friend, Canon Barnett of Toynbee Hall: 'He wore an obsolete tall hat and buttoned shoes that lacked half their buttons, and he carried a derelict handbag tied round with a piece of rope in place of fastening. . . . To the end no man ever gave less thought than he did to personal upholstery.' Masterman's widow, who did not doubt 'the detailed accuracy of this description', recounted that her husband's dishabille thereafter grew worse, as it became his habit to cram 'a large twelve-and-sixpenny book into each of his sidepockets, accompanied very often by a six-inch pencil with a sharpened point and no protector, with disastrous effects on the appearance of any suit'.[2]

But it was immediately apparent that Masterman, despite his absurd costume, demanded to be taken as seriously as he took the world. To him, Gardiner wrote, 'joy was a fleeting illusion playing over the tragic comedy of man, and his emotions were strained and tortured by the agony of things'. The product of 'a dark Puritan upbringing', he confessed to the Cavalier Chesterton that he was 'the sort of man who goes under a hedge to eat an apple'.[3] The burdens of humanity weighed heavily on him, and even the Liberal victory of 1906 failed to convince him that the promised land lay within reach. There were those who resented his tendency to dwell upon the obstacles to progress, and who mistook his foreboding for want of resolution. 'Damn the feller,' Campbell-Bannerman exclaimed in 1905 upon receiving a presentation copy of Masterman's *In Peril of Change*, 'I thought he wanted change.'[4] This was unwarranted, for Masterman's tone was one of sobriety, not despair, reflecting – as he took pains to explain in his introduction to that volume – 'an experience . . . spent in communication less with the triumphs of civilization than with its failures'. As a personality, he was charming even

1. The *Nation*, 26 November 1927.
2. Lucy Masterman, *C. F. G. Masterman*, p. 51.
3. Chesterton, *Autobiography*, pp. 123–4.
4. Lucy Masterman, p. 56.

in his melancholy, and jovial in his pessimism. Gardiner, who considered him 'one of the most generous souls of this generation', exulted in his comradeship, and remembered the excitement in Bouverie Street when Winston Churchill, who ran 'neck and neck' with C. F. G. 'as the man of the future', dropped by 'to see Masterman and in the high spirits of the time would accept a challenge to finish the leader on which Masterman was engaged'.

Others who owed their start to Gardiner, or whom he helped along the way, included E. C. Bentley, who doubled as an author of detective stories and who gave his middle name (Clerihew) to a double-couplet verse that he invented, Wilson Harris, editor of the *Spectator* from 1932 to 1953, Robert Lynd, whom readers of the *New Statesman* knew as 'Y.Y.', S. K. Ratcliffe, an astute observer of the American scene, H. M. Tomlinson and R. A. Scott-James, both distinguished literary critics, Margaret Bryant, one of the best women journalists of her day, and Stuart Hodgson, who followed as editor in 1919. Drama reviews were contributed by William Archer, the Ibsen scholar, poetry by John Masefield and William Watson (then much in vogue in Liberal circles), and periodic essays by Hall Caine. L. G. Chiozza Money, whose *Riches and Poverty* (1905) had a profound impact on Edwardian consciences, began by writing the 'Life and Labour' column in collaboration with P. W. Wilson, who graduated to become parliamentary correspondent. Hilaire Belloc was an early contributor, whose later attitudes confirmed the worst of Gardiner's apprehensions.

Gardiner looked with greater affection, although by no means unalloyed approval, on Bernard Shaw and H. G. Wells, and he was pleased to publish their letters (provided that they were not too long) and articles (provided that the price was not too steep). Wells professed his willingness to accept less than his normal fee out of 'affection . . . for the editor of the Daily News',[1] and Arnold Bennett, whose terms were ordinarily cash and carry, refused a lucrative offer from the Cadburys to continue his connection with the *Daily News* after Gardiner's departure. Like Bennett, many members of the staff owed a personal loyalty to the editor sufficiently strong to overcome their antipathy to the paper's proprietors and, in some cases, to its principles. Chesterton, invited by Gardiner's eldest

1. Wells to Gardiner, n.d., G.P.

daughter to inscribe a page in her autograph album, impishly penned 'Some Revelations of Journalism', which conveyed a better sense of his colleagues' *bonhomie* than of their dedication:

> It is as well that you should know
> The truth about that empty show,
> That vast and histrionic ruse,
> Which calls itself 'the Daily News'.
>
> 'Tis a dark truth, if truth be said.
> We tried at every other trade
> And we have found (with joy I sing)
> That we were bad at everything.
> When upon any work our wit
> We tried, we made a mess of it.
> When your Papa, exultant, sailed
> A pirate, he distinctly failed.
> When Wilson's dancing seemed to pall
> Upon the Empire Music Hall,
> When Spender found, and also Nash
> They were not meant to haberdash,
> When simple Bentley first began
> To see he was no sandwich man,
> When I myself perceived that I
> Must work, or I should shortly die,
> We all abandoned worldly strife,
> And chose this simple mode of life.
>
> One secret more: one person writes
> All the whole paper all the nights.
> He writes on war and war's redress,
> On literature and ladies' dress.
> Upon the commerce of Hong Kong
> He is particularly strong.
> His beard is long, his gestures free,
> And his initials G. K. C.

With relatively few exceptions, those who worked with Gardiner became his friends for life. Some, like Harris and Lynd, acknowledged him as their mentor, although he was always too humble to claim them as protégés. In later years, he was always available at the

Reform Club or the Institute of Journalists to reminisce about old times. For those who shared either his literary interests or his enthusiasm for sport, he reserved special attachment. In 1928, at the age of sixty-three, he joined Wells and Bennett for a tennis match in Cadogan Square, across from Bennett's house, where they changed their clothes. A reporter from the *Daily Mail*, who was an uninvited (and, until later, an unsuspected) spectator, related with amusement that A. G. G., 'tall, erect, white-haired and spectacled', looked by far the most 'professional' of the three, and twice beat Wells, a year his junior, only to lose to Bennett, who was the youngest at sixty-one.[1]

The disparity among his colleagues, no less than among his friends, was a tribute to Gardiner's tolerance and a measure of his delight in the richness of humanity. As editor, he saw himself as the helmsman of a crew whose members, by virtue of their intellects and personalities, would inevitably cross oars and pull in competing directions. Always holding passionately to his own beliefs, he did not expect to agree on every issue with those close to him, nor did he require those who served him to agree with him. For this reason, he could continue to enjoy the company of Wells, whose morality differed sharply from his own; of Massingham, Harris and J. A. Hobson, who lapsed from the Liberal faith to which he remained wedded; and of Bennett, who consorted with the unsavoury Lord Beaverbrook. 'Men never appeal to me by reason of their opinions but by virtue of something much more deep and enduring,' he told Chesterton.[2] He did not shrink from controversy, either in conversation or in print, recognizing it as an ingredient that personal relationships and newspapers thrived on. All he asked of his associates was that they extend the same courtesies to him and to one another that he was prepared to extend to them. To be sure, the *Daily News* was a professed organ of advanced Liberalism, which only the most masochistic Tory would have wished to join. But advanced Liberalism was a label with a kaleidoscope of meanings; it embraced a variety of antithetical causes whose advocates often reserved their greatest suspicions and most savage denunciations for one another.

1. Stanard, *With the Dictators of Fleet Street*, pp. 181–3; also *The Journals of Arnold Bennett*, iii, 277, entry for 3 October 1928.
2. Gardiner to Chesterton, 12 February 1913 (copy courtesy of Miss D. Collins).

Garvin, an editor to whom Gardiner may be compared in professional if not in political terms, observed to Kingsley Martin, then a novice, that 'the policies of a paper must change from time to time, but it is wiser for an editor to proceed in curves rather than right angles'.[1] Gardiner, who could not have better described what he assumed to be his essential task at the *Daily News*, had all he could do to steer a middle course between the Cadburys, on the one hand, whom he was obliged to satisfy, and the Nevinsons and Brailsfords, on the other, whom he had to restrain from moving too quickly in new directions. Although he generally handled such situations with skill and forbearance, they taxed his energies and diverted him from the work for which he considered himself best qualified. 'I'm not an editor, you know,' he once confessed to Lynd, who explained that Gardiner 'was not greatly interested in the organizing side of a newspaper, and that it was the political and literary features that alone engaged his whole heart'.[2] There was no assignment that suited him more ideally than the chairmanship of the Reform Club library committee, which he held from July 1928 to May 1942, and which permitted him to browse at leisure through the volumes entrusted to his care, and to enjoy the conversation of men of similar disposition.

Nevinson, who perceived the pain that their 'discrepancies' (as he politely called them) inflicted on Gardiner's 'pacific temperament', found him 'at heart . . . a temperate and conciliatory editor . . . [who] follow[ed] the straight path of honest and definite principle to the utmost of his position's limits'.[3] He would not have been unfair to have added to Gardiner's personal limits as well. Unequipped by nature to engage in the professional and political struggles that intruded upon him, A. G. G. was incapable of self-restraint when he ultimately took to the warpath. On such occasions, most notably in his eventual conflict with Lloyd George, he would strike quixotically in all directions, losing a sense of proportion and a degree of credibility. Aware of the passions that seethed within him, he made a conscious effort to keep them in check. 'Don't get excited. Keep cool,' he preached to his daughter. 'It's the cool people who are masters of themselves & therefore of circumstance. I'm the most excitable

1. Kingsley Martin, *Editor* (Penguin ed, 1969), p. 49.
2. Robert Lynd, 'A. G. Gardiner', *News Chronicle*, 4 March 1946.
3. *More Changes, More Chances*, p. 288.

person in the world: that's why I know so much about the virtues of coolness.'[1] Like many men of peace, he responded to the disillusionments of wartime with a ferocity that surprised others more than himself and that he was powerless to control.

To do him justice, it was not simply a case of nerves too easily jangled. The pressure of events was overwhelming, and it was intensified by the anomalies of his position. Unlike Garvin or Scott, who exercised undisputed authority over their respective papers, or H. A. Gwynne, to whom the proprietress of the *Morning Post* conceded a free hand, Gardiner was required to justify his policies to the Cadburys, who were occasionally known to countermand his instructions and engage personnel without consultation. In this respect, he resembled R. D. Blumenfeld at the *Daily Express* and Geoffrey Robinson (later Dawson) under Northcliffe at *The Times*, each of whom suffered considerable proprietorial interference. Following the precedent established by Lehmann in 1901 Gardiner was not accorded a seat on the paper's board of directors. It did not go unnoticed, however, that when the *Morning Leader* was absorbed in 1912, Ernest Parke, its former editor, 'became a director of the *Daily News and Leader*, which Gardiner was not, . . . [a] rather unsatisfactory situation being thus created'.[2] Not that Gardiner had anything to fear from Parke, whom certain members of the combined staff continued to recognize as their supreme chief. But the arrangement was a careless one, indicative of the difficulties that Gardiner experienced and a source of further confusion.

George Cadbury was too advanced in years and too immersed in his business and philanthropic activites to take a direct hand in the paper's administration. But it would be wrong to conclude that either the contents of the *Daily News* or developments in Bouverie Street escaped his surveillance. Gardiner's mail was filled with letters of comment and suggestion from his proprietor, who invoked the Almighty at every turn, and from his proprietor's wife, who disputed his analysis of Thomas Hardy heroines ('Tess would never have gone back'), lectured him on the merits of Mrs Humphry Ward, and criticized the paper's religious coverage ('Mr Cadbury says you are a a member of the Church of England; I wish the writer of the Religious

1. Gardiner to Gwen Gardiner, 7 July 1914 (courtesy of Miss Gwen Gardiner).
2. Harris, *Life So Far*, p. 93.

Column were! It is trash!')[1] As a replacement for Ritzema, who retired to the north in 1907, Cadbury designated his third son, Henry Tylor, who had studied agriculture at Cambridge and whom he could spare from the concern at Bournville. Henry invited Bertram Crosfield, his friend and subsequently his brother-in-law, to assist him as managing director; and Edward Cadbury, the eldest of the brothers, presently assumed the chairmanship of the board. To an extent that Gardiner could not have anticipated when he first accepted his appointment, he became a participant in a family operation. As such, he was treated generously and, as a rule, with deference. Nevertheless, the Cadburys were not the easiest of masters, and problems arose which can best be investigated, like his achievements, in the context of his editorial career.

1. Elsie Cadbury to Gardiner, various undated letters, G.P. George's second wife, Elsie, was later better known as Dame Elizabeth.

4. Early editorship

In the closing weeks of 1904 W. T. Stead's *Review of Reviews* took an inventory of London editors, their papers, and the influence they commanded.[1] As one might have predicted, G. E. Buckle of *The Times* and J. A. Spender of the *Westminster Gazette* headed the list, both editors of party journals 'read by men of both parties'. In the next, more crowded category, came – in order of decreasing importance – the editors of the *Standard* (soon to convert to evening publication and then to perish), the *Daily News*, the *Morning Post*, the *Daily Chronicle*, the *Morning Leader*, *St James's Gazette*, the *Daily Graphic*, the *Star*, the *Globe*, the *Echo*, and the *Pall Mall Gazette*. Under a third heading, that of papers which 'combine the maximum of advertising and of circulation with the minimum of influence', appeared the *Daily Telegraph*, the *Daily Mail*, and, 'hobbling painfully after', the *Daily Express*. And, finally, with neither revenues nor editorial authority to their credit, there followed the *Morning Advertiser*, the *Daily Mirror*, the *Sun*, the *Evening News*, and the *Evening Standard*.

Of the London dailies that had made the transition to the new century, neither the *Sun*, the *Echo*, nor *St James's Gazette* (which merged with the *Evening Standard*) survived to report the death of King Edward in 1910. Two years later, the *Morning Leader* was amalgamated with the *Daily News*. The number of papers upon the news stands remained high, especially if one counted the 'specialized' dailies, which catered to a particular trade, activity, or social group. But the number of popular dailies decreased steadily, largely as a result of financial pressures that took a disproportionately heavy toll on the evening ones. The decade's single significant attempt to reverse the trend, the founding of the *Tribune* in 1906, was a costly failure that demonstrated, among other things, the extent to which the market, particularly for Liberal journals, had been saturated.

1. 'His Majesty's Public Councillors', December 1904.

It was against this background of fierce competition and sustained losses that the *Daily News* improved its relative position. However much Fleet Street officials might have quibbled about the order in which Stead ranked the newspapers of his day, few would have disputed his assertion that the *Daily News* stood close to the top, and that it retained its standing throughout the period of Gardiner's editorship. It made its appeal not, like the *Westminster*, to the gentlemen of the Pall Mall clubs, nor, like the *Manchester Guardian*, to the educated upper middle class,[1] but, more widely, to the amorphous suburban classes whose self-regard and dedication to self-improvement set the tone for the era. Not that circulation statistics alone provided either an index to the influence that Stead described or, for that matter, an assurance of financial solvency: the *Westminster*, for example, provided striking proof that a paper could enjoy prestige without pretence to popularity. But in terms of sales, the record of the *Daily News* was undeniably impressive: after the Boer War, its circulation rose to 80,000; by 1907, its price reduced to a halfpenny, to 151,000; and after 1909, with the simultaneous publication of a northern edition at Manchester, to nearly 400,000.[2] Each increase in sales, however, brought corresponding expenditures upon plant and personnel, with no assured gain in advertising revenues. George Cadbury, happy to take his profit in moral currency, was reconciled to a loss on each ten, twelve, or fourteen-page halfpenny paper. 'It is a big undertaking,' he wrote to Gardiner, weighing the pros and cons of a halfpenny paper,

but I can enter into it with real pleasure and joy, as . . . the opportunity for good is *vast*. The churches have not preached ethical christianity & we must do it & bring them up to a higher standard, this must be the case before

1. A. Yates (whom Peter Clarke identifies as 'very probably a printer on the paper') analysed the *Manchester Guardian*'s readership in a letter (10 August 1912) to C. P. Scott: 'Among cultured and earnest people, on the one hand, and mere commercial men, on the other, the "M.G." is undoubtedly a great force. But the majority of the electors belong to the working class, and working men do not read the "M.G." ' Quoted in Clarke, *Lancashire and the New Liberalism*, p. 155.

2. These statistics, which appear in Gardiner's *Life of George Cadbury*, pp. 228–9, and Derek Hudson, 'Reading', in *Edwardian England*, ed. S. Nowell-Smith, pp. 320–1, do not appear to take into account the return of unsold copies.

'The kingdoms of this world shall become the kingdoms of our Lord, and of His Christ.'[1]

Gardiner's personal contribution to his paper's success cannot be exaggerated. He recruited the foremost Liberal journalists, whom he provided with a showcase for their talents and whom he assiduously kept in delicate balance with one another. The literary features, which were his special interest, maintained a consistently high quality. The leader page, over which he maintained an ultimate control, was force- ful without being obsessive. The news coverage was extensive; the correspondence columns were recognized as a forum for serious debate; and the typography was lively, while avoiding the excesses that characterized most of its halfpenny rivals. The *Daily News* wore a look of dignity that was consonant with its sense of purpose, but the impression with which it left its readers was nonetheless one of vitality.

In the day-to-day management of the paper, Gardiner exercised his authority with a light hand. His function, as he conceived it, was to blend the features of each issue, not to dictate them. Trusting to the judgment and discretion of the men whom he hired, he left them to go their respective ways, provided they did not stray too far from the appointed path. As a rule it was not he but the Cadburys who called a wayward colleague to heel. Nor did his signed articles appear as regularly or prominently as Spender's in the *Westminster Gazette* or Garvin's in the *Observer*. When the occasion presented itself, he would write a light essay (usually under a pseudonym), a book review, a few stanzas of verse, or an obituary notice. Each edition of Ben- jamin Franklin's autobiography, an old favourite, elicited further praise and reflection from him. When he travelled, at home or abroad, he kept detailed journals that yielded material for columns. In 1907 he began the first series of 'character studies' of the public figures with whom he came into contact, eventually alternating them with the Saturday columns that continued until his connection with the paper came to an end in 1921. It was his practice more to inspire than to write leaders. In short, there was no department with which he did not concern himself and which did not feature his work. Following further in Hazlitt's footsteps, he provided anonymous reports of

1. Cadbury to Gardiner, 11 February 1904, G.P.

sporting events, especially boxing matches, which won him Nevinson's sincere (but much resented) accolade as 'the pugilistic expert of the *Daily News*'.[1]

No sooner was Gardiner ensconced in Bouverie Street than he was approached by party stalwarts eager to enlist his services. Herbert Spencer and Sir Charles Dilke proffered arguments to be used against the Government's educational proposals, an affront to nonconformist sensibilities, and others suggested ways to attack such evils as indiscriminate licensing and the importation of Chinese indentured labour to South Africa. Gardiner's position brought him into frequent contact with Herbert Gladstone, the Liberal chief whip, whom he accommodated on certain issues and confronted on others. Gladstone responded sniffily to the *Daily News*'s demand that Liberal MPs spend more time at the House, where they had missed valuable opportunities to challenge and embarrass Tory ministers: 'It is very good for us all to receive rebuke and criticism on the frequent occasions when we need it,' Gladstone advised Gardiner. 'But may I suggest that it is quite impossible either to secure a full or anything like a full attendance of our men every day, or to enact that there shall be no pairs. . . . At least 25 per cent of our men by infirmity, occupation or temperament cannot attend from day to day.'[2]

Like its elected representatives, the Liberal Party in the early years of the century was prevented 'by infirmity, occupation or temperament' from giving effective focus to the growing national opposition to the Balfour Government and its policies. In these circumstances, Liberal editors rendered valuable service of which the politicians, in their disarray, seemed incapable. One sees this most clearly in matters of social reform – unemployment relief, housing, and a minimum standard – where men like Gardiner and Spender took the initiative. And by their insistence, even in the darkest days, that a Liberal renaissance was inevitable, these editors kindled hopes that eventually gave reality to the wish.

1. Nevinson, *More Changes, More Chances*, p. 289
2. 24 June 1902, G.P. As late as 2 March 1905, a group of Liberal MPs – among them Henry Labouchere, Reginald McKenna, David Lloyd George, J. E. Ellis, and Winston Churchill – complained to Gardiner that Liberal absenteeism made it 'almost hopeless to attempt to turn out the Ministry', and asked him to run daily lists of members who had not been present to vote in divisions. G.P.

Despite his age, provincial background, and self-effacing manner, Gardiner quickly ingratiated himself with the 'Certain people of importance' who were later his subjects in that and other volumes of cameo portraits. Francis Hirst introduced him to John Morley, whom Hirst was then assisting in the preparation of a three-volume life of Gladstone. There were modest lunches at Morley's Wimbledon home, where Gardiner brought Philip Snowden and listened enthralled to reminiscences of Gladstone and John Stuart Mill. 'On one occasion,' Gardiner wrote long afterward,

the talk turned on perorations, and Snowden . . . revealed a remarkable facility of remembering famous examples. I was asked to make a contribution & confessed that I cd. only recall one. 'It happens to be one of your own,' I said, turning to Morley. 'Would you care to hear it? . . . It was at the end of a speech which I heard you make in Lancashire at the end of the '80s.'

Morley, more moved by the recollection than by the recitation, identified the passage as part of a speech he had delivered in support of John Slagg's candidacy in a Darwen by-election. Gardiner corrected him: the speech was made at Blackburn, and Slagg had stood not at Darwen, but at Burnley the year before. Unable to agree, the two men bet a penny on who was right, 'and in due course' Gardiner received payment, accompanied by 'an acknowledgement (in Greek) that in this case my memory was better than his'.[1]

There were meetings, too, with Sir Henry Campbell-Bannerman, who recognized in Gardiner a kindred soul and a loyal lieutenant. With typically Scots candour, Sir Henry confided his impressions of several politicians who were to be his colleagues in the 1905 Liberal Government: 'Master Haldane? I haven't spoken to Master Haldane in two years.' The mention of Asquith prompted Sir Henry to remark that 'Asquith *qua* Asquith is a fine fellow, an honest man and a sincere Liberal. But Asquith *cum* Margot is a lost soul.' With a talent for character analysis that Gardiner might envy, Sir Henry went on to describe Sir Robert Reid who, as Lord Loreburn, became Lord Chancellor in 1905: '"Bob Reid?" (closing one eye, he looked reflectively at the ceiling). "Bob Reid is a stout fellow, a good Liberal

1. Gardiner quoted from this peroration in his portrait of Morley in *Prophets, Priests and Kings* (p. 152), but made no mention of this personal exchange, which he recorded in a memorandum among his papers.

and an excellent colleague – if he has his own way. If he doesn't have his own way, he sulks for a month".' Gardiner, who gave Campbell-Bannerman credit for a Lincoln-like 'wisdom clothed in home-spun', was always first to defend him against contemporaries or historians who underrated him. On this score, he was fond of quoting Margot Asquith's backhanded tribute that 'the man who could outwit Haldane, could outwit anybody'. [1]

As his reputation and that of his paper increased, Gardiner's circles widened: J. M. Barrie, who applauded his stand on education, asked to meet him ('I have long liked your outlook on things'); and the Webbs, although piqued by his early criticisms of their proposals for the London School Board, valued him as a champion of progressive causes including, later in the decade, their minority report on the Poor Law. In May 1902 Wilfrid Scawen Blunt requested space in the *Daily News* to address the nation on 'matters of the highest public importance', and, eighteen months later, Bernard Shaw appealed in vain for a full two columns: 'My letter would lose its opportunity in any other paper. . . . However, you might be right in concluding that what I have to say . . . is not worth the space it requires. I am not an impartial judge in the matter.' [2] As with Shaw, to whom he was drawn by a common interest in literature and social problems, Gardiner was soon on intimate terms with Augustine Birrell, who was temporarily excluded from the House of Commons and passing his time 'birrelling' – writing the gentle essays on human nature that were to be 'Alpha of the Plough's' speciality – and presiding over the National Liberal Federation. Faithful, with equal intensity, to the same political leaders and books (Birrell bequeathed Gardiner his copy of Gibbon's autobiography), the two also shared what 'Alpha' considered the most noble of human attributes, 'an umbrella conscience'. [3] Hurrying to catch the last bus to Hampstead after a late dinner party at Lord Portsmouth's, Gardiner realized that he had exchanged his own shabby umbrella for a more elegant model embossed in gold with Birrell's initials. 'I do not deny I have had some uneasy hours brooding over my loss,' Birrell replied to Gardiner's note of apology,

1. Various memoranda, G.P.
2. Shaw to Gardiner, 30 November 1903, G.P.
3. 'Umbrella morals', in *Pebbles on the Shore*, pp. 52–3.

turning over the names & so far as I knew them the antecedents of my fellow guests. . . . But I had faith & was content to wait, relying upon the twangs [?] of Conscience. Your excuse is quite sufficient. Indeed, what with the flunkey who handed me my hat, the flunkey who hitched me into my coat, the third who put me into my cab, I never thought to look what kind of an umbrella it was that the fourth thrust into my hand. Not till I got home did I discover that my golden umbrella with its gold-mounted pencil (the gift of a lady, *Honi Soit* &c.) had undergone a change. . . . Now that once more we are both honest men, we can wait with colossal calm the result of the [by-election] fight at Reading between a Modern Jew [Rufus Isaacs, later Marquess of Reading] and a Christian Antiquarian [Charles Keyser]. [1]

It was not, however, Gardiner's custom to keep such late hours in society or to frequent such formal gatherings. Six nights out of seven, he was on duty in Bouverie Street, where he remained until the last headline was written and the early edition of the next morning's paper was 'put to bed'. After his race against the clock, he was grateful for the opportunity to unwind aboard a bus that meandered past some of London's most famous landmarks and eventually deposited him close to his door in Finchley Road. As 'Alpha', his alter ego, described it: 'The pleasantest hour of my day is the hour about midnight. It is then that I leave the throbbing heart of Fleet Street behind me, jump on to the last bus bound for a distant suburb, and commandeer the back corner seat', which afforded him an unrestricted view of his fellow passengers, the sights along the route, and, weather permitting, a starlit sky. [2] His wife and children were already asleep, and he was usually too tired to share their breakfast a few hours later. He spent his mornings at home, and did not return to central London until after lunch, unless he had an engagement to keep or a story to track down at the National Liberal Club or the Reform Club. By mid-afternoon, he was stationed behind his desk, issuing instructions, approving copy, and readying another edition.

With its proud Cobdenite tradition, there was no doubt of the position that the *Daily News* would take in May 1903, when Joseph Chamberlain unfurled his Tariff Reform banner at the Birmingham

1. Birrell to Gardiner, 5 August 1904, G.P. John Gross, who has written with insight about the Liberal tradition of 'birrellers', is less than fair when he dismisses Birrell, the politician and Irish Secretary, as 'a benign old bookworm'. *The Rise and Fall of the Man of Letters*, pp. 118–22.
2. *The Star*, 6 December 1916.

Town Hall. Although it was not yet apparent how disruptive Chamberlain's latest tack would prove to the Unionist Government, in which he continued for the time being as Colonial Secretary, Gardiner recognized this fortuitous occasion as an opportunity to unify and galvanize the Liberal Opposition. Not for a moment did he seriously consider the economic validity of Chamberlain's attacks on the Free Trade system: this was, to him, purely a moral and, as such, a political question. As a spokesman for Radical causes, he considered this Chamberlain's ultimate treachery; as one who had experienced deprivation, he condemned 'stomach taxes' as a cruel hoax upon the labouring poor; as an internationalist, he found the concept of retaliatory duties morally repugnant. Like many Liberals, he reduced the whole affair to a sinister attempt by Chamberlain to capture the limelight and thereby mastery of the Unionist machine. Worse, it seemed to him a shameful stunt to divert the country's attention from pressing social needs. Campbell-Bannerman, himself not inactive in defence of Free Trade, gave praise to Gardiner's tone and tactics: 'You appear to me to be taking, if I may say so, quite the right line.' [1]

For the first time, Gardiner found himself in league with Asquith, the most vigorous and eloquent of Chamberlain's Liberal antagonists, whose Liberal Imperialist connections had hitherto obscured the literary and temperamental affinities between them. It was still too early for him to absolve Asquith from the machinations of the previous decade, and some of their most serious quarrels lay ahead; but he came to prize Asquith's quick intelligence and oratorical gifts. Gardiner, too, assumed an active part in the rebuttal to Chamberlain. On the evening of 15 December 1904, he travelled to the Edinburgh Castle Hall in the Limehouse section of east London, where he heard the high priest of protectionism deliver 'his Imperial dithyrambs with a counterfeit solemnity which was not in its way ineffective'. His readers the next morning were treated to an on-the-spot account of his adventures:

'Why do you lock the door?' I asked the guard at Blackfriars station as he turned his key in the door of my compartment. 'To keep the workmen out,' he replied laconically. The answer comes back to mind as I glance round on the dense throng that crowds the Edinburgh Castle Hall. The meeting is in the East-end, but not of it. The East-end is outside in the

1. Campbell-Bannerman to Gardiner, 18 December 1903, G.P.

mean, dim-lit streets, watching the constant processions of carriages and motorcars which bring up the Protectionist battalions from the West.

Gardiner's intense commitment to a programme of social re-construction along advanced Radical lines made it difficult for him to credit the humanitarian sentiments of Chamberlain, whose political fortunes were too closely linked to vested interests that impeded progress. George Cadbury, like Chamberlain a Birmingham manu-facturer of nonconformist background, appeared to Gardiner a more disinterested and purposeful reformer, whose business career testified to the benefits, moral as well as material, of Free Trade. In a private capacity, Cadbury had long agitated for subsidized housing, for non-contributory old-age pensions,[1] for extensive land reform in favour of smallholdings (a prominent feature in Chamberlain's 1885 'un-authorised programme'), and for an end to the infamous sweated industries. Gardiner, whose deep concern for the execrable living and working conditions of the poor owed more to the inquiries of Charles Booth and Seebohm Rowntree than to his employment by Cadbury, counted among his colleagues and acquaintances some of Edwardian England's most persuasive propagandists against social injustice, who used the *Daily News* to help their contemporaries to discover the nature and extent of poverty. He did not exaggerate when he de-scribed the paper as 'the vehicle in the press of the new spirit of social reform which was soon to change the current of politics', and 'a vehicle not merely of opinion but of action'.[2]

It is necessary to recall that although most of the problems that Gardiner helped to publicize were eventually the subject of Liberal legislation, he acted without the direct encouragement (and, in some cases, against the wishes) of his party chiefs. Campbell-Bannerman, whatever his sympathies, could not afford to alienate either his Whiggish followers or the more orthodox Gladstonians by sanction-ing an implicit attack upon the rights of property. Moreover, as in the matter of old-age pensions, the remedies that Gardiner proposed were often far more ambitious than the schemes subsequently adopted by Liberal ministers, who had a Tory-dominated House of Lords as

1. See Bentley B. Gilbert, *The Evolution of National Insurance in Great Britain*, pp. 190–1, which specifically contrasts Cadbury's attitude with Chamberlain's.
2. *Life of George Cadbury*, pp. 222, 225.

well as backbench conflicts to take into account. Resigned to such disappointments, he reasoned that, while official policy could not hope to keep pace with advanced opinion, the spokesmen for advanced opinion nonetheless had an obligation to forge continually ahead.

A self-taught student of history, Gardiner subscribed to the contemporary Radical view (given currency by his friends J. L. and Barbara Hammond) that the ills of industrial society were largely the result of the systematic exclusion of smallholders from the land. The enclosure movements of the late eighteenth and early nineteenth centuries were held to be the prelude to the growth of slums, to a fall in real wages, to a general deterioration in the quality of life, and, still more problematically, to a decline in agricultural productivity. What did it matter if the scholarship of the Hammonds, like the arguments with which Lloyd George was to defend his People's Budget, appealed more to conscience than to fact? Each side in the Edwardian class conflict had its theory of history, and neither sacrificed rhetoric for objectivity. To his credit, Gardiner did not go as far as some Radicals in romanticizing the preindustrial past. For one thing, his knowledge of eighteenth-century literature did not permit him to believe that that had been an age of self-sufficient yeomen among whom poverty was unknown. For another, his concern with world problems, particularly the situation in India, impressed on him the essential benefits of an industrial economy. He took up the cry for land reform not simply as a means to redress an historic grievance, but, more constructively, to alleviate early twentieth-century agrarian distress. Combining salient features of the Fabian programme with the old Radical 'three-acres-and-a-cow' demand, he campaigned for a more equitable taxation of land values, for the reallocation of property to the greatest extent practicable among independent owner-occupiers, and for the adoption of 'collective methods which have revolutionised agriculture on the Continent'.[1] He wrote leaders and columns in the *Daily News* on the subject – some of the best were reprinted in pamphlet form – and on one occasion (8 December 1903) offered a

1. Gardiner, introduction to C. F. G. Masterman, *et. al.*, *To Colonise England*; the 'land campaign', as an ingredient in Edwardian politics and especially in Lloyd George's career, is analysed by H. V. Emy in *Lloyd George*, ed. A. J. P. Taylor, pp. 35–68.

poem, more distinguished by social commitment than by literary merit, which mournfully concluded:

> How long, O Lord, shall the people be
> Aliens in their own country?
> How long shall the Squire from his park gate see
> Giles follow the plough to the workhouse door?

Like other agents of the 'new Liberalism', with its advocacy of greater state intervention, the *Daily News* aroused concern for the physical welfare of the working classes by 'publishing facts and exploring values'.[1] Not that all humanitarians had the same party loyalties: in the winter of 1904–5 Sir John Gorst, the Tory democrat, conducted his well-publicized tours of the East End slums to much the same purpose and effect. During the same months, which witnessed the introduction of various relief schemes, the *Daily News* launched a fund for the residents of the London dock area at West Ham, where chronic unemployment was intensified by seasonal layoffs and by heavy fogs that paralysed commerce along the lower Thames.[2] An estimated 50,000 persons, living beyond the boundaries of the City of London and therefore ineligible for aid from such charities as the Mansion House Fund for the Unemployed, were 'reduced to a condition of impoverishment unexampled even in a district where extreme poverty is the normal condition'. Masterman, adopted to stand for an adjacent constituency in the next general election, brought the appalling situation to the attention of his editor. 'Distress broods like a black cloud over Canning Town and South West Ham', the *Daily News* told its readers (the style was early A.G.G. at his turgid best), and, beginning on 21 December, it issued daily appeals for cash, food, and clothing. The first response, an anonymous contribution of £250 from G. P. Gooch, was more than double the amount that the trade unionists of West Ham had modestly hoped to raise. 'By Christmas,' Mrs Masterman later recalled, '£5000 had been collected and the staff of the *Daily News* worked as volunteers all night on Christmas Eve to send off the quantities of parcels that

1. Asa Briggs, 'The political scene', in *Edwardian England*, ed. Nowell-Smith, p. 58.
2. Except where otherwise noted, this paragraph is based on Lucy Masterman, *C. F. G. Masterman*, pp. 53–6; Gardiner's *Life of Cadbury*, pp. 226–7; and his introduction to Copping, *Pictures of Poverty*.

arrived.' Interest was kept alive by the serialization in the *Daily News* of Arthur E. Copping's heart-rending sketches of life among the East End poor, and the total receipts eventually approached £12,000.

Sensitive to charges in *The Times* (6 January 1905) that indiscriminate alms-giving produced 'greed and demoralization among those who received it and corruption among those who handled it', the sponsors of the fund endowed projects to 'improvise employment'. Accompanied by Masterman and Will Crooks, Labour M.P. for Woolwich, Gardiner toured the afflicted area and spoke to mayors, corporation officials and the Epping Forest commissioners, who agreed to various schemes by which some 32,000 days of work were provided for unemployed dockers. Old playgrounds were asphalted, and new ones laid out, an open air bath was constructed, West Ham hospital was painted and decorated, levelling and draining work was carried out in Epping Forest, and in other directions useful and permanent work was accomplished, all with the *Daily News*'s bounty. Proud as they were of their efforts, the organizers of the fund were aware that private munificence could hope neither to eliminate the problem nor to indemnify the greater number of its victims. On 19 January the paper cited the West Ham project as 'a striking object lesson of the desirability of previous preparations and the scheduling of work of national importance which would be undertaken in these times of scarcity'. The success of the enterprise, no less than the grave conditions that had occasioned it, gave impetus to the movement for labour exchanges and unemployment insurance, and accelerated the retreat from the classical *laissez-faire* position.

Following the dictates of conscience, the *Daily News* entered fearlessly into the most sensitive of areas, that of Edwardian industrial relations. In the aftermath of the 1901 Taff Vale decision, which effectively disabled trade unions by making it prohibitive to strike, the morality and legality of a given situation were often in conflict. One of the fiercest and most devastating disputes raged at Bethesda in the Frangeon valley of North Wales, where Lord Penrhyn (whom Gardiner likened to Sir Anthony Absolute) closed down his giant slate quarries sooner than bargain with trade union officials. To be sure, all of the intransigence was not on one side, but the fact remained that Lord Penrhyn, although considerably inconvenienced, did not face starvation. Bethesda's only remaining source of income was the town choir, which gave benefit performances around the country. The *Daily News*, unable to impress on the Balfour Government the necessity for mandatory arbitration, formed a committee to solicit charitable contributions. In all some £30,000 was raised. It was obvious that Lord Penrhyn was less concerned with obtaining a satisfactory settlement than with breaking the backbone of the trade union, which, without reserves of capital or influence, finally capitulated in December 1904. He subsequently brought a successful legal action against W. J. Parry, a local adversary who had dared to accuse him of 'tyranny', and the *Daily News*, through the renewed generosity of its readers, provided a further £2500 to save Parry from certain bankruptcy and probable imprisonment. Again, the need for remedial legislation was incontrovertible.

No catalogue of the *Daily News*'s attempts to awaken the national conscience would be complete without an account of the campaign to expose and put an end to the abuse known as sweated labour.[1] In the spring of 1906 the paper sponsored (at Cadbury's expense) a six-week exhibition at the Queen's Hall, London, that drew 30,000 spectators. Merchandise was displayed alongside reports of the wages paid for its manufacture: 'Button roses made at 1s. 4d. a gross, with buds thrown in; . . . cardboard boxes at a wage which worked out at 1s. 3d. for twelve hours; hook and eye carding at 1s. 4d. for 384 hooks and 384 eyes; . . . a heavy day's work of eleven hours at chain-making which gave an average wage of 6s. to 8s. a week.' Here was demonstrable proof that 'sweating . . . did not make goods cheap: it only made human life cheap'.

But it was one thing to indict a practice, and another to abolish it. A National Anti-Sweating League was founded to press for a minimum wage in those crafts or industries where workers, often dispersed in their homes, lacked the means to organize in defence of their interests. Cadbury was president of the League, and paid the rent on its headquarters in Mecklenburgh Square. Lord Beauchamp, not yet a Liberal minister, was treasurer, and Gardiner was president of the

---

1. Except where otherwise noted, this account is based on Gardiner's *Life of George Cadbury*, pp. 224–5; his introduction to Clementia Black, *Sweated Industry and the Minimum Wage*; his introduction to C. F. G. Masterman *et. al.*, *To Colonise England*; *The Christian Commonwealth* (special supplement), 5 February 1908; and reports in *The Times*, 22 July 1908, and 23 July 1909.

executive committee, which included Lord Henry Bentinck, Chiozza Money, Shaw, and Sir Arthur Steel-Maitland. Among the vice-presidents were Beatrice and Sidney Webb, Herbert Gladstone, Keir Hardie and Wells.

Gardiner, one of the League's most effective propagandists, agreed with Beauchamp that there existed 'a number of people . . . sincerely anxious to do what they can to prevent sweating but not knowing how to set about it'.[1] The League's purpose was therefore one of education as well as agitation. Gardiner deprecated the suggestion that tariff reform might indirectly provide a remedy, and pointed to evidence that 'the horrors of sweating in Protectionist America go deeper even than those in Free Trade England'. Instead, he called on the state to protect the victims of exploitation and, 'in protecting them, protect itself also'. The League adopted as its primary objective the promotion of Dilke's Sweated Industries Bill. On 28 January 1908 it held a 'Great National Demonstration' at the Queen's Hall at which the Bishop of Birmingham took the chair and speeches were delivered by Dilke, Shaw, Gardiner, Arthur Henderson, Will Crooks, and Mary Reid Macarthur, editor of *The Woman Worker*. The following July Gardiner presided at the League's annual meeting and proclaimed to his colleagues that 'they now stood . . . in the presence of victory'. It was not a complete victory, but nonetheless one that afforded considerable satisfaction. Winston Churchill's Trade Boards Bill, modelled on the Dilke proposals, set a minimum wage in specific industries – tailoring, lace finishing, cardboard box making and chain making – and passed its third reading in the House of Commons in time to be celebrated at the League's third and final annual session. 'Not one of them could doubt the success of the Bill when it became an Act,' Gardiner told his associates, and he confidently (and accurately) predicted not only its prompt acceptance by the Lords, but also the 'extension of its principles to other trades needing it'.

More than any of Gardiner's other philanthropic or reformist activities, his campaign against sweated labour won him a respect and gratitude apart from that accorded to his paper. Most notably, his chairmanship of the League's executive committee strengthened his bonds with Beatrice Webb. Before her marriage and 'conversion' to

1. Beauchamp to Gardiner, 16 July 1906, G.P.

Fabian socialism, Mrs Webb assisted Charles Booth in his investigation of conditions among East End tailors, whose suffering, she had reported in 1890 to a select committee of the House of Lords, 'could scarcely be exaggerated'. Through the League he was also brought into lifelong collaboration with the young J. J. ('Jimmy') Mallon, already a champion of the London poor, who in 1913 became warden of Toynbee Hall and eight years later Gardiner's son-in-law. Reformers of every stripe and intention looked to Gardiner for publicity and often advice, among them 'General' William Booth of the Salvation Army, who sought to enlist his influence on behalf of an ill-fated scheme to colonize Rhodesia as a means 'of providing a way of escape for many of the deserving poor and suffering classes in this country'. [1] Whatever prominence he attained inevitably attached to his paper, which, in the opinion of A. M. M. Methuen, the progressive-minded publisher, had 'improved enormously' by early 1905: 'It seems to me to have something which few papers possess – a soul.' [2] By encouraging and articulating a demand for social change, the *Daily News* made a substantial contribution to the Liberal Party's spectacular success at the polls the following year. But Gardiner, even in his elation, did not confuse the shadow of victory with its substance. In the ensuing decade, as much to his annoyance as to theirs, he was frequently moved to remind Liberal ministers of their campaign pledges and the nation's social priorities.

As we shall see, Gardiner's criticisms of governmental policy did not abate, and in several crucial respects intensified, after the return of his own party to power. One of the essential qualities of the Radical tradition, and a source of its perpetual frustration, was an inveterate distrust of official attitudes. One of the characteristics of a conscientious journalist, and a measure of his self-respect, was a refusal to subordinate truth (as he saw it) to party interest. Yet Gardiner, however impatient he might become with Liberal spokesmen, invariably preferred them to their Tory counterparts, who seemed to him narrowminded, self-seeking, and cynical.

To an unusual degree, political controversy in the early years of the century turned towards, indeed hinged on, personality. As exemplified perhaps most famously by Lytton Strachey, the age was one that

1. Booth to Gardiner, 29 September 1906 and 15 April 1908, G.P.
2. Methuen to Gardiner, 27 February 1905, G.P.

defined itself and preceding generations in terms of 'eminent' individuals. It was much the fashion to write thumbnail sketches of public figures, each of whom was held to embody a particular policy or attitude. Along with Gardiner, those who tried their hand at the game included W. T. Stead, Herbert Sidebotham, Harold Begbie, G. W. E. Russell, Bryce, and Churchill. In contemporary politics, Chamberlain's name was synonymous with protectionism, Milner's with the glories (and extravagances) of empire, Lord Roberts's with conscription, Morley's with residual Gladstonianism, Sir John (later Lord) Fisher's with the 'Blue Water' school of naval defence, Lloyd George's with Jacobinism, John Redmond's with Irish Home Rule, and Rosebery's with Liberal Imperialism.

It is noteworthy that neither of the official party leaders, Campbell-Bannerman or Balfour, possessed a public image as readily identifiable as some of their confederates. The *Daily News*, despite George Cadbury's recommendation 'that personalities be avoided as far as possible',[1] was too much a product of the times to defy fashion. Its editor, of course, made his reputation as a delineator of personality and a diagnostician of its effect upon policy. It was therefore too much to expect that the paper would debate topical issues without reference to the individuals who were popularly identified with them.

The death in October 1904 of Sir William Harcourt, who had given long and devoted service to the Liberal cause, inspired Gardiner to write a lengthy tribute, part of it in verse, that was obviously intended to promote a reaction in favour of the principles which Harcourt had vainly struggled to establish. His detailed review of Harcourt's parliamentary career, with special emphasis upon the prolonged leadership crisis of the 1890s, affirmed the patriotism of the 'Little Englander' position and reflected unfavourably on Rosebery and the Liberal Imperialists.[2] Harcourt, had he survived, might well have been an impediment to Liberal reunion; but the heirs to his memory mourned him as a victim of factionalism and a guardian of their party's historic values.

1. Cadbury to Alfred Harmsworth [spring 1904], cited in Pound and Harmsworth, *Northcliffe*, p. 283.

2. *Daily News*, 3 October 1904; Sir William's son, 'Loulou' (later the 1st Viscount Harcourt), expressed gratitude 'for your welcome and ready sympathy' to Gardiner, whom he later commissioned to write the official biography of his father (5 October 1904, G.P.).

The *Daily News* boasted its villains as well as its heroes. Alfred Harmsworth, who received his baronetcy on the same occasion that Edward Elgar was made a knight (the *Daily News* icily noted the 'disparity of public service' between the two), was already regarded as an agent of corruption within the profession and a potential danger to national life. Kipling was denounced as much for his influence on poetry as for his base appeal to popular emotions. But it was the 'prancing pro-consuls' of the empire, Lords Curzon and Milner, for whom the greatest indignation was reserved. Both neared retirement from their respective imperial assignments as the general election approached, and in the opinion of Bouverie Street each personified in his own way the worst attributes of empire: Curzon, the Viceroy of India, by his swagger, his costly border aggressions, and his disdain for mass sentiment; Milner, the High Commissioner in South Africa, by his prejudice against democracy, his reliance on force, and his obdurate refusal to compromise. It is doubtful that any Liberal figure at this time suffered greater abuse in the right-wing press than Milner did in the *Daily News*, where he was systematically pilloried as the man who had burned Boer farmhouses and whose importation of Chinese 'coolie' labour had displaced white workers. 'The British Empire has never, perhaps, produced a ruler who has been so consistently wrong,' it reflected in a leader on 13 October 1904:

He has never shown any width of outlook or breadth of sympathy. From first to last he has acted, not as the representative of the whole South African people, but as the tool of a set of parasites, whose presence is a curse to the country . . ., and it will be written of his retirement that it was the only boon he ever conferred on the country which he misruled.

It was not, however, until 2 March 1905 that the *Daily News* had the satisfaction of formally announcing Milner's retirement, which it regarded 'as inevitable as the coming Liberal victory. His retention of office a day after the accession of the Liberals to power would be impossible. . . . He represents the war and all the waste and ruin and bloodshed it created.'

The second of the 'inevitabilities' to which Gardiner looked forward – Balfour's departure from office – did not occur until 4 December. A string of by-election defeats that portended certain disaster convinced the Unionist Prime Minister to hold on until the last possible moment in the hope that his Liberal opponents might discredit themselves by their wrangling. On 31 March, and regularly thereafter, the *Daily News* rebuked Balfour, 'who by refusing to appeal to the country has continued to govern in defiance of popular will'. But neither such demands nor occasional embarrassments in the House appeared to ruffle Balfour, whose majority remained more than ample for him to survive the full term of the present Parliament. The longer the Liberals waited, the more feverishly they intrigued against each other, nearly creating the very situation that was his desperate hope.

In August Gardiner took the opportunity of Parliament's recess to enjoy his first holiday on the Continent. His travels in Germany were intended to acquaint him with social conditions there (the following spring's Anti-Sweating Exhibition acknowledged its debt to a similar presentation in Berlin), and, not least, to allow him to replenish his energies for the political struggles that lay ahead. Although he spoke neither German nor any other foreign language, he was a warm admirer of German culture and had never hesitated to proclaim himself an advocate of improved Anglo-German relations. The previous March, when the Kaiser's visit to Morocco had 'occasioned a flutter in the dovecots', he had attempted to allay his countrymen's fears by stressing the fundamentally pacific nature of German foreign policy: 'The Kaiser is always histrionic,' he wrote on the 27th, 'and his orations will be awaited with much curiosity and little concern.'

During his three-and-a-half weeks in Germany, Gardiner kept an encyclopaedic journal, which he mailed in instalments to his wife at Bournemouth with instructions to read it to the children and to 'take it home if only that I may have some materials for an article or two afterwards'. Where words failed him, he supplied a drawing or a diagram in the margin. He saw a good deal of the country, much of the southern region by foot, and was favourably impressed by the living conditions, if not by the scenery: neither the Tyrol nor the Black Forest could compare to either the Lake District or the wild beauty of North Wales, but their populations were better fed, better housed, and appreciably more sober. 'Everybody', he reported, 'drinks beer, but it is the light lager & there is apparently no drunkenness.' It also struck him that 'everybody in Germany seems to have a cigar in his teeth', his being the only pipe in evidence. It was impossible to get a cup of tea, but that was the only inconvenience. The state-operated railways were a joy, the people outgoing and friendly, and, unlike Stonehenge at this time, the monuments of the countryside were 'open to all and not shut off with notice boards & circled with ring fences'.

Not everything in Germany, however, was worthy of emulation. Standing in 'the courtyard of the castle' at Heidelberg, he saw

some little boys engaged in a game which seemed to throw a flashlight on German life. It was a game of soldiers, but it was played with a seriousness I have never seen equalled in England. One of the half dozen boys was got up in the uniform of a lieut., red cape gloves complete, & he was drilling a couple of others while the captain, helmetted & carrying a wooden sword, looked on, and another also in helmet carried a card on which he marked the point. It was all done with immense gravity. Militarism is bred in the bone of the Germans & conscription nourishes & keeps it alive.

Elsewhere in the same city, he saw disturbing evidence of militarism in one of its most sadistic manifestations among the university students, whose 'duelling idiocy' filled him with revulsion.

But these were not the aspects of German life that he chose to dwell on either privately in his journal or in his published accounts. Rather, he pointed to Germany's achievements in education, her burgeoning trade union movement, and her expanding commercial contacts, all of which he expected to exert a salutary influence. In this respect, he was typical of a generation of English Radicals, who trusted to the en-lightened self-interest of nations and who saw in German growth not a threat but, on the contrary, an invitation to greater cooperation. His tendency when abroad to find reassuring confirmation of Britain's inherent superiority brings to mind John Stuart Mill's dictum that 'in history, as in travelling, men usually see only what they already had in their minds'. On the last Sunday before his return, he attended Roman Catholic worship in Bavaria: 'Happy England to have been delivered from such a blight. . . . Tomorrow we are going to a German Evangelical Church to take the taste of this morning's mummery out of our mouths.'

Impatient to return to his family, to his desk, and to the political barricades, Gardiner preceded home the last of his dispatches from

Germany. Surprisingly little had changed in his absence. With considerably more anxiety than amusement, Liberals occupied themselves at the parlour game of cabinet-making, shifting various designees from the Exchequer to the Home Office to the Board of Trade and back again. It was a game without rules in which the key players held their cards close to their chests and, for the most part, gave no indication how high they were prepared to bid. Each contender had his team of self-proclaimed experts, among whom journalists figured prominently. The croupier was Balfour, who set the stakes by his refusal to declare whether he intended to resign or dissolve. Throughout the autumn, Gardiner pressed for the second alternative, which would permit the Liberals to come to office with a general election behind them and their ranks presumably solidified by success. But that was not to be the case, and, on the morning of 5 December, Campbell-Bannerman had the unenviable task of assembling a team that would appeal to the nation in the name of a revived and reunified Liberalism.

5. The Liberal revival

The formation of the 1905 Liberal Government, preceding as it did a general election, was a task of the utmost delicacy. On the one hand, Sir Henry Campbell-Bannerman had to assemble a viable team from the disparate talents at his disposal; on the other, he had to convince the electorate, which had not returned a Liberal majority since 1892, of his party's competence to govern. On neither score could he afford to dispense with the Liberal Imperialists, whose exclusion would have deprived the Cabinet of some of its most respected and effective members, and, at the same time, would have been widely regarded as a signal of the party's continued debility. The question, however, was which Liberal Imperialists he was prepared to invite, which ones would accept his invitation, and what terms they might extract from him.

For that matter, it was not clear in many minds whether Campbell-Bannerman ought to retain his command – indeed, whether he intended to do so – or, if he did, whether his leadership would continue beyond the general election. Back in 1903 he expressed doubts about his physical powers that gave rise to persistent speculation that he would conveniently step aside on the threshold of office, possibly in favour of Lord Rosebery. In recent months, Asquith, Grey and Haldane, the three most active Liberal Imperialists, had come to doubt the wisdom, let alone the feasibility, of a Roseberyan restoration. Meeting in September at Relugas, Grey's retreat in the northeast of Scotland, they formalized an alternate strategy, the terms of which Haldane was deputed to convey to the King at Balmoral. They professed their willingness to join a Campbell-Bannerman ministry on receipt of assurances that the Prime Minister would retire to the Lords, that Asquith would receive the Exchequer and the leadership of the Commons, that Grey was assigned either the Colonial or Foreign Office, and that Haldane was made Lord Chancellor. There was a distinct possibility that, with royal connivance, such an arrangement might have been imposed on Campbell-Bannerman and the majority of the parliamentary Liberal Party. That the strategy failed reflected less Campbell-Bannerman's mastery of the situation than the fact that Asquith retreated from his demands sooner than endanger his acknowledged position as heir apparent to whom the succession would assuredly pass before long.

Gardiner was among those who took upon himself the task of fortifying Campbell-Bannerman against the Liberal Imperialist assault. Unlike *The Times* and even the *Westminster Gazette*, the *Daily News* insisted that the man who had led the party through recent years of adversity was not only entitled but also admirably equipped to assume the full powers of the premiership. Gardiner had expected to encounter stubborn resistance from imperialists of both parties, who feared the Liberal leader's Radical connections and his alleged 'pro-Boer' sympathies; what he had not anticipated was the self-effacing attitude of Campbell-Bannerman, who, in the words of his biographer, 'joined cheerfully in discussing the various ways of eliminating himself'. [1]

On the morning of Tuesday, 5 December, Campbell-Bannerman was duly summoned to Buckingham Palace, where the King commissioned him to form a ministry, and offered the friendly advice (which was instantly recognized as Haldane's work) that it might be best for his fragile health to take a peerage. Asquith, who had accepted without condition the offer of the Exchequer, urged consideration of the King's suggestion on the grounds that 'the combination of leading the House and being Prime Minister . . .[was] practically two men's work'. Besides, with Lord Spencer's illness and Lord Rosebery's probable defection, the Liberal forces in the upper House stood badly in need of reinforcement. The new premier listened sympathetically, but neither these arguments nor the threat of Grey's unavailability appeared to move him. A day passed, during which Campbell-Bannerman unsuccessfully offered Lord Cromer the Foreign Secretaryship, and Asquith, probably embarrassed by his failure to stand as firm as he had promised the other Liberal Imperialist triumvirs, interrupted an engagement at Hatfield to press his case. He called on Sir Henry in Belgrave Square and, more candidly than before, cited his own discomfort rather than his concern for his

1. Spender, *The Life of the Rt Hon. Sir Henry Campbell-Bannerman*, ii, 138.

leader's physical welfare: 'It is no use going over the same ground again, my dear C.B. I make a personal appeal to you, which I've never done before; I urge you to go to the House of Lords and solve this difficulty.' According to Margot Asquith, who recorded her husband's accounts of these interviews in her diary,[1] Campbell-Bannerman genially agreed to lay the matter before his wife, who was due to arrive from Scotland that evening. It was supposedly her declaration of 'no surrender', delivered at the dinner table, that made him determined to stand his ground.

There are reasons to suspect, however, that the issue was more complicated and the deliberations more prolonged. Gardiner, when he arrived at his office the next afternoon, found a message from Herbert Gladstone, who asked him to 'be good enough to ring me up as I wish to speak to you on an urgent matter'. Gladstone left perplexing instructions that Gardiner was to telephone at precisely a quarter past ten ('I say 10.15 because an early hour will probably suit you best but I shall be at home after 10.15') and that the caller was not, at any time in the conversation, to pronounce the name of the party to whom he was speaking. Barely able to restrain his curiosity, Gardiner rang the specified number at the appointed time, and Gladstone himself answered. He asked whether Gardiner had seen the leader in that morning's *Times*, which strongly endorsed the proposal of a peerage for Campbell-Bannerman and the designation of Asquith as leader of the Commons, and he assumed that the *Daily News* contemplated a reply. 'May I suggest,' he cryptically told Gardiner, 'that you should not dismiss the idea too absolutely.'

Gardiner was dumbfounded. 'Gladstone', he later wrote in an unpublished account of the episode, 'was one of the most loyal of C.B.'s supporters & had already accepted the Home Secretaryship & I was puzzled by the singular request.' On whose behalf was Gladstone acting? The request for clarification met with no response. Gardiner, whose 'intention had been to insist in the strongest terms on C.B. staying in the H. of C.', did not know how to proceed. 'If H.G. was in favour of C.B. going upstairs,' he reasoned, 'then C.B. himself must have given way.' At a loss for an explanation, and with the next day's paper ready to go to press, he sought the advice of

1. Quoted in her *Autobiography*, ii, 71 ff., which Roy Jenkins has described as 'the fullest account of [these] days', *Asquith*, p. 154.

Masterman, who agreed that, despite the lateness of the hour, 'the best thing was to put the question bluntly to C.B. himself'. Gardiner dashed off a note 'referring to *The Times* leader, but not, of course, to the telephone communication, and asking for a word of guidance'. His secretary took it to Belgrave Square. Campbell-Bannerman, who had already retired for the night, came downstairs in his dressing gown and gave his approval for 'a reply to *The Times* [that] was not wanting in vigour & firmness'.

Greatly relieved by the Prime Minister's response, Gardiner none-theless remained puzzled by Gladstone's seemingly disloyal behaviour, and disquieted by the possibility that Sir Henry would prove unable to withstand the subtle pressures of those closest to him. On Thursday, the 7th, he expressed his concern to John Sinclair (later Lord Pentland), Campbell-Bannerman's former private secretary and close friend, again taking care not to reveal the source of his worry:

> I am extremely anxious to take a strong line against the Lords idea. In this matter I know that we have the party with us. C.B.'s withdrawal at this moment will be a wet blanket over the General Election. It will take the heart out of all of us. It will be taken as [a] sign of weakness & it will leave us without anyone to state our policy. . . . To the rank & file, C.B. is the leader who has kept the flag [flying] & has at last won through. . . . I should like him to know if possible how widespread & deep this feeling is & if I could see him I should be glad. [1]

It is not clear whether Campbell-Bannerman spared time from the rigours of Cabinet construction to gratify Gardiner's request for an interview, but the leader pages of the *Daily News* could leave him no doubt of its editor's sentiments. In any case, Gardiner's fears were allayed by the composition of the Cabinet as it was made known on Friday. The Prime Minister, who remained a commoner, had ultimately prevailed over Grey, who went to the Foreign Office, and Haldane, whom he mischievously dispatched to the War Office, that infamous graveyard of reputations. The woolsack, which Haldane had coveted, was assigned instead to the faithful Sir Robert Reid, now Lord Loreburn. Also among the appointees were such Glad-stonian fundamentalists as Morley, James Bryce, Lord Ripon, and

---

1. Gardiner to Sinclair, 7 December 1905, Campbell-Bannerman Papers, Add. MSS 41,230, fols 91–92.

Herbert Gladstone (the last, his paternity notwithstanding, the least effective exponent of the creed), such Whigs as Lords Elgin, Carrington, and Crewe, such representatives of the Radical left as John Burns and Lloyd George, and such lesser Liberal Imperialists as Sydney Buxton and Henry Fowler (later Lord Wolverhampton). Winston Churchill, Lord Randolph's son, was named Under-Secretary for the Colonies; at least on the face of things, there were others with far better claims to consideration, but the inclusion of a Churchill in a Liberal Government afforded an irresistible satisfaction. Campbell-Bannerman had performed a masterly job of neutralizing one influence with another, and of accommodating the widest possible range of talents and personalities within the framework of an effective administration. Still, Gardiner continued to brood over Gladstone's 'inexplicable' telephone conversation on the night of the 6th, and he liked to think that he might have been to some degree responsible for influencing the course of events. He never broached the subject with Gladstone, of whose Home Office policies he was a relentless critic, and pondered to the end of his days 'the meaning of his intervention in favour of the other side'.[1]

The novelty of office and, presently, the pressures of electioneering were a welcome distraction from the party's internal dissensions. With polling scheduled to begin on 12 January Campbell-Bannerman officially opened the campaign on 21 December with a well received (but, for the most part, inaudible) speech at the cavernous Albert Hall. Although most politicians did not join the fray until after Christmas, the party press had neither time nor patience for seasonal formalities. Even before the last Cabinet appointments had been made, the battle already flared. The *Daily News*, with renewed vitality, revived its cry against 'Chinese slavery' in the Transvaal. At the risk of opening wounds among its fellow Liberals, it denounced the late Government's jingo excesses, and recalled the iniquities of Balfour's licensing and educational schemes. But, most of all, it

1. In addition to his memorandum on the subject, written many years later, Gardiner wrote a brief account of the incident as a footnote to Gladstone's message, which he preserved among his papers. He allowed Massingham to publish a belated and guarded report of the conversation in his 'London Diary' (The *Nation*, 4 June 1921), but if his intention was to elicit an explanation from Gladstone, he was not successful.

thundered against the inherent evils of protectionism as preached by Chamberlain, whom, it alleged, a Tory victory would bring to a position of overweening authority: 'Science, democracy, Radicalism, Liberalism, yes, and true Conservatism are hostile to this plausible demagogue, who during the last six years has so grievously misled, and so sadly injured the people of Great Britain', a typical leader proclaimed on 4 January. Five days later the paper implored its readers to 'realize that Chamberlainism and Balfourism are dying forces, and [to] take care by their votes next week to give them the fatal stroke'.

With a sure sense of impending triumph, the *Daily News* threw its full weight into what it described (6 January) as 'by far the greatest electoral struggle of our generation'. It made polite, but comparatively brief mention of campaign appearances by Liberal Imperialists, while the least impressive remark from the Prime Minister received extensive coverage and frequent reiteration. The greatest prominence was accorded to those politicians with whom it identified: Lloyd George, for one, and, more curiously, Morley and Burns, the former praised for imparting his 'old faith' to the struggle, and the latter for contributing his 'experience and sound, practical wisdom'. Burns won special gratitude by travelling to north Worcestershire, where Cadbury was an elector, to speak on behalf of J. W. Wilson, a defector from Unionism who now stood in the Liberal interest.

The Liberal floodtide began tentatively enough on the 12th, with the gain of a single seat at Ipswich. It was in fact the second day of polling that proved the 'first day of the deluge', with Balfour heading the list of Tory casualties. On the comparable day of the previous general election, the *Daily News* reckoned, the Unionists had captured twenty-six constituencies and the Liberals and Labourites only fifteen; now, the Unionists had won a mere five contests, and the parties of the left, between them, carried thirty-six. The ultimate pattern was thereupon established. A leader on the 19th noted with glowing self-confidence that, 'so far from abating, the Liberal deluge is covering the whole electoral earth'. At the end of three weeks, the Liberals had attained an exclusive majority of 136, made still more impressive by the fact that they could generally count upon the support of eighty-three Irish Nationalists and fifty-three Labour members.

In what better atmosphere could the *Daily News* have commemorated its Diamond Jubilee? With ten polling days yet to come, and a stunning victory assured, a celebration banquet was held at the National Liberal Club on Saturday evening, the 27th. Gardiner, who presided, pointed proudly to the fact that three members of his staff (Masterman, Wilson, and Chiozza Money), 'to say nothing of half a dozen former members', had obtained seats in the new Parliament. Less fortunate was David Williamson, whose valiant assault upon the 'Tory citadel of Dulwich', incurred a defeat 'almost more honourable than victory'. Among the guests were George and Henry Cadbury, and various Liberal politicians and journalists. The presence of such editors as Donald of the *Chronicle*, Parke of the *Star* and *Morning Leader*, and Hobhouse of the newly founded *Tribune*, was taken to imply 'that the Liberal Press of London will have no rivalry except that noble one of seeking how best to serve the people's cause'. Gardiner, in his after-dinner remarks, reviewed the paper's history of sixty years, and paid eloquent tribute to Dickens, Bright, and Harriet Martineau ('the first and the greatest of women journalists'), whose contributions to the Liberal tradition entitled them to be ranked among the architects of the present triumph. 'The great battle of the hungry forties was approaching its crisis,' he declared,

the forces of feudalism were dying in the night, and vast horizons of human rights were opening up to the sight of men. The 'Daily News' embodied the two motives which were behind that birth – the political motive and the social motive. It represented political Manchester and it anticipated that social policy to which Manchester was cold, and which was only now emerging from the realm of the dreamer into the sphere of practical politics. [1]

Here is an indication that, in certain Liberal quarters at any rate, equal stress was placed on the third element in the party's catch-phrase of Peace, Retrenchment, and Reform. On this score, a 'pro-Boer' like Lloyd George was in rare agreement with a Liberal Imperialist like Haldane.

Historians in their quest for irony have long debated the significance of the 1906 returns: did the Liberal plurality reflect no more than an indignation with Tory methods, a repudiation of runaway imperialism, a distrust of Chamberlain, and a boredom with Balfour;

1. *Daily News*, 29 January 1906.

or, more significantly, did it constitute a mandate for social change? To what extent did the Liberals arrive in office committed by conscience, if not necessarily by explicit campaign promises, to the concepts of a welfare state? 'Social reformers', it has been justly argued, 'were certainly elected to Parliament [in 1906] in some numbers: but by and large they were not elected because of their propensity to reform, but because of their partisan hostility to the retiring Government.'[1] How many elections, one wonders, are decided on essentially negative grounds, out of opposition to a personality, a party, or a programme? Is there in fact an inconsistency (Gardiner saw none) between a rejection of Toryism and an endorsement of social reform? Is there necessarily a contradiction (there was none in Gardiner's mind) between Retrenchment, on the one hand, and Reform, on the other? By his definition, not an uncommon one, Retrenchment meant not simply the curtailment of expenditure, but the curtailment of expenditure on armaments and the consequent reallocation of revenues. Massingham, writing in the *Daily News* on 9 March, agreed with his editor that the Radical desire for economy reflected substantially more than a Cobdenite passion for thrift: 'It arises from the moral objection to militarism and secondly out of the necessities of the programme of social reform to which the Government is committed.'

Surely the Liberals deserve more credit than blame for drawing attention to their opponents' weaknesses rather than to their own often yet unresolved intentions. Spared the embarrassment of acknowledging publicly the many sources of friction and disagreement that persisted among themselves, they amassed a majority that exceeded all reasonable expectation. Although signs had pointed unmistakably to a Liberal success, its huge extent had not been anticipated by the party leaders, who, with the single exception of the aged Lord Ripon, had never known the satisfaction of holding office in a strong Liberal ministry. 'Some say all will end in a tie, as in 1885: *i.e.* Liberals = Unionists + Irish,' Morley wearily informed a correspondent on the eve of polling. 'Others give us a clear majority of 30 or 40 over the two.'[2] A veteran of seven general elections, the first

1. Bealey and Pelling, *Labour and Politics*, p. 266.
2. Morley to Lord Ampthill, 4 January 1906, cited in Koss, *John Morley at the India Office*, p. 54.

as long ago as 1868, he could remember no precedent for the 1906 windfall.

Gardiner was less impressed by the magnitude of the electoral victory than by the opportunities it presented for creative policy. Particularly gratifying to him was the return of so large a complement of Labour members, who could be depended upon to press for welfare legislation. It was his considered opinion, delivered seven years later to an audience at the Solvay Institute of Sociology at Brussels,[1] that 1906 ranked as 'one of the great permanent landmarks in the social history of Great Britain . . ., the opening of a new and remarkable chapter in the development of the State.' True, the Liberals had begun slowly, even timidly; but, after all, they had languished in opposition for an extended period and needed time to settle into office. Judged by the context and conventions of their own political society, they lacked neither imagination nor enterprise. Gardiner, who lived long enough to witness (and deplore) the Labour landslide of 1945, never ceased to regard 1906 as a watershed. A signal 'that the reign of *laissez-faire* was at an end', that election had paved the way for schemes of 'internal reorganization under the general title of Social Reform': measures for the care and maintenance of the aged poor, protection for the ill or unemployed worker, child welfare, public health, improvements in the administration of justice, and new principles of taxation intended to rectify the 'unequal distribution of wealth'. Speaking in 1913, he did not pretend that Liberal legislation had been sufficient to cure the ills of society, but he asserted that an intelligent start had been made, and that the party's capacity for reform was far from exhausted.

The election results necessitated a reorientation in the policy and presentation of the *Daily News*, which, under its present management, had functioned only as an opposition organ. Until this time, Gardiner had seen no reason, either moral or tactical, to restrain his criticism of the Government and its officials. Now, however, such criticism might be construed as an implicit attack on Liberal doctrines. Time and again his problem was to maintain his independence without damaging the political interest with which he identified.

Other editors and their papers attempted to accommodate themselves as best they could to the new situation. Unionist journals, if

1. 'The social policy', in *The Policy of Social Reform in England*.

they did not retreat into misanthropy like the *Morning Post*, comforted their readers with the supposition that Liberal ministers, being human and British, would act in all crucial respects much like their predecessors. *The Times*, which for decades had assiduously impugned the Liberal Party's capacity to administer an empire, lost no time in pledging its support to the Government in matters of diplomacy and defence which, it patronizingly suggested, ought never to be brought into the political arena. The *Daily News*, doubting whether any Liberal policy commended by *The Times* was worthy of its name, remonstrated on 29 January that the Foreign and War Offices were precisely the departments most in need of Liberal refurbishing. Noting uneasily the presence at these key ministries of Liberal Imperialists, whom it feared were least equipped by personality and ideology to resist the 'blandishments' of Printing House Square, it called upon the Government to 'obey the spirit that called it into existence, not the defeated powers against whom a tremendous national verdict has been secured'.

Gardiner, for one, would have no truck with the argument, so often propounded in the prewar years by permanent officials and Tory politicians, that national honour and safety required the maintenance of 'continuity' between one Government and the next. He doubted both the prudence and the political sagacity of J. A. Spender's semi-official assurances in the *Westminster Gazette* that the Liberals, now safely installed in office, could be depended upon to recognize their responsibilities to the Empire and to the 1904 entente with France. Had Gladstone, he asked, ever compromised himself or hamstrung his colleagues by upholding, for the mere sake of 'continuity', policies inherited from Disraeli or Salisbury? The Liberal victory of 1880, the last before 1906 upon which the party could reflect with unalloyed satisfaction, had brought a sweeping repudiation of Tory foreign and imperial policies. A member of the Eighty Club, which commemorated that proud occasion which he was too young to recall firsthand, Gardiner cited the unhappy record of Rosebery's brief premiership as proof that bipartisanship could be attained only by mortgaging Liberal principles and by accepting uncritically the assumptions that had produced, among other disasters, the Boer War.

Determined to influence a rechannelling of national policy in a decidedly more Liberal direction, Gardiner initiated campaigns in the early weeks of Liberal rule from which he was diverted only by the outbreak of war. To a surprising extent, these efforts were aimed against various members of the Cabinet who lacked the energy, perhaps even the inclination, to realize the potential of a revived Liberalism. Some of these weaknesses might have been predicted; others not. Entombed at the India Office, to which he referred resentfully as a 'gilded pagoda', Morley displayed little of the generosity and none of the courage that he had previously brought to Irish affairs. 'He is the guardian of the victories of the past', Gardiner wrote of him. 'He points to no far horizons, and stands icily aloof from all the eager aspirations of the new time. . . . The gravity and apprehensiveness of his mind revolt against the irrevocable word and make decisive action an intolerable pain.'[1] Gardiner's contacts with such Indian nationalists as Surendranath Banerjea and Lala Lajpat Rai, and his 'outspoken & really sympathetic utterances' on their behalf,[2] brought him into mutually painful collision with the venerable Indian Secretary.

With less compunction, Gardiner promptly identified himself as a persistent critic of other ministers. As Home Secretary Gladstone seemed to him a conspicuous failure, distressingly unresponsive and hidebound. Successive First Lords of the Admiralty – Lord Tweedmouth, McKenna, and Churchill – conveniently forgot the slogans of economy that they themselves had preached in other capacities. Haldane at the War Office made a greater effort to effect reductions, but his tedious and abstruse speeches ('His oratory', Gardiner observed, 'is like an interminable round of beef – you may cut and come again'), his lingering affiliations with Rosebery and Milner, and indeed the very nature of his office (Lloyd George, with studied malevolence, dubbed him 'the Minister for Slaughter') made him suspect.

Undoubtedly Gardiner's most severe disappointment was Burns, the 'man with the red flag' in the 1889 London dock strike, whose progressive impulses had long since gone the way of his jaunty straw hat. As a minister of the Crown, Burns did nothing to justify either the confidence reposed in him by organized labour or the dread that his reputation continued to inspire in more privileged circles.

1. *Daily News*, 28 December 1907, reprinted in *Prophets, Priests and Kings*, pp. 148–9.
2. Banerjea to Gardiner, 11 July 1907, G.P.

Gardiner, who recognized a tame lion when he saw one, nonetheless held vain hopes that Burns's working-class background and trade unionist connections would inspire the Local Government Board and the Government as a whole. To his consternation, Burns revealed an engrained conservatism that acted repeatedly as a brake on reform. It was not simply that Burns was ineffectual as an innovator, but rather that he was alarmingly effectual as an obstacle to innovation. Gardiner, whom he would often meet at lunch at the National Liberal Club and with whom he would stroll afterwards along the Victoria Embankment, trading impressions of books or apprehensions about the 'vulgaring [*sic*] of public life, Americanizing of Press, and materializing of politics generally',[1] was slow to write him off as a total loss to the cause: 'If he will only check the tendency to intellectual hardening which some of us observe, guard against the subtle advances of the official spirit, suspect the flatterer, and occasionally listen to old friends who will not flatter, he has a long career of service to the people before him.'[2]

Burns, whose invariable response to criticism was intensified rigidity, was disappointed in turn by the *Daily News*. His association with George Cadbury during the Boer War and, earlier, in the heyday of the new unionism, had fostered the hope that the paper might plead his case with the fervency with which the *Manchester Guardian* defended Lloyd George, with the dependability with which the *Westminster Gazette* supported Asquith and Grey, or with the unabashed pugnacity with which *The Times* soon came to champion Churchill. Instead he found the *Daily News* an equivocal ally, more often than not ranged among his antagonists. The fault, in his opinion, lay in Gardiner's inconstancy, and specifically in what he derided as the paper's 'indiscriminate support of Labour right or wrong'.[3] Good-naturedly, he brushed aside an invitation to reply in a guest column: 'Cabinet Ministers must not write for money, they must only work for abuse.'[4] But, however flippant his response, there can be no doubt

1. Burns's diary, 14 October 1909, Burns Papers, British Museum, Add. MSS 46,327, fol. 43.
2. *Daily News*, 30 November 1907, reprinted in *Prophets, Priests and Kings*, p. 296.
3. Burns to Gardiner, 1 November 1906, G.P.
4. Burns to Gardiner, 5 November 1907, G.P.

that he was nettled. 'Sir,' he jokingly addressed a communication to Gardiner after reading a sketch of himself in the *Daily News*: 'Writ for libel issued for publication of Saturday last. Will you name your solicitor?'[1]

Egotistically, Burns imagined himself as the pivotal figure in a Government which could not survive if he were denied adequate support. 'If Tariff Reform and Reaction win at [the] next Election by 100 to 200 [seats]', he reproached Gardiner at a time when the House of Lords was proving implacable and by-elections were going steadily against the Government,

the reasons . . . will be 7
  Vaughan Nash
  H. W. M[assingham]
  C. F. G. M[asterman]
  A.G.G.
  P. W. W[ilson]
  W. T. Stead
  K[eir] H[ardie]
And the worst of all [is] A.G.G. because he runs a paper and himself is run. Our Press urges us to bring in Bills. When done, they at once take the bloom off all our peaches, or when the Bill is passed they reveal to our enemies not what it has done, but what it did not do. . . . Why the D.N. is an enemy of Progress! Why its Editor should be ————, etc.[2]

Accused of listening to false friends, Burns retorted that it was his critics and not he who had gone astray. 'Every Paper wants its own tame Cabinet Minister', he complained, and he ascribed the animosity he had incurred to the fact that, unlike certain colleagues, he did not cultivate particular journalists either by leaking information or by writing prefaces to their books.[3]

Was it wishful thinking that prompted Burns to begin his diary for 1909 by recording the unfounded rumour 'that Gardiner of DN was retiring'?[4] Perpetually irritated by the failure of the *Daily News* to pay him homage, he waxed indignant at its tendency to take the part of the ILP leaders, whose influence within the Trades Union Congress

1. Burns to Gardiner, 2 December 1907, G.P.
2. Burns to Gardiner, 22 June 1908, G.P.
3. Burns to Gardiner, 7 July 1908, G.P.
4. 1 January 1909, Burns Papers, Add. MSS 46,327, fol. 1.

he had long contested. 'Between the intervals of wearing crepe for J. R. M[acDonald] and sobbing over K[eir] H[ardie]', he wrote caustically to Gardiner on 14 April 1909, 'don't hesitate to notice a very good Blue Book I am issuing next week on the Social Life and Conditions of the People.'[1] At this juncture, Burns was making a forlorn attempt to recapture the limelight from the Webbs, his erstwhile allies (he recalled with a shudder how Beatrice had tried to 'governess' him during his Fabian days), whose minority report on the Poor Law he had officially rejected. Gardiner, whose pen Shaw had enlisted for the minority position,[2] won Sidney Webb's gratitude for his 'magnificent backing . . ., which has done much to influence Liberal opinion everywhere'.[3] The *Daily News* demanded a sweeping reform of Poor Law administration and, at Webb's request, featured reports of particular situations – the workhouse nursery in Renfrew Road, Lambeth, for example – which were an acute embarrassment to the Local Government Board. Burns, needless to say, was incensed, and tactlessly disclaimed any intention to oblige his critics with 'a great Poor Law measure'. Was this 'a mere joke'? the *Daily News* asked on 17 May. Was Burns not a 'democrat', but 'on the contrary a

1. G.P.

2. Shaw, who kept Gardiner abreast of developments within the Poor Law Commission, declined his invitation to defend the 'sensationally interesting' minority report in the *Daily News:*

'Strictly between ourselves, my hands are not quite free on the subject of the Poor Law Commission Reports. As you perhaps know, there is a laborious comedy going on there. Lord George Hamilton imagined that he was going to rule the roost and attached no importance to the fact that Mrs Sidney Webb was a member of the Commission. Of course the poor devil has had no more chance against her than if he were a mouse in a python's cage at the zoo.

. . .

'I have read much of it (confidentially, of course), as the Webbs, when they have worked themselves so completely to a standstill that they are incapable of getting a fresh view of what they have been doing, often ask me to read their stuff through and tell them where they have left a hitch in their arguments, or omitted a useful illustration, or, generally, left any point open to improvement. Unluckily, though this qualifies me especially to write about the report, it also disqualifies me of availing myself of the opportunity. So I think it best to give you this private information, which will enable you to put the reports into the hands of one of your young lions, and coach him in its main points.' Shaw to Gardiner, 24 November 1908 (copy), G.P.

3. Webb to Gardiner, 27 February 1909, G.P.

bureaucrat of a very extravagant type'?[1] Mrs Webb, glad to see the inflated Burns so effectively punctured, solicited Gardiner's 'counsel' for 'uniting the Progressive forces in a sustained crusade' on behalf of 'the principles of the Minority Report'.[2] He attended Sunday night working suppers at her home, where guests were treated to a nourishing repast of statistics and strategy, and he contributed to the propaganda for the National Committee for the Break-up of the Poor Law, soon retitled the National Committee for the Prevention of Destitution. Under either name, such an agitation was anathema to Burns, who considered the 'New Liberalism' only slightly less odious than the old socialism. By the end of the year, his notes of protest to Gardiner, while no less frequent, had lost any trace of humour or friendliness. 'Really, Gardiner,' he exclaimed on 2 November, exasperated by charges that he was too willing to entertain amendments from the Lords to his Housing and Town Planning Bill, 'your article, written before our attitude was known, is a shameful disgrace. You, H. W. M[assingham], and the junkers are going to get an awakening.'[3] Nor did he appreciate the praise that the *Daily News* lavished on Lloyd George and Churchill, whom he regarded as irresponsible demagogues. 'I have never spoken better in my life', he boasted during the second election campaign of 1910, 'but the trail of Limehouse, Lambeth & Mile End has lost us many seats and our papers have done us badly.'[4] Surely he was aware that the *Daily News*, while virtually ignoring him, had applauded each platform appearance by Lloyd George, whose ducal metaphor Gardiner had borrowed for an immensely successful series of campaign dialogues, 'The Duke goes canvassing'.[5] Gardiner was inclined to blame the decreased majorities

1. 'How pitiful that the DN will put its foot into it nearly every time', Burns privately rebuked Gardiner for 'your screamingly funny yet rather vulgar article' that morning. He subsequently related that 'Poor Nevinson', presumably the author of the 17 May leader, '[had] blushed like a peony the other night at N[ational] L[iberal] C[lub] when he saw me'. Burns to Gardiner, 17 and 29 May, G.P.

2. 4 May [1909], G.P.

3. G.P.

4. Burns to Gardiner, 29 November 1910, G.P.

5. These weekly columns appeared as a series in the *Daily News* during the last months of 1909. Collected in pamphlet form, they sold a quarter of a million copies within a fortnight at the time of the first general election of 1910: *Institute Journal*, October 1914, p. 483.

of 1910 not on the fiery Chancellor of the Exchequer, whom only a Tory might fear, but rather on the pusillanimous President of the Local Government Board, who had hardly made it seem worth the effort to cast a Liberal vote.

There was, however, one area in which Burns claimed Gardiner's respect. A failure in the administration of his own department, he was, for what it was worth, a consistent critic of Grey's diplomacy. It was frequently the case that a minister who incurred Radical disapprobation in one capacity redeemed himself in another: parliamentary allies of Indian nationalism, who denounced Morley as a reincarnated Strafford, could not help but admire his continued devotion to Irish Home Rule; many who attacked Haldane's army estimates welcomed his conciliatory gestures toward Germany and respected his educational proposals; Churchill confounded his backbench critics by alternating fierce growls against striking workers with evidence of what Gardiner recognized as a 'passion for humanity'. Grey, alone among frontbench figures, offered no sop to Radical opinion. Refusing to acknowledge any relationship between foreign and domestic problems, he had no wish to concern himself with general Cabinet business and expected his colleagues, in return, to allow him to operate in splendid isolation.

Neither Grey's antecedents nor the favour he continued to enjoy in Tory circles was likely to endear him to conscientious Radicals, who, to one extent or another, advocated a measure of popular or parliamentary control over foreign policy. Gardiner agreed that Grey was a statesman of unimpeachable integrity ('His aims are high, his honour stainless'), but he doubted Grey's powers of application, and, above all, resented Grey's refusal to disclose facts: 'Sir Edward Grey's view of foreign affairs . . . is that it is a close bureaucratic preserve into which he will allow no impertinent trespassers. . . . There is no right of way through his woods, and he is the keeper with a gun.' Unlike certain Radicals, who anticipated the clamour for 'open covenants openly arrived at', Gardiner was prepared to concede that Grey's might be 'a just view so far as the conduct of delicate negotiations is concerned, but it is assailable,' he insisted, 'when applied to the spirit of national policy'. [1] His complaints were not without substance. It remains, of course, open to serious question whether a

1. *Daily News*, 25 April 1908; reprinted in *Prophets, Priests and Kings*, p. 76.

foreign minister more responsible, if not necessarily more responsive to the Commons might have averted the catastrophe of the 1914 war. But it is obvious that, by publicizing the nation's commitments and his own apprehensions, Grey might have better prepared his country-men for that eventuality. Historians have since demonstrated that, 'Though the number of pressure groups and the demand for infor-mation increased during the Liberal period, Grey did not attach great importance to public opinion and was even less generous in his treatment of Parliament than his predecessors'. [1]

Without holding Grey personally responsible for war when it came, Gardiner nonetheless faulted him for failing to discipline his subordi-nates, who were allowed to convey the wrong impression of British intentions to foreign chancellories and to preserve the Foreign Office as a bastion of aristocratic control and anti-German bias. It would have required, Gardiner saw as early as 1907, 'a more imaginative sense and a swifter instinct' for the situation to be taken in hand. It would also have needed a Foreign Secretary with a stronger commit-ment to Liberalism. Grey conferred an element of respectability on the Government and incidentally made things easier for himself by preaching the virtues of 'continuity' in foreign policy. As Lord Edmond Fitzmaurice, himself a symbol of 'continuity' – parliamen-tary under-secretary from 1905 to 1908, this veteran official was the younger brother of Grey's predecessor, Lord Lansdowne – explained the Government's 1906 proposals on the Turkish customs: 'Our hands were largely tied when we came in.' [2] Gardiner, who could never bring himself to acknowledge any obligation to Unionist pre-cedent, rejected this logic. To him 'continuity' smacked of collusion between the two front benches. The Liberal Imperialists, he recalled, had urged a 'clean slate' to emancipate themselves from Gladstonian burdens; he in turn asked to jettison Tory survivals. Without a free hand, it would be impossible to exercise the moral authority vested in a Liberal Parliament: 'Our foreign policy must be one which leaves us free to use our power in the world in the world's service.' [3]

Attracted, as we have seen, to German culture, although mindful

1. See, for example, Steiner, *The Foreign Office and Foreign Policy, 1898–1914*, pp. 197–8.
2. 3 July 1906, G.P.
3. *Daily News*, 23 June 1909.

of its unpleasant undercurrents, Gardiner sent the eldest of his children, his daughter Stella, to a finishing school at Mecklenburg. His Germanophilia, reinforced by his typically Radical hatred of Tsarist Russia, made him wary of commitments, real or implicit, to France, whose statesmen he distrusted as unscrupulous and corrupt. As a journalist, he devoted himself to the task of allaying popular fears of Germany and thereby restoring a balance in Britain's diplomatic position. Stead, long a Fleet Street crusader, shared his disquiet and agreed that the solution was to provide the English reading public with a more accurate knowledge of German life and opinion. There was great difficulty, however, in finding a qualified Berlin correspondent for the *Daily News*, especially one who could combine a command of the German language with the proper contacts to 'keep our people posted concerning the evolution of practical socialism in Germany'.[1] One after another, candidates were recruited on the spot or dispatched from London, but none proved wholly satisfactory. Hirst of the *Economist*, who perhaps unreasonably expected a popular daily to act with the singlemindedness of a weekly journal of opinion, lamented the failure of English papers to convey an adequately sympathetic picture of Germany: 'The *Daily News* man', he complained to Sir John Brunner, the newly elected president of the National Liberal Federation, 'is as bad as anyone.'[2]

Along with J. A. Spender, to whom one cannot impute hostility to Grey, Gardiner played host in 1906 to a delegation of German editors who had detoured through London on their way home from the Algeciras conference. The next spring, the Germans returned the hospitality, and among those who made the journey were Gardiner, Spender, Stead, Sidney Low, Lucien Wolf, and J. S. R. Phillips of the *Yorkshire Post*. It was on this occasion that Spender 'first got to know' Gardiner, 'a warm friend in after years', who shared his devotion to cricket and his facility to toss off long articles under the pressure of an impending deadline. Travelling together through Germany, they basked in the glory of an 'uproarious' welcome and in the 'beautiful June weather'.[3] The visiting Englishmen were shepherded through schools and industrial works, entertained at the opera, and, in a

1. Stead to Gardiner, 4 July 1906, G.P.
2. 5 December 1911, Brunner Papers.
3. J. A. Spender, *Life, Journalism and Politics*, i, 202–3.

single afternoon, honoured at a lunch given by the Kaiser at Potsdam and at a garden party given by Prince von Bülow, the Chancellor. They were introduced to various public figures, among them Beth-mann-Hollweg, then Prussian minister of the interior and eventually Bülow's successor, but they were kept at a frustrating distance from representatives of the Social Democratic Party whom Gardiner was especially anxious to interview. His account of the tour appeared in the July number of the *Albany Review*, and concluded with an appre-ciation of 'how deep and abiding are the common interests of the two nations, how superficial the causes of irritation, and how much the happiness and progress of the world depends upon a friendly under-standing between Great Britain and Germany'. An official at the Wilhelmstrasse assured him of Bülow's admiration and contrasted the article with Austin Harrison's inflammatory remarks in the *Observer* of 30 June, which, he only hoped, the German press would allow to pass unnoticed.[1] Gardiner, too, regretted the effects of the 'incendiary Press' on each country's perception of the other:

> Every irresponsible word of violence printed in our Press duly reappears in the German newspapers, where it has all the authority of British opinion. *En revanche*, the bitter attacks on England which are common in a certain section of the German Press are served up in this country as representing the general feeling of Germany. . . . It is a factitious Press campaign which has no popular backing.

So far as he was concerned, there was nothing more despicable and, in a profound sense, more unpatriotic, than the tendency among publishers and journalists to build circulations or reputations by playing on popular anxieties, and so helping to create the perils against which they warned.

It would be wrong to conclude that Gardiner sacrificed either principle or perspective in his campaign to promote Anglo-German reconciliation. Within a year, he had published in the *Daily News* character sketches of the Kaiser (9 November 1907) and Bülow (9 May 1908) which, though basically respectful, could have given only qualified satisfaction to the two men. 'Prince Bülow's politics . . . are the politics of the Foreign Minister,' Gardiner said, with a guarded thrust at Grey:

1. H. Bunche (?) to Gardiner, 3 July 1907, G.P.

Human rights and human wrongs do not interest him. He dwells, like his Emperor, outside them in the realm of Imperial dreams. . . . In all this he represents the spirit of German policy, with its large ambitions and its divorce from the humanising tendency of modern politics. . . . But with all his Imperialism Prince Bülow would seem to love war as little as the Kaiser.

Gardiner's appraisal of Bülow's master appeared in the *Daily News* on the day that its subject arrived in England for a state visit to Windsor. 'Is he a menace or a safeguard?' Gardiner asked of the Kaiser.

Let his past be his witness. For twenty years he has had the peace of Europe in his keeping and for twenty years not a German soldier has fallen in war. . . . He is a militarist, but he is not a warrior. . . .

He keeps his powder dry and his armour bright. But he stands for peace – peace armed to the teeth, it is true; peace with the mailed fist; but peace nevertheless.

What were the chances of a lasting peace so long as a single man, who owed his power to birth and an explanation to no one, might act capriciously in the name of a mighty nation? 'Germany will not cease to be a disturbing element in world politics', Gardiner stated, 'until the Kaiser has stepped down from his medieval throne and derives his power from a free and self-governing people.' By the same reasoning, Great Britain could best operate as an agent for peace by giving full rein to the emergent forces of democracy, on which the Foreign Office, like the House of Lords, imposed a check. The best way to render the world safe for democracy was in fact to concede to democracy the full responsibilities to which it aspired. How else might Liberal England take its place, as Campbell-Bannerman had pledged in his 1905 Albert Hall address, 'at the head of a league for peace'?

Looking back, Gardiner was too much inclined to ascribe the misfortunes that befell the party and the nation to the loss in the spring of 1908 of Campbell-Bannerman. Asquith's ascent to the premiership, long in prospect, accorded a greater degree of ministerial freedom of which the Liberal Imperialists, who now controlled the three vital organs of prewar government, quickly seized advantage; but however much Gardiner later hesitated to acknowledge the fact, the basic problems had existed while 'Good Old C.B.' held command. The last weeks of 1907 saw the first symptoms of the illness that brought Campbell-Bannerman's resignation and death the following April. Vaughan Nash wrote from Downing Street, requesting Gardiner

to take some opportunity of pointing out that his [Campbell-Bannerman's] removal to the House of Lords (as to which a tremendous crop of rumours has lately sprung up again) so far from being helpful to him from the point of view of comfort and health would be the very reverse. The transition from the leadership of a large and loyal majority in the Commons to that of a small & feeble minority in the Lords would be like going from the temperate zones for a rest cure at the North Pole![1]

Four months later, Campbell-Bannerman died a commoner. Asquith, whose claims to the premiership went uncontested, easily surpassed him as a parliamentarian; he could never replace him as a comrade-in-arms.

Was Gardiner mistaken in his assessment of Campbell-Bannerman's qualities and achievements?[2] One may posit that Asquith's premiership gave him a more valuable ally in Downing Street, particularly in matters of social reform. But Gardiner had difficulty warming to the

1. 14 December 1907, G.P.
2. In 1923 Gardiner wrote a review in the *Nation* of J. A. Spender's life of Campbell-Bannerman, and drew a spirited rejoinder from Asquith, who revealed that his predecessor had 'often admitted' that the 1901 'methods of barbarism' speech, which Gardiner celebrated as a stroke of genius, 'was his worst *gaffe*'. According to Asquith, 'C. B. . . . was, au fond, in all the troubles from 1892 to 1904, a Roseberyite [who had had] . . . all that he could do to purge himself from . . . the deferential feeling of the son or grandson of a bourgeois Glasgow trader towards a blue-blooded Scottish Lord'. Asquith demurred at the suggestion that Campbell-Bannerman had been the architect of either the 1906 electoral victory ('If you had sat in the Cabinet, or behind the scenes, . . . you would have known better') or the 1908 South African settlement for which Gardiner assigned him exclusive credit. 'He was a far subtler character', Asquith recalled, 'than Spender . . . has thought it opportune to depict. He had a very strong touch & even flavour of the cynic.'
Margot, Asquith's irrepressible wife, took even stronger exception to Gardiner's portrait of Campbell-Bannerman as a man of lofty principle and no guile. 'When I read your C.B. today, I rubbed my eyes', she told him. 'We got to know the dear old boy *xtremely* [sic] well & I loved him. Much of what you say is absolutely true', she conceded, but she strenuously denied that Campbell-Bannerman had lacked cunning: 'I wd. back him if he were alive to-day to have outmanoeuvred Ll[oyd] G[eorge].'
Spender, whose future projects included an official life of Asquith, responded

alliance. 'He creates confidence and carries conviction', he wrote of Asquith, not yet Prime Minister, on 29 February 1908,

but he does not inspire men with great passions. His eloquence keeps to the solid earth; it does not fly with wings. It assures you victory: but it denies you adventure. . . . Mr Asquith does not utter great thoughts. No Balliol man of the Jowett tradition does. The Balliol mind distrusts 'great thoughts' even if it thinks them. . . . Balliol, in fact, is really atrophy of the heart. It is exhaustion of the emotions. It has produced the finest mental machines of this generation, but they are sometimes cold and cheerless. . . . We admire them, we respect them: we do not love them, for we feel that they would be insulted by the offer of so irrational a thing as love.

Convinced that 'great thoughts' and 'great passions' provided the sustenance of Liberalism and the only hope for world peace, Gardiner undertook to remedy the deficiency from Bouverie Street. It is to these activities that we must turn.

---

more favourably to Gardiner's review: 'I could wish that a large part of what you have written were in the book, for I have not said it half as well myself.'
Asquith to Gardiner, 28 October 1923; Margot Asquith to Gardiner, 29 October 1923; Spender to Gardiner, 29 October 1923, G.P.

6. 'Tip-toeing amidst the eggshells'

Throughout the period of Gardiner's editorship, even before its operating deficit had been reduced to manageable proportions, the *Daily News* could legitimately advertise itself as London's best selling Liberal daily. By any standard, it was unquestionably the most outspoken. What did this mean in terms of Gardiner's influence and responsibilities? What does it tell us about the organization of the press and the issues of the day?

Like the House of Lords, the British press survived the 1906 Liberal landslide as a preponderantly Tory domain. Here was a situation that perplexed and irritated Liberals, who continually complained that they lacked adequate means to appeal to the democracy of which they were the elected representatives. To be sure, Liberal journals existed in profusion, commanded large and loyal followings, and counted among their contributors a majority of the celebrated names in contemporary journalism. Yet however long established, well endowed, or widely read, they could not pretend to the authority of some of their Tory rivals, who enjoyed an influence disproportionate either to quality or circulation. The *Manchester Guardian*, for all its eloquence, spoke with a dialect (what better proves the point than its proscription of the word 'provincial'?) and not with the imperial resonances of *The Times*. The *Daily Chronicle*, eminently well-tempered and informative, carried little weight. The *Economist* was too specialized and too much the prisoner of its Cobdenite heritage. The *Nation*, infinitely livelier, was too transparently partisan to be taken as seriously as its case often deserved. And neither Gardiner, who articulated the sentiments of the Liberal backbenches, nor Spender, who was privy to Cabinet deliberations, wielded half as much political power as the mighty Garvin, whose public platforms were not nearly so impressive. Small wonder, therefore, that Lady Horner, the confidante of Asquith and Haldane, was prompted to wish that the Liberal press 'were stronger and that someone read it!' [1]

The Liberal predicament was put most clearly in a letter addressed to 'My dear Old Daily News' by a reader, who wrote not for publication, but for its editor's enlightenment:

This is the first time I have written to you, the friend of my youth & all my days & I am now approaching 60. Yes, I disagree with you about Vivisection & various other things, but you are sound & healthy & going strong.

But what about 'The Times'? Like many other radicals I take in 'The Times'. I take it for its news & its letters. Is it not possible to get up a Liberal paper which will attract the best letter writers? (Yes, your letters are good, but there are other kinds of letters.) Have you any idea of the number of people there are, like me, who take in 'The Times' because of the news & the letters? The country is overwhelmingly Liberal. We need the halfpenny 'Daily News', but we also need the other kind of paper.

No! I am really not a snob. I ask for a liberal paper which will command the attention of the well-to-do liberals who are now compelled to take in 'The Times'.

You will say that the tax I pay, 3d a day, for 'The Times' is not great. But it is a *tribute* paid to the enemy and I had rather pay ten times as much for a liberal paper. [2]

Gardiner shared his reader's concern, as did a great many Liberal editors, publishers, and politicians, and wondered how best to remedy the situation. As recent experience had demonstrated, it was difficult to launch new publications and impossible to guarantee them either a market or a sphere of influence. The *Tribune*, with Hobhouse as its editor, was a fiasco. In 1907 the weekly *Speaker* was at last put out of its misery, and superseded by the *Nation*. Arnold Bennett, admittedly 'flattered' by an invitation to contribute to its pages, nonetheless agreed with H. G. Wells 'that though the "Nation" was admirable', particularly on labour questions, '[it] was a failure because it had no circulation'. [3] Early in 1908 there were hopes that *The Times* might be acquired by a Liberal syndicate. Spender recalled that 'Campbell-Bannerman was one of the leading spirits' in the venture, 'and the

1. Lady Horner to Elizabeth Haldane, [13] January 1910, cited in Koss, *Lord Haldane, Scapegoat for Liberalism*, p. 143.

2. William Perry to 'My dear Old Daily News', 9 January 1908, G.P.

3. Entries for 2 March 1908 and 26 November 1909, Arnold Bennett's journal, Berg Collection, New York Public Library.

last communication I ever received from him was a message from his sick-room to say he hoped it would go through and would result in my being editor of a Free Trade and independent *Times*'.[1] What enormous satisfaction it would have given the Liberals to capture control of this enemy citadel: better than a trumpet to bring down the Tory Jericho, it would have established them within the walls themselves. But, for reasons which remain unclear, the scheme seems to have died with Campbell-Bannerman. The property was presently annexed by the Harmsworth empire, conferring on its new owner extraordinary powers of which he took full advantage, much to the future detriment of the Liberal cause.

Various other schemes were mooted in 1908, reflecting a general intensification of political debate at this time. With one exception, they came to nothing. William Robertson Nicoll, the editor-proprietor of the free church *British Weekly* ('a journal of social and Christian progress'), reported to C. P. Scott 'a strong movement . . . to establish a penny morning Free Trade daily', again under the editorship of Spender. According to Nicoll, 'Sir George Newnes [had] become weary of the Westminster Gazette', which he hoped to sell for £50,000 to raise capital for the new venture. As a businessman, Nicoll doubted whether the project would succeed: 'After the experience of the Tribune it is most desirable that no false step should be taken', he told Scott, and he furthermore cited 'the complete failure of the Pall Mall Gazette to establish itself as a morning daily'. As a Radical, he was inclined to think that the situation required a more full-blooded enterprise than any that Spender might edit. Instead, he joined those who urged Scott to consider a London edition of the *Manchester Guardian*, whose early edition the railway often did not deliver to the capital before midday.[2] This was a suggestion often heard in prewar years, and one which Lloyd George continued to promote; but the right investors, men who would neither limit the paper's independence nor impair its image, were not forthcoming; besides, as Scott may well have reasoned, the *Guardian* had as much to lose as to gain from such a transformation.

If Manchester would not come to London, the *Daily News* was prepared to bring London to Manchester. Its northern edition,

1. *Life, Journalism and Politics*, ii, 164–5.
2. Nicoll to Scott, 31 March 1908, *Guardian* Archives.

produced at up-to-date premises in Dale Street, made its debut on 11 January 1909; publication thereafter continued without interruption for a dozen years, with a brief resumption in 1928. The move had been 'a good deal rumoured' as early as the previous May, when John Scott predicted to his father that 'it would be foredoomed to failure'.[1] Not that the Scotts had reason to fear competition: there existed a large, untapped Lancashire market from which the *Manchester Guardian* had excluded itself as much by content as by price. Publicly and privately, the proprietors of the *Daily News* took every opportunity to 'emphasise . . . the fact that our coming [to Manchester] is in no spirit of rivalry to that great national champion of good causes, the "Manchester Guardian"'. G. G. Armstrong, who was brought from the *Northern Echo* at Darlington to preside over the Dale Street operations, submitted for Scott's approval a circular which he and Henry Cadbury had drafted for distribution among Liberal agents, trade union officials, and nonconformist ministers in the area.[2] Professing a 'desire to supplement . . . [the] efforts' of the *Guardian*, Armstrong and Cadbury argued 'that a penny Liberal paper cannot adequately counteract the influence of its halfpenny Tory rivals. As you are well aware,' they told prospective readers,

Conservatism and Protectionism are powerfully aided by halfpenny journals published in Manchester, which, by their price, or place of publication, or both, are able to reach the masses in the North with very much greater ease than any of their competitors. It is this advantage which our firm desires to neutralise by its present step.

In large part, the northern edition of the *Daily News* was a replica of its London-based parent, although columns were reserved for 'North country news and comment'. Its success can be better measured by its immediate popularity than by any political ramifications. Issues varied in size from twelve to sixteen pages, and the staff had expanded to two hundred by the time that publication ceased in 1921, when 'duplicate publication' was considered 'no longer a commercial proposition'.[3] Gardiner was not directly involved in these proceedings, which

1. John Scott to C. P. Scott, [15 May 1908] (copy), *Guardian* Archives.
2. Armstrong to Scott, 22 December 1908, and draft circular, *Guardian* Archives.
3. Manchester Press Club, *Fifty Years of Us*, pp. 54–5.

gave him a vastly expanded and more widespread reading public. His immediate responsibility was to sustain the high quality of the features that appeared simultaneously in both editions. Shifts in personnel, occasioned partly by the rise and fall of other Liberal journals, compounded his difficulties. Early in 1907 Massingham departed for the *Nation*, which, with Joseph Rowntree's munificence, rose from the ashes of the *Speaker*. In parting, he expressed admiration and continued support for Gardiner, whom he humbly assured that there would be 'no difficulty in the "D.N." securing a successor to me' as parliamentary correspondent: 'I have been too much of the House,' he declared, '& a fresher eye & style will be a good change.'[1] Later that year, Hammond resigned the position which he had managed to combine with the editorship of the *Speaker*. 'I am strongly disinclined to leave the "Daily News",' he told Gardiner, 'where I have found it very pleasant working with you for a paper in whose success I am deeply interested.' His health, however, was poor, and his doctor had prescribed a stint at Whitehall as a restorative. Campbell-Bannerman had thoughtfully invited him to serve as secretary to the Civil Service Commission, 'a very comfortable post . . . with a salary beginning at £800'. He was all the more reluctant to refuse the appointment after overhearing George Cadbury mutter that the *Daily News* might be sold if Henry Cadbury did not soon make 'a success of it'.[2] As much as Gardiner wished to retain Hammond's services, he could say little to allay his anxieties. The paper's fate was indeed uncertain, and more or less remained so until the northern edition was successfully established. Hammond was 'touched' by Gardiner's words of tribute, and grateful for his candid assessment of the paper's prospects; 'it is of a piece with all your treatment of me', he replied: 'I had no idea how grave the situation was. I am very very sorry. It is very hard on you after all the trouble & devotion with which you have made it so good a paper. What you tell me makes me hate the idea of leaving you.'[3] Nonetheless, Hammond had no choice but to accept the Prime Minister's offer, which promised him a less strenuous and more secure future.

The *Daily News* suffered a third major loss in April 1908, when

1. 26 January 1907, G.P.   2. 26 August 1907, G.P.
3. 29 August 1907, G.P. Gardiner's 'kind letter' to Hammond is, unfortunately, not preserved among the Hammond Papers.

Masterman, a member of Parliament since 1906, began his ministerial career as under-secretary at the Local Government Board. Nevinson, who had long been waiting for a suitable vacancy to occur, saw the announcement on the 12th 'that Masterman had been summoned to Asquith, which almost certainly means I shall be offered his place on the D.N.' Five days later, Nevinson 'cycled early to Gardiner's house', a steep descent through the streets of Hampstead. He was greeted by the 'children and Mrs Gardiner', who preceded A.G.G. down to breakfast, and who appeared to Nevinson 'all rather indistinguishable, but with [a] soothing air of simplicity & virtue'. According to the account that Nevinson recorded in his diary, Gardiner soon 'came down & we talked for about an hour'. Although the purpose of his visit was obvious, Nevinson scrupulously avoided any reference to Masterman's departure. Instead, he made it a point to deny a recent item in the *Manchester Guardian* that imputed an anti-Cadbury bias to his crusade against the importation of slave-grown cocoa from Portuguese Africa. It was in fact Gardiner who finally broached the subject uppermost in Nevinson's mind, and declared he 'hoped to hear something definite on Tuesday when Henry Cadbury wd return from a family consultation'. Nevinson pedalled home from Finchley Road reassured that Gardiner 'was very straight & sensible'. [1]

Nevinson was an unlikely candidate to succeed Masterman in Gardiner's affections. Nor could he be expected to counteract the militancy of Brailsford, his friend and ally, who had shared leader-writing assignments with Masterman. The prospect of Nevinson and Brailsford in joint possession of the leader page was not a comforting one. 'What a pair to drive tandem,' Parke of the *Star* remarked to Gardiner, whose own misgivings proved more than justified. Cantankerous and devoid of humour, Nevinson clashed to one extent or another with every editor for whom he worked. Gardiner told him that 'he ought to have been a soldier', which Nevinson accepted as 'partly true'. [2] He in turn censured Gardiner for buckling under to the Cadburys, and, on certain vital issues, to the politicians. His diary, which provides a more accurate description of his experiences than his three volumes of autobiography, reveals the extent to which he misrepresented Gardiner on both scores: in the published version,

1. Nevinson diary, 12 and 17 April 1908, Bodleian Library.
2. *Ibid.*, 24 January 1909.

for example, he catalogued Gardiner's attempts to prevent him and Brailsford from agitating in favour of a boycott of Angolan cocoa until Brailsford bravely 'threatened resignation, and his leading article appeared in May, 1908'; in the privacy of his diary, however, he described how Gardiner 'had faced [the] D.N. directors on [the] Angola question & secured freedom of publication'. [1] For that matter, even George Cadbury, the accomplice of 'the cocoa slavery', appears to have behaved more reasonably than Nevinson was later given to admit. In a conversation on 5 November 1908 Cadbury volunteered 'his reasons for not boycotting . . ., but agreed it was a good thing to rouse public opinion'. He especially commended Nevinson and Brailsford 'for the time we took on social reform in our leaders, & we parted in great amity'. Nevinson grudgingly concluded that perhaps he and Brailsford 'had both been too suspicious' of their employer, to which Brailsford 'agreed, adding he had been worse than I, which is true'. [2]

Not all partings were taken as amicably as those of Massingham, Hammond, and Masterman. As we shall see, Nevinson and Brailsford quit the *Daily News* in a flurry of self-righteous indignation. More painful to all concerned was the departure in 1913 of Chesterton, whose relations with Gardiner (like his commitment to the Liberal Party) had grown increasingly strained. The days had long since passed when G.K.C. and G.B.S. tilted lances in the paper's correspondence columns, Shaw insisting privately to Gardiner that Chesterton responded so vehemently only 'because he eats too much, and feels my slender figure and my vegetarianism to be a standing reproach to him. Tell him so,' Shaw mischievously suggested; 'and give him notice that you will not allow contributions from young men of more than 16 stone after the 30th June, or 14 after this year, or 11.7 (my own weight in my clothes) after Lent, 1908.' [3]

Chesterton was better able to abide Shaw's impudence than to suffer the moral imperfections of Liberal government. Or, as he put it in his *Autobiography*, although he continued to believe in Liberalism, he 'was finding it dimly difficult to believe in Liberals'. His disenchantment was evident as early as July 1907, when he lumbered to

1. *More Changes, More Chances*, p. 86; Nevinson diary, 5 May 1908.
2. Nevinson diary, 5 November 1908.
3. Shaw to Gardiner, 11 March 1907 (copy), G.P.

the defence of H. C. Lea, a Radical backbencher, whom Lord Robert Cecil alleged to have committed a breach of privilege by writing to *The Times* in denunciation of jobbery and title-mongering. Gardiner thought it advisable to hold over Chesterton's column in support of Lea, 'not [he explained] because I do not entirely agree with its point of view but because just at this moment it would look like backing Lea's unmannerly attack on C.B.' [1] Chesterton, who was not mollified by assurances that the article would be kept in reserve for a later occasion, lodged a vehement protest:

> Lea is to be humiliated & broken because he said that titles are bought: as they are; because he said that poor members are reminded of their dependence on the party funds: as they are; because he said that all this was a hypocrisy of public life: as it is. And all this is to be done by that well known champion of Liberalism & C.B., Lord Robert Cecil, supported by the silence of the 'Daily News'.
>
> One thing is certain. Unless some Liberal journalists speak on Monday or Tuesday, the secret funds & the secret powers are safe. . . . I would willingly burn my article if I were only sure that you would publish one yourself tomorrow on the same lines. [2]

At very least, Chesterton begged licence to publish a brief letter to the editor on the subject. Gardiner granted the request, and Chesterton made his point as a private individual and not in his capacity as a member of the *Daily News* staff.

Chesterton's 1907 campaign on behalf of Lea presaged his subsequent rampages against ministers who trafficked in Marconi shares, who sold peerages, and who otherwise perpetuated the dreaded 'party system'. He knew that sooner or later, he and Gardiner must have 'a row about right & wrong', but he hoped that it would prove possible to salvage their friendship from the debris of their professional relationship. 'If I leave the "Daily News" I shall not forget that I leave a friend there – & a godson,' he assured Gardiner. 'I ask you therefore to tell me, not as an editor to a contributor, but as a friend to a friend, whether I can in decency & self-respect go on writing for it, thinking what I think, & writing what I think.' In a faltering hand, which, he explained, was due to 'a complicated fracture at the elbow

1. Gardiner to Chesterton, 12 July 1907, cited in Ward, *Gilbert Keith Chesterton*, pp. 293–5.
2. Chesterton to Gardiner, 14 July 1907, G.P.

. . ., but not to any further softening of the brain, or any sort of relaxation of my bigoted and deadly purpose', Chesterton indicted a Liberalism that no longer seemed to tolerate the dissent on which it had once thrived:

I think the Insurance Act not only a tyranny, but one of the historic turning-points of tyranny, like Ship Money or the persecution of Wilkes. I believe our children will remember it against us. As to why I think this, I will tell you that if you will let me. But unless I may tell it you in public, we must instantly decide to have all our future arguments in private. I like writing for the 'Daily News' selfishly, because I have a large pulpit; but also affectionately, because I like so many men & memories connected with it, & was so heartily in sympathy so very short a time ago. . . . Hitherto I have hung onto the jolly old paper on the principle that Liberalism must . . . allow for open questions. As so it does, in some cases. Anybody is allowed to abuse the Government in the name of the microscopic minority of Suffragettes. You allow Massingham, week after week, to damn & blast the Liberal Party to infinity, merely because we are on the side of France, where (one would think) any free Western citizen might naturally be. It is surely tenable that Grey is Liberal in fighting for the French Republic against Bismarck & the Mailed Fist – at least as tenable as maintaining that Lloyd George is Liberal in imposing a State stratification of rich & poor practically imposed on Germany by Bismarck himself. . . .

If I have to follow the Liberal Government, I cannot write for the paper: nor could Massingham. But if I can attack it as he does, I will go on attacking it as he does. May I now & henceforth speak of the Liberal policy in Insurance as he speaks of the Liberal policy in Persia? May I champion the resisters to English insurance service as he would champion the resisters to Russian (or Australian) military service? May I damn Lloyd George as he damns Grey? Until you answer this, I shall hold myself ready for Saturday as usual: but I seriously ask you to answer it as soon as you can. It has troubled my sense of honour for some time. I would rather write for the 'News' than anything; if I can leave on record that I wrote on the right side.[1]

Strictly speaking, it was not a political dispute that brought Chesterton's connection with the *Daily News* to an end. In 1913 he published elsewhere his 'Song of Strange Drinks', which was widely taken as an attack upon the Cadburys. The middle stanza of the poem would certainly lend credence to such an interpretation:

1. Chesterton to Gardiner [1911], G.P.

Tea, although an Oriental,
Is a gentleman at least –
Cocoa is a cad and coward,
Cocoa is a vulgar beast,
Cocoa is a crawling, cringing,
Lying, loathsome swine and clown,
And may very well be grateful
To the fool that takes him down.

Gardiner, who tactfully professed 'too much respect for your sense of decency to suppose you would stoop to so gross an outrage on those with whom you have been associated in journalism for years', called upon Chesterton to correct the 'impression' ('baseless, as I am sure it is') to which the poem had given rise 'in some quarters'.[1] Chesterton lamely protested that he had intended nothing personal: 'Was the verse against tea an attack on Lipton? Was the praise of wine a puff for Gilbey?' Still, he concluded, 'it is quite impossible for me to continue taking the money of a man who may think I have insulted him. . . . Therefore I see no other course but to surrender my position on the paper quite finally.'[2]

Chesterton's resignation came as a relief, not least of all to G.K.C. himself, who had had enough of Shaw's taunts that he was 'Cadbury's property'. To Gardiner, on whom he knew the affair inflicted considerable pain, Chesterton offered the consolation that the result was not

a separation, but rather the removal of one. I can now say what I could never have said while there was a hint of my hanging on to the paper. I not only never felt anything but friendly to you, but I never had any but friendly feelings for the Cadburys. They were always nice to me; and I have known no case of their being nasty to anyone else. That their moral philosophy is remote from mine I feel no more at this moment than I did the first moment I met them, when we were all packed together by the necessity of a Pro-Boer paper. That they are wrong I believed then. That they are insincere I do not believe now. I could call many witnesses to prove that I have defended them from the blind charge of hypocrisy brought by many of my friends with whom I agree in politics. I think my friends right about politics, but wrong about people – especially people they don't know. . . .

1. 28 June 1913 (copy), G.P.
2. [n.d.], G.P.

I believe my brother & Belloc & the rest are right about the future of England: & so there is nothing for me but to back them up. But let us meet sometime soon and express our one common view of politics by talking about something else. [1]

Their subsequent meetings were neither as frequent, nor for that matter, altogether as cordial as Gardiner would have liked. But he held to his farewell promise that Chesterton, no longer a columnist, would 'be welcome as a correspondent', and except for a manifesto on the Marconi scandal, Chesterton's letters – all 'morally important' – were inserted 'fairly' and prominently. [2]

Gardiner's recurrent difficulties with Chesterton, like his successive differences of opinion with Nevinson and Brailsford, reflected certain basic problems inherent in his position at the *Daily News* and in the role that that position accorded him in Liberal politics. It was his primary responsibility to serve the interests of the Cadburys, who employed him, and to defend their honour to the extent that it merited defence. As editor of a prominent Liberal daily, it was no less incumbent on him to promote the party programme, even if there were ingredients to which he took exception and ministers with whom he regularly disagreed. With the revival of Tory opposition and the erosion of Liberal support in the country, there was the risk that criticism of official policy, however constructive or tempered, might be construed as an attack on the Government, whose existence was sometimes as precarious as that of the newspapers on which it relied. This was a risk that Gardiner was prepared to run: as a conscientious Liberal and a self-respecting journalist, he had no choice. But, unlike some colleagues, he was not inclined to indulge in argument for argument's sake, and preferred to concentrate his paper's limited resources where they might do most good. Inevitably, he was caught in the crossfire between contributors and directors, or between journalists and ministers, among whom he attempted to negotiate compromises that would allow the *Daily News* to function and the Liberal Government to retain credit.

The issue of women's suffrage provides a case in point. As President of the Board of Trade, Lloyd George aroused a degree of antagonism. His manner bore an unflattering resemblance to that of the young

1. [n.d.], G.P.
2. Chesterton to Gardiner, various undated letters, G.P.

Chamberlain, and his 'astonishingly fertile' mind often seemed sadly deficient of principle. 'He is always improvising,' Gardiner complained in the *Daily News* on 11 April 1908. 'You feel the theme is of secondary importance to the treatment.' Yet Lloyd George, raised to the Exchequer, soon became Gardiner's shining knight, *sans peur et sans reproche*, who attacked the dragons of privilege in town and countryside. The old 'pro-Boer' alliance was resuscitated, much to the satisfaction of George Cadbury, whose high regard for Lloyd George remained constant. Gardiner was reluctant to shake this alliance, which promised to achieve so much, by embarrassing Lloyd George on other matters.

On the evening of 5 December 1908 the Chancellor of the Exchequer addressed an Albert Hall meeeting on women's suffrage. Gardiner was among those on the platform, and Nevinson was in the audience. Lloyd George, himself not the least unsympathetic to the question, cautioned against the adoption of extremist tactics that were likely to discredit the cause. A phalanx of militant suffragettes, scorning his advice and attempting to disrupt the proceedings, were ejected – in the words of the *Manchester Guardian* – with 'nauseating brutality'. Nevinson delivered a stinging rebuke to Lloyd George, whom he somehow held accountable, and, 'on reaching home that night, . . . found a note from Gardiner "suspending" me from service on the *Daily News* until further notice'. Mounting his principles and his bicycle, he proceeded at once to Gardiner's home 'and told him I had done only what he or any other decent person would have done – rather an unfortunate defence, seeing that he had been sitting behind Mr Lloyd George all the time'. [1] Nevinson's suspension was rescinded by the board of directors; but the impression persisted, which his writings did much to foster, that Gardiner cared more for ministerial reputations than he did for the rights of his countrywomen.

Yet, was this a fair conclusion to be drawn? Surely Gardiner, like any editor, deserves to be judged by what appeared in his paper and not as an ornament on public platforms. The *Daily News* made clear its support of proposals to extend the franchise to women. It relentlessly condemned the methods by which suffragettes were apprehended, and pleaded for greater leniency in the courts and better treatment for those found guilty and imprisoned. These forthright

1. Nevinson, *More Changes, More Chances*, pp. 322–4.

appeals, if they failed to satisfy Nevinson, were nonetheless sufficient to enrage Gladstone, the Home Secretary, who defended existing procedures to Gardiner:

Suppose Home Rulers, or Social Purity reformers, or anti-Vivisectionists – who we all know to be very emotional people – take to Suffragette methods – strike constables, break windows, try to 'rush' the H. of C., collect great crowds & block the traffic, etc., etc.; are these people to be entitled to the legal right to escape all punishment except mere detention? The Suffragettes have posed as martyrs. They make it their object to induce a too gullible public to think that they have to suffer untold hardships & indignities which really do not exist. To alter the law in the direction wh. appears to be indicated wd. be a most dangerous step leading all sorts of people to disorderly methods. And where are you to stop? What is your limit to the political offence wh. is not to receive punitive treatment?[1]

Gardiner, who was not unique in the opinion, thought so little of Gladstone's administrative performance that he did not bother to dispute his statement that 'you suppose the H. O. in general & myself in particular incapable of rational judgement on some matters'.[2] It was not, therefore, out of consideration for the Home Secretary, but for those closer at hand that Gardiner hedged on certain issues and hesitated to condemn too strongly in print the practice of forcible feeding which he privately described as 'repugnant'. Nevinson and Brailsford, who threatened to resign if the *Daily News* did not echo the 'excellent leader' that had appeared in the *Manchester Guardian*, had several long sessions with their editor, who provided a 'pathetic account [of] how he was torn between Mrs Cadbury on one side' and themselves on the other. To no avail, Gardiner attempted to demonstrate that the policy pursued by the *Daily News* 'was a compromise' between the two positions, and that he, to the utmost of his ability, had taken their part. Brailsford tendered his immediate resignation, 'so that G. might use it to coerce the Cadburys if he liked'. Nevinson agreed to stay on as leader-writer for a few weeks, but his decision to leave was unalterable, notwithstanding 'G's personal consideration in dealing with my imaginary violence'.[3]

1. 20 July 1909, G.P.
2. Gladstone to Gardiner, 29 July 1909, G.P.
3. Nevinson diary, 27–30 September 1909.

Nevinson failed to appreciate the strong influence of the Cadburys, Elsie included, who were unusually sensitive at this time, and particularly in matters where he was concerned. Weeks later, they brought a successful libel action against the *Standard*, which had pilloried them as supporters of slavery in the Portuguese cocoa plantations. Acknowledging the evils of that system, they testified that they were working to reform it and had provided the Foreign Office with valuable information. It was their view that a boycott along the lines that Nevinson and others had proposed would inflict further suffering on African labourers and disrupt negotiations with the Portuguese authorities. The jury awarded the plaintiff, represented by Rufus Isaacs, a farthing damages and costs; the counsel for the defence, incidentally, was Sir Edward Carson. All the same, criticism continued of the Cadburys' import practices, and there was intensified ridicule of the 'cocoa press', the so-called syndicate of journals owned by them and the Rowntrees. On 7 December the *Daily News* gave prominent attention to the verdict of the Birmingham jury, but withheld editorial comment. Not so that morning's *Times*, which, 'without impeaching the sincerity of any members of the plaintiffs' firm', pointedly expressed 'regret that the newspaper which was not unconnected with them did not reserve a little of the fierce indignation which it poured upon Chinese slavery for the unmistakable form of it which existed in San Thomé and Principe'.

The 'cocoa press' – the designation was consciously intended to imply an insipid quality – was alleged to propagate the cosmopolitan and pacifist creed of its Quaker proprietors at the expense of national greatness. It incensed its enemies, particularly those on the Tory right, by its fidelity to Free Trade, its advocacy of improved relations with Germany, its dogged opposition to preparations for war, and, not least of all, by its bourgeois concern for social improvement. Surely its various interests were not unrelated. The agitation for *rapprochement* with Germany had as its logical corollary a demand for reduced army and navy estimates, which, as they rose, threatened welfare programmes with impoverishment, if not extinction, and made the prospect of war both more terrifying and more inevitable. The *Daily News* pressed the case for disarmament more ardently than any other London daily and, with the exception of the *Manchester Guardian*, more than any other major daily in the country. It had sporadic assistance from the *Westminster Gazette,* always careful not to embarrass Grey, and from the *Daily Chronicle,* which correctly gauged the limits of its influence. But its chief ally in the metropolis was the *Nation,* another 'cocoa' byproduct.

Given the urgency of the situation and their similarities in outlook, it is perhaps surprising that Gardiner and Scott made no serious effort to coordinate their propaganda; the circumstances of Gardiner's appointment may have been in some measure responsible. Closer ties existed between each of the dailies and the *Nation,* whose editor, the taciturn Massingham, had served on both staffs and recruited many of his contributors from among former colleagues. Like Hirst of the *Economist,* his equal in pertinacity but neither in contacts nor resourcefulness, Massingham actively identified himself in print and in party councils as an advocate of neutrality abroad and disarmament at home.

Liberal editors, 'cocoa' and otherwise, tended to champion Sir John (later Lord) Fisher, whose naval reforms promised financial relief and adequate defence without recourse to National Service, which they naturally detested on grounds of principle. Their esteem for Fisher was shared, for perhaps different reasons, by persons as diverse as King Edward and Garvin, the latter 'a sort of journalistic Fisher', [1] impetuous, passionate, and unconventional in his allegiances. Gardiner, far more prosaic than either Garvin or Stead, nonetheless got on famously well with the admiral, who had seen battle in the China Seas before Gardiner was born. 'Jacky' Fisher summoned him for frequent briefings and, as was his custom with men he liked, rambled on and divulged more than he had intended. 'Lots of things I remember now I ought to have told you!' he wrote to Gardiner shortly after one of their sessions; 'but kindly . . . don't remember anything I said!' [2]

His glorification of Fisher ensured Gardiner the hostility of Lord Charles Beresford, Fisher's arch enemy, and contributed to his misgivings about successive First Lords of the Admiralty, who gave way to public pressure allegedly in disregard of Fisher's advice. The naval scare of 1909, induced by exaggerated reports of German shipbuilding, left Gardiner with an unfavourable opinion of McKenna,

1. Marder, *From the Dreadnought to Scapa Flow,* i, 77.
2. 20 June 1909, G.P.

previously an exponent of economy and now a self-proclaimed 'Big Navy' man, whose inability to dictate to admiralty officials was evident. Asquith improvised a compromise – four dreadnoughts were to be constructed immediately and four more the following year if the German schedule was not modified – that restored order in the Cabinet, but bitterly disappointed Radicals outside. Nevinson submitted a strong leader against 'the 4 "contingent" Dreadnoughts', and Brailsford, true to form, announced that 'he wd. walk out of [the] office if G. smoothed it over'. To their 'astonishment', Gardiner read the piece and 'came in asking if I was not too mild!'[1] What had happened to Lloyd George, Morley, Churchill, and others, who had vowed to resist increased estimates? The front-bench politicians, Hobhouse complained to Scott, 'really owe something to their Press which incurs all the obloquy. Morley ought to speak, and lecture the whole country on the subject of Panics.'[2]

In 1911 a second Morocco crisis fanned anti-German sentiments and revived the popular outcry for naval expansion. Fisher had meanwhile attained the age of seventy and, with due honours, retired temporarily from active service. McKenna's transfer from the Admiralty could not long be postponed, and Haldane intimated his interest in going there to carry out reforms comparable to those he had accomplished at the War Office. Instead, the Prime Minister replaced McKenna (whom he made Home Secretary), with Churchill, an appointment that filled Gardiner with foreboding. Until the provocative appearance that summer of the German gunboat *Panther* at Agadir, Churchill had been among the most truculent 'Little Navy' men in the Cabinet; but his ground had since shifted. Gardiner had always been sceptical about the depth of Churchill's Liberalism ('He is a personal force and not a party instrument, and he will never be easily controlled except by himself'), and doubtful of Churchill's ability to see himself and his work in perspective. Nor had the egregious Winston distinguished himself as a master of tact. Most distressing was Churchill's tendency, which Gardiner had detected by the early days of 1908, to infuse politics with a military spirit: 'It is impossible to think of him except in the terms of actual warfare. The smell of powder is about his path, and wherever he appears one seems

1. Nevinson diary, 26 July 1909.
2. 7 April 1909 (copy), *Guardian* Archives.

to hear the crack of musketry and to feel the hot breath of battle.'[1] The length and vicissitudes of Churchill's career allowed Gardiner to return to him periodically as a subject for character study, and to write some of his most percipient sketches which, strung together, constitute a classic in Churchilliana and a superb commentary on nearly a half century of political life. Understandably, he wrote far more often on Churchill than on any other public figure, and although his emphasis varied with the issues of the day, his approach remained constant: admiration for Churchill's phenomenal energy which, he feared, might too easily burn itself out or, worse still, generate ruin. 'Remember,' he concluded a 1912 essay on Churchill, 'he is a soldier first, last, and always. He will write his name big on our future. Let us take care he does not write it in blood.' The judgment was severe, and intentionally so, but Gardiner said no more than what many Liberals were then thinking. Nearly three decades later, he heard Churchill, as Prime Minister, deliver a wartime broadcast on the BBC. 'What a man!' he exclaimed. 'I venture to say he embodies in his own person Caesar, Napoleon & Lincoln, with a few other fellows from Demosthenes to Gladstone thrown in to make weight. . . . Of course he loves the war game: no one who didn't love it could have saved us.' The occasion stirred 'proud' memories of his earlier 'forecast', which he saw no reason to repudiate: 'And so perverse are events,' Gardiner reflected, 'that now I thank God [Churchill] has been spared to write [his name] in blood.'[2]

Churchill's pugnacity, which Gardiner ultimately came to regard as the nation's greatest asset, seemed to him a distinct liability in the uneasy years that preceded the First World War. Here was a sabre-rattler as potentially dangerous as the Kaiser, a First Lord whose disdainful reference to the German fleet as a 'luxury' was an insult to

1. 'This is true as I know him', Walter Runciman, soon to join the Cabinet as President of the Board of Education, responded to an advance proof of Gardiner's first Churchill essay, which appeared in the next day's *Daily News*, 'but aren't you rather hard on him when you say he has not the love of humanity in him? I am not sure about that. What I think would be fairer, would be to enquire if ever he has been or even can be *disinterested*. Self sacrifice is not one of his ideals! And yet he has a pathetic & tender way of securing affection. Your analysis (barring these points) is the best thing ever done on him'. Runciman to Gardiner, 17 January 1908, G.P.
2. Gardiner to Swinnerton, 9 February 1941, Swinnerton Papers.

German patriotism, and whose spiralling estimates exacerbated tensions. Masterman, on a single day, subjected himself to 'lunch with Gardiner, who was quite cheerful and cursing Winston's speeches' on naval and foreign policy, and dinner 'with Massingham, also cursing Winston'. [1] Fisher, who retained a seat in the Committee of Imperial Defence and a lively interest in events at Whitehall, sought to allay Gardiner's distrust of the new Churchill, who plied him with invitations and requests for guidance. A strong navy, he reasoned, would provide an irrefutable argument against compulsory service: 'Give the Navy every d—d thing they want! Let there be no loophole for saying the Navy is short of anything & so that we must have an Army.' [2]

Gardiner was not convinced that further expenditure upon sea defence was justified either by the German menace or by Fisher's logic that this would weaken the case of those who demanded nothing less than a large professional army equipped for continental warfare. He nonetheless found much to admire in the old sea-dog, who returned his affection by defying his 'Nelsonic' motto – 'never ask advice' – with an appeal for help on the volume of memoirs he had begun to write. 'I think the reason I suddenly ask your advice', Fisher confided, 'is that not only are you a man of the world, which King Edward said I was not and never would be! "that I had gone all round the world but I had never been in it!" (which was rather nasty of him!) but you are also a man of literature and that I am not either.' [3] Gardiner encouraged Fisher to pursue the project: 'Not to do so would be to deprive the world of one of the most entertaining books I can imagine.' He recommended 'absolute frankness and fulness', which he could count upon Fisher to supply, and also a second reading of the manuscript by 'some thoroughly judicious person' before publication. [4]

The comparative calm of his retirement, interrupted by the outbreak of war, afforded Lord Fisher the leisure not only to contemplate his past heroics, but also to peruse old newspapers which he had

1. Masterman to his wife [September 1912], cited in Lucy Masterman, *C. F. G. Masterman*, p. 244.
2. Fisher to Gardiner, 19 January 1911, G.P.
3. Fisher to Gardiner, 18 March 1911, G.P.
4. 24 March 1911, cited in Marder, ed., *Fear God and Dread Nought*, ii, 265n.

saved unread. In the stack he found 'an old number of the "Daily News"' containing an article that 'fires my imagination'. Perhaps Gardiner had written it, he wondered:

> The gist of it is that some fifth rate diplomatic fool supported by his 'Sisters and his Cousins and his Aunts' at the Foreign Office (whose *permanent sustained* pressure none but a Cromwellian Secretary of State for Foreign Affairs could resist) is able to plunge our Great Empire into a beastly mess before the public have any power to intervene! My pretty big experience of our diplomats is that their habitual residence abroad & their marriage with foreigners leads to their ceasing being Englishmen (To put a man like Bryce from the outside is a very rare occurrence!) . . . *Our Diplomacy is effete!*[1]

It would have been impossible for Gardiner to identify the particular article, so much had it gained in the retelling, and so typically did it reflect the line that the *Daily News* had taken since the Boer War. Gardiner, as we have noted, held tenaciously to the view that national policy ought never to be determined by either permanent officials behind closed doors or accredited agents 'on the spot'. He would have hastened to add, however, that neither ought policy to be dictated by admirals, generals, or members of the House of Lords, none of whom were directly responsible to the people. Sovereignty, as he defined it, lay in the House of Commons, which derived its power from the electorate and, to the greatest extent possible, reflected the national will. Needless to say, this was not a theory that enjoyed universal acceptance, and it was frequently put to the test during the prewar period.

A strong Liberal majority in the Commons, met by Tory intransigence in the Lords, made for inevitable collision. The Lloyd George budget of 1909, and its consequent rejection in the upper House, crystallized issues. Out of the ensuing crisis came, within the space of a single year, two bitterly contested general elections, followed by an Act to shear the House of Lords of its powers, and a shake-up in the Tory leadership. The Liberals emerged with diminished majorities and were henceforth compelled to rely heavily on Irish and Labour support. The Tories registered substantial electoral gains which, if insufficient to impede Government legislation, inspired confidence

1. Fisher to Gardiner, 5 October 1911, G.P.

that the tide had turned in their favour. In these circumstances, Gardiner saw the need to mute his criticism of Liberal policy so as not to increase the party's vulnerability in Parliament or at the polls.

Ten days into the first of the two 1910 elections, J. A. Spender wrote to Gardiner, whose recent attitude toward the Prime Minister had been noticeably cool:

Will you let me tell you quite privately what I hear about the Tory strategy during the next few months [?] It is, shortly, to get in, to propose a hundred million loan for the navy, to dissolve again, & to make the election turn on this – in fact to hold a Khaki election.

It seems to me that we ought to prevent this at all costs, if possible, for reasons of international & domestic politics alike. But the only way we can prevent it is by keeping the present Government in. If they go, the command of strategy passes to the Tories & they will endeavour to make the issue what they choose.

Asquith will, I hope, get through on his pledge . . . [of a] promise of Royal support for a Bill giving finance to the Commons. But if the Lords check that, we are all right & make our own issue; if not, we recover finance & get the Budget & then advance to the Second Chamber question more at leisure. But the King will not give guarantees on the legislative veto Bill; indeed, on the present showing, it would not be fair to expect it for a Bill which has never been drafted & if we give the other side ground for dragging the King in & saying that we are treating him badly & threatening the monarchy, we shall be playing a very bad card.

I suggest, then, that we journalists should not make it too difficult for Asquith to hold on. It will be no remedy to defeat Balfour on the address if we once let him in. That would look factious and throw on us the onus of financial confusion, & leave him free to dissolve & have his Khaki election. I thought you would forgive me if I tell you what I know to be the present Tory plans on some of these matters. [1]

Gardiner, who regarded as 'villainous' the accommodating line that Spender took in the *Westminster*, dismissed Spender's appeal as 'full of timid alarms'. [2] Nonetheless, Spender was apparently assuaged by Gardiner's prompt reply. 'I don't think we disagree', he wrote the next day. 'The great thing to my mind, at the moment, is not to make it difficult for Asquith to go on, or we should not even get the Budget

1. 24 January 1910, G.P.
2. Gardiner's diary, 24 January 1910, G.P. Gardiner considered that day's leader in the *Westminster* an 'evident reply to me'.

through.'[1] Gardiner would not dispute Spender's strategy, although he had considerably more on his mind than the Budget, however staunchly he defended it. In the wake of the general election, he forwarded to Downing Street a reminder of campaign promises that remained unredeemed since 1906, and he called for a reaffirmation of Liberal priorities. Vaughan Nash, serving there in a secretarial capacity, promised to bring the document to Asquith's attention: 'You may be sure that he realises all the difficulties of the situation & the danger of disheartening people.'[2] Following the precedent set in 1906, the *Daily News* celebrated the election returns at a dinner on February 26. As befitting the occasion, it was a smaller, less festive gathering than the last – Henry Cadbury represented his family and Chesterton was among those in attendance – and Gardiner vacated the chair in favour of E. C. Bentley, his deputy.

Radical MPs, who had been able to speak with virtual impunity when the Liberal majority was overwhelming, now thought twice before raising issues that might divide the House. Their ranks depleted by the elections of 1910, they were acutely conscious of their weakened position within the parliamentary Liberal party, and feared, not without reason, that the Opposition might take advantage of a backbench revolt to turn out the Government. As a result, Radicals were forced to fall back on a proliferation of subsidiary and extraparliamentary agencies: the Foreign Policy Committee, the National Reform Union, the International Arbitration League, the Committee for the Reduction of Expenditure on Armaments, and, pre-eminently, the National Liberal Federation. One of the most active, though least durable, was the Gladstone League, in which Gardiner, as chairman of the executive committee, was a moving force. On 23 March 1910 it held its inaugural meeting at the Queen's Hall, with Lloyd George, as president, giving an address on the land question, 'perhaps the most poignant tragedy of English life'. Although Gardiner, who took the chair, thought the speech 'disappointing', the *Daily News* dutifully praised it as a 'great' one. Masterman also spoke, and seemed to Gardiner to fall 'flat'.

Gardiner was a good deal less critical of his own performance:

1. 25 January 1910, G.P.
2. 17 February 1910, G.P. Gardiner's letter does not survive among the Asquith Papers.

'General opinion I did very well', he jotted with satisfaction in his diary. The Prime Minister did not attend, but sent a letter which the chairman read aloud to the 'great audience'. After the meeting, Lloyd George, Masterman, and Gardiner went 'to Gatti's for oysters. Remained till after twelve, George talking all the time, quoting Welsh sermons, Welsh hymns, Welsh stories.'[1] Despite the enthusiasm with which it was launched, it was decided that the Gladstone League could best achieve its goals in concert with other groups, into which it merged later in the year.

Radicals also relied on their few newspapers for the exposure that was no longer available to them in parliamentary debate. The *Daily News*, more reluctant than before to come out officially against the Government, allowed its correspondents considerable freedom to take issue with specific Government policies. Always sympathetic to Indian demands for self-determination (the 1909 Morley–Minto reforms had seemed to Gardiner sadly lacking in foresight) the paper irritated Edwin S. Montagu, Morley's successor at the India Office, by its condemnation of sedition trials and other acts of repression. In this area, Gardiner worked closely with Roger Casement, a champion of subject nationalities including his own, who arranged interviews for him with Indian nationalist spokesmen. The ill-fated Casement, a frequent visitor to Bouverie Street, also published anonymously in the *Daily News* his celebrated exposé of the Peruvian Amazon Company. 'The signature is wholly fictitious,' he explained in a letter that accompanied one of his articles, 'a sort of hybrid corruption of my name. . . . You need not be afraid of libel suits if you print this. I'll see you through, that I can promise you, if any-one or the P.A. Directors dared to take action. But they won't – they'll only shiver in their skins for fear of what else may be coming.'[2] Shaw, another crusading Irishman, found the *Daily News* an attrac-tive market place for his wares, but sent notice that 'Bernard Shaw items' would be in short supply at the end of 1910, when he would be sailing to Jamaica.[3] Christabel Pankhurst, too, was a featured con-tributor to the correspondence columns, and provided Gardiner with 'documents' to support the case for women's suffrage. Early in 1912,

1. Gardiner's diary, 23 March 1910, G.P.; also *Daily News*, 24 March 1910.
2. [1910], G.P.
3. 23 December 1910, G.P.

there was a series of letters on Irish Home Rule by Erskine Childers that won Casement's commendation: 'I hope there will be more of them & that you won't cut them short.'[1] Frederic Mackarness, an indefatigable ally of the Irish and Indian freedom movements, applauded the *Daily News*'s service to 'undefended peoples', among whom one might presumably include the female population of Great Britain: 'I should be ungrateful indeed if I did not warmly recognize how often I have been helped by the D. N. The paper has a great & long tradition in this respect: one which I hope & pray it will always maintain with the courage & ability of old.'[2]

Not that the *Daily News*, preoccupied with its humanitarian concerns, turned its back on the Liberal Party in its hour of need. Idealistic, the paper and its editor were not foolhardy. Happily, the Liberals chose to fight the December 1910 election on grounds which any Radical could easily support. Alexander Murray, the Master of Elibank and chief Government whip, could not allow the campaign to close without sending Gardiner

sincere thanks for all the help which you have extended to me during my somewhat difficult year of office.

I feel that the results in London are largely attributable to the stimulus of your leading articles, and the care and tact with which you have dealt with delicate situations.

. . .

You have no idea of the difference it makes to me here to feel that one has a friend directing a great Liberal journal. It is so much easier to discuss matters freely and frankly.[3]

The dominating figure in the second 1910 election, as increasingly within the Cabinet, was Lloyd George, who had precipitated the constitutional crisis, whose invective against the 'dukes' reached a new pitch, and whose blueprint for social reform drove his Tory enemies to distraction. Gardiner not only recognized Lloyd George as the man of the moment ('his is the crest around which the battle rages'), but pinned his hopes to him as the man of the future. Lloyd George, yet to acquire his legendary reputation as a master at manipulating

1. Casement to Gardiner, 2 February 1912, G.P.
2. Mackarness to Gardiner, 14 December 1911, G.P.
3. 17 December 1910, G.P.

the press, already relied on Gardiner to do his bidding. 'I am looking forward to seeing you tomorrow', he had written in his most charming vein to Gardiner the previous 15 June, calling his attention to F. E. Smith's letter in that day's *Times* endorsing the compromise proposal for an inter-party conference to break the constitutional deadlock. 'I hope you will rub it in – it is a very important letter. I wish you could see your way to call special attention to it in tomorrow's *Daily News*.'[1] When they met the next day, Gardiner was able to gratify Lloyd George with a copy of that morning's *Daily News*, in which he had written and inserted a leader in praise of Smith and his 'letter worthy of the eve of a serious and important meeting'.

The Chancellor's efforts to ameliorate the lot of the unemployed and the needy earned him Gardiner's greatest respect and most devoted service. It was in the *Daily News* (27 August 1908) that Lloyd George first aired his views on national insurance, and the paper thereafter took his part in controversies with critics in the medical profession, the friendly societies,[2] and titled matrons. Gardiner, as chairman of a debate between Ramsay MacDonald (pro) and Hilaire Belloc (con), was no honest broker but a fervent advocate of the controversial scheme, which, as much as its author, he expected to 'reclaim [a] huge tract of humanity now sodden in wretchedness'. The *Daily News* 'has helped Insurance', Lloyd George assured him on 29 March 1911, two days after the appearance of a lavish spread on the proposals:

> I can see evidence of that in all the papers today. Many thanks. Vested interests in this as in all reforms are potent & pernicious. They can be successfully fought in one way – by rousing the public conscience to the wickedness of exploiting human distress to satiate greed. In such a struggle I feel confident I can always rely on the powerful influence of the Daily News.[3]

On 16 December, the Insurance Bill received the royal assent, and Gardiner celebrated by publishing in the *Daily News* the second of his portraits of Lloyd George, who that day 'add[ed] to his record the most far-reaching legislative achievement of our time'. In his exultation, Gardiner forgot his earlier reservations about the hero of the

1. G.P.
2. See issues of 1 and 2 December 1910.
3. 29 March 1911, G.P.

hour; his effusions, later recalled to him, caused him considerable embarrassment. Lloyd George, he wrote, had singlehandedly 're-habilitated' Liberalism by his unique 'combination of imagination and courage': 'His eye ranges over wide horizons. He sees the future with the literalism with which the general sees the battlefield. He calculates forces and possibilities as another man calculates his profits and losses, and having decided on his line of attack no fear or hesitation palsies the ardour of the onset.'

Again, he compared Lloyd George to Chamberlain, but only to contrast the 'spirit' of the two men. Lloyd George, he insisted, 'bears no enmities. When he has cut you down with his sword he will pick you up with his smile. He carries himself with a boyish gaiety that is irresistible.' In summary, Gardiner hailed his subject as

the portent of the new time – the man of the people in the seat of power. He has no precedent in our political annals. Our politics have been governed by men who have studied the life of the people as others have studied the life of ants or bees, objectively, remotely. Even Bright, Cobden, Chamberlain were not of the people. They were of the middle class and knew the poor as the instruments of the great employer. Mr George like Mr Burns comes out of the great hive itself. In him democracy has found its voice and to him it will be loyal so long as he remembers.

There was no doubt in his mind that Lloyd George would remember, and he discounted the danger, which he had seen so clearly from a further distance, that Lloyd George might go the way of Chamberlain. At the time, it seemed inconceivable that the man who had known poverty in his Welsh boyhood might 'forget from whence comes his authority and his commission. . . . For however much the glitter of the great world delights him, his heart, untravelled, always turns back to the village between the mountains and the sea.'

A magnificent victory had been won, but there were other battles, which Gardiner was proud to fight beneath the Lloyd George standard. Breakfasting with the Mastermans at the Chancellor's Downing Street residence, he heard Lloyd George describe how, when first adopted at twenty-five to stand for Carnarvon, he had been asked 'whether I would go out against Gladstone on the subject of Welsh Disestablishment'. Their host recollected that he had replied 'in the words of Cromwell: "If I meet the King in battle I will fire at him with my pistol." Great is the cheek of youth!' To which Gardiner, making a note of the anecdote, responded: 'It has not deserted you yet!' [1] In addition to frequent breakfasts at Number Eleven, Gardiner joined Lloyd George at sessions to plan the campaign for land reform, in which he and George Cadbury took keen interest. Their relationship was a close one, and Gardiner donned his formal attire to accompany Lloyd George to dinner at the Hotel Cecil ('You know what a large place the Hotel Cecil is,' he wrote the next morning to his daughter. 'Well, the dinners there are just as large as the Hotel'). [2] For personal as well as political reasons, therefore, he was dismayed by charges levelled at Lloyd George and other ministers during the so-called Marconi scandal of 1912–13.

The charges, although gravely serious, could be answered; not so the innuendoes, against which any appeal to fact was futile. Lloyd George and Sir Rufus Isaacs, the Attorney-General, denied that they had held shares in the Marconi Company, which the Postmaster-General had engaged to erect an imperial network of wireless stations. They subsequently admitted, however, having invested in the company's American affiliate. The Master of Elibank, too, was implicated, both as an individual and as the custodian of party funds. It was an unsavoury business, and for a time it looked as if several ministerial careers – Lloyd George's chief among them – had been ruined. Masterman, who called on the Prime Minister 'when Mr Lloyd George's career was in the balance', reported to Gardiner that he had found him 'walking to and fro in the deepest agitation and murmuring, "I cannot save him; I cannot save him."' [3] But Asquith, if he had doubts, took care not to betray them publicly. Lloyd George, to whom friends were often pawns in the game of power politics, was visibly moved by the way that his associates stood securely by him. Throughout the ordeal, the *Daily News* continued to proclaim his innocence. 'I am off to a game of golf,' he buoyantly told Gardiner when the storm had at last abated,

but I could not enjoy it without writing you to tell you how deeply I appreciate the warm & loyal friendship you have proved during the last

1. Lucy Masterman, *C. F. G. Masterman*, p. 139.
2. Gardiner to Gwen Gardiner, 13 October 1912 (courtesy of Miss Gwen Gardiner).
3. Gardiner, 'Asquith', the *Nineteenth Century and after* (November 1932), p. 616.

few days. The more thoroughly this business is probed the cleaner and more straightforward the transaction will appear. At the same time, it has worried me a good deal. What compensates for all however is the fact that it has demonstrated to me that I have true friends whom I can always rely upon.

P.S. The article you wrote was tip top. It was a triumph of tact & judgment.[1]

But he had spoken too soon. Early summer brought a recrudescence of attacks as further evidence seeped out. Harold Spender, in his haste to clear the Chancellor's name, made matters worse by writing a piece in the *Daily News* that unwittingly raised more questions than it answered. Gardiner apologized to Lloyd George for the blunder, which he ascribed to 'the tendency of the author to get a little off the rails. He has seen no one on the subject except yourself & believes that he was stating your view. Unfortunately I was so pressed that I didn't see the article until it had gone to press.' Lloyd George proposed to confront his critics in his next public appearance, and Gardiner urged him to 'err on the side of gravity rather than of brilliancy'. The speech should be addressed to the nation, he sagely counselled, and should emphasize

the real motives of the attack, glancing lightly at the difficulties of investment for a Minister & at the vulnerability of the enemy on the subject. . . . The chief object, it seems to me, is to establish in the mind of the country that the attack is not promoted by a concern for the standards of public conduct but by a desire to break you & through you the party & its policy. . . . I have no doubt that your own instinct will guide you aright, but on this occasion I should try to avoid impromptus. They are delightful but dangerous.[2]

Lloyd George accepted Gardiner's explanation for the Spender article ('He is a well-meaning but clumsy fellow'), and welcomed his advice: 'I think your line is quite right; and if "retaining grace" is vouchsafed unto me I can guarantee to follow it – but I need lots of grace, so pray for me!'[3] Gardiner, who trusted more to the power of the press than to the power of prayer, kept to the defence, and by autumn had the satisfaction of serving as 'Drummer boy' in the

1. 26 March 1913, G.P.
2. Gardiner to Lloyd George, 25 June 1913, Lloyd George Papers C/9/4/65 (Beaverbrook Library, London).
3. Lloyd George to Gardiner, 26 June 1913, G.P.

successfully launched land campaign. 'We've really got "a move on",
this dear old land at last & it is you who have done it,' he declared to
Lloyd George, whose rousing speech at Swindon had left 'Limehouse
standing still. Wherever I go I find men brimming over with good
spirits. . . . 'Tis good in this dawn to be alive – and kicking.'[1]

These were indeed happy days for Gardiner, before the intrusion of
international events that destroyed the Liberal order and sundered his
alliance with Lloyd George. Yet, looking back, one can detect signs
of the developments that soon crippled his party and cost him his
editorship. In November 1911 he paid tribute to William Jeans, a
Fleet Street regular who was retiring after some forty years of service
in the press galleries of Westminster, 'a journalist of the old school,
. . . which considered its duty to be to inform the public, to give
trustworthy reports and sound information, and not to be in any way
sensational'. Gardiner, who felt increasingly an anomaly in the age of
Northcliffe, 'was not sure that those old virtues had not still some
uses in the modern world'.[2] A month later, plans were revealed to
amalgamate the *Daily News* with the smaller *Morning Leader*. He was
not immediately affected, but his relations with colleagues and directors were inevitably altered, to the extent that there were recurrent
rumours of his impending resignation. The amalgamation necessitated proportionate reductions in both staffs. Ted (Edward Taylor)
Scott, a writer for the *Morning Leader*, 'survived the massacre', but
decided in any case to move to the *Manchester Guardian*, where he
succeeded his father as editor in 1929. Others were less fortunate in
their range of alternatives. R. C. K. Ensor, who had spent two years
writing leaders for the *Daily News*, was given notice: an 'ugly business', thought C. E. Montague, C.P.'s son-in-law and a director of
the *Guardian*, for a man 'with two or three children & no other work
& hardly any but Conservative papers in London.'[3] Gardiner, who
apparently had no voice in the matter, trusted that the Cadburys had
conferred a 'satisfactory' settlement on Ensor, whose 'services & . . .
comradeship' he was sorry to lose. He hoped that their association
would 'be renewed at some time &, in the meantime, that we may not

1. 23 October 1913, Lloyd George Papers, C/10/1/59.
2. *The Times*, 28 November 1911.
3. Montague to Francis Dodd, 19 December 1911, Montague-Dodd Correspondence, British Museum Add. MSS 45,910, fol. 67.

wholly lose sight of one another'. [1] Ensor soon found employment on the *Daily Chronicle*, where he remained until 1930, when it merged with the *Daily News* to become the *News Chronicle*.

The *Daily News and Leader* started publication in May 1912. Its appearance, like all else, was overshadowed by the previous month's *Titanic* disaster. The first edition featured interviews with such prominent politicians as Lloyd George and Haldane. Ramsay Mac-Donald replied that he was 'so filled up at the moment' that he could not contribute, although he offered 'to write a series of articles' as a retort to Graham Wallas's views on syndicalism. Meanwhile, he hoped that Gardiner would 'do something to revive an interest in the . . . continued depression of labour'. [2] John Burns, still smarting from old wounds, refused Harold Spender's request for material on the grounds that he was too immersed in important projects at the Local Government Board: 'Apart from this the DN cannot be interested in anything I say or my Dept. does.' [3] In its new incarnation, the *Daily News* proceeded to placate MacDonald and to alienate Burns further by its sympathetic treatment of industrial unrest. Gardiner, who was always anxious to promote accommodations between Liberal and Labour party organizations in the constituencies, insisted that the essential conflict was not one between 'Labour and Capital', but 'between anarchic labour and organized trade unionism'. Acknowledging the existence of legitimate grounds for grievance, he implored workers to cease the 'irresponsible guerrilla warfare' that menaced the trade union movement. [4] Nor was it likely that he endeared himself to Burns by his persistent tributes to the Webbs, who, 'although their labours have been confined to the material fabric of society', seemed to him to have 'done as much as the poets to cleanse its soul as well'.

If Gardiner had reason to resent his subservience to the Cadburys, he might well have consoled himself by comparing his lot to that of J. A. Spender, whose paper had passed to the hands of a syndicate

1. Gardiner to Ensor, 5 December 1911, Ensor Papers (The Library, Corpus Christi College, Oxford).

2. MacDonald to Gardiner, 8 May 1912, G.P.

3. Spender to Burns, 6 May 1912 (with marginal note by Burns), Burns Papers, Add. MSS 46,302, fol. 147.

4. See particularly A.G.G.'s Saturday columns of 22 November and 6 December 1913, and 9 May 1914.

headed by Sir Alfred Mond (later the 1st Baron Melchett), a Liberal politician of vast wealth and commensurate ambition. In October 1912 the *Daily News* had launched a fund to relieve Balkan war victims, and Mond was among those who pledged support. 'And he didn't send a copper', Gardiner inscribed unforgivingly at the foot of Mond's promise of assistance. [1] The same day that Mond offered his unsigned cheque to Gardiner, Arnold Bennett spied him closeted with Spender at the Reform Club. 'Spender looked as dry as he is', Bennett noted, and 'the employed and the employer', taking leave of each other, 'shook hands like not too intimate friends'. [2] It was far preferable, Gardiner knew, to draw one's salary from cocoa than from alkali.

Various Liberal associations proposed to adopt him as their parliamentary candidate, but, like Spender, he wisely declined on grounds that he could serve the cause more actively and meaningfully from outside the House. The British political tradition offered no counterpart to the breed of journalist-statesman that flourished across the channel under the Third Republic. Morley, a distinguished student of French culture, had been inspired to enter Parliament 'exactly because I hope to become a thoroughly useful political writer'. [3] No sooner had he arrived at Westminster in 1883 than he found, to his lasting regret, that his two vocations were incompatible. More recently, Scott had returned to full-time journalism after ten frustrating and undistinguished years as member for Leigh. Gardiner's place at the *Daily News* afforded him a perspective on men and events that would have been difficult to improve, as well as the opportunity to speak his mind more freely and on more subjects than any backbencher. Best of all, he was not required to take the whip and could dissent from his party chiefs – he hoped with some effect – on questions of foreign policy or defence, on social issues, and, early in 1914, on the negotiations over Home Rule for Ireland. Ford Madox Hueffer (soon driven by the pressures of wartime opinion to repeat his first name as his last), neither espoused Gardiner's politics nor envied his position. 'I have always thought', he confessed in what was osten-

1. Mond to Gardiner, 16 October 1912 (with note by Gardiner), G.P.
2. Arnold Bennett's Journal, 16 October 1912.
3. Morley to Chamberlain, 3 January 1878, cited in Koss, *John Morley at the India Office*, p. 2.

sibly a review of Gardiner's latest volume of portraits,

that of the queer things in this queer world the queerest of all must be to write political or social articles for the *Daily News*. I do not mean to say that it must be disagreeable, for it must be so funny – the odd obstacle race of a thing that such writing must be. For just imagine what, exactly, must be prescribed for you. You have to be extremely anti-Romanist, for your supporters are Nonconformist; at the same time you must be pretty fairly Papist, or you will displease the followers of Mr Redmond, Mr Belloc, and the tolerant. You must generally slam the Church of England; at the same time every now and then you must assure that Church, for the sake of the Bishop of Hereford, the Dean of Durham, and Archdeacon Lilley, that you only desire Disestablishment in order that Anglicanism of the Low variety may eventually triumph throughout this realm of England. You must rejoice in the triumphs of Fabianism, Labour, Syndicalism, Anarchism, Forcible Feeding, Feminism, and Strong Government by turns. You must talk for ever of the imbecility of Toryism, and you must never hit Mr Balfour very hard. For one thing, you think the country will not stand hearing very much against Mr Balfour; for another, you think that every word uttered in praise of the former leader is a kick delivered to the address of Mr Bonar Law.

. . .

Of course, if you are a writer on things of the intellect you may be as impartial as you please. You might uphold the sanctity of marriage, or praise a book extolling Free Love à la P. B. Shelley; for in the *Daily News* public there are many mansions. Except for Mr Kipling, at whose head, I think, you must whack whenever he bobs it up, you may praise any writer, musician, or painter, and your readers will like it the more if he is one of les jeunes. That is quite jolly.

So the *Daily News* walked delicately, its writers tip-toeing amidst the eggshells, holding their breaths beneath avalanches. I dare say it and they still do so, but I never see it now. I gave it up because of its treatment of Suffragette news. Buts its delicate treading; its bright niceness; its feeling of unreality – all these things were due to Mr A. G. Gardiner. [1]

If Gardiner had had enough of the 'obstacle race', the strain did not show. To the contrary, congratulating his daughter on her twentieth birthday, he remarked that 'I never remember feeling

1. The *Outlook*, 10 January 1914. Hueffer was no stranger to Gardiner, who invited Wells to join him on holiday at Hythe in 1908: 'Hueffer & his wife are coming over – I mention this as a supplementary & superior attraction'. 18 August 1908, Wells Papers (University of Illinois Library).

younger than now. I am beginning to think that growing old is only a delusion. . . . It is a question of keeping the heart fresh – looking out at the world & not brooding over one's self.'[1] It was not 'tip-toeing amidst the eggshells' that wore him out, although that was admittedly part of the job; it was the pressure of incessant deadlines. But that, too, was part of the job. Pausing to write again to his daughter, before he left the office late one night, he urged her to 'think of me . . . on the top of the "bus" [to Hampstead], looking up at the patient stars, wondering . . . how the dickens and what the dickens I am going to write to-morrow – for to-morrow is black Thursday when I have to squeeze a special two col[umn]s out of my worried brains or die in the attempt. And now I must bolt.'[2] Some-how, the London sky always did its work, and after a morning with his family, he faced the world with renewed spirit.

A more accurate, if less amusing portrait of Gardiner soon appeared anonymously – he revealed the author to members of the family as Margaret Bryant of his staff – in the *Everyman*:

If, armed with the necessary credentials, you penetrate of an evening up the broad, old-fashioned staircase of the *Daily News* to see the Editor, you will find him in a small room, dark with a single heavily shaded light, hung over a huge desk littered with innumerable letters and papers. It is the room of a man intent on affairs, a room in which there is sensibly present the tension which is inherent in 'going to press'. . . . The man himself is un-hurried, urbane, genial, with nothing in his manner to suggest that he wears concealed about him the rapier with which he has attacked ducal patronage, the censoriousness of the *Spectator*, the decorous culture of Mrs Humphry Ward, the jovial effrontery of Mr Roosevelt, or the heavier weapons with which he attempts a breach in the Milner fortress. . . . He has more the air of a man of letters than of a politician. He will find time to talk to you of books, or to tell a good story. Still it is plain that he is keenly alive to the moral and political issues of the monent; he has his share in the fight, but does not in any sense wave a red flag.[3]

Five months later, the nation was plunged into the war that Gardiner had long dreaded.

1. Gardiner to Gwen Gardiner, 21 January 1913 (courtesy of Miss Gwen Gardiner).
2. Gardiner to Gwen Gardiner, 14 January 1914 (courtesy of Miss Gwen Gardiner).
3. *Everyman*, 6 March 1914.

7. The holy warrior

There is no figure more vulnerable to attack – and indeed none that more invites it – than the disabused idealist. He may repudiate his former beliefs, now called into question by events, but only by tacitly conceding the faultiness of his judgment. He may cling unrepentantly to past convictions, but only by sacrificing any claim to be regarded as a realist. Or he may do his best to reconcile principle and circumstance, knowing that he will most likely alienate his friends without appeasing his enemies.

War came in August 1914 from a direction that few, if any, had anticipated. But it broke with a fury that gave undeserved credit to those who had warned of its inevitability. Gardiner, as his antagonists readily perceived, exemplified the Liberal dilemma and mirrored its perplexities. Conditioned to an element of irrationality in domestic affairs, he had remained confident that reason would prevail in the settlement of international disputes. In the public mind he stood compromised as one who had vouched for Germany's pacific intentions, who had unilaterally opposed schemes for national preparedness, and, not least, who apparently lacked the determination (some would say the inclination) to inflict a crushing defeat on the enemy. At the same time, his cautious attempts to exonerate British statesmanship incurred the fierce resentment of pacifists,[1] who saw him as a traitor to the cause.

He could not, like Lord Courtney and other leaders of the prewar peace movement, trim his sails until the initial storm had passed. '. . . I must choose the moment for speech or writing even at the risk of being too late', replied Courtney, whom Gardiner had called upon

---

1. Like G. H. Hardy, I have used the term 'pacifist', with some misgivings, 'in the sense in which [it] came gradually to be used by the public and the press during 1914–1918, that is to say as applicable to all individuals and organizations whose views about the war were in any way unorthodox or unpopular'. *Bertrand Russell and Trinity*, p. 3n.

to rally the faithful: 'I am afraid the *Daily News* must be left to fight a good fight much alone.'[1] Courtney could not be blamed for his reluctance to mount public platforms before the issues were clear and he had had time to come to grips with them. Gardiner, unhappily, had no choice. Neither his temperament nor, more important, his professional duties would permit him to suspend judgment or withhold comment. Courtney might cancel engagements or absent himself from the House of Lords. Morley might retire to his suburban library, there 'to imitate Michelangelo's figure of the Pensieróso' and to compose an apologia for posthumous publication.[2] Lloyd George, whom some had mistakenly expected to resign from the Government with Morley and Burns, might grapple with his conscience, a supple one to be sure, behind the closed doors of the Cabinet room. But Gardiner had a paper to produce six mornings a week, and was expected to address himself to events as they unfolded. More than any memorandum or volume of memoirs, his leaders and columns in the *Daily News* provide us with evidence – as Lloyd George justly (if unkindly) pointed out – 'of the change which came over public opinion' and the painful process by which the vast majority of Liberals 'came tardily to the conclusion that war was justifiable'.[3]

Gardiner's assorted critics on the right, stifled by the conventions of the party truce to which they had been nominally committed by their front-bench leaders, called attention to the inconsistency of his pronouncements as a means of discrediting Liberalism. What confidence could one repose, they asked, in a party whose popular spokesman had often praised the Kaiser's restraint, had greeted the war with an appeal for a 'just and prudent and statesmanlike' declaration of British neutrality, and who, seemingly overnight, had decided that belligerence was a moral imperative? To a comparable extent, Gardiner's critics on the left, many of them his former political allies, singled him out as a personification of the 'insolvency' of 'Liberal idealism' and ridiculed him as a purveyor of myths.[4]

1. Courtney to Gardiner, 30 July 1914, G.P.
2. Morley, *Memorandum on Resignation*, p. 32.
3. *War Memoirs*, i, 41.
4. Active among them was Irene Cooper Willis, a wartime convert to Labour and a member of the general council of the Union of Democratic Control, who passionately rejected the beliefs of the party she had abandoned. According to her,

Gardiner solicited no defence against those who charged him with inconsistency. Only a charlatan or a warmonger, he would insist, could maintain equability in the face of such calamitous events. Consumed by the issues of the moment, he had no time to consider how posterity would look upon him. 'I have been guilty, so far as I can recall, of only one axiom: Life is adjustment,' he told his grandson many years later. 'And that,' he added, 'is so obvious that I suppose something like it must have been said in the days of the cave dwellers.'[1] With this disclaimer in mind, is it either fair or relevant to fault him for shifting his ground as statesmen and societies revealed themselves in a quickly changing light? Given the speed with which one crisis overtook another, it was unavoidable that he should occasionally contradict himself. Given the frequent difficulty of ascertaining truth, it was understandable that he should come up with conflicting answers. And, given his political tradition, which was one that permitted considerable latitude, it was natural for him to alter his allegiances according to new priorities. It would be futile to deny these discrepancies, and meaningless to apologize for them; instead, we shall examine them in the context in which they occurred as a means to appraise the impact of war upon the Liberal conscience.

Before proceeding further, it might be useful to review briefly the salient points of Gardiner's prewar 'pro-Germanism'. A careful reading of the evidence suggests that he was hardly the uncritical apologist for German world ambitions that his various critics liked to portray. Rather, his sympathetic words for Germany, far from being gratuitous, were deliberately intended to influence British opinion: his repeated praise for Bismarckian social legislation, for example, was an implicit exhortation to his countrymen to adopt similar schemes; his respectful references to German industrial

there was 'no more pitiable spectacle in the war than the spectacle of Liberals, at sea in reaction, clinging to the myth that their aims were supreme'. And it was the *Daily News*, whose columns she ransacked for quotations, that she held 'more responsible for that myth than any other paper'. Using Gardiner as her prototype ('"A.G.G." ought not, I am well aware, to stand alone. . . . But his attitude has been typical . . . of the "enlightened Liberal" '), she wrote three treatises: *How We Went Into the War, How We Got On With the War,* and *How We Came Out of the War.*

1. Gardiner to Patrick Gardiner, 23 October 1939 (courtesy of Mr Patrick Gardiner).

growth were designed to promote the expansion of British higher education and a more efficient use of national resources; on the other hand, his fierce denunciations of the 1913 Zabern affair, in which the German military successfully asserted its freedom from civilian control, were meant to be taken as an attack upon British officers who, concurrently, were threatening to resist government orders in Ulster.

It was Gardiner's contention that the situations in Germany and Great Britain were analogous, and that, with due allowance for cultural disparities, essentially the same problems afflicted the two societies. German and British progressives, whatever party label they affixed to themselves, had much to learn from one another, and, by cooperation, might jointly triumph over the gutter journalists and armaments contractors who were their common bane. By 13 November 1913 he had despaired of a Liberal initiative and pleaded for an act of 'statesmanship that will unite the Labour Party in England and the Socialist party in Germany to destroy the octopus that is bleeding both countries white'. In no area was the need for mutual assistance more imperative than in the conduct of foreign affairs. Here, German parliamentarians enjoyed a relative advantage that was the envy of British Radicals: they possessed, at least in theory, the constitutional mechanism to call Wilhelmstrasse officials to account. It was to the absence of parliamentary controls over British foreign policy that Gardiner ascribed the 'intolerable' fact that 'the country has been woven into a web of international politics which involves us in alarming activities and mysterious silences'. On 27 November 1911, in a signed front-page article, he vigorously endorsed the resolution in favour of Anglo-German friendship that the National Liberal Federation had passed by acclamation four days earlier. It was then unusual for him to accord himself such prominence, but – as he put it – the time for 'polite make-believe' had passed. The previous summer's Moroccan crisis had raised disquieting questions, for which Radical journalists and backbenchers had since pressed in vain for answers. 'What is the principle', he demanded to know, 'which makes us dumb when Russia invades Persia, when Italy invades Tripoli, when France invades Morocco, and [yet] stings us into action when Germany sends a ship to Agadir? Is the entente the pacific understanding we have been led to suppose, or is it a military and naval alliance with a definite objective?'

Better than any other product of his pen, this article not only put his case against prewar Foreign Office procedures, but also helps to explain what some have regarded as his incomprehensible vacillations in the early days of August 1914. Far from being an isolationist, which was a popular misconstruction of the Radical position, he wished to avoid diplomatic entanglements that needlessly exacerbated tensions and that jeopardized, more than they protected, legitimate British interests. Furthermore, he was wary of alliances, however informal, that, without declaring specific conditions, made British involvement a foregone conclusion. 'It is idle', he maintained, 'to talk of [Germany's] supposed designs on Belgium and Holland. If those designs ever mature – which is extremely doubtful – Liberal England will not fail in its duty to small nationalities; but it needs no alliances against that contingency.' We may, with good reason, dispute his strategy, but there is no reason to suppose that he was anything less than sincere in his 1911 proclamation that in the unhappy (and to his mind improbable) event that Germany violated Belgian neutrality, he would support British intervention. Who, after all, took more seriously than a 'pro-Boer' the rights of defenceless peoples?[1]

If for no other reason than that he lacked confidence in the British Foreign Office, Gardiner did not rule out the possibility of an eventual clash with Germany. War, he feared, would result not from commercial or colonial rivalry, but from the incessant provocations of which both sides were guilty. He relied, however, on Lord Fisher's authoritative assurances that, if all else failed, British naval power would prove amply sufficient to repel invasion, to patrol vital sea routes, and, if necessary, to ferry the British Expeditionary Force across the Channel. Retired from active service, Fisher remained a member of the Committee of Imperial Defence and a force to be reckoned with. '*I have not been idle!*' he told Gardiner on 7 March 1913, citing as proof the 'fact' that he was 'being vilified now beyond all past experience and that is saying a lot!' As much as Gardiner, whom he greatly influenced in such matters, Fisher railed against the War Secretary's 'insubordinate subordinates who', in league with Grey's permanent officials, 'are trying to turn us into a Continental

1. Indeed, four years earlier (20 December 1907), the *Daily News* had suggested a joint guarantee of Belgian and Dutch neutrality as the first step toward Anglo-German cooperation.

Power when God made us an Island'. [1] A year later, and a year closer
to war, he trumpeted that he had 'absolutely succeeded in pulverising
Conscription', [2] which he interpreted as a sinister plot to raise British
troops for service along the Rhine.

Gardiner, like all pupils, borrowed selectively from his master's
teachings. While he accepted Fisher's 'Blue Water' theory that
Britain's power must rest ultimately on her navy, he did not agree
that the navy required further expansion. His view, based as much on
moral as on strategic grounds, was not without a certain logic. 'If
there is no pause in this crazy competition in building ships for the
scrap-heap,' he warned his readers on 17 January 1914, 'national
suicide is surely our doom.' Like many Liberals who spoke out at this
time – on public platforms, in the press, and through various Liberal
associations and chambers of commerce – he was responding to a
New Year's Day appeal by Sir John Brunner, president of the
National Liberal Federation. The Government was known to be
deeply divided over the increased naval estimates that Churchill had
submitted, and Gardiner, like Brunner, was hoping to strengthen the
hand of the 'Economists' within its ranks, who stood opposed to 'this
unnecessary expansion of destructive expenditure'. [3] By his calculation, 'in the eight years since the Liberals came into power the naval
expenditure of the country has gone up from £34,600,000 to
£47,000,000, an increase of over 12 millions sterling a year'. Had such
appropriations been put to domestic use, 'every slum in the country'
could be eradicated, and with the balance, 'we could solve the education problem by building provided schools wherever they are needed'.
There was no better investment than social improvement that would
'regenerate the race', for 'it is upon its citizens and not upon its ships
that the security of this country ultimately depends'.

It was by no means exclusively on fiscal grounds that Gardiner
rested his case. A self-professed Cobdenite, although a highly unorthodox one, he was no practitioner of what the *National Review*
derided as 'penny-in-the-slot politics'. Each acceleration in the naval

1. G.P.   2. Fisher to Gardiner, 31 March 1914, G.P.
3. Charles Hobhouse (then Chancellor of the Duchy of Lancaster) to Lewis
Harcourt (then Colonial Secretary), 15 January 1914, Harcourt Papers (Stanton
Harcourt, Oxon). For Brunner's appeal and the wide response to it, see Koss, *Sir
John Brunner: radical plutocrat*, pp. 264 ff.

race seemed to him to render more improbable the chance of rapprochement between Britain and Germany. If either of the rivals was
to call a halt, it was only fitting that it should be the established power,
whose *beau geste* could not possibly be interpreted as a tacit acceptance of inferiority. Far from wishing to shutter the Foreign Office, as
certain Radical firebrands proposed, he hoped to expand its vision:
'If we can . . . initiate the true Triple Alliance of England, France,
and Germany, we shall not only bring down our Navy Estimates, but
we shall secure the peace of the world on the only enduring basis that
can be found for it.' The obstacle to so logical an arrangement was
not the duplicity of statesmen, and surely not economic competition,
but rather the prejudices and uneducated self-interest of 'the militarists and the Jingoes who are the common enemy'. Convinced, as we
have seen, that social conflicts transcended national boundaries, he
reasoned that only societies at peace with themselves could live in
peace with their neighbours. It was not coincidental that 'in both
countries . . ., the fire-eaters, the people who cry out for more ships,
and still more ships, are the anti-social gentry – the Junkers in
Germany, "The Spectators" and "National Reviews" here. They keep
alive these animosities as part of the machinery for controlling the
democracy', and there could be 'no compromise' with them on any
score.

Six months later, a Habsburg archduke was assasinated by Slav
nationalists in the Bosnian capital of Sarajevo. Gardiner deplored the
incident, although, as a Radical, he naturally sympathized with the
plight of subject nationalities. As an editor, he did not deem the
affair worthy of more than cursory attention. One can hardly blame
him for his failure to anticipate the subsequent flow of events. Recent
years had witnessed a spate of Balkan wars, none of which had
required the direct intervention of the great powers. Who could have
predicted that the present incident, its origins obscure, would put
European statesmanship to so severe a test?

Like his countrymen, Gardiner was promptly diverted by what
appeared to be a more significant death, that of Joseph Chamberlain.
Incapacitated by a stroke in 1906, at the moment that he had been
tipped to oust Balfour from the Unionist leadership, Chamberlain
had since continued to inspire fierce loyalties and to exert a profound
influence upon British political life. His followers mourned him as the

man who ought to have been prime minister, and who, had his advice been heeded, would have given unity to the nation and new meaning to the Empire. His opponents, who found little to commend in the Chamberlain of more recent decades were moved by the occasion to pay fond tribute to 'Radical Joe' of the seventies and eighties. Gardiner, who came upon the scene too late to recall the younger Chamberlain, could not forgive him his apostasy. Still, he recognized in him an adversary as much to be respected as feared. Writing on 4 July, he likened him, not unflatteringly, to Charles James Fox, another 'great disturber' whose capacity for good had gone largely unrealized. Had Chamberlain possessed the quality of patience, Gardiner wrote, 'there would have been nothing for Mr Lloyd George to do now, for Joseph Chamberlain would have done it all'. But Chamberlain had not been content to wait out the Liberal succession, which assuredly would have accrued to him before long. More seriously, he had lacked 'a governing philosophy to check his drift to reaction once his moorings had broken loose'. Gardiner acknowledged that Chamberlain 'destroyed much that was outworn and . . . set in motion tendencies that are destined to make a juster and a better State'. But it staggered the imagination to contemplate how much more might have been accomplished had Chamberlain put his enormous talent and energy to more purposeful use. There is no reason to suspect that, in reviewing Chamberlain's career, Gardiner was making insinuations about Lloyd George. Yet it did no harm to remind those who occupied or aspired to high office of the futility of action 'divorce[d] from doctrine'.

If, as the cliché would have it, war clouds were gathering, they were not yet the least visible over London, where skies throughout the month continued deceptively blue. Saturday, the 11th, found A.G.G. basking in the summer radiance of the metropolis: 'Merely to work in it, to walk its streets and loiter in its parks, is to feel its magic and to become a sharer in its large and liberal life.' A week later, his tone was more sombre, but his gaze was focused on distant Japan, where he detected the existence of a class of 'wartraders' who, like their European counterparts, kept 'the war fever raging in order that they may raid the public purse in the pursuit of dividends'. He obviously did not suspect the danger to be near at hand.

On the 25th, the *Daily News* appeared without a customary

Saturday column by its editor. It was not often that Gardiner was at a loss for words, which, after all, were his stock in trade. No explanation was offered, but presumably he could neither bring himself to ignore the international crisis, by this time acute, nor yet pass judgment on its perplexities. Two days earlier Austria–Hungary had delivered an ultimatum to Serbia, whose reply that day, although unexpectedly conciliatory, did not deter a declaration of war on the 28th. Thereafter, events moved with a rapidity that 'outstripped' statesmanship. Grey proffered his services as a mediator, despite his 'instinctive feeling', soon proved justified, 'that this time Germany would make difficulties about a Conference'. [1] The Russians mobilized in support of Serbia, the Germans in reply to Russia. On 1 August Germany declared war on Russia and demanded tangible assurances of French neutrality. A German declaration of war against France followed on the 3rd.

What were Britain's commitments, moral as well as diplomatic, in these circumstances? Opinion differed widely, even within the Cabinet, which was engaged in prolonged deliberation and, at intervals, bitter recrimination. On 27 July Lloyd George, who was known to be among those ministers inclined to neutrality, assured C. P. Scott that 'there could be no question of our taking part in any war in the first instance', and he deplored the view taken by *The Times* that the entente constituted a full-scale alliance. [2] As late as 2 August, Asquith instructed Bonar Law, the leader of the Opposition and an avowed interventionist, that, despite a 'long standing and intimate friendship with France', Britain was 'under no obligation, express or implied, either to France or Russia to render them military or naval help'. [3] Nonetheless, it was unmistakably clear in which direction national policy was leading, and distressed Radicals made a desperate attempt to reverse the trend. Gardiner's position is best understood in relation to this feverish activity.

On 29 July Arthur Ponsonby served Grey with a petition, signed by twenty-two Radical backbenchers, calling for Britain to hold aloof from Continental entanglements. It was his 'opinion', volunteered the next day in a letter to the Prime Minister, that no less than 'nine-

1. Viscount Grey of Fallodon, *Twenty-Five Years*, i, 304 ff.
2. Scott's diary, 27 July 1914, in *Political Diaries*, pp. 91–2.
3. Cited in Blake, *The Unknown Prime Minister*, pp. 223–4.

tenths of the party are behind us', and he warned that 'before long we may see fit to ask them all to express their opinion openly'. [1] Various groups of academics, trade unionists, and businessmen registered their dissent, and the Radical press spoke with new urgency. The *Manchester Guardian*, in a leader on the 31st that won plaudits from Lord Loreburn, decried the apparent fact that 'England had been committed, behind her back, to the ruinous madness of a share in the wicked gamble of a war between two militant leagues on the Continent'. Massingham, in the 1 August number of the *Nation*, thundered his disapproval, and, in that morning's *Daily News*, Gardiner enumerated the reasons 'Why we must not fight'.

Silent the previous Saturday, he could no longer hold his peace. 'The greatest calamity in history is upon us – a calamity so vast that our senses are numbed with horror', he began a column of unusual length and solemnity.

We hardly dare look into the pit that yawns at our feet and yet any hour, any minute may plunge us in beyond all hope of return. At this moment our fate is being sealed by hands that we know not, by motives alien to all our interests, by influences that if we knew we should certainly repudiate. Every step at this hour may be irrevocable. The avalanche trembles on the brink and a touch may send it shattering into the abyss.

It was not yet the Kaiser whom he feared, but rather the Tsar, 'who at one word can let hell loose upon the face of Europe'. Nicholas II, a despot who had been alternately the captive of 'inhuman philosophers' and 'mystics and charlatans', hardly qualified to him as 'the man whom the free peoples of France and England can trust with their destiny'. And yet western statesmen, by tacitly encouraging Russian intransigence, had made the Tsar master of their common fate. There was no question in Gardiner's mind that Serbia had 'wholly inspired' the Sarajevo murder, and that 'Servia is the instrument of Russia'. What was to be gained, he asked, by helping Russia to achieve her 'hegemony of the Slav world'? It was unthinkable that any Englishman should 'wish the Russian civilisation to overwhelm the German

1. Ponsonby to Asquith, 30 July 1914 (copy), Ponsonby Papers (Shulbrede Priory, Haslemere, Surrey). Ponsonby (later Baron Ponsonby of Shulbrede) has been identified as 'the foremost [prewar] critic of the system and organization of the Foreign Office and Diplomatic Corps': Swartz, *The Union of Democratic Control in British Politics during the First World War*, p. 15.

civilisation', which would mean 'the triumph of blind superstition over the most enlightened intellectual life of the modern world'. Besides, Britain had settled by negotiation all outstanding disputes with Germany, while 'with Russia we have potential conflicts over the whole of South-Eastern Europe and Southern Asia'. In the last analysis, however, strategic considerations were incidental. It was the moral issue that weighed most heavily. Despite the Germanophobic rantings of Lord Northcliffe, 'speaking through his myriad gramophones', Gardiner saw no reason for Great Britain to commit herself and every reason for her to stand aside.

It is because England is free that Europe hesitates. It is our neutrality which is the only protection Europe has against the hideous ruin and combustion on the brink of which it trembles. Let us announce that neutrality to the world. It is the one hope. There is no other. Let us make it clear that unless and until British interests are attacked we will have no part in this world insanity, that we will not shed a drop of English blood for Tsar or Servia, that our one obligation is the interests and peace of this land, and that we refuse to recognise any other. We can save Europe from war even at this last minute. But we can only save it by telling the Tsar that he must fight his own battles and take the consequences of his own action.

If the British Government does this it will do the greatest service to humanity in history. If it does not it will have brought the greatest curse to humanity in history. The youngest of us will not live to see the end of its crime.

Had Gardiner delayed his column until Monday, or, better still, Tuesday, there can be no doubt that he would have expressed himself differently. At very least, he would have avoided any sentimental reference to Germany's cultural superiority. But there was no time to lose, and he could not default on his responsibility to his readers. Writing on the evening of 31 July, he addressed himself to the situation as it had thus far revealed itself. Although he invoked history, he was of course writing journalism, and could not take into consideration events yet to occur. The immediate response was encouraging. 'Your article is superb', J. L. Hammond privately assured him. 'Miles and away the best thing that has been written on it.'[1] Other prominent Radicals concurred. Monday morning's correspondence columns were filled with letters of endorsement, one of them from

1. 2 August 1914 (postmark), G.P.

G. M. Trevelyan, the Cambridge historian, and another from Gilbert Murray, the Oxford classicist. But by the time that Monday's paper was upon the newsstands further complications had arisen. The previous evening Germany had demanded free passage through neutral Belgium, and the Belgian King appealed that morning for British support. According to Lloyd George, on whom the pacifists had banked, 'only two members of the Cabinet had been in favour of our intervention in the War' on Sunday, 'but the *violation of Belgian territory* had completely altered the situation. Apart from that it would have been impossible to draw us into war now.'[1] Still, there were Radicals who clung to the remnants of peace: Massingham, in a letter to the editor of *The Times*, casuistically argued that Germany's invasion did not technically violate Belgium's neutrality; Joseph King, Liberal MP for North Somerset, argued the case against British involvement in a letter to the editor of the *Manchester Guardian*; and Courtney, Loreburn, and Bryce employed the same dubious logic in the House of Lords. P. J. Baker, subsequently better known as Philip Noel-Baker, contributed to the *Daily News* of 4 August a letter entitled 'Belgian neutrality; why England is not bound to fight'. By this time, however, there were few who listened. The previous afternoon, Grey had addressed the House of Commons. His words, grave and unexpectedly eloquent, had had a profound effect on the majority of his former critics. Murray, for one, admitted that he found it 'difficult to resist Grey's case . . . [and to continue] to oppose Government action when the German Government has plainly run amok'.[2] Gardiner, too, reportedly had second thoughts as a result of Grey's patient exposition.[3] The Foreign Secretary's speech made considerably less impression on policymakers at Berlin, who ignored his ensuing demand for assurances that Belgian rights would be respected. At 11 p.m. on the 4th the nation was at war.

Instead of the popular indignation which the 'peace men' had anticipated, and indeed which they had hoped to stimulate, there was overwhelming exultation. Instead of the mass exodus from the Cabinet that some had predicted, only two members resigned, neither of whom had the intention, let alone the resources, to rally the stray

1. Scott's diary, [4] August 1914, in *Political Diaries*, p. 96.
2. G. H. Mair to Scott, 1.30 a.m., [4] August 1914, in *ibid.*, p. 95.
3. Harris, *Life So Far*, p. 102.

forces of disaffection. The few who dared to maintain their opposition to war clearly spoke only for themselves and no longer for any important segment of public opinion. Scott, like Morley and presumably others, was 'reminded . . . terribly of all that went before the Boer War'. [1] Again the 'pro-Boers' had failed, and this time with infinitely greater consequence.

Where had they gone wrong? Why had they so completely misjudged the temper of their countrymen, the intentions of their Government, and the realities of international diplomacy? For one thing, they had lacked a Gladstone to appeal, as in 1876, to the higher instincts of the nation. Lloyd George, the best they had, was no substitute. Then, too, they were generally politicians of advanced age, whose energies had been dissipated in earlier campaigns, and whose strategies, based on Victorian precedent, were hopelessly outmoded. As men of reason, they had neglected to take into account prevailing anxieties and prejudices. As men of faith, they had trusted too much to enlightened self-interest or, in some cases, to divine mercy. Few, if any, among them had had any inkling of decisions taken at the Foreign Office, at the Admiralty, and, especially, in the Committee of Imperial Defence. When the crisis came, they felt nearly as betrayed by their own Government as by Germany's breach of international law.

Confronted with 'a challenge more fierce than anything experienced in the past', the Radical 'community', as Gardiner described it, was further paralysed by its own divisions:

> On the one side were those who, regardless of the merits of the quarrel and regardless of the consequences of the issues of the quarrel, stood immovably for the doctrine of non-resistance; on the other, in varying degrees, were those who, while preserving their abstract hostility to war, found in the circumstances of the war with Germany so clear an issue between right and wrong as made a departure from the strict letter of the doctrine justifiable and necessary. [2]

Those most despondent quietly withdrew from public life, which had lost for them its purpose and, needless to say, its savour. Some,

1. Scott to Hobhouse, n.d. ['soon after 4 August 1914'], in *Political Diaries*, p. 99.
2. Gardiner, *Life of George Cadbury*, p. 273.

who persisted in their belief in a people's diplomacy, variously defined, founded the Union of Democratic Control, and, by stages, gravitated into the Labour Party, which promised greater fidelity to principles of internationalism. But the vast majority of pacifists, at least for the time being, continued to identify themselves as Liberals of one stripe or another. Without leadership, and subject to constant abuse in the right-wing press, they struggled to come to terms with a situation that was as painful to contemplate as it was maddening to explain.

Gardiner, too young to retire and too old to seek a new profession, retained his editorship and, with it, his commitment to Liberalism. There is no indication that he gave serious thought to any alternative. Significantly, he did not join the UDC, of which the Cadburys were benefactors, although he sympathized with its aims and, usually without solicitation, helped to publicize its ideals. 'Secret diplomacy belongs to the traditions of personal and autocratic government', he wrote on 29 August. 'It has no place in a democratic world, and the example of the United States must become the model . . . if Europe is to be free from menace in the future.' To his mind, it was not Liberalism that was responsible for bringing the country to war, but, on the contrary, a failure to apply Liberal teachings. He therefore saw no reason either to regret his previous actions or to apologize for his present position, which was one of supporting the allied effort without condoning the origins of the alliance. 'We have no need to be ashamed', George Cadbury soon assured him in a letter that might stand as their joint manifesto,

but to rejoice in the fact that we did what we could to prevent war, a war which has brought desolation and misery to millions of homes, and which we still believe might have been avoided if England had maintained her old position as a friend of Germany. Now that we have entered into the war it is as impossible to stop it as to stop a raging torrent. The anger of the people naturally has been roused, and we must secure restitution to Belgium for the injuries inflicted. [1]

The *Daily News* was pledged by precedent to the restitution of Belgium, for which it had raised a relief fund of £30,000 in the aftermath of the Franco–Prussian War.

1. Cadbury to Gardiner, 27 November 1914, cited in *ibid.*, p. 274.

Like every area of English life, operations along Fleet Street reflected the exigencies of wartime. As supplies of newsprint dwindled, papers charged more, usually for editions of fewer pages. *The Times*, which had sold at a penny before the war, maintained its customary size, but only by increasing its price first to a penny-halfpenny, then to twopence, and in March 1918 to threepence. The *Daily News*, which had begun modestly at a halfpenny, had to resort to eight and even six-page issues (much to the disapproval of George Cadbury) despite its rise to a penny in January 1917. Within weeks, comparable increases were announced by the *Evening News*, the *Star*, the *Daily Telegraph*, and the *Manchester Guardian*. Mechanical difficulties frequently arose from an inability to replace faulty plant, and as compositors, responding to recruiting appeals that they set into type, departed for military service. The *Westminster Gazette* alone sent ninety employees to the war, many of them never to return.

Budgeting its space as carefully as possible, the *Daily News* was forced to jettison many of its familiar features, including much of the literary content in which Gardiner had justly taken such pride. Fiction was among the first ingredients to be sacrificed. Early in the summer of 1914, Arnold Bennett had been commissioned to write a serial, 'The Price of Love', but his contract was cancelled and he was instead invited to contribute 'topical articles', which he did on a weekly basis during the first two years of the war. Nor was there room, in a paper of diminished size, for the daily photographic studies that, in happier days, had graced the back page.

In addition to Bennett, whom he especially prized as an acquisition, Gardiner hoped that other literary and public figures would adopt the *Daily News* as their forum. The results, on the whole, were disappointing. One after another, those from whom he solicited views either replied that they had nothing to say or else expressed reluctance to speak out. Thomas Hardy affectionately declined the request, expressing certainty that his 'general opinions . . . would be laughed at: e.g., such a highly rational one as that all the Churches in Europe should frankly admit the utter failure of theology & put their heads together to form a new religion which should have at least some faint connection with morality'. [1] Sidney Webb apologized that he 'had no time to write an article', but quickly added that, given a free choice

1. 25 August 1914 (copy), G.P.

of subjects, he 'might be tempted' to reconsider, 'should [he] be thought worth Arnold Bennett's price'.[1] Bryce thought it best to confine his public remarks to the 'small pamphlet' he had produced on the status of neutral nations. 'I shall not forget your wish should any occasion arise when any word could, so far as I am concerned, be usefully said', he vaguely promised. Meanwhile, he lectured Gardiner on the necessity of devising 'some means . . . of testing the numerous stories of atrocities . . ., many of which (one must hope & think) be exaggerated'. But even on this subject, he had 'no suggestion to make', although he admitted 'fear . . . that some shocking things, entirely against the Hague Conventions, have certainly been done in Belgium upon non-combatants'.[2] G. M. Trevelyan, too, called on Gardiner to counteract the mischief caused by unconfirmed atrocity reports (often accompanied by unidentified photographs) in the *Daily Mail* and elsewhere. Specifically, he asked Gardiner to 'edit out' from front line dispatches any allegations 'that [do] not seem to you sufficiently proven. . . . There will be a reaction', he warned, 'if we state more than we can prove', and he pointed to the distinct probability that Belgian sources 'exaggerate greatly, when exaggeration is not necessary to move indignation, the truth being bad enough'. Neither Bryce nor Trevelyan had any reason to fault the *Daily News*'s coverage; and the Reverend William Temple, who, as Archbishop of Canterbury, was to condemn indiscriminate aerial bombings in the next war, thanked Gardiner on behalf of a 'number of men drawn from all denominations – mainly ministers' for his judicious approach to an inflammatory subject.[3]

A.G.G.'s own Saturday column continued as a wartime feature, retaining its popularity and its outspokenness. One week after he had unsuccessfully appealed for British neutrality, he took consolation in the fact, more apparent than real, that the nation had 'embarked' on its mission 'united in one thought and one object as, perhaps, it has never been united before. . . . There is only one party in the State. The Government represent that party and Tories are as proud as the Liberals of the amazing efficiency and swiftness with which it has met the challenge of an unprecedented emergency.' It did not suit his

1. 15 November 1914, G.P.   2. 15 October 1914, G.P.
3. Both Trevelyan's letter (undated) and Temple's (dated 13 September) were apparently written in the early months of the war. G.P.

purpose – or the nation's – to concede that there existed any degree of 'panic or hatred. This is not a war of peoples', he averred, 'but of despots and diplomatists. . . . We have no quarrel with the German people. In all the centuries we have never fought them before, though we have often fought by their side.' As he saw it, the British people had gone to war to save their German brethren from 'the tyranny which had held them in its vice – the tyranny of personal government, armed with the mailed fist, the tyranny of a despotic rule counter-signed by Krupps.' In 'fighting for the emancipation of Germany', Britain was defending 'the liberties of Europe', which would not be secure until the tyrant of Potsdam had been toppled from his throne. 'War Gods', he knew, were not confined to any single nationality, and it was his hope that 'in destroying the devil-worship of Nietzsche' among Germans, we 'may release the great spirit of Tolstoy' in Russia. Recalling that Kant had 'founded his vision of Perpetual Peace on the Rock of Republicanism', Gardiner, as a loyal subject of George V, was willing to tolerate kings provided that they neither 'wore a uniform [n]or pranced at the head of soldiers'.

Like all effective journalism, Gardiner's weekly columns treated a limited number of themes in an infinite number of variations. Repetition, ordinarily a stylistic sin, was a tactical device that enabled him to revive in his readers' minds ideas which they had probably not contemplated since the previous weekend. Written late on Friday, published on Saturday, and, presumably, discarded on Sunday, his pieces were intended to stand on their own and not to be read seriatim. It is noteworthy that, when he selected the best of them for an anthology,[1] he scrupulously expunged many of the rhetorical flourishes and reiterations that had appeared in the originals.

In retrospect it is possible to discern certain general patterns in his wartime writing and in the issues with which he directly concerned himself. These did not reflect fundamental changes in his own thought so much as permutations in the political and social conditions of the time. In the early years of the war, at least until the formation of the first coalition in May 1915, he was supremely confident that the sacrifice, however enormous, was not in vain: the country would emerge from 'the Shipwreck', he predicted on 29 August 1914, with 'a new social fabric . . . on a collective basis' ('I can almost hear

1. *The War Lords* (1915).

Mr Sidney Webb purring as he looks on at the swift and silent revolution'), and with its Liberal traditions redeemed. Gradually events robbed him of his certainty, although not yet his hope, and the circumstances of Lloyd George's takeover in December 1916 demonstrated that he had underestimated the resilience of the concerted forces of reaction. Neither the Russian revolution nor, ultimately, Woodrow Wilson's new diplomacy fulfilled their initial promises, and it soon became evident that the Liberal Party, as he had known it, had perished with the old order. His writing acquired a mordancy, some thought a distemper, that shocked his employers, but which those closest to him recognized as another side to his character, one which he had hitherto taken pains to shield from public view. His last regular Saturday column for the *Daily News* appeared in March 1921, eighteen months after he had been deposed as editor, and concluded a phase of his career which, like each of those that had preceded it, provides a commentary on the Liberal predicament.

Before proceeding to an analysis of Gardiner's eventual disillusionment, it would be useful to ascertain his earlier views on the origins and significance of the war. Writing in the *Everyman* on 14 August, he expressed doubt whether 'posterity will attribute all the diplomatic blame to Germany. The entente with France', he reasoned, 'was a wise and well-intentioned scheme; but it contained a perilous possibility. It was meant to secure friendship with France, not to establish hostility to Germany. But it canalised our policy in that direction.' Ironically, as the crisis neared, Britain had enjoyed more cordial relations with Germany 'than had been the case for years, and those who had had dreams of an Anglo–French–German friendship began to think that the dream might become a reality'. Peace was betrayed not by conscious design, but by the inadequacy of those in power, chiefly the Kaiser (the Tsar was now pardoned, if not exonerated), who had not sought war, but whose 'vanity and impulsive folly' had been translated into national policy. With his 'machine mentality', the Kaiser was unable to respond to the 'spiritual factors' of the situation: 'national feeling, personal values, the psychology of men and peoples, the play of accident'. Here was proof that 'there can be no enduring peace in a world which is subject to personal rule', and that Germany's crimes were not to be avenged on the German people, but on the dynasty that had instigated them. By 19 December 1914

European society had 'passed . . . beyond the range of etiquette and flunkeyism', and Gardiner, anxious to focus resentment as narrowly as possible, suggested that the Kaiser ought to be brought to trial as 'an example . . . [that] will strike the imagination of the world and show that humanity has ceased to be the sport of despots'. Again on 1 March 1916, writing as 'Alpha' in the *Star*, he recommended that the culprit 'be summoned like a common criminal before the civil courts of the countries whose laws he has outraged'. These words were inconveniently recalled to him during and after the 1918 election, when he fulminated against those who proposed to 'Hang the Kaiser'.[1]

To the best of his ability, Gardiner attempted to arrest popular passions, to which he found even himself responding unpredictably. 'I never thought that a time would come', he admitted to his readers on 5 September, 'when I should look on the soldier's uniform with envy and when my one grievance against the year of my birth would be that it forbade me to join the throng outside the recruiting office.' Yet to take arms against the enemy was one thing, to persecute the innocent another. Neither as an individual nor as an editor did he succumb to the hysteria that vented its fury on resident aliens, on those with German-sounding names, and, more generally, on the products of German industry and culture. As one who, weeks before the war, had likened Richard Wagner's creative genius to Shakespeare's (he was capable of no greater tribute), he was not ashamed to admit (30 September 1916) that he had gone to a Promenade concert at the Queen's Hall to hear the *Tannhauser* overture ('Familiarity cannot make that immortal thing vulgar'); it took him another quarter of a century to hear in the strains of Wagner 'the very soul of Nazism'.[2] Hatreds between societies, he asserted more than once, 'were political creations, not racial tendencies', and he had only contempt for those who either attained public influence or sold newspapers by

1. Deploring Lloyd George's postwar statement to the House of Commons that the Kaiser should be tried in London, Gardiner declared that he was 'less sure to-day than' formerly 'of the wisdom of the dock and the scaffold so far as the large and enduring interests of the world are concerned'. Furthermore, 'even the greatest and most indubitable of criminals are entitled to a fair trial by an impartial court', which hardly seemed possible in the circumstances: *Daily News*, 5 July 1919.

2. Gardiner to Swinnerton, 15 January 1942, Swinnerton Papers.

exploiting irrational fears. Was it worth the price to defeat barbarism abroad by sacrificing civilization at home? Surely England had more worthy weapons in her armoury than the venomous and misdirected barbs of Northcliffe, Gwynne, Maxse, and the incorrigible Bottomley.

Gardiner, whose aversion to the 'new journalism' has been noted, had not expected better from its practitioners, who now, in his opinion, threatened to demoralize the country much as they had already debased the profession. Among intellectuals, the popular press had fallen into a disrepute that can be glimpsed in the case of Julian and Quentin Bell, Clive's precocious sons, who daily prepared their 'New Bulletin', a single typewritten sheet, for the amusement of their family's luncheon guests (their aunt, Virginia Woolf, among them) at Charlestown. The boys advertised their product as 'unique among daily papers in being controlled by no millionaire or political party. It is perhaps not unique', they conceded, 'in having no principles.'[1] Their youthful cynicism, no doubt strongly influenced by the attitude of their Bloomsbury elders, was more than justified. The stresses of wartime revealed, as never before, the dangers of a national press monopolized by individuals who were given to unscrupulous methods, defamatory reporting, and overweening ambitions.

Historians have since convincingly argued that the press and, specifically, the men who dominated it served a 'vitally important' function during the war, when, too often, 'the politicians were not speaking out'. On the subject of conscription, to cite an obvious example, 'the Press represented the feelings of the nation' and in turn impressed those feelings on the Government.[2] Gardiner, needless to say, would have disputed such a thesis, although he would have been the first to agree that there were frequent occasions when journalists, usually for the worse, forced the hands of politicians. Newspapers were of course entitled, even required, to take a stand; it seemed to him, however, that some of his rivals were governed less by conscience than by ulterior motives, that they did not so much reflect as distort public opinion, and that they deliberately inspired the emotionalism that they then reported as fact. Northcliffe, to his mind, was the prime offender because of his mammoth scale of operations, his dubious

1. Stansky and Abrahams, *Journey to the Frontier*, p. 25.
2. Gollin, *Proconsul in Politics*, p. 284.

ethics, and the unbounded influence that he craved. It was understandable that many common people, 'fumbling darkly for an explanation of an inexplicable world', should lend credence to rumours about mysterious Russian soldiers, arctic snow still clinging to their boots, travelling the length of Britain on their way to service on the Western Front. But there was no excuse for Northcliffe, whose *Daily Mail* featured blurred photographs of the trains that allegedly sped these mythical cossacks through the night. It was the duty of any self-respecting newspaperman, Gardiner proclaimed on 19 September 1914, 'to bring Rumour to the challenge of definite proof. For the true twilight of the gods came with the printing press. Mythology and the newspaper cannot co-exist.'

No less an affront to Gardiner's canons of professionalism, indeed to his sense of decency, was the tendency on the part of Northcliffe and others to victimize those who had German or simply suspicious antecedents. Convinced that the Home Office, under Liberal management, was incapable of taking sufficient precautions against subversive elements, they fostered the notion of a spy peril. Their prominent attention to mob outrages against 'German-owned' shops and businesses, unaccompanied by any hint of admonition, was undeniably an incitement to further violence. At the same time, vicious campaigns were waged against public figures, the most prominent being Lord Haldane, whose patriotism was impugned. True, the Liberal press retaliated with innuendoes about Sir Edward Carson and Lord Milner (was his father's name Charles or Karl?), but it was no match for its competitors in the art of vilification. On 26 October George Cadbury 'noticed an attack in the "Daily Mail" . . . on the "Daily News"', which had lodged a vigorous 'protest against poisoning the minds of the people against those with German names and Germans who are settled in the country. This shows', he declared prophetically to Gardiner,

the spirit that we must expect when the time for settlement comes, and when probably the unscrupulous papers will cry out for revenge without any regard as to what the results for the future may be. . . . The present war may either cause a backward movement, or, if a wise peace can be arranged, a movement forward. We can but do our duty remembering that God works slowly and that 'A thousand years with Him are as but one day'.[1]

1. 26 October 1914, G.P.

Less willing than his employer to await the unfolding of God's plan, Gardiner seized the initiative and, in his column on 5 December, addressed an open 'Letter to Lord Northcliffe'. It was subsequently reprinted as a penny pamphlet that also contained his follow-up piece in the *Star*, and bore on its titlepage a quotation from North-cliffe's *Evening News* (17 October 1913) that 'acknowledge[d] the Kaiser as a very gallant gentleman, whose word is better than many another's bond'. Ostensibly, Gardiner wrote in reply to 'a book of newspaper scraps' that Northcliffe had recently issued (*Scare-mongerings from the 'Daily Mail', 1896–1914*) to justify his daily boast that the *Daily Mail* was 'the paper that persistently forewarned the public about the war'. It was not Gardiner's purpose to deny him that honour, although, as indicated, it would have been easy enough to cull an anthology of 'pro-German' statements from the prewar columns of the *Mail* and its various sister publications. 'Your claim to be the true prophet of war does not call for dispute,' he baited Northcliffe:

It had always been your part to prophesy war and cultivate hate. There is nothing more tempting to the journalist than to be an incendiary. It is the short cut to success, for it is always easier to appeal to the lower passions of men than to their better instincts. There is a larger crowd to address, and you have never deserted the larger crowd. The student of your career will find it difficult to point to anything that you have done and to say 'Here Lord Northcliffe sacrificed his journalistic interests for the common good, for the cause of peace, for some great human ideal that brought no grist to his mill; here he used his enormous power not to enrich himself but to enrich the world.' But he will have no difficulty in pointing to the wars you have fomented, the hatreds you have cultivated, the causes you have deserted, the sensations, from the Pekin falsehood to the Mons falsehood about the defeat of the British Army, that you have spread broadcast. You have done these things, not because of any faith that was in you, not because of any principle you cherished. You have done them because they were the short cut to success – that success which is the only thing you reverence amidst all the mysteries and sanctities of life.

Identifying his adversary as 'the most sinister influence that has ever corrupted the soul of English journalism', Gardiner went on to indict Northcliffe as 'the preacher of discord and hate at home'. The third Marquess of Salisbury, he gleefully recalled, had had the 'final word' when he described the *Daily Mail* as a paper 'written by office boys for office boys', and, since acquiring *The Times*, Northcliffe had 'succeeded in staining it with the dyes of the office boy's mind'. But the issues at stake were more personal. If, as Northcliffe maintained, the *Daily News* and other organs of Liberal opinion 'were working for a lost cause' by woiking for peace, they had been no more deluded than such Unionist leaders as Bonar Law, who, in a 'memorable speech in November 1911 . . . [had] repudiated the doctrine of the inevitable war'. Even more outrageous was Northcliffe's charge that the editorial policy of the *Daily News* was dictated by the 'horrible commercialism' of its proprietor. 'No,' Gardiner remonstrated,

we did not work for peace because it paid. It does not pay to go against the popular tide. No one knows that so well as you . . . who have spent your life in an infamous servitude to the changing passions of the hour, We worked for peace because we believed that that was the duty of a responsible journal. We worked for peace because we wanted to see a better and a juster world, because we believed that the fulcrum of human society is international co-operation, and not international enmity, that civilisation cannot co-exist with barbarism, that war would ruin all the hopes of that social readjustment, that alleviation of the lot of the poor, that was the purpose for which the 'Daily News' was founded and for which, whatever its failures, it has lived.

The guns of Fleet Street, thundering as furiously as those across the Channel, were no more successful in moving the enemy from his entrenched position. The following Saturday, Robert Blatchford came to Northcliffe's defence in the *Daily Mail*, and on Monday morning, the 14th, Gardiner's 'rejoinder' appeared on the front page of the *Daily News*. Maintaining the offensive, Gardiner ignored 'the eccentric Socialist' whom Northcliffe employed, and instead spoke, as before, to the master himself. 'You say that I have resorted to abuse', he recounted.

The public will judge. . . . If to indict you is to abuse you, then the charge is just. If to tell the plain facts of your career, which you would have forgotten but which you dare not disown, is to abuse you, then I am guilty. I have shown that you have preached war and exploited international hatreds as a trade; that you have attacked every country in turn and that you have attacked it for the basest reasons; that you have supported every cause when you have thought it would win and deserted it when you have thought it would lose. . . . I have shown that you have made journalism a by-word for sensationalism, and a thing of reproach to those who are engaged in it. Do you deny it? There is hardly a man in Fleet-street who does not know it and deplore it. There is not an audience in the country, of any party whatsoever, that does not receive your name or the name of the 'Daily Mail' with a shout of derisive laughter. The people read you; but they despise you.

Had Gardiner truly believed that Northcliffe was a mere laughing stock, a gallon-size Bottomley and no more, it is doubtful that he would have wasted his invective. On the contrary, he recognized with Shaw an alarming tendency, even among men whose 'own experience . . . reduced to utter absurdity the ravings and maunderings of . . . [their] daily paper . . . . yet [to] echo the opinions of that paper like a parrot'. [1]

In any case, Northcliffe was not prepared to perpetuate the debate, which his sympathetic biographers have put down as 'a scathing polemical exercise which produced back-patting approval at the Reform Club'. [2] Nor did he encourage Lovat Fraser, a contributor to the *National Review* as well as to various Harmsworth properties, to unmask the Cadburys as hypocritical profiteers. 'My object in showing up the *Daily News*', he professed to Fraser on the 15th, 'is to spike their guns when the settlement comes, and I think I have done that. I do not in the least mind personal attacks, nor do I care what the public think about me.' [3]

Gardiner, too, was overridingly concerned with the eventual peace terms, and feared that right-wing journalists would inflame passions to the point that a rational settlement would be impossible. At the same time, Tory 'ultras' were spurred to greater fanaticism by their suspicion that Liberal politicians, possibly with the connivance of certain top-ranking Unionists, were seeking to negotiate a compromise peace, probably at Belgium's expense. By pillorying the Liberals as the party of myopia, Northcliffe, as he candidly admitted, hoped to deprive them of any credit at the international conference table. Gardiner, who dreaded the prospect of war *à outrance*, defended his party's devotion to peace as a potential asset. His object was to

1. *Heartbreak House*, preface.
2. Pound and Harmsworth, *Northcliffe*, pp. 470–1.
3. Cited in *ibid*.

justify not so much Liberalism's past performance as its future uses.

His rebuttal to Northcliffe won Gardiner the gratitude of 'many hundreds' of readers, whose letters he acknowledged the following Saturday. In addition, he received messages of appreciation from prominent Liberals who shared his preoccupation with the conditions that would prevail when peace was restored. 'I greatly rejoice in the spirit of your letter', Masterman, himself the object of scurrilous press attacks, told him. 'They that love the Lord must get together as time goes on, and see what can be saved out of the general catastrophe when we have won the war abroad and come to the far more difficult and critical war at home.'[1] Alexander ('Alex') Shaw, soon to enter the House as Liberal member for Kilmarnock and later a Lloyd George Liberal, reported that

> I meet many good Liberals in Midlothian & elsewhere who are prone to take the view that we pacifists made a mistake & the jingos were right all along; & such a letter as yours will make many of these reflect on the sham which the jingos are foisting on us & will arm them against the coming jingo campaign which will be a feature of our politics at the conclusion of the war.[2]

Edward Cadbury, eager for 'any further opportunity of exposing the Harmsworth press', anticipated that 'in a few months' time, when people get tired of the war, we shall be able to rub in the responsibility of Northcliffe for it'.[3] His father, equally confident that a victory had been achieved, continued to ponder its significance in a Christmas message to Gardiner:

> You have had a very stormy and critical time and a tremendous responsibility resting upon you. It has been extremely difficult to know exactly the right course to take. We all hate personalities, but there are times in the interests of truth, and certainly in the interests of the paper, when they seem necessary, [as] only by attacking Lord Northcliffe himself can we attack the 'Times', 'Daily Mail', 'Evening News', 'Weekly Despatch', &c. I expect you are looking forward as I am to the time when peace is to be declared, and before then we must if possible educate men to think. We shall be doing not only a national but a world-wide good if the terms of settlement are such that it can be seen we have acted disinterestedly in the whole affair. To unduly humiliate Germany would simply be to lead to another war in time to come, if we can be guided by history.[4]

1. 9 December 1914, G.P. 2. 9 December [1914], G.P.
3. 7 December 1914, G.P. 4. 21 December 1914, G.P.

Neither Gardiner nor the Cadburys were naïve enough to suppose that they had heard the last of Northcliffe, whose methods and motives they were pleased to have brought into question. It did not, therefore, come as a surprise to them when attacks upon Liberals intensified, and when, the following May, the Prime Minister was forced to capitulate to what appeared to be, on the face of things, a 'press intrigue'. Gardiner bemoaned the dismemberment of the Liberal ministry and its supersession by a coalition, all the more because he detected traces of Northcliffe's 'sinister influence'. It was too much of a coincidence that the crisis was attended by mysterious disclosures in *The Times* of a scandalous munitions shortage. Discounting the usual explanations – that Cabinet reconstruction had been necessitated by a personality clash between Churchill and Fisher at the Admiralty, or by 'the deficiencies of Lord Kitchener' (a recent Northcliffe target) at the War Office – he concluded instead that the 'chief factor' was, 'that in the midst of the most stupendous struggle in the history of the nation, the issues of life and death are the sport of a sensational journalist'. The choice, he told his readers on the 22nd, was 'between responsible Government and a Press dictatorship. . . . The freedom of the Press is a great thing, but that freedom involves responsibility, and there comes a time when even the freedom of the Press must give place to the safety of the State.' It was obvious to him that 'there has been foul play in quarters where foul play will never be forgotten or forgiven', and although 'Lord Northcliffe may rejoice at the confusion he has done so much to create', the country could no longer permit such individuals to play havoc with its 'destinies'.[1]

Despite appearances to the contrary, Gardiner was poorly equipped by nature for the fierce struggles in which he engaged. He did not enjoy his exercises in vituperation, and would have been grateful had events not required them of him. Unfortunately, the voices of Liberalism were too few and too feeble for him to permit himself the luxury

1. Only a fortnight earlier, Gardiner had castigated *The Times* and other antiministerial journals for irresponsible criticism that Germany, without the tradition of a free press, might take as evidence 'that the purpose of this country is weakening'. All the same, he argued that it would be 'regrettable' for the Government in any way to stifle criticism: 'That right is the very breath of Liberalism, and a challenge to it would be a precedent that would be used ruthlessly against democracy in the future.'

of silence. Others accepted the situation more philosophically, the more cynical even finding amusement in the follies of mankind. 'Look at Massingham,' Wells would chuckle when the editor of the *Nation* showed his gloomy countenance in the smoking room at the Reform Club, 'afraid there's some good news!'[1] Gardiner, by contrast, never suffered greater pain than when his own dire prophesies were vindicated.

In a world that afforded few pleasures, he found two sources of consolation. The first was his sanctuary in the Chilterns, where he acquired 'a tiny week-end cottage' that he later rebuilt as The Spinney, his family home. He had been on the lookout for such a retreat at least since the summer of 1911, when John Lane, the publisher, had invited him to stay at Wendover, near Aylesbury, and to inspect various properties in the vicinity. In the autumn of 1914, enjoying 'a couple of days tramp' in the countryside with his eldest son, he found what he was looking for:

> When, having plunged down the steep slopes of Bullpit Hill & traversed the golf links below, we turned into the Icknield Way and found the lovely hamlet of Whiteleaf, with its sixteenth-century thatched cottages sheltering under the deep woods of Whitecron Hill and looking over Princes Risborough and the wide Wycombe valley to Bledlow Ridge, I knew that something had happened to me.

Jimmy Mallon, his friend and future son-in-law, 'had already found his "spiritual home" here', and helped him to find a place 'with the hills encompassing it behind and the great landscape stretching to the Thames and Berkshire downs in front'.[2] As he told Wells, whom he invited to substitute for him one Saturday, it was the perfect place to get some rest, 'to read nothing later than the 18th century, & not to put pen to paper for at least a week'.[3]

Another 'pleasant distraction from the anxieties of the War', although generally a less effective one, was his weekly masquerade as 'Alpha of the Plough' in the *Star*. That paper had accompanied the *Morning Leader* on its 1912 migration to Bouverie Street, and its editor, James Douglas, had since made occasional use of Gardiner's

1. Swinnerton, *Autobiography*, pp. 303–4.
2. Autobiographical note (n.d.), G.P.
3. Gardiner to Wells, 3 August 1916, Wells Papers.

services. In the closing days of 1914, Douglas assembled 'a constellation' of literary talents 'which was to illuminate his journal every
evening of the week'. It was arranged that Gardiner would shine on
Tuesdays, but how was he to identify himself? Given 'all the firma-
ment' from which to select his pseudonym, he could not resist the
'sublime image' of 'Alpha', the star 'at the head of the Plough . . .
that points to the Pole'. Appropriately, his debut on 5 January was a
recapitulation of his difficulties in 'Choosing a name'. Other writers
in the series, each similarly disguised, were E. V. Lucas, A. A. Milne,
and J. C. Squire. The constellation soon disintegrated when 'Arcturus'
left for military service, but 'Alpha' continued on his own. Innumerable editions of his collected essays were published,[1] and school-
children at home and abroad came to know him as their guide and
companion.

Gardiner's heavenly excursions in the *Star* afforded him the welcome 'opportunity to go on holiday with my pen & [to] escape for an
hour or two once a week from the maelstrom of the war'. Leaving
topical issues to A.G.G. in the *Daily News*, he was again free to dote
upon the joys of nature and the foibles of his fellow creatures. Like
any good letter-writer, 'Alpha' excelled at 'intimate triviality':
accounts of country walks and back-fence gossip; thoughts 'On being
tidy' and 'On talking to one's self'; reminiscences of cricket matches
and boyhood romances; and periodic re-evaluations of the books
upon his shelf ('If I affirm that the *Brothers Karamazov* is the greatest
achievement of the imagination since Shakespeare, I do not promise
not to say the same thing for something else, *David Copperfield* or *Les
Misérables*, when, after a due interval, I express my view again.')
His pieces were distinguished by a sensibility that precluded mawkish-
ness, by a rhythm and clarity of prose, and, not least of all, by an un-
grudging affection for mankind. It would be too much to expect
'Alpha' to have been immune to the disorders that afflicted his age.
Reference to the problems of the day crept into his columns, making
them 'a sort of informal diary of moods in a time of peril'. Disclaim-
ing 'pro-Germanism' (the *Morning Post* branded Gardiner a leading

1. *Pebbles on the Shore* (1916) was followed by *Leaves in the Wind* (1919).
Windfalls (1920) was described as 'a third basket from a modest orchard', and
probably the last. But Gardiner's publisher, J. C. Dent, prevailed on him to
produce a fourth volume, *Many Furrows* (1924).

'exponent of Pro-German propaganda'), he was moved to protest against the abuse of people accused of German sympathies. More likely than A.G.G. to credit the fears that preyed upon men's minds, he agreed that wartime hysteria was induced by unconscionable journalists, in whose hands truth was a malleable substance.

Never acknowledged in print, the identity of 'Alpha' was not too difficult to guess. His carefully routed walks through London must have seemed instantly familiar to faithful readers of the *Daily News*; so, too, his literary and historical allusions. There were indications that 'Alpha' was a veteran of Fleet Street, an intimate of Liberal politicians, and someone sufficiently close to Arnold Bennett to write knowingly of the novelist's teatime habits. Yet many failed to make the obvious connection. Arthur Lee (soon to become Lord Lee of Fareham) was 'keenly interested' in meeting 'Alpha', and instructed his publicity officer at the Board of Agriculture to make inquiries. By coincidence, Lee's deputy wrote to Gardiner, whom he asked to confirm his supicion that 'Alpha' was really S. L. Bensusan.[1] It took another decade before Bennett could describe 'Alpha' – who had irritated him by dismissing James Joyce as 'muck' – as 'a pseudonym which now fails to hide the personality of one of our most illustrious journalists'.[2]

One wonders, however, whether Gardiner, in adopting a pseudonym, had wished so much to hide his personality as to preserve an aspect of it which was then threatened with extinction. At the time that 'Alpha' was born, Gardiner could find little comfort in the conduct of human affairs. Serving the first of two separate terms as president of the Institute of Journalists (Garvin succeeded him in 1917), he felt all the more acutely the shame of his profession. 'Alpha', with his undimmed optimism and his delight in the complexities of character, pointed each week to the survival of homely virtues which A.G.G., in his anguish, would otherwise have tended to overlook.

1. W. Purvis to Gardiner, 7 January 1918, G.P.
2. *Evening Standard*, 24 May 1928.

8. At war with Lloyd George

In the welter of personal and moral conflicts in which Gardiner found himself, there was none more acutely painful or, in effect, more self-destructive than his well publicized feud with Lloyd George. He would not have taken it so deeply to heart, nor would he have been driven to such extremes, had his antagonist been anyone else. His was the hatred of a jilted suitor, embittered by the realization that the long romance would never be consummated. It was in Lloyd George that he had invested his hopes for the rejuvenation of Liberalism as a social and political force. In 1910, for example, he had given a luncheon for the 'Morrells, Wellses, and Hammonds', at which it was agreed that there would be a better 'chance' for meaningful reforms 'when George comes to [the] throne', and Wells proposed the formation of a '"G.R.G." League (Getting Ready for George)'.[1] Unlike other Radicals who could not bring themselves to forgive Lloyd George for his eleventh-hour endorsement of the war effort, Gardiner had since clung to him as a brake on Liberal Imperialist diplomacy and, particularly, as the eventual architect of postwar reconstruction. Slowly, however, he came to the conclusion that Lloyd George was more a threat than an ally to the causes they had once both served. By his reckoning, the war produced no greater single casualty, and certainly none that better illustrated its maleficent spirit 'working through the principals whom events have brought into the fierce light that plays upon the European stage'.[2]

One might have expected Gardiner, of all people, to have seen the writing on the wall; indeed, he himself had once put it there. His 1908 portrait of Lloyd George had raised certain doubts that ultimately proved more than justified. But, by the time he returned to the sub-

1. Gardiner's diary, 6 March 1910, G.P. The Morrells were Phillip, soon to resume his parliamentary career as Liberal MP for Burnley, and his wife, Lady Ottoline.
2. *The War Lords*, p. 3.

ject three years later, he had willingly suspended disbelief and sung the praises of the Welsh David, who undauntedly attacked the Goliath of Tory privilege. Any misgivings he may have had about Lloyd George's methods or associates were dispelled by the squeals of protest that issued from the enemy camp. Weeks before the outbreak of war, writing to congratulate his daughter for winning a botany prize at school, Gardiner facetiously suggested that she restrain her talents 'or we shall swell to vanity to such a size that we shall have to go into a bigger house &, really, times are so bad, what with Mr Lloyd George & other things, that we cannot afford it'. [1]

Despite their earlier collaboration and mutual esteem, Gardiner and Lloyd George emerged from the war as implacable enemies. To Gardiner, Lloyd George had come to embody the triumph of the worst elements of wartime society: he was a demagogue, whose perfidious and piratical behaviour won him power at the expense of principle. As a journalist, Gardiner found especially reprehensible the way that Lloyd George had 'squared the Press', and he contrasted the front-page glorification of Lloyd George ('The man who won the war') with the nation's virtual neglect of Sir Douglas Haig, who had the misfortune to be too much 'a high-minded soldier and gentleman' to have got 'rich profiteers to put up money to buy newspapers to "run" him'. Gardiner did not doubt that Haig, had he been so inclined, might easily have arranged 'breakfasts at which all the newspaper men who wanted titles, jobs for their friends, pickings for their relatives, would have daily appeared'. [2] Lloyd George, for his part, had grown equally disdainful of Gardiner, whom he looked on as a perpetual irritant, wholly ignorant of practical necessity. Undoubtedly he had the *Daily News* uppermost in mind when he complained to Lord Riddell, the proprietor of the more compliant *News of the World*, that 'Newspapers are continually misrepresenting the state of public affairs. They suppress information regarding things that are well done and magnify mistakes which are inevitable in the conduct of life.' [3]

The two men knew each other too well for the hostility between

1. Gardiner to Gwen Gardiner, 7 July 1914 (courtesy of Miss Gwen Gardiner).
2. *The Star*, 11 December 1919.
3. Entry for 22 August 1919, Riddell, *Intimate Diary of the Peace Conference and After*, p. 111.

them to have been generated by any simple misunderstanding. Nor for that matter, was it any single event that sparked their differences: by the time that Lloyd George supplanted Asquith in the premiership, his relations with Gardiner had already degenerated into a mutual enmity that was intensified by subsequent developments. Gardiner's gradual disenchantment with Lloyd George was a crucial factor in his response to wartime conditions and, implicitly, an index to the Liberal dilemma. As such, it merits close scrutiny.

At the onset of war, Gardiner would have been the last to predict his estrangement from Lloyd George, let alone his bond with Liberals like Reginald McKenna, whose previous performance had inspired him more with scepticism than enthusiasm, He accorded loyal support to Asquith, as for that matter did Lloyd George, more out of consideration for national unity than out of any sense of personal devotion. His advocacy of parliamentary control over diplomacy was, in fact, a tacit criticism of the Prime Minister, and his various recommendations for collectivism far outdistanced Asquithian policy. No one was more pleased by Gardiner's early wartime columns than Lloyd George, who professed himself an avid reader, and who took time to send the author a 'word of warm congratulation' for his 'brilliant' analysis (10 October 1914) of 'the issues of the war'. Lloyd George warmly commended the article as not only 'far and away the best thing I have read till the present' on the subject, but also 'your very best, and that is the highest praise one could give to any journalist. I feel as if another talk were long overdue', he added. 'Unfortunately, Downing Street in the hands of the repairers looks like the morrow of a German invasion. London workmen can give many points to the Uhlans in the way of devastating a comfortable home!'[1]

The European collapse, Gardiner observed on 24 October, was due in large measure to the 'fact that the wonderful material advance' of recent generations had 'been unaccompanied by any moral growth'. Not only had social relationships been embittered and disturbed, but technical advances had had the effect 'on the one side to make the globe a unit and on the other side to intensify its separatisms. . . . We have seen every new triumph of science diverted into channels of competitive destruction.' Concentrating his fire on enemies whom

1. Lloyd George to Gardiner, 12 October 1914, G.P.

Lloyd George had yet to embrace as his friends, and employing the rhetoric of Limehouse which Lloyd George was now inclined to disown, he struck out at 'the powerful, anti-social influences bound up with the Army', and reminded his readers that it was 'only a few short months ago', at the time of the Curragh incident, 'that the aristocracy [had] revealed the ultimate source of its arrogant claims over the democracy'. Expecting 'to find that challenge much more defiant after the war', he alerted his countrymen to the designs of those who would use the international crisis as an 'instrument for destroying democracy':

> If you wish to understand the war of ideals which is being waged behind this war of the battlefield read a paper like the 'Morning Post'. . . . It is fighting for militarism. It believes, like Treitschke, that war is an eternal condition of society. . . . For nearly ten years the 'Morning Post' and the society it represents have groaned under the heel of a Government which has set itself to the task of establishing social justice in this country. . . . Now they see the restoration of the old aristocratic rule in sight. . . . Militarism is going to 'teach us all our proper stations'. Conscription is to come so that our men may be drilled into subservience to our Prussian Junkers; Protection is to come so that taxation shall fall on consumption and not on possessions – that is, on the poor and not on the rich.

It is inconceivable, given his sources of information, that he failed to discern the direction in which Lloyd George was moving, his flirtations with Unionist editors, and his modified stand on conscription. Rather, Gardiner sought to rekindle the fires of earlier controversies in the hope of returning his wayward leader to the appointed path.

On matters of economic policy, Gardiner remained wedded to the classic Liberal position, subsequently popularized by F. W. Hirst,[1] that the war was an unmitigated disaster. Any trace of 'vigour' in the wartime economy, he argued on 28 November, was 'due to temporary and unproductive causes. . . . We are blowing our resources out of the cannon's mouth, and though there is activity in trade it is the activity of fever and not of normal health.' Lloyd George, at the Exchequer, took a decidedly less cataclysmic view of the situation, in

1. *The Consequences of the War to Great Britain*; also Hirst and J. E. Allen, *British War Budgets*.

which he saw grounds for encouragement and even confidence. His press secretary found it

interesting to record that while discussing the questions arising from the War with all manner of men, I find the greatest optimism among the practical business men who, though vitally affected one way and another, are extremely hopeful. Our greatest pessimists are among our own rather academic friends (Gardiner, Massingham, Hirst, etc.) who, I think, are rather upset at finding that in spite of the calculations they made in figures showing the impossibility (on financial grounds) of the war being continued a month, things are so normal. [1]

Less alarmed than Gardiner by the growth of 'non-productive wealth', Lloyd George welcomed the opportunities that presented themselves for creative management and directed social change. Their divergence transcended immediate economic views and reflected, as Gardiner soon came to realise, two mutually exclusive views of the nation's predicament.

Fiercely proud of his own independence, Gardiner was most rankled by the extent to which Lloyd George courted newspaper editors and proprietors with flattery and often titles. [2] In a front-page interview in the *Christian Commonwealth* (3 March 1915), he recalled that Hazlitt, by the order of his essays, had given precedence to footmen over editors. Were Hazlitt writing now, he would be obliged to revise his sequence, for editors had become 'amongst the very greatest of mankind, . . . rank[ing] with Prime Ministers, peers, and princes of the Church: *primus inter pares*'. Neither in his personal capacity nor as president of the Institute of Journalists did Gardiner celebrate the new status conferred on certain members of his profession, who placed their calumnies at the disposal of the highest bidder. Less culpable, but no less irresponsible in his opinion, were those like Scott and Sir William Robertson Nicoll, who served Lloyd George in the pathetic hope that they might exert a salutary influence upon him: Scott struck him as well-intentioned, but hopelessly deluded; Nicoll, on the other hand, had never been highly regarded

1. Sir William Sutherland to Frances Stevenson (later Lady Lloyd-George), 31 December 1914, Lloyd George Papers C/8/4/14.
2. On Lloyd George's dealings with the press, see A. J. P. Taylor's pungent remarks in 'Lloyd George: rise and fall', the 1961 Leslie Stephen Lecture, reprinted in *Politics in Wartime*, pp. 130–2.

by Gardiner, who once heard him speak on literary criticism and thought him 'as false & sleek as ever', although undeniably 'very clever'. [1]

It is more than unlikely that the various press barons figured as prominently in wartime events as Gardiner presumed, or, for that matter, as they themselves liked to think. Lord Northcliffe, the epitome of the breed, was not instrumental in the formation of either coalition, although he contributed to the crisis of confidence that preceded each of them. Surely he was too much the captive of his own destructive energies to seek dictatorial powers. Lord Beaverbrook, a later arrival on the scene, was (at least at this stage of his career) content to work on behalf of others. Sir Henry Dalziel, Riddell, Nicoll and the rest, were dangerous only in so far as Lloyd George chose to listen to them. Yet it was difficult to avoid exaggerating the importance of a phenomenon that so much exaggerated itself. The disillusioning experience of the Anglo-French entente left Gardiner inclined to suspect collusion where there was, more usually, only mutual accommodation. Lloyd George was never actively in league with Northcliffe, as Gardiner supposed and as he encouraged others to believe. His fears, however, were too widely shared to be dismissed as paranoia. And he was not mistaken when he maintained that these men, whom Lloyd George cosseted, exerted a corrupting influence on policy and opinion.

The first winter of the war, ending in a stalemate that shattered hopes of a quick and easy victory, subjected friendships and political allegiances to untold strains. Gardiner was nettled by many of his former comrades, including Wells, who proposed 'an eternal economic war on Germany', and Shaw, whose 'sublime cocksureness' inspired him to write 'pamphlets and letters and articles which for vanity, pertness, ignorance of men and pompous perversity of opinion leave one breathless with amazement if not with indignation'. [2] Bennett earned his editor's rebuke by basing a column on an unconfirmed report in the *Daily Telegraph*. [3] The rantings of literary men were, of course, more easily discounted than the promulgations of Cabinet ministers. Once shown the error of their ways, Wells, Bennett,

1. Gardiner's diary, 28 January 1910, G.P.
2. *Daily News*, 27 February 1915; *Star*, 23 March 1915.
3. *Daily News*, 21 May 1915; also Bennett to Gardiner, 21 May 1915, G.P.

and even Shaw were restored to Gardiner's good graces whether or not they obliged him with a recantation. Lloyd George was another matter. His sins dictated by expediency and not by conviction, he forfeited any chance of pardon and remained Gardiner's arch villain as long as he lived.

It took many months of soul-searching for Gardiner to formalize his break with Lloyd George, to whom he always assigned credit for having 'changed the whole current of British politics'. Unfortunately, Lloyd George ultimately proceeded too far, perverting the democracy to which he had given a supreme voice. As soon as war was declared, he established himself as the 'inspiration' of the Government (Asquith was its 'brain' and Grey its 'character'), and even his 'fiercest foes' joined loudly in his praise: 'The city bankers', Gardiner noted with gratification, 'are, half in jest, but half in earnest, suggesting that his services should be rewarded with a dukedom.'[1] Gradually, however, it became apparent that he was endearing himself to his former opponents by turning his back upon the issues previously identified with his name. Never irretrievably committed to the orthodoxies of Free Trade – Gardiner was hard pressed to 'recall one really weighty contribution that he had made to the . . . case' – he did not hesitate to proclaim himself an advocate of wartime controls, many of which ran counter to the Liberal tradition. His 'independence of all theory and doctrine', which Gardiner had once applauded, now revealed its dangers. His counsellors, always recruited from the back corridors, came increasingly to include men of disreputable background and dubious intention. Prominent among them were journalists whose vicious attacks on his ministerial colleagues he might have silenced by a public statement or a private admonition; that he declined to do so raised serious questions about the nature of his informal alliances with Northcliffe and other press magnates. Still, he was an arresting figure, whose campaign to curb drunkenness among munitions workers persuaded not only the King but even 'Alpha' (the *Star*, 13 April 1915) to pledge not to 'touch anything stronger than water' until the Kaiser had been brought to his knees.

For the time being, Lloyd George's activities were a distraction and not an obsession for Gardiner, whose primary concern remained

1. 'The British Cabinet', *Atlantic Monthly*, cxv (1915), 677; reprinted in *The War Lords*, p. 71.

the war and the ways in which the *Daily News* could contribute to its successful conclusion. As much for historical as strategic reasons, he applauded the March invasion of the Dardanelles, which he saw as the revival of the Gladstonian mission against the unspeakable Turk. Essentially, however, he remained a 'westerner', who believed that the war could only be won by inflicting direct defeat upon the Prussian autocrat, who 'sees in democracy the spirit of rebellion against himself and against the Almighty' (1 May 1915). For this reason, he was reluctant to expend Allied resources in diversionary campaigns. McKenna, who concurred, thanked him for his 'much needed and ... very opportune' remarks.[1] It was significant that by May it was he, and no longer Lloyd George, who communicated approval.

McKenna was perhaps second only to Haldane in the violent abuse he suffered in the right wing press. 'Mr McKenna must go', insisted successive banner headlines in the *Daily Express*, whose editor was no less outraged by the Home Secretary's reluctance to impound potential spies than by his order to release detained suffragettes. The *Morning Post* reserved its vitriol for Churchill, and Northcliffe for Kitchener, the War Secretary whom he had helped to foist upon the Government at the inception of the war. But Simon, Harcourt, and the Prime Minister himself were not spared, and Haldane, of course, was fair game for all.

What was the connection between this press agitation and the fall of the Liberal Government in mid-May? The Cabinet crisis was 'as obscure in its origins as it was sudden', and Gardiner, for one, saw neither the logic nor the utility of the coalition that emerged.[2] In particular, 'the throwing of Lord Haldane to the wolves' seemed to him 'an indelible stain' on the new administration and on Asquith, who remained to preside over it. But there were a number of puzzling features about the new ministry, the appointment of F. E. Smith and Sir Edward Carson 'as the law officers of the crown' not the least among them. Gardiner hoped that Lloyd George had not been a party to the apparent intrigue, but he suspected otherwise. On the central question of an alleged 'deficiency in the supply of munitions', there were unmistakable signs of 'a very direct conflict between the

1. McKenna to Gardiner, 1 May 1915.
2. Gardiner's formal assessment of the episode appears in *The War Lords*, pp. 79–84.

Prime Minister and his chief lieutenant'. Gardiner restrained himself from leaping to conclusions, but the episode left him all the more suspicious of Lloyd George and Churchill, about both of whom mysterious rumours circulated, and whose traffickings with Northcliffe provided sufficient grounds for indictment.

A visit to the House of Commons on 3 June confirmed the worst of Gardiner's apprehensions. Despite the recent creation of an all-party coalition, partisan emotions ran higher than ever: 'The old sense of coherence, unity, gravity, had disappeared.' If the object had been to allay press criticism, the exercise was a conspicuous failure. The enemies of the late Government were not appeased by the formation of a ministry in which Liberals retained the key positions, in which McKenna was elevated to the Exchequer, and in which Asquith, Grey, Birrell, and even Kitchener were allowed to continue in their respective places. Asquith's twenty-minute explanation to his followers, *ex post facto*, shed little light on the proceedings and left Gardiner unsatisfied. 'No one, I think,' he lamented on the 5th, 'looking at the new Government with a knowledge of real values will feel that the position of this country has been strengthened.'

The creation of a Ministry of Munitions, with Lloyd George as its head, was the only development of any considerable consequence. It had tremendous repercussions on the wartime economy and propelled Lloyd George toward the premiership. Gardiner, who recognized the suitability of the appointment, chose not to regard it as an adverse judgment on the voluntary system, which had yet been seen to operate at full capacity. In any case, he dismissed the question as an academic one: 'It is foolish or disingenuous for us to cry out against Democracy because it is not so efficient for war as Despotism. It would not be Democracy if it were. One might as well expect the quiet householder to be as efficient at burglary as the professional burglar. He is not; but he does not turn burglar to adjust the balance.' He enjoined his readers to safeguard their 'liberty . . ., the one weapon that makes you the equal of Kings'. But, at the same time, he called on them to demonstrate greater self-sacrifice, whether in terms of subscriptions to the War Loan or extended work hours in collieries and workshops. Above all, he implored young men (26 June 1915) to enlist in defence of King and country: 'Compulsion is the weapon of Prussia: we shall meet it and break it by the weapon of freedom.'

There were those who derided such faith in the voluntary principle, and who argued that the time had come for the imposition of regulatory and coercive measures. Gardiner, in turn, denounced (31 July 1915) the infernal 'pessimist', who was 'more to be feared than the enemy himself, for he is the enemy in our midst. He is poisoning the blood of the nation, and, still worse, he is poisoning the mind of our Allies against us and filling the enemy's papers with cheerful tidings.' Those who agitated for conscription, military and industrial, underestimated the resolve of their countrymen, perhaps because they mistakenly imputed to them their own lack of patriotism. The voluntary system had amply proved its capacity to harness the talents and energies that were essential to victory. To back up his case, he quoted on 31 July from a letter he had received from an officer at the front, who offered £25 for the reprinting of an article 'describing the spirit of this country—not slandering it, but painting it soberly', so that he might distribute it among his men 'as an antidote to the poisonous effect which "The Times" and the "Daily Mail" is doing out here'. Three weeks later, he featured another letter that a private in the RAMC had sent to his parents in Somerset: 'I sincerely hope one thing, and that is that the Conscriptionist Party do not get the upper hand in England, for if they do we might as well be under German rule.'

Thanks to a Hampstead shopkeeper, who wrapped his deliveries in newspapers 'that are otherwise strangers to us', a copy of the *Daily Mail* crossed Gardiner's threshold. Its 'baseless' and 'reckless' charges inspired him to write his column of 21 August on 'The Great Slander', which was soon reissued in pamphlet form, possibly with the unidentified officer's £25 helping to defray costs. The system of voluntary recruiting 'is subjected to this outrage', he averred, not because it had failed, but because it was succeeding so well. Conscription, he explained, would produce a 'cheap army', at reduced expense to the wealthy taxpayer. 'Scratch a Conscriptionist,' he declared axiomatically, 'and you will find an enemy of the people.' Those who preached compulsion were, in may cases, less concerned with 'an expedient for meeting the needs of war', than with 'an expedient for controlling democracy when peace returns. It is the instrument by which Trade Unionism is to be kept in check, and [by which] the people are to be organised for the suppression of their own liberties.' Military authorities had gone on record to the effect that present arrangements were sufficient and that any departures would prove demoralizing and disruptive. But the 'enemy Press in our midst' discounted such testimony, and was 'prepared to imperil the victory of the Allies rather than forego the chance of imposing Prussianism upon this country'.

Lord Northcliffe's fulminations distressed the accredited spokesmen for National Service almost as much as they infuriated Gardiner. Lord Milner revealed that he had 'discouraged' his erratic ally 'for all I was worth, foreseeing that, as Northcliffe is a "red flag to a bull" not only to the Liberal but to a large section of the Unionist press, the fact of his making himself prominent in the agitation for National Service would create a reaction against it'. His fears were well grounded: there was 'a great deal of fuss', with the result that virtually 'the whole Press – the *Morning Post* is almost the only exception – has joined in the hue and cry against Northcliffe'. Milner took pains to distinguish between two sets of responses:

1. A great many papers, while denouncing Northcliffe & declining to press the Govt., yet make it clear that they would support National Service, if the Govt. & especially Lord Kitchener wanted it. . . .

2. On the other hand some papers like the Daily News, the Daily Chronicle, the Nation & the Star have thrown themselves furiously into the anti-Northcliffe agitation with the obvious intention of using the unpopularity of Northcliffe to damage the cause of National Service. [1]

Northcliffe, by Milner's calculation, had done the cause irreparable harm; with friends like him, the National Service League needed no enemies.

Gardiner, unlike some with whom Milner was inclined to bracket him, had never been a proponent of *laissez-faire* individualism, although on certain moral issues he had lately found his allies among those who were. Conscription, by his definition, was precisely such a moral issue; it implied an ulterior threat to the rights of the citizen and to the premises of the Liberal state. His aversion to compulsion, as it was variously mooted, did not blind him to the imperative need for other, less blatant controls. Insinuating himself into a public debate between Bennett and Wells, he acknowledged (7 August 1915)

1. Memorandum of 29 August 1915, written at Windsor, 'most probably for the information of the King': cited in Gollin, *Proconsul*, pp. 283–4.

that 'hatred of the enemy's motives should not prejudice us against all his methods. . . . If we are to win this struggle . . . we have to prove that Democracy and organisation can co-exist, that political freedom is consistent with material efficiency.' Englishmen, he told his readers, had traditionally 'not thought enough of the State, and the supreme lesson of the war is that we have to readjust the relations of the individual to the community'. His difference with Milner was essentially one of degree: to what extent should society be organized and for what ultimate purpose? Consistent with his prewar views, he prescribed the readjustment of social relationships 'not in order to make the State, as in Germany, the facile instrument of a despot, but in order to make it an effective guarantee of the personal liberties which we enjoy and which can only be preserved by co-operative action.'

Within the Cabinet, of which Milner was not yet a member, the 'great underlying conflict . . . between freedom and control'[1] soon surfaced. Like Asquith, who counted on one minister to balance the influence of another, Gardiner relied on McKenna, a trusted Free Trader and an anticonscriptionist, to hold the line against 'panic-stricken interference with that great machine of industry on which the issue of the war depends'.[2] Lloyd George, who had come out as an advocate of conscription and other more stringent wartime controls, disliked McKenna as much on personal as ideological grounds. He suspected McKenna of 'fomenting mischief against him among the Liberals', and, in particular, of impugning his loyalty to Asquith. 'Evidently someone has been supplying the Daily News with information,' Lloyd George's private secretary seethed in her diary on 17 September, 'and that someone is no doubt McKenna.'[3]

The next day the *Daily News* carried two signed articles by its editor: his usual Saturday column (apparently written in the middle of the week), and, more prominently, an open letter to Lloyd George on 'The present crisis' (obviously written at the last minute). On its

1. Taylor has thus described the forces that shaped 'Politics in the First World War' in his 1959 Raleigh Lecture, reprinted in *Politics in Wartime*, p. 20; see also Gollin's illuminating discussion on the subject, *Proconsul*, ch. xi.

2. *Daily News*, 4 September 1915; see also his 'appreciation' of McKenna in *Pearson's Magazine*, xli (January 1916), 93–7.

3. *Lloyd George: a Diary by Frances Stevenson*, p. 60. There is no evidence among either the Gardiner or the McKenna papers of such collusion.

own, his regular column might have given Lloyd George a measure of encouragement: it provided a sweeping survey of the social changes (including the 'emergence of woman') that had occurred, and concluded with an 'indictment' of the Government, which had left too much to private initiative and had failed to offer any plan for 'the resettlement of society'. But Gardiner had no intention of allowing the Minister for Munitions to infer either approval or acquiescence. 'Our relations in the past', he reminded Lloyd George in the accompanying letter,

have been such as to give me the assurance that you will understand the spirit in which I write and the motives by which I am governed.

. . .

It would be folly or worse than folly to blind one's-self or the public any longer to the fact that the peril to our domestic peace comes from you. . . . Without you the cause of Conscription was negligible; with you it is a danger more to be feared than Prussia.

He refused to believe that Lloyd George found anything but 'painful and revolting' the recrudescence of press attacks against Asquith, who had stood firmly by him in the Marconi scandal, and against Kitchener and other anti-conscription ministers: 'But you cannot be unaware that your name has been used to give point and emphasis to them, that your virtues have been exalted to throw your chief and your colleagues into deeper disrepute.' The Government, he argued, had thus far resisted the outcry for conscription because the majority of its members realized

that in the complex functions of this country in the war the free energies of the people are vital to success. . . . You have only one supporter from among your old colleagues, Mr Churchill. I say nothing in regard to him. Mr Churchill is – Mr Churchill.

For the rest, who are the leaders in this crusade? They are Lord Milner, Lord Curzon, and Lord Northcliffe.

How, he asked, could Lloyd George possibly reconcile himself to an alliance with these three peers, who personified respectively the forces of 'Prussianism', 'Imperialism', and restless self-aggrandizement?

Whatever your motives may be, they are not anti-democratic. They may be emotional, personal, anything, but they cannot conceivably be that. . . .

Beyond all men you have the ear of the democracy and the power of moving it to great issues. But the people of this country will not take the message of Lord Milner even from your lips. . . . They look to you to preserve the spirit of the nation from a deadly rupture, and I believe that they will not look in vain.

If Gardiner, as he was eager to imply, nursed hopes that Lloyd George could be tempted (or shamed) back to the fold, there were others who had given him up for lost. Vivian Phillipps, a lifelong Asquithian, acquainted Gardiner with a conversation he had had at Crowborough on the 18th with W. H. Cowan, MP, 'who is one of the group who are pressing for conscription'. Cowan revealed 'some interesting things', which Phillipps attempted to 'set . . . out in his own words as near as I can recall them.'

1. We are going to get conscription at once.

2. We cannot wait and do not intend to wait until Kitchener comes down and says definitely that the voluntary system is no longer sufficient to give us what we want. To agree to do this would be to waste time. Kitchener would probably want to make an appeal to the country to make a final effort to save the voluntary system. This would take time and nothing could be done – say till the New Year. By that time we should have lost *three valuable months*. (I underline these last words – because as you will see – they 'jump' with Lloyd George's 'preface' statement about 'what we do in the next three months'.)

3. There will have to be changes in the Cabinet. Asquith and Grey will have to go – possibly Kitchener and others.

4. The loss of Asquith and Grey will not weaken the country. Lloyd George in command will provide a driving force which will more than compensate for their removal. Kitchener has already made enough blunders. He could quite easily be replaced.

5. If organized labour resists the change, so much the worse for it. We have a big army in this country, quite sufficient to deal with any attempts to thwart our policy.

6. The plea for a united nation is a fudge. No nation was ever united in the prosecution of a war – vide the Boer war.

7. Possibly a General Election may have to be fought on the question. No one really believes that this would embarrass us in the least in the conduct of the war.

8. In any case the thing has now reached a point at which either Lloyd George must win or he must go. The country cannot afford to lose him, therefore it must back him and give him what he wants.

Phillipps professed a natural reluctance to accept Cowan as an authoritative source. Nonetheless, the information Cowan had volunteered seemed to him significant as an indication of 'the kind of thing which is evidently current talk among the conscriptionist gang'. Gardiner, too, took the matter seriously, as evidenced by the fact that he promptly forwarded Phillipps's letter to an unidentified third party (possibly John Gulland, the Liberal whip), adding only the marginal inscription: 'Here is the whole plot. Please return.'[1]

In retrospect one is tempted to see this episode, like the Cabinet crisis of the previous May, as a dress rehearsal for the convolutions of December 1916. Had Lloyd George merely intended to pressure the Prime Minister, or had he aspired to depose him? Historians, much like contemporaries, may only speculate. Events failed to move as speedily as Cowan had confidently predicted; but, after all, it was common for wartime politicians to under-estimate the time it would take to effect their aims. Conscription ultimately came through Asquith, and not in spite of him. Kitchener was eventually removed by a fatal accident which no one could have foreseen. Yet there remains every likelihood that a plot had been afoot, and that Lloyd George was its beneficiary if not, strictly speaking, its agent. Once again, Asquith survived by astutely combining private concessions with a public appeal to national unity. The price he paid, as yet undisclosed, would leave him bankrupt fifteen months later, when, at last, Cowan would have his Lloyd George conscriptionist Government without Asquith, Grey, and Kitchener.

Well aware of Lloyd George's support for conscription, Gardiner had not expected him to throw down the gauntlet with such force. His unease was intensified by the fact that he had been out of the country during the fateful week in which Parliament reassembled and Lloyd George issued his 'preface'. Early in September, permission was obtained for him to visit the western front. 'Don't be killed,' George Cadbury thoughtfully instructed, urging him to make contact with his son Laurence, who was serving at Dunkirk with the Friends' Hospital Unit.[2] After a year of describing the military situation from afar, Gardiner was grateful for the opportunity to obtain firsthand experience. His early autumn columns in the *Daily News* reflected on

1. Phillipps to Gardiner, 20 September 1915, G.P.
2. 5 September 1915, G.P.

the sights he had seen, and 'Alpha', in the *Star* on 14 September, movingly described the mood that prevailed 'In a dug-out'. General Sir William Robertson, then chief of the General Staff, hoped that the visit would result in more than good copy, and invited Gardiner to 'exercise [his] considerable influence over a large body of our fellow-countrymen in regard to giving us the support, both in men and material, which we *must* have to enable us to bring this business to a satisfactory end'.[1] More than ever, Gardiner was convinced that he could best fulfil Robertson's request by giving credit to the voluntary system that had raised the armies to whose spirit and valour he could now personally attest.

With all due respect to Robertson, Gardiner tended to doubt whether 'men and material' would suffice. Given the nature of Britain's commitments to her Continental allies, and her extensive trade with non-combatants, it seemed to him 'almost more important to have money'.[2] With public expenditure fast approaching the daily level of six million pounds, he deplored not only the sums that were wasted, but also the devious ways in which members of the privileged classes managed to escape commensurable burdens. McKenna's first budget, introduced in September, marked a 'courageous beginning', but it failed – notwithstanding its increases in direct taxation and its levy on excess profits – to deal as effectively as Gardiner had wished with the perennial problem of 'superfluous wealth'. Significantly, he raised no strenuous objection to the so-called McKenna duties, by far the most controversial ingredient in the budget package, which imposed surcharges upon enumerated 'luxury' imports. Trusting implicitly to the Chancellor of the Exchequer, who had emerged as Lloyd George's opposite number, he accepted this departure from Free Trade practice as a temporary expedient that promised to yield needed revenues, and he scorned the notion that it represented the thin edge of the Protectionist wedge. All the same, he feared that any impediment to the flow of natural market forces would have a crippling effect upon British power: 'If Jefferson Davis could have got his cotton to Lancashire,' he circuitously reasoned on 13 November, 'Lee's armies would not have been reduced to rags and misery and defeat.'

1. 18 September 1915, G.P.
2. *Daily News*, 9 October 1915.

Nor was he satisfied with wartime censorship, which, although admittedly necessary, appeared to him to operate on a false assumption. 'The true function of the Censorship is to conceal from the enemy things which we do not want the enemy to know. But . . . our Censorship has concealed from us things that the enemy did know.' As a case in point, he cited the 'excision' from John Buchan's recent *Times* dispatch of a passing reference to German bravery. 'Could anything be more fatuous?' he asked his readers on 16 October. 'If the Germans are brave we cannot conceal it from them by concealing it from ourselves. . . . Let us have fearless criticism and drastic remedy, but do not let us cultivate panic and pessimism, least of all for political ends.' Yet he himself soon came up against the complexities of the issue. Anxious to stave off conscription, he 'kicked' against publishing an article in which Arnold Bennett calculated 'the financial danger'[1] of the Derby scheme, which, despite its unlikely auspices (Lord Derby, the newly appointed Director-General of Recruiting, was an avowed conscriptionist), was hailed by many Liberals as their salvation: if a sufficient number of eligible men came forth to 'attest' their eventual willingness to serve, there would be no conceivable reason to institute compulsion. Gardiner was therefore eager to publicize the merits of the scheme and to encourage the widest possible response. On 28 October Derby officially thanked him 'on behalf of the Recruiting Staff throughout the Kingdom . . . for the assistance you have already given to recruiting', and he appended a few lines of personal gratitude: 'You have already been so good and kind to me in this campaign that I feel certain that without any such letter you would do all you could to help. P.S. Come and see me whenever you want to.'[2]

Others, including the ten Liberal backbenchers who voted against it, more readily perceived the implications of the Derby scheme, which hastened the dreaded inevitability of universal military service. Even the most devoted Asquithians began to recoil at the cruel necessities that they were called on to sanction in the abused name of

1. Gardiner 'printed it in the end', Bennett recorded in his journal on 26 October, 'unfortunately cutting out the very part in which I saved myself by blessing the present recruiting campaign and expressing the hope that only at the end of the 6 weeks' trial would recruiting be stopped': *Journals*, ii, 148.
2. G.P.

national unity. 'There are some of us that would go to hell or any other place of worship for the Prime Minister *himself*,' Walter Runciman – was it the president of the Board of Trade or his father? – angrily notified the party whip, 'but we are not prepared to go in the company of *his* enemies and ours at their bidding.' What Runciman particularly resented was the 'persistent domination' of the Government 'by an anti-national bloodsucking press', whose 'decrepit panaceas' were accepted by an unwitting public. He nursed the vain hope that the Prime Minister, with all the force and eloquence of which he was eminently capable, would speak out in Parliament against these enemies of the nation.[1]

Asquith, however, entertained a more dignified view of his responsibilities. Supremely confident of himself as 'the indispensable man', he declined to descend to the level of his opponents, to whom he refused to give the satisfaction of a reply. Gardiner, for one, marvelled at his self-control, and, as 'Alpha', likened him to the noble Pitt, beneath whose statue Asquith addressed the Lord Mayor's banquet at the Mansion House in early November: Pitt had known, 'Alpha' wrote on the 11th,

what it was to have the curs yapping at his heels, slandering his name, impugning his capacity. But he went on his way heedless of the Fat Boys of his day. And in his patient, unfaltering loyalty to the State, and his scorn for the rabble of snarling critics that beset him, Mr Asquith is not unequal to the great example that Pitt has left to the rulers of men.

How much happier 'Alpha' and his creator would have been had Lloyd George acted more like Pitt and less like Chamberlain. Even J. L. Garvin, whose support for National Service was tempered by a keen sense of political reality, 'spoke rather sadly of Lloyd George', whom he took to task 'for quarrelling with his own party', and for going out of his way to affront 'the Labour men, the Irish and the Radicals. . . . A man should always stick to his own party because there lies his influence', Garvin told Scott, to whom he questioned 'the use of Lloyd George breaking with the "Daily Chronicle" and

1. Runciman to Gulland, 28 October 1915 (copy), G.P. The peppery language, if not the sentiments expressed, was more typical of the elder Runciman, but it is difficult to explain why Gulland should provide Gardiner with a typescript copy of a letter from a backbencher.

"Daily News" and cultivating the "Daily Mail" and "The Times".'[1] Before the Derby scheme had had the opportunity to prove its worth, the Prime Minister hinted broadly to the House that conscription on one basis or another was a foregone conclusion. His introduction on 5 January of the Military Service Bill, a limited measure of compulsion for single men, therefore came as no surprise. Gardiner was deeply disappointed in Asquith, but the possible alternatives were too frightening to contemplate. Reluctant to say anything that might further jeopardize Asquith's position, the *Daily News* remained strangely silent, much to the annoyance of those who counted on it to resist evil from any source. 'What has become of the *D.N.* these days?' W. Llewelyn Williams, the Liberal member for Carmarthen, asked its editor:

Here we are 'at the parting of the ways,' & no clear note in the Radical organ! I had a talk with A. P. N[icholson, the paper's Lobby correspondent] on Wednesday. Indeed his article on Thursday was a pale reflection of my lurid talk! But I thought I detected a marked falling-off in his ardour against compulsion. I hope it isn't symptomatic of the paper's policy. Believe me, 'compulsion of single men' will be used by Ll. G. to justify all round compulsion later on. That poor weakling of a P.M.! It is too pitiful. How can you make an invertebrate stand up? I remember your woe-begone face in the Strand six weeks ago, when you told me – incredulous! – about Ll. G. and the weakness of Asquith. Little did I think that before the year was out we shd. be writing 'Ichabod' over so many shining names. But I hope the *Daily News* will remain staunch.[2]

Williams, resisting strong pressure from all sides, joined the forlorn band of Radical, Labour, and Irish members who denied their vote to the Military Service Bill.[3] Gardiner, too, thought it ironic that the

1. Scott's diary, 'probably 13–15 November 1915', in *Political Diaries*, p. 157.
2. Williams to Gardiner, 29 December 1915, G.P. Williams's letter to the editor of the *Daily News* (18 November 1915) was published as an appendix to Gardiner's recent pamphlet, *The Great Slander*.
3. See *Parliamentary Debates* (Commons), lxxvii, col. 1035 (5 January 1916). Sir John Simon was the only member of the Cabinet to carry out his threat to resign on the issue. He was soon writing to Gardiner to request publicity for his 'practical suggestions for the relief of married men from civil liabilities. . . . I don't want to be a mere critic, & the Govt. seem to have no plan ready.' 24 March 1916, G.P.

Bill was prefaced by 'hosannas to the voluntary system' to which it dealt a death-blow. Yet he reasoned on 8 January that:

If we are to accept this dangerous innovation in our national life it is better that we should accept it from his [Asquith's] rather than from any other hand, for we know that he has come to his decision unwillingly, that he has yielded to considerations which are above suspicion, and that he will limit the operation of the system strictly to its present military needs.

On the 29th at the close of an otherwise humiliating parliamentary session, he noted with relief and wry amusement that Asquith had once again outmanoeuvered his enemies: 'How many times during the past year, indeed during the past eight years, has the end of Mr Asquith been foretold, the manner of that end arranged, the date of his execution fixed, his political grave clothes prepared, his successor crowned in the ante-chamber?'

The Prime Minister, according to Gardiner, had survived by virtue of his 'patient wisdom and large statemanship', his loftiness of character, and the trust he inspired in all quarters, except perhaps 'society', where 'alone will you hear the voice of detraction, slander, and fierce hostility raised'. In the circumstances, Gardiner was prepared to forgive Asquith's surrender on conscription, even his earlier sacrifice of Haldane: 'Mr Asquith was big enough to do a base thing when he believed that something greater than his own honour was at stake.' Given time to reconsider, even the stout Williams came to extol the rare qualities of Asquith, 'that brave, patient man, the greatest Englishman of all time'. [1]

One must resist the temptation to ridicule Gardiner and others like him for their mistaken strategies and misplaced allegiances. There were not many Liberals, Trevor Wilson has pointed out, who 'could . . . bring themselves to force Asquith from office when the consequence might be even worse than divided government and diluted conscription: the annihilation of the Liberal party at a "khaki" election, and the accession to office of a Lloyd George–Carson administration capable of much greater inroads on personal liberty'. [2] Political ambition, not in itself reprehensible, was not the only motive. There was the vain hope that the first dose of compulsion, a moderate

1. Letter to the editor of the *Manchester Guardian*, 4 December 1916.
2. *The Downfall of the Liberal Party*, p. 83.

one, would be the last, and Asquith seemed the best available guarantee against further ministrations. If he were removed, the way would be open for the enactment of a host of antidemocratic measures, including Protection, which the *Spectator* now recommended as an expedient 'for the period of the war'. Other Liberal ministers could not possibly continue in office without their chief: McKenna and Runciman would undoubtedly be replaced with Tariff Reformers; Birrell, soon to be counted among the casualties of the Dublin Easter uprising, with an Irish Secretary who might obstruct Home Rule. Gardiner especially feared the departure of Grey, whom he had come to regard as the 'keystone' of the western alliance: 'The fall of Paris', he wrote on 22 January, 'would hardly give more joy to the Germans than the fall of Sir Edward Grey.' There were, then, diverse and complex reasons for upholding Asquith, who, at very least, had 'the audacity to treat' Northcliffe 'as the irresponsible office boy that he is'. That was more than one could say for some politicians. Indifferent to the abuse showered upon him by 'the Markhams and Dalziels, the McNeills and the Carsons, the Northcliffes and the Bathursts', Asquith reminded Gardiner of Lincoln, who 'held on his way with a magnanimous calm that never permitted his purpose to be deflected or his vision to be clouded by the malice and frenzy that raged about his path'.[1] It is noteworthy that it was precisely when Asquith was under heaviest attack that Gardiner paid him these fulsome tributes. Clearly, Asquith won them less by merit than by default. So great was Gardiner's aversion to Lloyd George that he would gladly have praised the devil if the Minister of Munitions would suffer in the comparison.

During April the political situation deteriorated to an extent that men of conscience, regardless of party label, were filled with disgust. 'There is a cabal every afternoon and a crisis every second day', complained H. E. Duke (later the 1st Baron Merrivale), the Unionist member for Exeter: 'It is time an end was made to them.' The Prime Minister, absent from the country for ten days to consult with Italian officials, returned on the 7th to face a badly divided Cabinet, renewed pressures for universal conscription (which came early the next month), and impending disorders in Ireland. Informed observers expected either Lloyd George to join Churchill and Carson in opposi-

1. *Daily News*, 1 April 1916.

tion, or Asquith, his frock-coat laid out in readiness, to deliver his resignation to the Palace.

Like Asquith, Gardiner looked on Lloyd George as 'the villain of the piece'. [1] There was, therefore, limited satisfaction to be obtained from the announcement that Kennedy Jones, another of Northcliffe's protégés, was defeated by 1800 votes in a Wimbledon by-election on the 19th. Gardiner's 'splendid assistance' to the coalition candidate earned him the gratitude of both the Liberal and Unionist whips. Buoyed by the Wimbledon result and, more specifically, by a meeting at the House on the night of the poll at which a hundred Liberal MPs affirmed their view that Asquith's 'continuation as the head of the Government is a national necessity', Gardiner decided that the time had come to seize the Goat (as Lloyd George was unaffectionately nicknamed) by the horns.

On Saturday, 22 April, Gardiner published 'A letter to Mr Lloyd George' in the *Daily News*; two columns long, it was reprinted in its entirety in that afternoon's *Star*. 'There is a time to speak and a time to be silent,' he began plaintively.

Your friends have been silent long. They have turned a deaf ear and a blind eye to many things that have happened. They have pretended not to know what they knew only too well. They have refused to see your figure flitting about behind the scenes, touching the strings, prompting the actors, directing the game, and have agreed to talk of Lord Northcliffe, Sir Henry Dalziel, and the Reverend Dr Sir William Robertson Nicoll when the name that has been in their minds has been the name of Mr David Lloyd George. They have done this for reasons you will understand and upon which you will have counted. They have done it because they remembered old associations, because they allowed much for the strain of this evil time upon an emotional mind like yours, above all because they were sensible of the gravity of doing anything that would shake the confidence of the country or imperil the Government.

But the time for these concealments has passed, and to-day I am going to talk about you. . . . The country has to make its choice – the gravest choice between men that any country was ever called upon to make – between Mr Asquith and you. It has heard much about Mr Asquith from your friends in the Press. . . . You have escaped not only insult; you have escaped exposure. You will escape no longer. If you are determined that

1. Roy Jenkins, *Asquith*, p. 392.

the country shall choose between you and Mr Asquith it shall not make its choice in ignorance of you.

At inordinate length and with excoriating effect, he proceeded to examine Lloyd George's methods and evaluate his attitudes. Crediting the absolute 'sincerity' with which Lloyd George believed himself 'the Man of Destiny', he pointed out that other aspiring Bonapartes, Churchill and Northcliffe prominent among them, entertained similarly 'inflated' views of themselves. 'Your brilliant success, your fascinating personality, your various, though wayward and superficial, powers encourage the belief,' he told Lloyd George. 'Still more do your deficiencies encourage it – your untutored empiricism, your casual and uninstructed habit of mind, your light hold of political principles or, as you call them, "dogmas".' It was only Asquith's tact and transparent 'good faith', Gardiner asserted, that had allowed the Government to avert a headlong conflict with trade unionism. Lloyd George, 'an agrarian agitator' without either patience or sympathy for problems of 'industrial organisation', had 'grossly exaggerated' reports of 'drunkenness and slackness' among munitions workers, and had otherwise unnecessarily provoked working-class antagonism to Government policy. But, most of all, Gardiner took Lloyd George to account for the misfortunes that had befallen the Liberal Party. Identifying him as 'one of the chief architects of the fall of the Liberal Government and of the establishment of the Coalition' in May 1915, he eagerly awaited the day when 'we shall know all the truth about that extremely obscure "shell" story' and about 'all the personal conflicts and ambitions behind that tornado of sensation'. One Government had been substituted for another, but the press attacks had not abated; nor had Lloyd George disavowed those who were responsible for them. Could one respect a politician who operated 'in close intimacy' with journalists who were the 'chief assailants' of his own colleagues? Could one entrust vital affairs of state to 'the victim of a feverish imagination', who had made the nation's 'agonies . . . the subject of political intrigue'?

Gardiner's column of the 22nd, like all bombshells exploded in the press, achieved at the same time rather more and less than intended. Bonar Law, dining with Riddell two days later, thought 'the attack . . . vicious and uncalled for', and put it down to 'political causes'. Far from inspiring confidence in Asquith, it seemed to him a further sign that 'the Government may break up at any moment'. Lloyd George, with whom Riddell discussed the matter on the 28th, assured his friend 'that the *Daily News* article had really served him a good turn. It had rallied the Conservatives around him and also a number of people who dislike personal attacks.' With no less satisfaction, Lloyd George acknowledged that the incident 'had also served to cut him off from "that crowd"', namely the Radical pacifists in whose company he had entered the war. The next day, Lloyd George re- peated for Riddell's benefit Bonar Law's felicitous remark that if the Minister of Munitions 'had paid Gardiner to attack him in the *Daily News*, the result could not have been more in his favour. The effect has been to show the public that he was the only Minister not re- sponsible for the recruiting muddle.'[1]

Instead of prodding Lloyd George into submission, Gardiner's assault had the incidental effect of driving him into closer alliance with the Tories. More grievously, instead of separating Lloyd George from his Radical followers, it tended to estrange Radicals from one another. The faithful Dr (later Viscount) Addison, citing the 'long open article by "A.G.G."' as the culmination of a week-long 'move- ment against L.G.' conceded that 'some of it was sound enough, but Gardiner missed the point of what is necessary to beat the Germans'.[2] Worse, he tellingly disputed its accuracy: 'Your article', he reminded Gardiner many years later,

was remarkably definite in its suggestions that L.G. in concert with certain others, some of whom were named, was or had been taking a certain course of action. I was myself at that time in daily contact with what was going on and had participated, particularly in connection with the crisis over re- cruiting, on several occasions in conversation with L.G. and others, and the line he was taking and the substance of conversations was quite different from what was suggested in your article; and, although I myself have suffered at his hands, I felt then, knowing the facts as to the line he was taking, that the article was seriously unjust and on re-reading it today I am still of the same opinion.[3]

Joseph Rowntree professed to have read 'with pain . . . Mr Gardiner's letter', which had 'evidently been written under great irritation, and

1. Entries of 24, 28 and 29 April 1916, in Riddell, *War Diary*, pp. 176, 179, 180.
2. Entry of 28 April 1916, in Addison, *Politics from Within*, i, 251.
3. Addison to Gardiner, 2 February 1934, G.P.

in lamentable forgetfulness of the splendid service to freedom which Lloyd George has given in the past'. As much for the sake of Lloyd George himself as for that of his critics, Rowntree enumerated the occasions when Lloyd George had rendered valiant service to the Liberal Party, which, 'but for his genius and courage, . . . might easily have sunk into decrepitude as Continental Liberal Parties have done'. The same service that entitled Lloyd George to greater courtesy made it regrettable that he should now throw in his lot with 'those who [had] opposed his great measures of reform' and who abused other Liberal ministers. In this respect, Rowntree soberly admitted: 'I think Gardiner's words . . . will meet with general response from thoughtful people.'[1]

However many 'thoughtful people' Gardiner might influence, he seemed to make distressingly little impact upon the public at large. The ubiquitous 'Mr Higgins', with whom 'Alpha' exchanged 'Words at the Pig and Whistle' (4 May), mindlessly continued to parrot the *Daily Mail*'s complaints of 'muddle, muddle, muddle, and wobble, wobble, wobble'. Perhaps with 'Alpha's' experience in mind, Gardiner renewed his attack in his Saturday column on 6 May. The Government's most conspicuous wobbler, he remonstrated, was none other than that Harmsworth hero, Lloyd George, whose recent statements as Minister of Munitions flatly contradicted the advice he had given as Chancellor of the Exchequer a year earlier. Then, Gardiner recalled, Lloyd George had agreed that it was more important to provide the alliance with adequate financial support and naval assurances than to put a Continental-size army in the field. Disputing Lloyd George's revised estimate of Britain's capability, as implied in his demand for universal service, Gardiner grimly prophesied that the nation would overextend itself if it 'tried, at Mr George's inspiration, to do what Mr George said we could not do'.

On the very day that Gardiner resumed the offensive, Lloyd George addressed a meeting of his constituents at Conway. There, on native soil, 'Cambria's uncrowned king' (as he was greeted in song) justified conscription as 'a democratic measure', and traced the steps by which he had come to that conclusion. Newspaper correspondents who had followed him to Conway hung on every syllable for a hint of his

1. Rowntree to E. R[ichard] Cross, Central Control Board, 26 April 1916, Lloyd George Papers, D/20/2/90.

political intentions, but Lloyd George had not travelled such a distance to raise the standard of rebellion. His references to the Prime Minister, if 'guarded' (to quote the special correspondent of the *Daily News*), were thoroughly respectful. In the ten years that he had served as Asquith's colleague, eight of them as his lieutenant, he had never hesitated to express his views 'freely, frankly, independently, whether they agreed with his [Asquith's] or not'. Adamantly denying that his differences with the Prime Minister in any way implied disloyalty, he pointedly asked: 'What use would I have been if I had not differed?'

His compatriots, who had waited trustingly and expectantly for him to speak in self-defence, cheered wildly at the first allusion to the press criticism of the past fortnight. 'I have recently been subjected to a cloudy discharge of poison gas,' he recounted with contempt. Although he declined to identify his 'assassin' by name, his audience was thoroughly familiar with the charges that had been brought against him and by whom. Under present circumstances, he insisted, he was not at liberty to give 'full reply', not that that mattered: '. . . If anyone believes that I am capable amid such terrible surroundings of making use of them for base and treacherous intrigue to advance my private ends, let him believe it.' Denouncing his assailant as one 'who publishes or invents private conversation in order to malign a friend', he 'hissed out' (again to quote the *Daily News* correspondent) the declaration that 'I seek neither his friendship nor his support'.

The report of Lloyd George's Saturday speech at Conway did not appear in the national press until Monday, and Gardiner therefore had the weekend to prepare a reply. He assured Lloyd George that he was more amused than wounded to be branded an 'assassin' and to have been 'dismissed . . . from the charmed circle of your friendship'. Far more painful to him was Lloyd George's attempt to obscure the issues that had been raised. 'It is much easier to say "assassin" than to meet an accusation which you know to be true and to which you have no answer.' He portrayed Lloyd George as a 'cuttle-fish', a stealthy creature that 'discolours the water with an inky substance in order to conceal his movements. It is an artifice which no politician employs with a greater skill than your own.' What distressed Gardiner, like so many of Lloyd George's erstwhile friends, was 'not your power of volition but your lack of judgment, not your enthusiasm about the war but your failure to understand your countrymen, not your loyalty to the cause but your lack of loyalty to the Government of which you are a member'. Particularly on the last score, Lloyd George's rhetoric had rung hollow. 'The charge against you is not that you have had disagreements with Mr Asquith,' whose past policies had often enough elicited strenuous objections from Gardiner, 'but that you have had agreements with Mr Asquith's declared enemies and the enemies of the Government.' According to Gardiner, Lloyd George's 'devouring egotism' had prevented him from uttering the 'one word of fearless repudiation' that might have put an effective end to 'the sneers and the venom' directed at various 'distinguished' ministers, most notably Asquith, 'whose loyalty to his colleagues is one of the splendid traditions of these times and whose loyalty to you has saved you in the past'. Instead, Lloyd George had allowed himself to be celebrated in the pages of 'the panic Press' as 'the little wizard of Wales'. It was surely 'not without significance', Gardiner noted in passing, 'that all the assailants of the Government are from the Celtic fringe – Sir Edward Carson, Lord Northcliffe, yourself and your entourage, Sir Robertson Nicoll, Sir Henry Dalziel, Mr Garvin and the rest'. Professing 'great respect for the Scotch and the Welsh and the Irish', and tactfully neglecting to classify Bonar Law, he contrasted the natural 'impatience of the Celtic mind . . . with the phlegm, steadiness, and obstinate patience of the English mind' as personified by Asquith, Grey, Long, Derby, and Kitchener. Yet despite the handicap of his national origins, Lloyd George might yet make amends, and Gardiner implored him to do so. English doggedness would win the war ('Let there be no mistake about that'), but it might manage more quickly with an injection of 'Celtic passion'. More than any other political leader, Lloyd George had it in his power to confer unity upon the Government and the nation. 'But you must make your choice,' Gardiner advised him. 'You cannot walk in step with Mr Asquith and Lord Northcliffe at the same time. You cannot have one foot in the camp of the Government and the other in the camp of its enemy. I hope you will make a wise choice, for we want to win the war with you and not without you.'

Gardiner, even before Lloyd George had publicly disowned him, had emerged as 'The Critic of Lloyd George'. He was so designated in the 20 May issue of *To-Day* by 'One who knows him', whom he in turn identified as Robert Lynd. 'Mr Gardiner', Lynd explained,

is in a broad sense a Puritan, in a very broad sense. His Puritanism is cheerful. He is more likely to quote Falstaff than Samuel Rutherford to you. He is curious about the arts and most of the pleasures. . . . He likes arguing about almost anything, indeed, from Scriabin to Charlie Chaplin. . . . He is, for a controversialist, exceptionally tolerant. He ceases to be tolerant, however, if anyone belittles Dickens. And he also ceases to be tolerant if anyone belittles the people.

By denigrating the voluntary system Lloyd George was said to have slandered the British war effort; by undermining the Government, he had intensified the attack upon democracy; and by the company he kept he had debased public life. Gardiner could find no excuse for such behaviour, tending as he did 'to judge the illustrious men of his own day as figures in history, and, to some extent, with an historian's charities and censures'.

For reasons of sentiment as well as expediency, Gardiner was still reluctant to advertise himself as a 'Critic of Lloyd George'. Rather, he preferred to be known as a champion of Asquith, and his columns in the *Daily News* and the *Star* won him that reputation. A character sketch of 'The Prime Minister' that he published anonymously in *Land & Water* (8 June 1916) ventured the 'not . . . very hazardous forecast . . . that the achievement of Mr Asquith will stand out as the supreme personal contribution to the victory that awaits us'. Whatever difficulty Gardiner experienced in writing off Lloyd George was obviously not reciprocal. At breakfast on 14 June C. P. Scott heard Lloyd George and Churchill 'talking . . . about and abusing the London Liberal papers', as they so frequently did for his benefit:

They had nothing to say about the 'Westminster' except that you always knew what it was going to say. The one thing about which Spender was really interesting was Education. The 'Chronicle' was fairly good but you never knew where you wd. have it. The 'Daily News' was a poor thing. 'I dislike its mentality,' said Ch[urchill]. Then with enthusiasm 'There's only one Liberal paper – the M. G.'

Lloyd George revived 'the old theme' of bringing out a London edition of the *Manchester Guardian*. 'What wd. it cost?' he asked

195

Scott, whose estimate of £20,000 a year did not strike him as too for-
bidding. ('All the same it is', Scott privately reflected.) It was not until
after their host had departed with 'the inevitable Lord Reading', that
Churchill 'complained' to Scott 'of the virulence and injustice of the
newspaper attacks' on him: 'He [Churchill] was a little sore that
George never said a word in his defence. It would be easy for him and
would have a great effect.' [1]

The political situation was radically altered on 6 June by news that
Lord Kitchener, within hours of embarking on a mission to Russia,
had drowned when his ship struck a mine. ('Providence is on the side
of the British Empire after all,' Northcliffe reportedly crowed to his
sister.) Lloyd George, who was to have accompanied Kitchener, had
luckily decided at the last moment to attend instead to Irish affairs.
The War Office, now vacant, was inevitably his, and on terms which
Asquith was in no position to refuse. Gardiner, alert to the implications, incongruously mourned Kitchener as 'not only a soldier but a
statesman', whose 'calculating wisdom' – best demonstrated by his
resistance to compulsion – had invoked 'a certain sense of greatness'.
Appealing to Kitchener's memory, which was to prove more potent
than Kitchener's assistance, he recalled the habitual abuse that the
late War Secretary had suffered. A recent visit to the French war zone
had convinced him (1 June 1916) that 'a journalistic discipline of the
severest sort' saved France 'from the Press-made sensations which
have kept this country in confusion'. Unavoidably, 'this stern muz-
zling of the Press' had kept the French public relatively uninformed
about the progress of the war, but the French Parliament had consequently acquired 'a degree of power unknown here'. The price was
worth paying to prevent 'the nation being made the sport of an irresponsible and incendiary journalism'.

Events soon proved Gardiner a more jealous guardian of his pro-
fessional liberties than his impetuous words may have suggested. In
July, he joined with various literary and public figures – including Sir
Arthur Conan Doyle, John Galsworthy, John Masefield, John
Clifford, Massingham, Bennett, Scott, Nicoll, and the Webbs – in a
vain attempt to save the life of Roger Casement, who had been

1. Scott's diary, 13–17 June 1916, Scott Papers, Add. MSS 50, 903, fol. 53.
For Churchill's successful efforts to restrain sniping journalists in the next war,
see Cudlipp, *Publish and Be Damned*, pp. 149–71 *passim*.

convicted for high treason for his part in Ireland's Easter rebellion. Shaw, who calculated that Casement would pose a greater danger as a martyr than as 'a reprieved and probably amnestied man', asked Gardiner to publish a letter for which *The Times* had declined to 'bear the burden'. The *Daily News*, for all its editor's sympathy, was equally unaccommodating. Shaw respected Gardiner's decision ('I dare say you are quite right'), and jested: 'I read your wild and reckless articles with great enjoyment. But what would they say of me if I went on like that?'[1] The question was a valid one. In the strongest possible terms, Gardiner accused the Government of bad faith in its relations with Irish nationalists, and deprecated the depths to which it sank in its efforts to discredit Casement. 'Alpha', too, was duly incensed; writing in the *Star* on 26 July he decried the madness that allowed grocers and tailors with German-sounding names to be victimized, while the Duke of Cumberland and the Duke of Albany, despite their overt pro-Germanism, retained their titles and their rights to the succession. Why should Casement be punished and not these 'Ducal Traitors'?

With the execution of Casement on 3 August Gardiner's tenuous alliance with Scott and Nicoll came to an abrupt end. Continued co-operation was impossible, given his suspicion of Lloyd George, to whose incidental acts he ascribed the most sinister intentions. Was it a coincidence that the War Office, which had expanded beyond the capacity of its premises in Whitehall, had ordered the 'compulsory acquisition' of the National Liberal Club? He and Massingham remonstrated that Lloyd George might have requisitioned one of the 'huge hotels' in Northumberland Avenue, or, better still, one of the Tory clubs in Pall Mall. Instead he had commandeered the head-quarters of the Radical opposition, and, to add insult to injury, had designated it for the purpose of compiling the national register of eligible conscripts.[2] Lloyd George's press secretary dismissed the incident as a tempest in a teapot: 'Massingham and Gardiner have been bitter,' he informed his chief, 'but they have a very small following.'[3] It is distinctly probable, however, that Lloyd George anticipated

1. Shaw to Gardiner, 7 and 13 July 1916 (copies), G.P.

2. Massingham wrote on the subject in the *Nation* on 9 September, and in letters to the editor of the *Daily News* on 9 and 12 September: Gardiner's major contribution was a leader on the 12th.

3. Sutherland to Lloyd George [September 1916], Lloyd George Papers, E/1/4/7.

the significance that would attach to his move, and that he might have mollified Radical opinion had he been so inclined.

Until the Somme offensive at last revealed itself as a staggering failure, Gardiner shared widespread hopes that the end of the war was in sight. On 2 September he predicted 'a rapid withdrawal on the western front', and cautioned against dismantling the alliance before Germany's capitulation was complete. The impression was enhanced by news from Berlin that Admiral Tirpitz had eclipsed Bethmann-Hollweg, whom 'journalistic wild men like Count Reventlow' had long disparaged as a 'namby-pamby blunderer'. What could better attest to the enemy's distress than the fact that her 'panic press' had gained the upper hand? 'We had our experience of this last year,' Gardiner recalled on 7 October, 'when the Northcliffes and the Pemberton Billings, the Carsons and the Dalziels had their innings and Mr Asquith was . . . buffeted by the waves of successive crises'. Although he was premature in his celebration of military 'success', he accurately prophesied a return of domestic strife: 'The "Last Phase" of the war threatens to be a long and trying phase, full of disappointments and checks, and fruitful of opportunities to the men who meet every emergency with hysteria and believe that the worst equipment of a captain in a storm is that he should have a cool head and a firm temper.' What Gardiner failed to appreciate was the immediacy of the threat and the extent to which Asquith's position had eroded. Military reverses and the submarine menace produced grave anxiety about the conduct of the war, and galvanized a parliamentary opposition which Bonar Law combined with Lloyd George to lead.

To what extent did Lloyd George conspire with fate (let alone with other, less reputable forces) to obtain the supreme position that he came to occupy in December 1916? Was his ascent to the premiership the product of a sordid intrigue, or was it a necessary response to Asquith's proved incapacity? Was he the captive of a vaulting ambition, or simply a natural leader of men on whom power inevitably devolved? The fascination of his personality, combined with the turbulence of his times, has inspired infinite variations on the Lloyd George enigma.[1] That he was the 'true person of the hour' was

1. Too often depicted as a snapdragon in the Liberal rose garden, Lloyd George has most recently been portrayed, no more convincingly, as something of a shrinking violet, whose 'years as [Asquith's] lieutenant had welded dependence to

admitted even by the *Nation*, which counted itself among his severest critics. The controversy has rested on the means by which he achieved his pre-eminence and the uses to which he put it.

To Gardiner, whose writings helped to give Lloyd George his Machiavellian image, it was self-evident that Asquith's downfall had been long and carefully plotted. There was not 'any doubt', he declared emphatically (but anonymously) in the March 1917 number of the *Atlantic Monthly*, 'that almost from the beginning [of the war] Mr George was seized with the notion of scrapping the old party system and creating out of the *debris* a new engine of political activity of which he would be the natural expression and director'. [1] Five years earlier, at a time when he had considered Lloyd George incapable of wrong, he had one day 'found him . . . full of Ferraro's "Greatness and Decline of Rome"', and observed that 'Caesar and Brutus, Cicero and Pompey and the rest only appealed to him as parallels' to contemporary politicians. To avoid embarrassment, Gardiner had declined to disclose who in Lloyd George's 'judgment is the Caesar, or the Cicero, or the Brutus of to-day', and had instead posed the question to his readers 'as an amusing speculation for the Christmas fireside'. [2] By December 1916 the time had passed for either reticence or sportiveness. Brutus stood revealed by his deed; Caesar, if only by his mortality.

Lloyd George's recent machinations had given pain even to those Liberals better disposed to him. The faithful Scott, belatedly aware that other press magnates had supplanted him in his hero's counsels, was profoundly distressed by 'a rumour going about – I shd. hope quite unfounded – that Northcliffe has some information', possibly about the Marconi affair, which he was using to hold Lloyd George 'in terrorem'. [3] Unlike Scott, who spent decades 'drearily dredging in

---

ambition', and whose 'loyalty was irreproachable': Hazlehurst, *Politicians at War*, p. 304.

1. 'Lloyd George and the coup d'état', *Atlantic Monthly*, cxix (1917), 392–401. Gardiner's authorship of this anonymous piece is confirmed by the existence of a draft manuscript among his papers.

2. *Daily News*, 16 December 1911.

3. Diary for 20–22 November 1916, Scott Papers, Add. MSS 50, 903, fol. 85. Trevor Wilson, who does not include the above passage in his published edition of the Scott diaries, acknowledges that Scott 'at this stage was an embarrassment', whom Lloyd George brushed aside: *Political Diaries*, p. 250.

a foul pond for the soul of Ll. G.',[1] Gardiner did not believe that it required blackmail to get Lloyd George to behave villainously. Nor, for that matter, did Lloyd George esteem Gardiner's professional conduct. On 21 November and again on the 22nd, he breakfasted with Scott and 'referred incidentally to Gardiner's earlier attack in the "Daily News", the unpardonable thing about wh. was that G. hd. made use of unguarded & only half serious remarks made in private conversation'.[2]

Gardiner's 'earlier attack' was a pale foreshadowing of what soon followed. Within the week, he sighted 'indications of what the sailors call "dirty weather" at Westminster', and he warned his readers of impending shipwreck. 'The disappointed place men, the incendiary journalists, and the wire-pullers', he reported on the 27th, 'are as active as bees on a warm spring day.' What did their stirring portend? It did not escape Gardiner's attention that the *Morning Post*, which had previously treated Lloyd George with contempt and derision, now designated him 'The Man' to whom it looked for victory. 'Mr Lloyd George must by this time have learned the meaning of the ancient warning about the gifts of the Greeks', Gardiner reflected more with hope than confidence. 'He will do well to refuse the proffered crown of the "Morning Post" and to beware of those who go about with lists of new Cabinets in their pockets.'

What Gardiner apparently did not yet know was that, two days earlier, Lloyd George and Bonar Law had formally proposed to the Prime Minister the creation of a three-man war council, its places reserved for themselves and Sir Edward Carson. In case Asquith, who took a week to deliberate, failed to understand the significance of the move, *The Times* put the matter to him bluntly in a leader on 4 December: the proposed council was to be 'fully charged with the supreme direction of the war', and he was to be disqualified from membership 'on the ground of temperament'. Leaping to the not unreasonable conclusion that Lloyd George had inspired *The Times's* article – it was in fact Carson who was the culprit – Asquith reversed himself and repudiated the scheme, by which allegedly he would have been 'relegated to the position of an irresponsible spectator of the

1. The description is Massingham's, quoted by Vivian Phillipps in *My Days and Ways*, p. 55.
2. Diary for 20–22 November 1916, Scott Papers, Add. MSS 50, 903, fols 83–4.

War'.[1] Technically, it was therefore he who provoked the ensuing crisis. Events moved with an inexorability that suggested that the ground was well prepared. Within a few days Asquith had terminated his extended lease on Downing Street, and Lloyd George had formed a new coalition.

'It would take a combination of Meredith, Browning, & Henry James to give you the story of our change of Govt.', remarked J. A. Spender, who, without pretence to literary distinction, subsequently provided more than one account of these confused proceedings: 'The old P. M. – bless his heart – never could see that by neglecting the art of advertisement he was handing himself over body & soul to the Northcliffe Press & its hero.'[2] His brother Harold, who was to be found in the opposite camp, offered a rival interpretation. 'It was certainly not the fault of Mr Lloyd George', he insisted, if he happened to be supported by various 'friends of the Press . . . [who] stood honestly and boldly for a more active prosecution of the war. . . . It was preposterous to expect that he should reject their help.' On the one hand, the younger Spender categorically denied that any 'working alliance' had been concluded between the new Prime Minister and Northcliffe; on the other, he acknowledged that they had reached 'a fortuitous temporary agreement in regard to the conduct of the war'. In any case, he would have no truck with 'mean and unworthy insinuations' that Lloyd George had been party to a press intrigue: 'There will always be men with their eyes fixed on the ground,' he sneered, 'when great signs are appearing in the heavens.'[3]

Gardiner, who stood somewhere between the two Spenders, was in any case too much of an agnostic to credit politicians with divine attributes. 'I do not, believe me, regard Mr Asquith as a godlike person', he wearily explained on 2 December, when the situation was hanging fire. 'He is a fallible human being. Whatever changes we make, we shall have to continue to rely upon fallible human beings.' Nevertheless, Gardiner remained 'profoundly convinced that Mr Asquith is the necessary man in this crisis, that he has qualities which

1. Asquith to Lloyd George, 4 December 1916, cited in Spender and Asquith, *Life of Lord Oxford and Asquith*, ii, 264.

2. Spender to ? [December 1916] (copy ?), Spender Papers, Add. MSS 46,392, fol. 251.

3. Harold Spender, *The Prime Minister*, pp. 239 ff.

are vital to our cause and which no one else can supply in equal measure, and that the day on which he lifted his hand from the helm would be a day of disaster to the Allies and a day of victory to the enemy.' To be sure, Asquith had made mistakes, not the least of which had been his abject failure to respond to the Northcliffe 'menace'; but it would be a mistake of infinitely greater consequence to substitute a 'Government which lives by the sanction of a Press dictator'. Because the present ministry, unsatisfactory as it had been in many respects, seemed to him 'the only combination that stands between this country and disruption', it won his grudging support. And because Asquith, inevitably to his own disadvantage, had refused 'to scrimmage in the gutter with the self-seekers and the adventurers', Gardiner pledged that he would never join 'the mongrel pack that yelps at his heels'.

On the evening of the 7th, Thomas Jones spied Gardiner at the Reform Club, where 'the whole atmosphere was very electric', and 'the prevailing feeling . . . was against L.G. and pro-Asquith'. Any hope that the old Prime Minister might again work a miracle was dashed around ten o'clock, when the tape brought word 'that L.G. had been asked to form a government with the cooperation of Bonar Law'.[1] Gardiner was too much of a realist to take refuge in the belief, sometimes imputed to Asquith, that Lloyd George would experience difficulty either in assembling a ministry or in obtaining requisite support in the Commons. Nor did he share the popular delusion that the new Government came equipped with readymade solutions to the vast problems that beset the nation. The resultant split in party ranks did not occur, in any meaningful sense, along ideological lines. Radicals divided in their loyalties, often on the basis of expediency or idiosyncrasy. All that one can safely say is that most (but not all) Liberals who favoured an all-out war effort sided with Lloyd George. Gardiner's friends, who did not, reflected various shades of party opinion. Privately, they gave vent to an acrimony which he dared not articulate in print. 'Did I not once write to you saying a certain person was a legitimate descendant of Judas Iscariot?' R. B. Cunninghame Graham, a former Radical MP who had since turned to literature, asked Gardiner. 'Who told the Cabinet secrets to Northcliffe? Who but Judas? . . . For the first time, I fear we shall lose the war, for

1. Thomas Jones, *Whitehall Diary*, i, 8.

the country looks as if it will be torn by factions. After the war, we shall have (I fear) civil war. . . . George will lead the pluto-aristocratic party.'[1] Sir Walter Runciman (later the first Baron Runciman), father of the ousted Cabinet minister and himself a Liberal MP, expressed the 'view . . . that LG could have got his ambition satisfied in a way that would have assured his future political position and he would have been beloved by everybody. Like yourself,' he told Gardiner, 'I was fascinated by him although many a time our differences were wide apart. I stood by him when he was bitterly attacked.'[2] Many of Lloyd George's Liberal critics might have been better able to credit his motives had he disassociated himself from the megalomaniac Northcliffe, who cast a portly shadow over the events of December 1916. 'It is no good omen for the future of England or of democracy that the press of one man, speaking with many voices to the mob of the streets and that of the clubs, should play the part of King-maker', Lord Bryce wrote forebodingly to Sir George Otto Trevelyan. 'How in the sixties & seventies we used to complain of Delane for infinitely less!'[3]

Although Gardiner had not confined himself to Saturday appearances when issues had suddenly presented themselves, he waited until the end of the week to broach the subject of the second coalition. Given the irretrievability of the situation, there was no reason for him to anticipate his normal column. Yet he did not wish his readers to think that he had been caught unawares:

> When I said a fortnight ago that the storm cone was hoisted at Westminster I had only external signs and hints and much past experience of the genesis of political storms to judge by. But the signs were infallible. I had seen so many of these tornadoes in the making that I knew the mechanism by heart. I could have written out the formula, assigned each man his part, taken you to where the thunder and the lightnings were being generated, . . . conducted you . . . to where the high explosive was awaiting the pre-arranged signal. It would make an astonishing comedy which I should love to write if we did not happen to be living in a world of unspeakable tragedy.

His purpose on 9 December was neither to redeem his reputation as an oracle nor to step into Northcliffe's shoes, now temporarily empty.

1. 6 December 1916, G.P.   2. 11 December 1916, G.P.
3. Bryce to Trevelyan, 22 January 1917, Bryce Papers (Bodleian Library), vol. xix, fol. 125.

He addressed himself not to the crisis that had passed but to the 'Perils ahead'. A Lloyd George Government, he postulated, would enjoy at least one advantage denied to its predecessor: 'It will be subject to a friendly, organised and responsible criticism which will aim at sustaining it and not destroying it.' The new Premier 'must, at all costs, have fair play from the Press and goodwill from all. He must not live under the menace of those screaming placards and those hysterical headlines that have made the past eighteen months a nightmare of shame and disaster.'

On the subject of the Prime Minister himself, Gardiner was firm but relatively restrained:

I do not doubt the energy of Mr George, but with all the emphasis at my command I counsel him to patience – patience with unalterable facts, patience with his advisers, patience with his colleagues. Let him fear his dramatic inspirations until they have passed the test of more cautious, more informed, more calculating minds. Let him remember that he is no longer in the engine-room. He is at the helm. Upon his wisdom and his caution no less than upon his energy the fate of everything we cherish depends. We look to him to remember the vastness of his trust and to walk cautiously however swiftly. We look to him, too, to place his whole confidence in Parliament. Let there be no terrorism from outside.

He noted a disquieting announcement that had appeared in the previous day's *Times* to the effect that 'Lord Northcliffe preferred sitting in Carmelite House and Printing House Square to sitting in the Cabinet'. Without passing judgment on Northcliffe's qualifications for office, Gardiner deplored the implication 'that having destroyed one Government Lord Northcliffe is going to exercise the powers of a dictator over its successor'. With renewed urgency, he warned that 'if the real power is not in the Cabinet but in Carmelite House, this country is lost'.

Bernard Shaw, who could always be depended on to hold strong views, urged his friend to speak less guardedly or, better still, to give him space in the *Daily News*. Gardiner tactfully declined Shaw's offer and advice, and, in the process, helpfully illuminated his own philosophy:

I am not courageous enough for the job, but I am courageous enough to have stolen a little of your raw spirits, added a substantial dollop of water & administered the dose to the public in tonight's paper. The truth (if I may speak frankly) is that you are a glorious but trying person for a timid editor. Your main theme, as I so often find, carries me with it entirely by its sanity & searching truth, but you mix it with so many asides that seem designed to arouse every sleeping dog & set it howling & barking at your heels that the wisdom of the main theme is lost on the dull-witted public who listen to the howling of the dogs & bark at your heels with them. Why stir up all the devils in hell at the same time? I always feel when I read you that if I had your genius & my pedestrian discretion I would civilize this country in a year. Anything cd. be done with your pen if it would cease stabbing every corn it can find on the flat foot of John Bull. [1]

Duly flattered by Gardiner's letter, Shaw was 'delighted' to read A.G.G.'s 21 December column on 'The Dynasts', which attacked 'Hohenzollernism' and, by implication, 'the British equivalent'. Having severed his link with the *New Statesman,* 'because the editor turned it quite simply into an organ of suburban Tory democracy', Shaw looked again to the *Daily News* to carry on the fight. 'Does Lloyd George mean to be the newest pet of the duchesses (Vice Joe Chamberlain deceased) or does he mean to be the first President of the British Republic'? he asked Gardiner, who shared his suspicion of the Prime Minister, but not necessarily his more corrosive passions. [2]

It was not only with regard to tactics that they differed. Gardiner continued to be a devoted follower of Asquith, whom Shaw had always tended to dismiss as a dry-as-dust lawyer, and whose resignation he had demanded when war was declared. Deprived of office, Asquith retained the constitutional right to submit a final honours list, and he proposed to reward Gardiner, probably with a knighthood. A.G.G. may have been tempted, but the 'Alpha' within him would have nothing to do with it. [3] 'I appreciate your reference to formal recognition,' he assured Asquith. 'That would have been distasteful to me at any time: in the present circumstances it would be unthinkable.' J. A. Spender, too, declined to be 'decorated'. Gardiner considered

1. Gardiner to Shaw, 21 December 1916 (copy), G.P.
2. Shaw to Gardiner, 28 December 1916 (copy), G.P.
3. 'Alpha' could never understand how a man of talent could prize 'a tag that any tuft hunter in public life can get', and confessed that he had had misgivings about J. M. Barrie since the novelist-playwright had accepted a baronetcy: 'On the Guinea Stamp', in *Pebbles on the Shore,* pp. 121–3.

himself sufficiently rewarded by 'the generous terms' in which his old chief had tendered the offer:

It has been a great privilege to me to have had some small part in advancing the causes & principles of wh. you have been the exponent. It is an infinite grief to me that those causes & principles have been overwhelmed by the unmeasurable disaster of the war. But though overwhelmed they are indestructible & the ground we have won will not be wholly lost. It is my hope, as it is the hope of all who have followed you & believe in you, that you will long be spared to lead us. The nation will need your wisdom & patience in the dark days before us as much as it has ever needed them in the past. [1]

Gardiner's adulation for the fallen Asquith was not without irony. Many of the achievements for which he generously assigned Asquith credit were in fact the work of Lloyd George, in whom he could no longer bring himself to see virtue. Among the principles that he identified with Asquith's name were many of those which, as late as August 1914, he had condemned Asquith for violating. Far from having resigned himself to the existence of a Lloyd George Government, as his December 1916 columns may have suggested, Gardiner was consumed by a bitter antagonism that he soon made little effort to suppress. Like Hazlitt, after whom he consciously patterned himself, he perpetually craved a hero. After 1916 the prospect of an Asquithian restoration was nearly as remote as had been that of the Napoleonic restoration for which Hazlitt had hoped a century earlier. Forced to look beyond Asquith to find an effective rival to Lloyd George, Gardiner, like Canning in Hazlitt's day, 'called the New World into existence to redress the balance of the Old'.

1. Gardiner to Asquith, 20 December 1916, Asquith Papers, xvii, fols. 266–7. Asquith's letter that so 'deeply touched' Gardiner does not survive among the Gardiner Papers, therefore one cannot be certain of the honour that was proposed.

9. Mr Wilson's disciple

It was only to be expected that British Liberals, their party shattered and their ideals in disarray, should turn westward to America's President Wilson, who was known to have drawn boyhood inspiration from a photograph of Gladstone that adorned the wall above his desk. Who could boast more impeccable credentials? With Asquith and Grey shunted aside, neither of them young or particularly effectual, Wilson appeared the statesman best qualified to infuse world politics with a Gladstonian sense of moral purpose. He commanded respect as a distinguished academic, an inveterate anti-jingo, and a social reformer who, true to his heritage, scrupulously respected the rights of the individual. Many British pacifists (again to use that term as broadly as possible) credited him with a superior wisdom that had kept his country free from entangling alliances and out of war in August 1914.

The President, to be sure, was pleased to be regarded as the heir to a tradition he had long admired. Without false modesty, he accepted the pedestal that was assigned to him in the Liberal pantheon, where several places now stood conspicuously empty. By the doctrines that he preached, he was eminently worthy of veneration. The Wilsonian principle of self-determination had been anticipated by Gladstone's persistent support of Balkan national movements. [1] Long before they had heard Wilson's name, let alone his message, Radical critics of the Foreign Office had pressed the case for open diplomacy. Likewise, they shared the President's disdain for Tsarist autocracy, his commitment to disarmament, and, above all else, his internationalist aspirations. Shocked and confused by circumstances beyond their control, British Liberals often heard in Wilson's tendentious pronouncements the reverberating echoes of their own self-righteousness.

Not that Wilson could claim a monopoly of the ideals that were popularly identified with his name. Many of the same policies had

1. A. J. P. Taylor, *The Struggle for Mastery in Europe*, p. 215n.

been promulgated by Grey (by now Viscount Grey of Fallodon) and Lloyd George, but the first was too much compromised by his part in the old diplomacy, and the second by his frequent lapses into Tory rhetoric. Wilson, however, spoke with an unsullied reputation and with the undisputed authority of American power.

For Gardiner, as for many, Wilson's heroic stature increased as the British political situation went from bad to worse.[1] Before the war, he had been mildly critical of the President, who resembled Joseph Chamberlain almost as much in manner as in 'feature'. Both men, Gardiner noted, exhibited 'a certain hard masterfulness'. Lloyd George, too, had a good deal in common with Chamberlain, but not as much as Wilson, who was more 'hard, combative, direct', a man of 'no compromise, no concealment, no finesse, but smashing drives straight from the shoulder'.[2] Ironically these were the very qualities that Gardiner celebrated in Wilson during wartime, and that he ultimately recognized as Wilson's gravest defects.

Many of Britain's most ardent champions of the so-called Wilsonian programme were among Gardiner's friends and acquaintances. They included, at least for the time being, his comrades in the prewar disarmament campaign, the most disaffected of whom joined the Union of Democratic Control. Gardiner confined his formal membership to the Writers' Group – its ranks included J. A. Spender, Gilbert Murray, Arnold Bennett, J. A. Hobson, G. Lowes Dickinson, Graham Wallas, and L. T. Hobhouse – which held periodic meetings, usually at the Reform Club, 'to give expression to Liberal views on the war and still more on the peace to follow'.[3] He had known General Smuts since 1906, when the South African statesman called at Bouverie Street late one evening to celebrate the 'pro-Boer' electoral victory.[4] Lord Bryce, an old ally, had tried to help the *Daily News* recruit a Berlin correspondent of American origin;[5] and Lord Robert Cecil, who emerged as the foremost British proponent of the League of Nations, corresponded with Gardiner in the most cordial

1. For the favourable response that Wilson elicited from disenchanted Liberals, see Swartz, *The Union of Democratic Control in British Politics during the First World War*, ch. 7; also L. W. Martin, *Peace Without Victory*.
2. *Daily News*, 9 November 1912; reprinted in *Pillars of Society*, p. 105.
3. Pound, *Arnold Bennett*, p. 273.
4. Smuts to Gardiner, 26 January 1906, G.P.
5. Bryce to Gardiner, 9 July 1915, G.P.

terms about the arrangements that were made for American journalists at the front.[1]

One would not wish to suggest that Gardiner required others to introduce him to Wilsonian-type principles, or even to fire his zeal. His prewar and early wartime columns in the *Daily News* proposed in substance, if not necessarily in detail, nearly all of the territorial adjustments and diplomatic changes that Wilson subsequently codified as his Fourteen Points. 'The greatest need in Europe to-day', he wrote on 3 August 1912, 'is the candid diplomacy which has been the tradition of the United States.' On 3 October 1914, he pleaded the case for 'an international court', similar in concept to the future League of Nations:

> If we emerge from this war with the Krupps and the Armstrongs and the Schneiders still triumphant, with despotism still among us, with the old gamblers of secret diplomacy playing their old games in the dark, the price that is being paid in the trenches on the Aisne will have been in vain. . . . We have to civilise the state as we have civilised the individual.

Early the following year, in the midst of a furious controversy over the maritime rights of neutrals whose commerce was allegedly supplying enemy markets, Gardiner declared himself in favour of maximum leniency. Unlike some other Liberals, he was less concerned with legal technicalities than with the possible effects on neutral, particularly American opinion. What was to be gained by giving substance to the anti-British feeling that was strongly rooted among certain communities in the United States? Why should the Allies make it more difficult for President Wilson to espouse their cause? 'I have a profound faith in [Wilson's] wisdom and his courage,' Gardiner proclaimed on 23 January, 'and I believe that he will act in the right way at the right time.'

It was not so much American military intervention that Gardiner desired, as American influence on the eventual terms of peace. If the war was to be fought to any constructive purpose, there would have to be a non-vindictive settlement, grounded on principles of democracy and self-determination. To the same extent that American troops would contribute to an Allied victory, American participation in the treaty-making would insure the likelihood of moderate war aims.

1. Cecil to Gardiner, 7 February 1916, G.P.

History, as usual, provided an object lesson. To commemorate the centenary of the Congress of Vienna, Gardiner recounted 'the story of 1815', and a tragic one it was. Prince Metternich and his accomplices, by effecting 'a peace with plunder' that ignored 'the interest of the peoples concerned', had created the rivalries and antagonisms that 'culminated in the universal catastrophe of to-day'. It was by no means too early to contemplate the task of international reconstruction if Europe was to avert 'a new century of armed peace and bloodshed', he told his readers on 13 Feburary 1915. 'The way of lasting peace is the path of democracy and not of despotism', of liberty and not of dynastic aggrandizement. With its evangelical tone, Gardiner's column commended itself to George Cadbury, who prayed: 'May it do some little to hasten the time when "nation shall no more lift up sword against nation, neither shall they learn war any more" '.[1]

Gardiner's employer was not his only admirer. Visiting London at this time was Colonel Edward M. House, President Wilson's counsellor and special assistant, who had been dispatched on a tour of European capitals. To Sir Horace Plunkett, the Irish statesman, House expressed an interest in meeting Gardiner, and Plunkett brought the two men together over dinner at the Wellington Club. 'House told me', Gardiner later recalled, 'that the President had been interested in some sketches of public men which I had published & had asked him to make my acquaintance. From this time onward my indirect contact with the President through Col. House was maintained.'[2] Unlike the other members of the 'peace party' whom he interviewed, Loreburn and Hirst among them, Gardiner served House not only as a source of information, but also as an introduction to the personalities of the day: meeting Lord Bryce for the first time, House quoted to good effect Gardiner's remark, which the President had read aloud to him, that Bryce, 'the greatest living Englishman', was in fact 'a Scotsman born in Ireland'.[3]

Flattered by the respectful attention he received from House and

1. George Cadbury to Gardiner, 14 February 1915, G.P.

2. Autobiographical memorandum, n.d., G.P.

3. Bryce declared that he 'had not read' Gardiner's essay, 'and was afraid to do so for fear his head might be turned; at the same time', House recorded in his diary, 'I noticed he asked me again the title of the book': diary entry for 25 February 1915, *Intimate Papers of Colonel House*, i, 383–4; see also entries for 9 February and 4, 7, 8 and 9 March 1915, *ibid.*, pp. 385, 390 and 448.

especially by the President's interest in his work, Gardiner began to explore the possibilities – professional as well as political – of Anglo–American collaboration. Already he made plans to join his friend S. K. Ratcliffe, a member of the *Daily News* staff and also the London correspondent for the *New Republic*, on a postwar American lecture tour. Ellery Sedgwick, the editor of the *Atlantic Monthly*, accepted with enthusiasm his first contribution to that journal. Paying tribute to its 'engaging brilliancy', Sedgwick could not 'help wondering how you come to know so much about the United States. Your portrait of Wilson is a masterpiece of the art of miniature.'[1] Other articles in the *Atlantic* followed, and eventually a syndicated American column that obtained a wide readership and exerted a subtle influence. Arthur Krock, whom Wilson provided with a letter of introduction to 'the great journalist', described Gardiner's effect upon American opinion as 'a relay. That is, American editors read him regularly and undoubtedly absorbed ideas which they in turn projected into their own writings.'[2]

But for the time being, while his trans-Atlantic following was more or less confined to the White House, Gardiner used his American contacts to help influence opinion at home. His 24 July column featured a detailed account of a conversation with a 'distinguished citizen of a neutral country' (presumably House), who had found in wartime Berlin exactly the situation that Gardiner had been describing. War to the bitter end, followed by a punitive peace, would betray the very cause for which the Allies professed to fight, this unidentified visitor agreed:

A humiliated Germany will not make for a democratic Germany. It will only make for a revengeful Germany. An honourable settlement, which would leave no wound to rankle, would be a more complete disaster to the militarists than a crushing defeat, because it would being them to a reckoning with the people. . . . The essential thing to remember is that you are at war with a system rather than with a nation. . . . If the aim is to destroy Germany Europe is in, not for a two years' war or a ten years' war, but for a hundred years' war, and Europe may go down into the abyss with Germany.

1. Sedgwick to Gardiner, 25 March 1915, G.P. Gardiner's article, 'The British Cabinet', appeared in the May number, cxv (1915), 672–82.
2. Krock to the author, 9 March 1970.

Gardiner's appeal, fortified by the testimony of a prominent and informed neutral, coincided with a strong movement in Liberal circles toward a negotiated settlement. Those who supported the war least enthusiastically or who pressed for moderate war aims were distressed by their Government's bellicosity quite as much as by the enemy's. With a stalemate on the western front and the Gallipoli campaign an admitted disaster, it seemed sensible to seek a solution at the conference table. Loreburn, spurred on by Hirst, concluded 'that the time may be ripe now for saying something that will make people think of the absurdity of fighting on till all the nations are utterly exhausted'. He proposed to publish a letter, signed by himself, Morley and Burns, the two men who left the Cabinet when the war was declared. Not that Loreburn was embracing the antiwar position typified by the UDC. 'We will do *everything* to support our men,' he insisted, 'but are not disposed to refuse peace if offered merely to support our Ministers.'[1] Gardiner could well appreciate his seemingly illogical distinction. Yet it was one that condemned such private initiatives to failure.

The intractability of the official party leadership forced Liberal dissentients into an increased reliance on President Wilson, and ultimately impelled many of them into the ranks of Labour. Of those who idolized the President, few had greater encouragement than Gardiner, who was given ample reason to believe that his admiration was warmly reciprocated. Presented with a copy of Gardiner's latest collection of essays, *The War Lords*, Wilson particularly savoured an anecdote about the Kaiser, who, after signing the declaration of war, 'suddenly flung the pen across the room, and looking up at the great military leaders assembled around him said: "there you've made me do it, and you are going to regret it for the rest of your lives"'. Wilson repeated the story to Henry Ford, who amusingly released it to the American press as a revelation from 'some high diplomatic authority'.[2] Gardiner, informed of the incident, defensively assured House that the report of the Kaiser's behaviour was 'as well authenticated as any statement of that sort can, in the present circumstances,

1. Loreburn to Burns, 26 July 1915, Burns Papers, Add. MSS 46,303, fols 171–2.
2. House to Gardiner, 6 October 1915, G.P. This was a reasonably faithful recapitulation of Gardiner's phraseology.

possibly be. It was told me by a member of the Government who, more than anyone else, is likely to be well-informed on the inner history of those thrilling days.' He looked forward to another meeting with House 'if not here while the war lasts, then in America when it is all over'.[1]

He did not have to wait long for the opportunity. The following February, the Colonel returned to London for another round of meetings with public figures. Inspired by the visit, as well as by the President's threat to break off relations with Germany if further American lives were lost 'through the sinking of an armed or unarmed passenger vessel by a German submarine', Gardiner undertook a stout defence of 'Mr Wilson's Policy'. Many Englishmen, members of the Government reportedly among them, had come to resent the President, whose moral strictures (no substitute for material assistance) seemed to imply an indifference to Britain's fate. Writing in the *Daily News* on 26 February, the day after House had sailed for home, Gardiner ascribed his countrymen's impatience with America to their failure to appreciate 'the enormous complexity of the American position'. The President, he explained, not only had to contend with congressional pressures, but also, to a far greater extent than any European statesman, had to satisfy a large and heterogeneous electorate. 'Through these tumultuous waters Mr Wilson has steered with a dexterity all the more admirable because it has never been the dexterity of the mere opportunist.' It was wrong for Englishmen to infer hostility on the part of the President, who, Gardiner consoled them, 'disappoints everyone in turn. He subjects himself to criticism from every quarter. . . . And in the midst of it all he pursues his purpose with an unflattering constancy that is indifferent of attack and careless of personal ambition.'

Gardiner sent House a cutting of his article, and diffidently expressed the hope that the envoy's return voyage had not been too much afflicted by the severe weather.[2] House, with the breezy informality that one would expect of a Texan, promptly responded with a letter of praise and gratitude. 'You have never written anything better,' he told the proud author, 'and that is saying much for, in my judgment,

1. Gardiner to House, 18 October 1915, House Papers (Yale University Library).
2. Gardiner to House, 27 February 1916, House Papers.

there is no English writer in your field comparable to you.' According to House, whose literary standards were obviously dictated by political strategy, Gardiner's eulogy of Wilson 'stirs one like an epic poem'. Gardiner received assurances that his piece 'will hearten the President on his difficult way. It's [*sic*] influence for good will be far reaching and in directions you little realize.'[1]

What exactly did House mean by his last cryptic remark? An astute tactician, he immediately recognized the advantages he could wring from Gardiner's contribution. His diary entry for 29 March describes a six o'clock 'executive session', after which Wilson and his colleagues retired to 'the sitting-room upstairs'. Comfortably settled, House asked Wilson

if he had read A. G. Gardiner's sketch of him in the London News which I had sent him about a week ago. I asked him to get it and read it aloud. When he finished, everybody commented upon the brilliancy with which Gardiner had written, and of the complimentary way in which he had brought forth the best features of the President's policy. The President smiled and said: 'I seem to see something of the Colonel's fine Italian hand in this article.'

House noted that Wilson was especially impressed and 'evidently stirred' by the tribute Gardiner had paid him for initiating a 'Pan-American Pact', designed to promote peaceful relations among the republics of the new world. 'As a matter of fact,' House recorded in his diary, 'Gardiner had merely repeated in this part of his article what I had told him, and had given my estimate of its [the Pact's] importance.'[2]

Although the subtleties of the situation probably escaped him, Gardiner had thus helped to strengthen House's hand in his contest with Robert Lansing, the traditionalist Secretary of State, who was cool to the idea of the Pact. But the resourceful Colonel had not yet exhausted the uses to which his English friend might be put. A copy

1. House to Gardiner, 15 March 1916 (copy), House Papers; the original has not been preserved among the Gardiner Papers.
2. House's diary, 29 March 1916, House Papers. House was perhaps too much inclined to claim credit, and historians have tended to take him at his word. (See, for example, L. W. Martin, *Peace Without Victory*, p. 104). Gardiner's covering letter does not sustain the interpretation that his column had been written at House's dictation.

of the *Daily News* column was sent to Ray Stannard Baker, a leading member of the 'informal brain trust of the Progressive movement', who had recently joined other intellectuals – including John Dewey, Jane Addams, Lincoln Steffens, Ida Tarbell, Max Eastman, and Walter Lippmann – in a migration to the Democratic Party.[1] Anxious to consolidate support among these influential converts, House pointed to Gardiner as an example of the high regard the President enjoyed among spokesmen for the British left. Baker read the cutting 'with great interest', and asked permission to 'retain it a little longer, in the hope that I may use some parts of it' in an article he was preparing to 'help in the coming campaign'.[2]

It would be a mistake, however, to presume that Gardiner's sympathies and talents were exploited. He was more than eager to render service, however indirectly, and trusted implicitly to House's discretion. On 27 May, in a major policy address at Washington to the League to Enforce Peace, the President pledged American power to the task of saving a Europe that was obviously incapable of saving itself. Gardiner cabled 'warm words' that were returned in kind. 'Yours is the most helpful voice that has yet come from across the Atlantic to cheer us on,' House wrote without too much exaggeration.[3] Lady Courtney, who noted that 'Wilson's speech . . . fills us with hope', nonetheless acknowledged that it 'was not well rec[eive]d here as a rule – jeered at'.[4] And Ratcliffe complained that British press opinion was, on the whole, 'simply beastly'.[5] Gardiner, who thought that the President had taken 'the only line of hope for the future of the world', was moved to 'regret that the response has not been more enthusiastic in some of the English journals; but I am confident', he told House, 'that as the idea is appreciated by the people there will be an overwhelming response'.[6]

Gardiner promptly dedicated himself to educating the British reading public so that Wilsonian ideals would command the wide acceptance they deserved. The President was not, of course, the sole

1. Hofstadter, *The Age of Reform*, pp. 154–8.
2. Baker to House, 8 April 1916, House Papers.
3. House to Gardiner, 29 May 1916, G.P.
4. Lady Courtney's diary, 13 June 1916, quoted in Swartz, *The Union of Democratic Control*, p. 132.
5. Ratcliffe to Graham Wallas, 31 May 1916, quoted in *ibid*.
6. Gardiner to House, 15 June 1916, House Papers.

repository of these ideals – indeed his 27 May 'speech might have been made by Sir Edward Grey'[1] – but by virtue of his background, his dignity, and his office, he eclipsed the others. It was therefore vital that he should win a second term in the November presidential election. On 16 June, as expected, Wilson's candidacy was endorsed by the Democratic Party convention at St Louis. The next day, no more surprisingly, Gardiner celebrated the event in the *Daily News*. A Wilsonian victory, he boldly asserted, would constitute nothing less than a mandate for a new world order. His lease on the White House renewed for a further four years, the President would be free to lead an international crusade 'to *change the purpose for which force is used*. It has been the instrument of war between nations: he will make it the instrument of peace to defend the community of nations.' Should Wilson lose, however, Europe would be left to

pursue the old path to ruin. The devil's engine of secret diplomacy will start weaving its webs on a new pattern, the old ambitions will take new forms, the despots will rearrange their alliances, the armaments ring will resume its international operations, the Press will be its corrupt instrument, the Parliaments will be left to play at democracy, the 'Morning Post,' Mr Maxse, and Lord Northcliffe, the Reventlows and the Bernhardis will clear out ashes of the fire that has devoured Europe and will heap up the fuel for a new sacrifice to the god they serve.

At the same time that Gardiner attempted to explain the President's motives to Englishmen, he communicated to Americans a better understanding of the British situation. Too often Washington officials relied uncritically on *The Times* as an index to British opinion on the war. Invited by the editor of the *Atlantic Monthly* 'to speak your mind with absolute frankness', Gardiner acquainted readers of that respected journal with *The Times*'s editorial biases, its proprietorial connections, and the alarming extent of its 'influence . . . upon public sentiment and, most especially, public men'.[2] Although there was no single American newspaper of comparable authority, the Americans had their share of press magnates, who lacked only a title before their names to complete their resemblance to Lord North-

1. House thought Gardiner was 'quite right' in this observation, 'for you and I both know that it expresses his views'. House to Gardiner, 29 May 1916, G.P.
2. Sedgwick to Gardiner, 21 August 1916, G.P. Gardiner's article, 'The Times', appeared in January: cxix (1917), 111–22.

cliffe, and who gave strong endorsement to the candidacy of Charles Evans Hughes, Wilson's Republican adversary. 'I think the President will win,' Colonel House instructed Gardiner mid-way through the campaign, 'but the reactionary forces have taken heart because of existing conditions, and here, as well as in England and elsewhere, they are striving for mastery under the cover of the great war.'[1]

No one on either side of the Atlantic could have been more delighted by Wilson's electoral success in November than Gardiner, who cabled a laconic message of 'Sincere congratulations and deep thankfulness'.[2] House 'greatly appreciate[d]' these few words, coming as they did from 'one of the few that realize what the President's re-election means. . . . The President's defeat would have heartened every imperialist here and abroad.' To assist Gardiner in interpreting the returns, House promised a map (which he somehow neglected to enclose) that showed 'the states which went for us and against us. It will doubtless interest you.' With questionable logic, he pointed out that:

A circle drawn within five hundred miles of Wall Street and another drawn within five miles of La Salle Street, Chicago, would practically cover every vote that went against us.

There has been some surprise expressed here and in Europe that those in charge of large business interests were against the President, since the country at this time is so prosperous. The answer I think is that for the first time in many years that element has no direction of government. They honestly believe that their property interests are so great that it entitled them to a hearing in the policies of the Government. They have resented the President's purpose to conduct the Government for the whole people rather than for the few.[3]

Even without reference to a map, Gardiner was sufficiently familiar with basic Tory attitudes – which did not vary considerably from one society to another – to appreciate the point that House was making. 'The facts you describe suggest a momentous fissure in the mind of the country,' he replied cautiously. 'I hope it is truly a fissure between the narrow idea of business interests and the greater ideal which the President stands for.' In any case, the contest had been won. 'Had it

1. House to Gardiner, 29 August 1916, G.P.
2. Gardiner to House, 10 November 1916 (cablegram), House Papers.
3. House to Gardiner, 13 November 1916, G.P.

gone otherwise,' Gardiner confided, 'I should have felt that the one visible hope in this sad world had been extinguished.'[1]

It is significant that Gardiner had settled on Wilson as 'the one visible hope' as early as 27 November, the day that he warned his *Daily News* readers of the 'dirty weather' that loomed over Westminster. Either he perceived that Asquith's long premiership would not survive, or, more probably, the Prime Minister had already forfeited too much credit to inspire further hope. Matters were only made worse by the substitution of Lloyd George, who, weeks earlier, had declared himself in favour of ending the war with a 'knock-out blow', and, making obvious reference to Wilson, had scorned 'outside interference'. His advent threatened a sharp break between British and American policy: 'the knock-out blow' *v.* 'peace without victory'. There was no doubt which alternative Gardiner and others of his persuasion found the more appealing. 'The whole fate of the world seems to me to depend on America,' Goldsworthy Lowes Dickinson, the Cambridge don, wrote to Arthur Ponsonby in a mood of bitter resignation.[2]

Lloyd George was not yet settled in office when he had his first brush with the 'outside interference' against which he had recently protested. On 18 December, Wilson addressed a note to the European belligerents, calling on them to define their war aims. His observation that the objectives of both sides were 'virtually the same' was taken to imply pro-German sympathies, and, as such, aroused the fierce indignation of Allied spokesmen and their American supporters. The situation was serious, although Colonel House surely exaggerated when he feared the possibility of war between the two English-speaking powers.[3] As the self-appointed guardian of the President's reputation,[4] Gardiner had all along maintained that Wilson's 'doctrine of neutrality', however strictly enforced, inevitably 'operated in our favour'.[5] Unwilling to acknowledge his hero's tactlessness,

1 Gardiner to House, 27 November 1916, G.P.

2. Dickinson to Ponsonby, 28 December [1916], quoted in Swartz, *The Union of Democratic Control*, p. 133.

3. Link, *Wilson: Campaigns for Progressivism and Peace, 1916–1917*, pp. 226–7.

4. Gardiner exchanged strong words with Owen Seaman, the editor of *Punch*, whom he took to task for publishing a 'chaff of Wilson'. Seaman defended the item as 'perfectly permissible'. Seaman to Gardiner, 22 November 1916, G.P.

5. 'America and the future', *Daily News*, 18 November 1916.

Gardiner insisted that Wilson's latest statement was being cynically misconstrued by those who sought to destroy the chances of a negotiated peace.

Late on the afternoon of the 21st, Gardiner was summoned by telephone to 10 Downing Street, where the new Prime Minister was that day taking up residence. Crossing the threshold, he met Sir Maurice Bonham Carter, Asquith's private secretary and son-in-law, who was 'clearing up'. Bonham Carter confirmed the story that Lloyd George had invited him to stay on: 'And I really think he meant it, . . . though how he cd. mean it . . . is beyond me.' Gardiner was less happy to see Sir George Riddell, who was dictating memoranda for his chief on the mining dispute, and who noted that the caller 'looked worn. All his ideals have been shattered.'

After a short wait, Gardiner was shown into the Cabinet room, where the Prime Minister was alone. 'I had not seen him since my open letter to him the previous Easter, & his attack on me at Wrexham [it was in fact Conway], where he called me "an assassin".' Gardiner found his host 'extremely agreeable', and as generous with his cigars as before. After an exchange of pleasantries, Lloyd George 'sat down before a document at the table', and spoke his mind:

P.M.: Well, a note addressed to all the belligerents has just come from President Wilson. It is very bad. It is a pro-German declaration.

MYSELF: I am sorry to hear that.

P.M.: Judge for yourself. Listen to this. (He then read the sentence in which the President sd. it seemed to him that the objects of both sides were the same, judging from the public statements of the statesmen of the various countries to their own people & the world.) That is a declaration that there is no difference between us.

MYSELF: I don't think so. It seems to me a natural inquiry. He is a neutral addressing both sides. So far as public professions are concerned, he finds no difference in them. He asks for a formal declaration to clear up the issue in his own mind & in the mind of his people who are directly involved & may any day have to intervene in the War.

P.M.: No, no. It is an unfriendly note, calculated to help Germany.

MYSELF: It is not an expression of opinion at all. It is an abstract inquiry. He is speaking not of his own view, but of the views put forward publicly by the belligerents. Will you read the sentence again? (He did so). Surely the meaning is quite clear. If you will transpose the last clause to the front of the sentence it may emphasize the meaning, but it will not change it.

P.M.: Well, I hope you will not support an appeal worked in these terms.

MYSELF: I am not anxious for a quarrel with America.

P.M.: Certainly not. Certainly not. But don't support this.

MYSELF: I shall certainly bear in mind what you have said when I write on the subject tonight. But may I, since you approached me from this aspect of the matter, make a suggestion from another point of view?

P.M.: Certainly.

MYSELF: I do not credit your reading of that passage, but I know that there are newspapers in London which will use it for offensive attacks on America. I think you ought to warn them against unnecessary & provocative language.

P.M.: I will do that. But don't support this.

Shortly after Gardiner had returned to Bouverie Street, he was handed 'a message . . . from the Press Bureau requesting editors in their comments on the American note to avoid personal attacks on the President'. His own leader, which appeared the following morning, stopped short of an outright endorsement of Wilson's efforts, but expressed confidence that the note would receive 'respectful attention' from all concerned. After all, the President, as he himself put it, was 'merely "taking soundings"'. To Gardiner's consternation, most other newspapers – and particularly the *Daily Chronicle* – were sharply critical, presumably as a result of having been incited by the Press Bureau communiqué. 'How many editors', he wondered uneasily, 'did Mr Lloyd George speak to that evening in the tones he employed to me?'[1]

Despite the relative cordiality of their meeting, mutual suspicions lingered between Gardiner and Lloyd George. On Christmas day, the

1. The above account of Gardiner's 21 December interview with Lloyd George is based primarily on Gardiner's memorandum, apparently written soon after the event, and preserved among the Gardiner Papers; also that day's entry in Lord Riddell's *War Diary*, p. 233. President Wilson asked Gardiner, when they met at the Peace Conference early in 1919, 'how his Note could have been so "widely misread"'. Gardiner 'was not able to tell him', but two years later promised 'to throw some light on this interesting theme' if Lloyd George granted 'permission to publish my record of my conversation with him . . . on December 21, 1916'. Permission was apparently not forthcoming. Gardiner's letter to the editor of the *Nation*, 12 March 1921.

Prime Minister repeated to Riddell the story that Gardiner had tried to persuade Robert Donald of the *Chronicle* 'to join him in urging discussion of peace terms', but that Donald was too 'sound on the war', and furthermore had a French wife who brooked no nonsense. [1] Yet, for all his derision, Lloyd George would have been glad had he been able to inaugurate his premiership with Gardiner back in his corner. According to Arnold Bennett, whose source was probably Gardiner himself, T. P. O'Connor had brought the editor of the *Daily News* 'a piece of information' which he had heard with his own ears: 'The other day Ll. George spoke of you in very friendly terms. He said you were not like the rest. Your difference of opinion was honest and he respected it. Yes, he spoke in the kindliest terms of you.' Shortly thereafter, Gardiner was approached at the National Liberal Club by 'another henchman of Ll. G.', who divulged that he, too, had 'heard Ll. George speak of you in the very friendliest terms the other day'. [2] But Gardiner knew too well the secrets of the Welshman's wizardry to be beguiled.

Although he ignored the overtures he received from Downing Street, Gardiner urged the Government to respond to those that came from Berlin. On 30 December, his 'new year' column took stock of the situation: 'We are all plunging down a steep place together, but Germany is ahead and has a nearer vision of the abyss.' What time could be more propitious for opening negotiations? Others disagreed. The *Morning Post* denounced his proposal in 'a column of rancorous misrepresentation', [3] while *The Times*, more ingeniously, sought to discredit him by describing the 'immense amount of space' that the *Frankfurter Zeitung* and other German papers had appreciatively devoted to 'quotations' from his column. [4] Irritated, but undeterred, he consoled himself with the thought that the right-wing press treated him no more outrageously than it treated the President, whom it had 'virulently assailed' on the basis of a 'deliberate mutilation of his text'. It would have been bad enough, he reasoned on

1. Entry for 25 December 1916, Riddell, *War Diary*, p. 233.
2. Entry for 4 January 1917, *The Journals of Arnold Bennett*, ii, 182.
3. The phrase is Gardiner's. 'The loan and the letter', *Daily News*, 13 January 1917. He referred to a leader, '"Before the cock crew twice"', in the 1 January *Morning Post*.
4. *The Times*, 6 January 1917.

13 January, 'if the misreading had been due to mere incapacity to understand English. . . . But it was something worse than ignorance: it was sheer incendiarism.'

Although the Allied reply to Wilson's note of 18 December was not notable for its magnanimity, the German response was by far the more intransigent. Gardiner was disappointed by both sides, but, like the President, he did not desist. On 22 January, in a speech before the United States Senate, Wilson renewed his call for a 'peace without victory' to be maintained by a League of Nations. Once again, he was hailed as a saviour by idealists at home and abroad, much to the distaste of Theodore Roosevelt, who blustered that the present occupant of the White House 'had become a rallying point for all the pacifists, cowards, and short-sighted fools which had plagued him since the war began'.[1] Gardiner, whom Roosevelt would probably have classified in all three categories, defended Wilson's right to assume an active part in European affairs. Writing in the *Daily News* on 27 January, he gave a Cassandra-like prophesy of what to expect if the President, his advice spurned, turned his back on the old world: 'Left to itself', Europe would 'return to its vomit, . . . and there will be a new struggle for that impossible thing, "the balance of power"'. Before long, there would follow 'another and far worse collapse into the horrors of war'. To whom would Britain then turn for support? 'We might, a generation hence, find Germany, Russia, and Japan with hands clasped across the hemisphere, joined together in a league against freedom, Imperialism running roughshod over the universal earth.' The prospect, too horrible to contemplate, was not too horrible to occur.

Recognizing the fact that, one way or another, America would determine both the length of the war and, ultimately, the shape of the peace, Gardiner watched events across the Atlantic with grave apprehension. Everything depended, he knew, on the President's maintaining a strong position. Lord Bryce, a justly respected authority, counselled a guarded silence: 'It is easy to do harm when things are in so critical a state as public opinion now is in the U.S.A.'[2] A more immediate appraisal came from Ellery Sedgwick, whose Boston

1. Quoted in Osgood, *Ideals and Self-Interest in America's Foreign Relations*, p. 150.
2. Bryce to Gardiner, 6 February 1917, G.P.

office had become an intellectual headquarters for intervention: 'This month is our August, 1914', he declared on 3 February:

If there is a division of opinion in this country, it has not yet come to the surface, and, thus far, the only plea for delay has come from a small band of radical peace men for whose sympathies I have great regard, but whose wisdom is generally distrusted. Undoubtedly, through the great inner reaches of the country, there is an immense reluctance, and, indeed, four Americans out of five are deeply, bitterly regretful of the Instant necessities of the case, but, God help us, we cannot otherwise.

Unlike Bryce, Sedgwick thought that Gardiner might make a positive contribution, and asked him to provide the *Atlantic Monthly* with 'a hands-across-the-water piece' that would have the virtue of 'coming from a radical liberal of the Bright school who understands America and does not make the familiar gibe of poltroonery against a people passionately devoted to peace'.[1]

Sedgwick, however, had misread the signs: America did not experience her 'August 1914' until April, when Germany's resumption of unrestricted submarine warfare and the incident of the Zimmermann telegram brought her into the war. In the meantime, Gardiner was among those who won Colonel House's further gratitude by 'maintain[ing] their equilibrium under such trying conditions'.[2] In part, Gardiner's restraint was due to the fact that he was diverted by other business, new and old. It was not long before he was once more embroiled in controversy with Lloyd George, who paid tribute to Sir Albert Stanley (later Baron Ashfield) for arranging the efficient transfer of railway equipment ('rolling stock') to the army in France. The *Daily News* (6 February) remonstrated that it was Walter Runciman, Stanley's predecessor at the Board of Trade, who deserved the credit. Assured by Runciman that this was the case, Gardiner refused the request of Lloyd George's press secretary to retract the leader that Wilson Harris had written at his dictation.[3]

1. Sedgwick to Gardiner, 3 February 1917, G.P. Such an article never appeared, although the March number contained Gardiner's anonymous account of 'Lloyd George and the coup d'état'. *Atlantic Monthly*, cxix (1917), 392–401.
2. House to William H. Buckler, an official at the American Embassy in London, 25 February 1917, quoted in Martin, *Peace Without Victory*, p. 129.
3. Sutherland to Gardiner, 7 February 1917, G.P.; also Harris, *Life So Far*, pp. 109–10.

In all probability, few readers of the paper discerned that Gardiner, by upholding Runciman's claims, was implicitly calling into question the Prime Minister's veracity. But it would have been difficult to mistake his attacks upon Northcliffe, which were brutally explicit. On 13 February a leader ('The idiot boy') assailed 'the thugs of Carmelite House', who, 'having destroyed one Government by the daily chorus of "Wait and see"', now appear determined to destroy another: 'Lord Northcliffe's affections rarely survive two months and we are not surprised to hear that he has already nominated a new Cabinet.' The dose was too strong for Edward Cadbury, who, identifying himself as one who 'always deprecated bitterness in controversy', informed his editor that 'this seems to me to overstep that mark'.[1]

That Northcliffe's name henceforth appeared less prominently in the columns of the *Daily News* owed little, if anything, to proprietorial injunctions. One possible explanation is that Gardiner was soon taken ill to the extent that, for three weeks, he was forced to discontinue his 'Alpha' column in the *Star*; he resumed on 22 March, having survived 'one of those chastening experiences which reveal to us how unimportant we are to the world'. But, more obviously the case was that he had been distracted from domestic affairs by the momentous events that had begun to occur in Russia, where 'the spirit of liberty' had at last awakened. On 24 February he could not resist pointing to the cruel irony that 'the principle of democracy and constitutionalism' which, in the west, was 'being triumphantly trodden in the mire', had taken root in the unlikely soil of Holy Russia. As the weeks passed, he grew more enthusiastic, even lyrical. 'There is spring in the air and there is spring in the souls of men', he proclaimed on March 17. 'Not since the Bastille fell has there been an event so full of splendid magnificence for men as the mighty happenings of this week in Petrograd. Russia is free.' For the sake of the alliance, he had had to mute his criticisms of the Tsarist regime;[2]

1. Edward Cadbury to Gardiner, 14 Feburary 1917, G.P.
2. On 6 March 1916, as president of the Press Institute, Gardiner chaired a meeting attended by visiting Russian newspapermen, whom he welcomed 'not merely as journalists, but . . . [as] unofficial ambassadors of a people with whom we are sharing in a common tribulation and a common glory. We have been separated from that people in the past by many things – by the hard, solid facts of geography, by the difficulties of an extremely obstinate language, and, to

now he could embrace Russia as a full-fledged partner in the coalition against autocracy. Her chains broken, Russia might be expected to realize her immense potential as a fighting power. Best of all, 'the example of Russia' was sure to prove 'irresistible' to the people of Germany.

Gardiner was not by any means the only one to be deceived by the initial promise of the Russian Revolution. Prince Kropotkin, a distinguished exile from Tsardom, received telegrams from his homeland that were 'full of hope'. He lauded Gardiner for having 'so admirably understood and interpreted the last changes in Russia. Yes,' he concurred, 'our country has now a great future before it, especially if the force for evil-doing in Germany and Austria is curtailed. You know, of course, what evil influences these two members of the 'Holy Alliance' and the Union of the Three Emperors have had throughout the 19th century in Russia.'[1]

As Russia's Provisional Government revealed its incapacity to revive that country's flagging war effort, it lost whatever support it may have had from the British right. Lord Alfred Douglas abused Gardiner in the most scurrilous terms for all the 'howling and whooping for the "glorious Russian Revolution"' that went on in the pages of the *Daily News*.[2] But Gardiner paid no heed to men of that disposition. He continued to celebrate at length the changes that had brought Russia into 'spiritual accord with her Allies' (5 May), particularly the overthrow of the Tsar, which he hailed (appropriately enough on 14 July) as a sure indication that 'the victory that is shaping itself is the victory we want and not the victory we feared'. The revolution, by changing the government of Russia, had consequently 'changed the character of the war from a war of nations to a war of an Idea'. It had become 'a People's War of Deliverance', and, as such, it was worthy of President Wilson himself.

---

some extent, by our insular habit of thought': *Daily Telegraph*, 7 March 1916. More typical of his attitude was his *Daily News* column of 8 November 1915, in which he condemned the Russian 'Government whose record is a blot on humanity and civilisation'.

1. Kropotkin to Gardiner, 22 March 1917, G.P. Kropotkin also wrote to Gardiner about Russian affairs on 28 Feburary and 6 June.
2. Douglas to Gardiner, 8 May and 25 July 1917, G.P.

On 6 April the United States entered the war as an 'associate' of the Allies. This 'happiest event', which seemed to Gardiner to exceed even the Russian Revolution in historic significance, was commemorated a fortnight later by a service at St Paul's. The Union Jack and the Stars and Stripes flew side by side in London streets, and the strains of the 'Battle Hymn of the Republic' echoed through the Cathedral, where spectators witnessed 'the King and the American Ambassador kneeling together in thanksgiving for the union of the two peoples in the task of emancipating the world from tyranny'. Gardiner, who captured the scene in his column on the 21st, was moved to lament the day that these two products of a common heritage had broken apart. The culprit, he recalled, was 'an obstinate King, trained in German ideas of kingship', and the issue at stake in 1776 was essentially 'the same issue as that of to-day – not an issue between this people and that, between the English and the Americans, but a collision between two systems of human governance, despotism and liberty'.

Not only was the struggle for liberty still being waged, but the British Cabinet was again a stronghold of reaction. There sat Carson and Milner, two self-acknowledged foes of the democratic order whose views on the prosecution of the war were assumed to be extreme.[1] In mid-April, when the German submarine threat was causing widespread anxiety, the Newspaper Proprietors Association issued an appeal to editors to 'take prudent and tactful steps with the object of explaining the position to the public'.[2] Gardiner responded on the 28th with a series of attacks on Carson's performance at the Admiralty, surely not what the author of the directive, Sir George Riddell, had had in mind. 'It may be that no one could have done better than Sir Edward Carson,' Gardiner conceded. 'I do not know. But no one could have done worse. . . . The regime must be changed – changed radically, changed at once.' Milner, in turn, was the recipient of an open letter on 12 May. Addressed as 'the most lonely and the most unrepresentative man in English public life', he was unkindly reminded that he enjoyed office only as 'the idol of the

---

1. On 17 October 1918, in an *Evening Standard* interview, Milner declared himself in favour of a negotiated peace, and thereby won the support of the *Daily News* and the enmity of Northcliffe. See Gollin, *Proconsul in Politics*, pp. 571–2.
2. Circular letter, signed and addressed by Riddell, 13 April 1917, G.P.

"Times" and the "Morning Post"' of whom the Prime Minister was 'the humble instrument'. Gardiner, sufficiently emotional to split an infinitive, begged Milner 'to avoid using your position to permanently Prussianise our life'.

There is no indication that Gardiner's outbursts had any adverse effect on circulation, which, to the enormous satisfaction of George Cadbury, grew at this time to 'be the largest of any newspaper in the Kingdom. May we use the influence that this gives us', he devoutly prayed, 'on behalf of suffering humanity here and abroad.' The man of faith was also a keen man of business, who, hoped to live long enough to see the *Daily News* sell a million copies a day: 'There is something far more impressive in reaching this figure than anything less,' he told Gardiner, 'and it is the chance of our lives of increasing the London sale, which is probably double the value of sales in the country from an advertising point of view.' Gardiner's elderly employer did not mind harsh words about Carson, so long as the *Daily News* 'dealt tenderly with Lloyd George, who has done much for the country by his finance bills and in other ways, and I do earnestly hope he may not be led astray, as Joseph Chamberlain was'.[1] But if the Prime Minister was shown any tenderness he was the last to suspect it. Resentful as much for his own sake as for that of his colleagues, he fulminated to a party of breakfast guests that 'Nobody cared what the "Daily News" and the "Nation" said, because they made it their business to find fault'.[2] That neither half of this statement was true, was proved by the fact that Dr Christopher Addison, who was present on the occasion, soon wrote to Gardiner to thank him 'for your kind reference to myself in the D.N. . . . It is some comfort to find a friendly word in these days of storm.'[3]

The spring and summer months of 1917 brought further incidents that demonstrated to Gardiner the diverse ways in which the war perverted opinion and debilitated institutions. 'Since April 1915, we have seen the Parliamentary system in this country thoroughly undermined,' he told his readers on 16 June. 'When Mr Lloyd

1. George Cadbury to Gardiner, 17 April 1917, G.P.
2. Scott's memorandum for 30 April–4 May 1917, Scott Papers, Add. MSS 50, 904, fols 7–8.
3. Addison to Gardiner, 23 May 1917, G.P. Addison wrote again in the same vein on 30 June 1917 and 8 April 1918.

George and Lord Northcliffe entered into partnership for the over-throw, first of the Liberal Government, then of the Coalition Government, they, consciously or unconsciously, embarked on a challenge to the Constitution.' It was only to be expected that others, trade unionists and Irishmen in particular, would follow in their wayward footsteps. Arnold Bennett, not an easy man to please, considered A.G.G.'s 16 June column 'the best political article of yours I have seen'.[1]

Was the Lloyd George–Northcliffe alliance a figment of Gardiner's tortured imagination, or perhaps a self-fulfilling prophecy? We learn from Lord Beaverbrook that although 'Lord Northcliffe influenced the course of politics profoundly', it was 'always from the outside'. True, perhaps; but Beaverbrook proceeds to acknowledge that, more than once, Northcliffe refused the offer of Cabinet appointment.[2] Even more frightening than the threat of Northcliffe's elevation to ministerial rank, was his being sent to the United States as head of the British war mission. What could have been a more calculated insult to President Wilson? There were fears in June 1917 that North-cliffe had been dispatched to America to supplant Balfour, and it was believed that the *coup* would have taken place had not embarrassing questions been asked.[3]

Recalling the happier days when Northcliffe had been confined to Fleet Street, where, to be sure, he was sufficiently a menace, Gardiner spoke with lingering nostalgia of Asquith, who, 'in the face of un-precedented difficulties and shameless slander, sought to bring us through'. With scant justification,[4] his 23 June column contrasted the present Government's stringent policies regarding conscientious objection with the Asquith Government's enlightened attitudes. And on 28 July Gardiner seconded Asquith's call for 'a re-statement of our aims in the light of the revolution in Russia and the advent of the United States'. If nothing else, Asquith could be depended on to subscribe with greater conviction than Lloyd George to the cardinal tenets of Wilsonian belief. Could a man who kept company with the

1. Bennett to Gardiner, 16 June 1917, G.P.
2. *Politicians and the Press*, pp. 15–16, 46–7.
3. Lord Buckmaster to Gardiner, 14 and 21 June 1917, G.P. Also see Taylor, *Beaverbrook*, p. 131.
4. John Rae effectively makes this point in *Conscience and Politics*.

likes of Milner, Curzon, and Carson, Gardiner asked on 27 October, be trusted 'to make the world safe for democracy'?

Although it is unlikely that Gardiner received direct encouragement at this time from the former premier, he was in close communication with Runciman and McKenna, Asquith's two principal lieutenants in the House of Commons, who fed him arguments and statistical information. [1] At the same time, he had his contacts in the other camp, chief among them being J. J. Mallon, his old friend and future son-in-law. Mallon was a charter member of 'The Family', a band of academics and civil servants who clustered around Lloyd George and who worked to infuse public administration with 'a new spirit'. [2] He was also a member of the Whitley Committee, whose report in June 1917 recommended the establishment of 'Standing Industrial Councils'. Gardiner received the Whitley proposals with enthusiasm. Industrial relations, he wrote on the 30th, required, much like international relations, a new 'machinery' to foster cooperation instead of conflict. As the war entered its fourth year, he began to profess more advanced social views, often quite antithetical to the Asquithian tradition. His reading of the Hammonds' *Town Labourer* inspired his column on 1 September:

> There has been no such social upheaval in our land since the Black Death swept it six centuries ago, and by creating a labour famine, broke the back of feudalism, and made the bond man free. This is the second Black Death and its consequences will be hardly less fateful than those of the first. That liberated the man from personal slavery; this, we may hope, will emancipate him from the slavery of the economic machine.

Severely critical of 'Mr Lloyd George's experiment in changing the mechanism of politics in this country', [3] Gardiner nonetheless lent an approbatory ear to suggestions for 'a new political formation' that would fuse the parties of the left. He had supported similar efforts before the war, but always with the hope that Lloyd George would lead such a progressive alliance. Now, however, Lloyd George was

1. Runciman to Gardiner, 28 and 30 July 1917; also McKenna to Gardiner, 29 and 30 October 1917, G.P.
2. Thomas Jones reported in his diary on 7 December 1916 that Mallon, like R. H. Tawney, 'had been agin Asquith continuing' in the premiership: *Whitehall Diary*, i, 8; see also pp. 2, 17n, and 21.
3. 'The revolt against Mr Churchill', *Daily News*, 21 July 1917.

the captive of the Tories, and a Radical–Labour coalition was designed as a weapon against him. According to Thomas Jones, a participant in the discussions, Mallon was deputed by his colleagues – among them G. D. H. Cole, R. H. Tawney, Arthur Henderson, and Arthur Greenwood – 'to find out how far the "Daily News" would support the new Party'. Gardiner complied with a column on 8 September ('How to pay for the War') in which the members of 'The Family' were pleased to detect 'traces of Sidney Webb'.[1] Some of his older friends were uneasy with the line he was taking. 'I expect you are right about the levy on capital,' Gilbert Murray advised him, 'though I am rather afraid of the enforced mortgages.'[2]

Others, who shared his eagerness for an accommodation with Labour, gave him warm support. 'I confess that I don't quite see where the old-fashioned Liberal Party is going to find itself,' Sir A. H. D. Acland, a past president of the National Liberal Federation, wrote after he had read Gardiner's 13 October column. 'I only hope the attitude of the capitalist Liberals towards Labour is going to be different from what it has been in the past.'[3] Walter Runciman, who toured the provinces in an attempt to revive the National League of Young Liberals, found 'the remaining members' of that organization 'most anxious' to meet Gardiner.[4]

It is difficult to credit the story, told by Lord Fisher to Lord Ranksborough on 2 September, that Gardiner – 'THE ABLEST LIVING JOURNALIST' – had recently 'been tête-à-tête' with Lloyd George, whom he was 'very sad' to find 'in a tight place, and in the complete grip of the Tories'.[5] As there is no other reference to such an interview, one must presume that the excitable Fisher got his dates wrong. Not that this assessment fails to do justice to Lloyd George's position at the time. Always scrupulously attentive to newspaper opinion – Lloyd George, Beaverbrook knowingly explained, 'likes a good Press

1. Entry for 10 September 1917, Jones, *Whitehall Diary*, i, 36–8.
2. Murray to Gardiner, 20 September 1917, G.P. 'Personally,' Reginald McKenna subsequently revealed to Gardiner, 'I am opposed to a capital levy; first, on the ground that it is impracticable and, secondly, that any attempt can only be made at the expense of the subscribers to War Loan in comparison with holders of other property.' McKenna to Gardiner, 16 January 1918, G.P.
3. Acland to Gardiner [October 1917], G.P.
4. Runciman to Gardiner, 22 October 1917, G.P.
5. Quoted in Marder, *Fear God and Dread Nought*, iii, 479.

as a shopkeeper likes a good customer'[1] – he was alarmed by the criticism he was then encountering. In particular, he was incensed by a 'gross attack' that appeared in the *Star*, the *Daily News*'s sister paper, which he ascribed to 'a violent and irrational spirit of personal bitterness' that had previously victimized Haldane and Churchill.[2] On its own, the *Star* was not worth the worry, but it soon enlisted an improbable ally in the person of Lord Rothermere, Northcliffe's younger brother and a press magnate in his own right. That autumn, Rothermere's assorted properties – most conspicuously the *Sunday Pictorial* – unleashed an offensive against the Prime Minister that did not abate until November, when Rothermere was named President of the Air Council.

Like the *Nation*, which the Government punished by proscribing its overseas sales, the *Daily News* remained a constant critic, sometimes at the price of condemning the good with the bad. Lloyd George's 12 November speech in Paris, a more than justified rebuke to British generalship, was torn to shreds in a leader on the 14th (unmistakably Gardiner's work) and again in A.G.G.'s Saturday column on the 17th. Geoffrey Dawson (formerly Robinson) was

roused . . . to maintain that the 'Times' [which he edited], the 'Telegraph,' and the 'Morning Post,' and possibly the 'Chronicle' were scrupulously careful to give the news honestly and in due proportion which is more than . . . can be said of the 'Daily News,' which . . . published the P.M.'s Paris speech and completely distorted it.[3]

Gardiner would have expected precisely such a response from Dawson, whom he contemptuously dismissed as Northcliffe's hireling, and whose editorship of *The Times* in the late 'thirties he was to regard as a national disgrace. Those who subscribed to Gardiner's views were, predictably, more complimentary. 'Loulou' Harcourt, for example, deprecated the Paris speech as an 'International Limehouse', and wrote to congratulate Gardiner upon his 'splendid articles on Ll.G. I suppose the man is mad with megalomania.'[4] More than a

1. *Politicians and the Press*, p. 108.
2. Scott's memorandum of 26–28 September 1917, Scott Papers, Add. MSS 50, 904, fol. 139.
3. Entry for 16 November 1917, Jones, *Whitehall Diary*, i, 39. Punctuation has been altered for intelligibility.
4. Harcourt to Gardiner, 18 November 1917, G.P.

month later, the Prime Minister continued to recall the episode with undiminished bitterness. There had been 'a conspiracy to defeat him on his Paris speech', he whined to Scott.

'It was an unholy alliance of the Generals' press and the partizan Liberals. . . . The "Daily News" & "Nation" joined hands with the "Morning Post" & "Spectator" in denouncing him for interfering with the soldiers, & very nearly succeeded in upsetting him.'[1]

Friends tried to temper Gardiner's wrath. 'Do *please* not mix up any Northcliffe–L.G. intrigue against the army with the great and enormously necessary reform that has just taken place in the Admiralty,' begged A. M. Pollen, the distinguished naval correspondent. 'You don't strengthen the very strong case . . . against assassination by Press clamour when you confuse it with an administrative reform brought about by constructive criticism.'[2] But A.G.G., unwilling to credit the Coalition with any saving graces, went so far as to hold it responsible for the November revolution in Russia that brought the Bolsheviks to power.[3] The Tory-dominated Government had denied the Kerensky regime 'moral help' in its struggle against 'the awful conditions which the Tsar had left behind'. Britain, to her shame and detriment, had thereby 'helped to make the Extremists triumphant in Russia as we have made the Sinn Fein cause a power in Ireland'. Writing on 10 November, Gardiner refused to concede that the situation was lost. With 'a great gesture from the Allies', Russia might still be saved from her 'wild men'. Successive weeks of 'enormous agonies and vast blunders' failed to shake him and the new year (5 January 1918) found him deeply moved by 'a spiritual splendour that blots out the follies and mitigates the crimes'. By this time, most Liberals had lost patience with the Russians, especially after the betrayal of Allied unity at Brest-Litovsk. 'The Russian Revolution with wh[ich] we were all so

1. Scott's memoranda of 16 and 27–28 December 1917, Scott Papers, Add. MSS 50, 904, fols 193–4, 225.
2. Pollen to Gardiner, 23 January 1918 (copy, courtesy of Mr J. A. Pollen).
3. 'Plain thoughts about Russia', *Daily News*, 15 September 1917. Gardiner was later proud to recall that Arthur Ransome of the *Daily News* was among the very few English correspondents in Russia to have 'supported the Revolution with unequivocal enthusiasm'. 'Mr Henderson and the Labor Movement', *Atlantic Monthly*, cxxii (1918), 224.

enchanted is turning out *very* badly alas,' Margot Asquith wrote haughtily to Gardiner, whom she reproved for paying too much regard to popular movements. 'Don't let us be fools. Look at our democracy & the way it *loves* Bottomley, Dalziel, Northcliffe, etc.'[1]

At very least, Gardiner owed a debt of gratitude to the Bolsheviks for publishing the secret treaties which had been filed away in Tsarist archives. Here was a stinging indictment of old-fashioned diplomacy and a fillip to a negotiated peace. It was surely no accident that a week later, on 29 November, the Lansdowne Letter appeared in the *Daily Telegraph.*

Lord Lansdowne was a ranking member of the Tory establishment, who, as Foreign Secretary, had negotiated the terms of the 1904 Anglo–French Entente. His appeal against futile prolongation of the war therefore carried no small measure of authority, despite the fact that *The Times* (which exluded it from its correspondence columns) 'believed it to reflect no responsible phase of British opinion'.[2] Most Tory journals were critical, some less politely than others, while Liberal reactions ranged from sceptical to wildly enthusiastic. Bennett, after 'having . . . reflected upon Lansdowne's letter & refreshed myself at the morning fountains of wisdom', sent Gardiner a detailed critique of the document, which he welcomed 'as a turning point in the expression of public opinion', but about which he had serious doubts 'as an actuality'. It was, he concluded, 'absolutely incredible' to suppose that Germany, 'if only she were properly approached, . . . would make an Allied peace or anything like an Allied peace now or soon'.[3] Gardiner, although he grasped this essential point, nonetheless hailed the Lansdowne letter as 'a torch in the darkness. I see', he remarked on 1 December,

that the 'Daily Mail' talks of it as a 'White Flag', that the 'Morning Post' denounces it as a surrender cloaked in the camouflage of hypocrisy, that the 'Daily Chronicle,' whose indictment of President Wilson a year ago on the occasion of his appeal to the belligerents to state what they were looking for still lives in the memory as one of the most reckless utterances of the war, now looks to the President to rebuke Lord Lansdowne (and himself), that the 'Globe' is seized with a fit of apoplexy (no uncommon thing), that

1. Margot Asquith to Gardiner [n.d.], G.P.
2. 30 November 1917.
3. Bennett to Gardiner, 30 November 1917, G.P.

the 'Daily Telegraph,' the 'Evening Standard,' the 'Manchester Guardian' cordially endorse the Lansdowne policy, in some cases with reservations on a single point, that the expression of Parliamentary opinion in the lobby is markedly favourable – that, in short, the cleavage between reason and unreason follows the lines that we might have anticipated.

Various Liberals, some new to the peace movement, searched desperately for ways to take advantage of this unique opportunity. Lord Buckmaster, a recent Lord Chancellor, requested 'to be allowed to use the Liberal Agencies for the purpose of circulating Lord Lansdowne's letter,' and met with 'a blank and rather curt refusal' from the party whip. He thereupon turned to Gardiner. 'Your support is absolutely invaluable,' Buckmaster affirmed:

> You have been engaged in your life in promoting many great causes, and you have suffered for your courage; but you have never put your hand to any task more noble and more difficult than the one you have now undertaken, and I do not envy the man with Liberal traditions in his blood who does not desire to stand by your side. [1]

Of the former ministers whom Buckmaster wished to bring down off the fence, none would have had greater impact than Grey. But, as usual, none proved more elusive. 'I agree about Grey,' Runciman told Gardiner on 5 December, 'and I wrote to him strongly yesterday & again today urging him to give tongue this week. He will probably write something now; & it will be, as you surmise, along the Lansdowne lines.' Meanwhile, Runciman settled back to wait for Asquith's scheduled address at Birmingham on the 11th. 'I *hope* Asquith will be definite enough . . .,' he declared, obviously none too sure, 'for the time has come when the dividing line is clear: *fight until the Germans surrender* (the usual expression is "Smash the brutes") on one side, and *fight until our 1914 aims are secured*, on the other.' [2] A week later, Asquith acquitted himself by blandly suggesting that Lansdowne had intended nothing more than to elicit a clarification of war aims. [3] Arnold Bennett, expecting as much, had written his weekly

---

1. Buckmaster to Gardiner, 2 December 1917, G.P.
2. Runciman to Gardiner, 5 December 1917, G.P. Grey's reaction to the Lansdowne letter was (in the words of his latest biographer) 'very guarded'; he replied to Runciman that he had no wish 'to get sucked into the whirlpool again': Robbins, *Sir Edward Grey*, p. 347.
3. H. H. Asquith, *A Clean Peace and National Reconstruction*.

column the day before instead of waiting to hear what Asquith had to say. More to his satisfaction was the fact that Rothermere's *Sunday Pictorial* 'sent me a long wire asking me to write an article defending Lansdowne's letter in its quality as an antidote to the "knock-out blow" speechifying business. I have written on war topics for the S.P. before,' he reminded Gardiner, 'but this is the first time they they have asked me to write on war politics, & I hope you agree with me in regarding it as a distinct sign of grace – especially after my last D.N. article.'[1]

The response to his columns – John Masefield praised them as 'splendid, calm, just & wise'[2] – was a source of encouragement to Gardiner; evidence of Lloyd George's acute discomfort was another. 'The "Thugs" were after *him* now,' he boasted to Bennett, whom he told the not improbable story that the Spanish press, which had lately quoted at length from his attacks on the Prime Minister, was officially informed by the British embassy in Madrid that the *Daily News* 'was pro-German and represented nothing in England, etc.!'[3] Of course, Lloyd George had more to fear than the effect of Gardiner's rhetoric upon Spanish opinion. To Scott, who defended the merits of Lansdowne's letter, he protested 'that one difficulty of stating our terms was the hostile attitude of the Opposition always lying in wait for an opportunity to upset him. And, he added, the other day . . . they came very near.'[4] Anxious to protect himself on every flank, he lunched privately with Asquith on 3 January and joined Asquith and Grey for breakfast two days later. 'My husband said he was amazed at Ll.G.'s deferential manner to him!' Margot reported to Gardiner. 'It is quite clear Ll.G.'s violent curve is to escape from his lot & regain ours. This was certain to happen: I betted on its coming sooner.'[5] Gardiner would have been far more impressed had he

1. Bennett to Gardiner, 6 December 1917, G.P.
2. Masefield to Gardiner, 15 December 1917, G.P.
3. Entry for 19 December 1917, *Journals of Arnold Bennett*, ii, 210.
4. Scott's memorandum of 16 December 1917, Scott Papers, Add. MSS 50, 904, fols 193–4.
5. 'Don't fail to let the political world know that Ll.G. went to *my* husband – Asquith did not go to 10 Downing St.', Margot implored. Margot Asquith to Gardiner, 7 January 1918, G.P. Runciman confirmed that 'LG & co.' were conducting 'secret conversations . . . with some other folk whom they wish to draw into responsibility': Runciman to Gardiner, 7 January 1918, G.P.

known that Lloyd George, at a Cabinet meeting on the 11th, issued a fierce denunciation of Northcliffe, whose *Evening News* had furnished 'excellent propaganda for use against us by the enemy'. Carson wondered 'whether some paper could not be got to go for Northcliffe', to which the Prime Minister replied: 'Only the *Daily News*, and it is always girding at him.'[1]

Dining at the Authors' Club with Mallon and his friends, Gardiner had to agree that Lloyd George's latest speeches had been something of a 'relief'.[2] Not that this prevented his Saturday columns from growmore explicit in their hostility to the Prime Minister, and in a way that keenly reflected the company he was keeping. 'If Labour's enthusiasm in the overthrow of the Prussian Baal is to be engaged to the utmost,' he postulated on 12 January, three days after the Mallon dinner, 'a means must be found to place the leaders whom it trusts – men of the type of Mr [Arthur] Henderson, Mr [Robert] Smillie, and Mr [J. H.] Thomas – in effective, if not titular, control of the war.' Lord Fisher was sufficiently aggrieved by the neglect he was suffering to agree with his friend: 'The Labour Party have the entire power in their own hands to oust the Government,' he asserted rather too precipitously. 'The whole mass of the people are indignant at being controlled by Carson, Curzon & Milner who got where they are by Fraud! They certainly are not *"the Elected of the people"*!'[3]

Lest his readers, like Fisher, interpret his message as a call for direct agitation, Gardiner hastened to make clear that he did not sanction the threat of Clydeside workers to 'down tools'. The idea of a strike 'on issues altogether outside the functions of a trade', he insisted on the 19th, 'is mere incendiarism' (an indictment he had hitherto reserved for Northcliffe), and a sure way to destroy organized trade unionism. Yet Gardiner remained convinced that 'in the present position the continuance of a Government so divorced from the mind of the nation and so discredited is a national peril'. By 2 February, his proposals had gained in specificity:

1. Entry of 11 January 1918, Thomas Jones, *Whitehall Diary*, i, 44. On the same occasion, Lloyd George proclaimed himself against suppressing the *Herald*, 'with its pro-Bolshevik line', and 'doubted' whether the suppression of the *Nation* had done the least good.

2. Entry of 9 January 1918, *ibid.*, i, 43. Gardiner's fellow guests included, besides Jones, Tawney, Greenwood, and Sir Arthur Zimmern.

3. Fisher to Gardiner, 15 January 1918, G.P.

If we are to hold our own democracy against Hindenburg we must have a Government . . . without any 'past,' a clear-cut expression of the determination of this country to have no part in a war of conquest and no dealings in secret diplomacy. It should rest firmly and absolutely on the democratic basis, and should be both nominally and actually a Labour administration, with men like Mr Henderson, Mr J. H Thomas, Mr [W.C.] Anderson, Mr Smillie, Mr [J.R.] Clynes at the head, with additions from sympathetic quarters from outside Labour's ranks, such as Mr [W.M.R.] Pringle, Mr [J.M.] Hogge, Lord Henry Bentinck, and Mr Waldorf Astor, and with the help of a few men still in office like Mr [H.A.L.] Fisher, whose work at the Education Office is too valuable to lose.

With a Government constituted on this basis, backed by the loyal support of Mr Asquith and Mr Lloyd George, the country could address itself to the war in a new spirit and with a new hope.

The following Saturday, he pursued the matter by publishing 'A letter to the Liberal Whip', whom he called upon to cooperate 'with men of good will of all parties' to form 'a Clean Government' that would enjoy 'the complete confidence of Labour'. He renewed that call on 9 March.

Some old-timers were perplexed by Gardiner's latest tack, and disturbed by the degree to which issues had become personalized. 'I have been most disagreeably impressed by the recent leading articles in the Daily News,' Sir George Otto Trevelyan told Lord Bryce:

There is a tone about them as if our real enemies were our Government, and not the Germans, and about a week ago there was a long, very long *communicated* article by 'A.G.G.' In this, after much abuse of the Ministry, it talked of a Labour Ministry, fortified by public men such as Lord Henry Bentinck, Waldorf Astor, and one or two others; I think Pringle and Hogge. . . . I now take the Chronicle, and like it well. [1]

The loss of a subscriber, even one so eminent, was a small price to pay for the freedom to speak one's mind. Lloyd George had to be removed, and there was no time to waste on supporting the claims of Asquith, whose return was improbable and not altogether desirable. Edward Cabury, who found Gardiner's articles 'most wise and statesman-like', admitted an inability to 'understand Asquith's attitude. I think he should be ready to sacrifice future position for present

1. Trevelyan to Bryce, 9 February 1918, Bryce Papers, xviii, fols 148–9.

danger.'[1] His father, always the most adventurous member of the family, began 'pondering the question of how far . . . [the *Daily News*] ought to go in for a large Labour Party in the House of Commons'. He knew that it would not be 'a popular thing to do among our middle-class readers', but he reminded his son Henry that 'we have always gone in for what we believed to be right, rather than for what pays'. Besides, as the Liberal Party 'evidently has no backbone', there was really no choice.[2] Gardiner saw things in much the same light. Invited to introduce Arthur Henderson to the readers of the *Atlantic Monthly*,[3] he elected to focus upon the 'palsy that has befallen the Liberal Party' and the drift of intellectuals toward Labour:

> A new alignment of forces is taking shape, with the interests on the one side, in possession of the machine of government and drawing to themselves all the predatory elements of society, and with the reconstructed Labor Party on the other, with a wider platform and a more comprehensive appeal, absorbing, not only the legions of the organized industrial army but all the scattered forces of democracy. Between the two the Liberal Party, condemned to sterile inaction, is in danger of being gravely squeezed.[4]

On 4 April, Gardiner stood with Bennett and J. A. Spender in the crowded press gallery of the House of Commons to hear the Prime Minister – 'the most supple politician that has ever appeared on the Parliamentary stage', A.G.G. called him nine days later – introduce his controversial Manpower Bill, with its contingency clauses for the extension of conscription to Ireland. Gardiner had warned against such a step, but, when it came, he accepted it with relative calm. A prolonged battle was raging on the western front, where the Germans had hurled their full force against Allied lines. It made good tactics, Runciman counselled, to wait until 'the great battle is over & the forces have exhausted themselves'.[5]

1. Edward Cadbury to Gardiner, 13 April 1918, G.P.
2. George Cadbury to Henry Cadbury, 29 April 1918 (copy), G.P.
3. Sedgwick to Gardiner, 4 April 1918, G.P.
4. 'Mr Henderson and the Labor Movement', *Atlantic Monthly*, cxxii (1918), 228.
5. Runciman to Gardiner, 25 March 1918. 'How dreadfully we have to pay for incompetence & conceit in running the war,' Runciman went on; 'even the qualities attributed to England's present Prime Minister are being shown at tragic cost to be the qualities of the Quack.'

There had been persistent allegations, now given more credence as the Allies were forced to surrender precious ground, that Lloyd George risked defeat in the west by diverting troops to his 'side-shows' in the east. On 7 May, there appeared in *The Times* – the same paper that had closed its columns to Lord Lansdowne – a letter from Major-General Sir Frederick Maurice, who defied the sacred canons of military discipline by accusing the Prime Minister of exaggerating to the House the number of troops deployed in France. Two days later, in the stormy 'Maurice debate', Asquith moved for a select committee to investigate the validity of Maurice's charges. This Lloyd George refused to concede, and, for the first and last time during the war, the Opposition divided the House (unsuccessfully) against the Government.

Lloyd George's critics required no select committee to tell them about their man. On the afternoon of the debate, a leader in the *Star* mocked him as 'the grand old camouflager'. Elsewhere in the same issue, 'Alpha of the Plough' held forth on the virtues of 'Telling the truth'. It was too early to predict the 'political consequences' of the Maurice 'bombshell', and, being the prudent chap that he was, 'Alpha' did not 'propose to discuss the merits of his case, for I know nothing about them'. Yet he could not help but 'rejoice' that Maurice 'should have compelled us, in this carnival of the devil, to consider the relations of truth to public conduct'. For taking such a line, he was vigorously upbraided by the *Daily News*'s 'quondam Military Correspondent', who dryly recalled 'a talk I once had with you about the Ulster troubles', when military insubordination was decried by Liberals as a crime against the state.[1]

Unlike 'Alpha', who only knew what he read in the papers, or Scott, to whom the 'Maurice affair' remained 'something of a mystery',[2] Gardiner enjoyed the benefit of a full explanation from Maurice himself. 'My object in making the statements I did was to compel [*sic*] the Government to accept responsibility for actions of theirs which directly affect the conduct of the war,' Maurice wrote the next day:

The Government decided it could not send enough men to France to keep the armies up to full strength & consequently large reductions had to

1. A.M.Murray to Gardiner, 11 May 1918, G.P.
2. Scott to Courtney, 10 May 1918, Courtney Papers, xii, fol. 131.

be made. The Government must take the responsibility. The Government decided to keep large numbers of troops in Palestine some of whom might have been in France & again they must take the responsibility. Mr Bonar Law's answer of the 23rd & the Prime Minister's speech of the 9th implied that the Government had taken every necessary step to meet the German offensive, the inference being that the responsibility for failure rested only with the soldiers. I fear I have made a great sacrifice in vain, but knowing what I did I could not remain silent. [1]

Gardiner, despite his respect for Maurice, knew better than to rush into print on behalf of a cause that had already come to grief in Parliament. As Edward Cadbury justly observed, until 'the German offensive has spent itself', it would be both mischievous and futile 'to advocate any change of Government'. Demands for Lloyd George's replacement would only serve to strengthen his position at a time when 'external attack' threatened. It was more important, he argued, for the *Daily News* 'to be in very close touch with President Wilson and be practically his organ in this country, expounding his international policy, and . . . do[ing] everything we can to keep in touch with him'. It would therefore be imperative to dispatch 'the right man' to Paris when the peace conference was held. 'We must not spare expense or trouble in getting him – it is extremely difficult I know, but one feels there must be a suitable man if we can only find him.' [2] Little did anyone suspect that the *Daily News*'s correspondent was to be General Maurice.

Biding his time, Gardiner devoted his columns to anticipations of the peace. On several occasions, he appealed to Grey to exert 'moral leadership', only to have the elder statesman reply from remote Fallodon that 'while the present German onslaught lasts, & while there is any hope in Germany of its resulting in German victory, there is little use in talking of anything but fighting'. [3] Week after week, Gardiner lamented the failure of the Allies to give meaningful endorsement to the Wilsonian programme. The chief culprit was Clemenceau, who had never bothered to disguise his scorn for the President. Now, to Gardiner's uneasiness, it was reported on good

1. Maurice to Gardiner, 10 May 1918, G.P.
2. Edward Cadbury to Gardiner, 10 May 1918, G.P.
3. Grey to Gardiner, 18 June 1918, G.P. Grey was replying belatedly to A.G.G.'s 11 May column, which J. A. Spender had brought to his attention.

authority 'that relations between Clemenceau and Ll.G. were very cordial'.[1] Dedicated to Wilson's principle of self-determination, he backed the Montagu–Chelmsford proposals for Indian reform,[2] and campaigned against Allied intervention in Russia. 'We cannot dictate to Russia what form of government she shall adopt,' he wrote on 29 June. 'That is her affair, and if she chooses to be Bolshevist, she will be Bolshevist, and we shall have to make the best of it.'

George Cadbury, too old to embark on further crusades, gave Gardiner his blessings ('May you have the needful wisdom and grace in the future'), and envied him the 'magnificent opportunity for reconstruction' that would come at the war's end.[3] But preparation began long before victory was in hand. With Gilbert Murray and Lord Buckmaster, Gardiner campaigned for the Atlantic Union. Spender pressed him into service on behalf of the peace and propaganda committee of the League of Nations Association; and Lord Beauchamp recruited him for the Lansdowne Committee, of which Beauchamp was chairman and Hirst the honorary secretary.

As the nations lurched toward peace, Gardiner worked to instil in the minds of his countrymen a knowledge and appreciation of the Wilsonian programme. At a time that the President was sometimes accused of playing God, Gardiner was proud to serve as his British Moses. The Fourteen Points, handed down at Washington the previous January, were his commandments; the League of Nations, his promised land. If men listened calmly and thoughtfully, he did not see how they could resist the irrefutable logic of the doctrines he preached. But a conducive atmosphere was not to prevail. That autumn, the country was plunged into an election campaign that gave vent to savage hatreds and stimulated a mood of frenzied vindictiveness. The golden calf had its day, and for this, above all else, Gardiner could never forgive Lloyd George.

1. Bennett to Gardiner, 17 May 1918, G.P. Bennett's source was Paul Cambon, the French ambassador.
2. See leader in the *Daily News*, 6 July 1918. Montagu wrote that day to thank Gardiner 'most sincerely for the assistance you are giving': G.P.
3. George Cadbury to Gardiner, 10 June 1918, G.P.

10. The khaki backwash

The Parliament that sat throughout the war was elected in the distant days of 1910. The issues that had then stirred men's consciences were now largely forgotten. There had since occurred a drastic realignment of parties which no one could have predicted. New elections would have to be held as soon as possible if democracy was to have any meaning. But when? Recalling the fate their party had suffered at the polls in 1900, most Liberals urged delay until the country had shed its khaki and recovered its equilibrium. Others pressed for an early contest to strengthen the Government in the House and at the impending peace negotiations. The ultimate decision rested with the Prime Minister, who called an election within hours of the armistice.

It is tempting to say that Lloyd George, borrowing another leaf from Joseph Chamberlain's book, capitalized on wartime feeling to cement his coalition. There is, however, reason to suspect that he had intended to go to the country that autumn in any event. 'I gather that things are not very easy between Ll.G. & his Tory colleagues on the subject of an election,' Vivian Phillipps, Asquith's private secretary, wrote to Gardiner in August. 'Ll.G. appears to have a programme that will out-Bolshevik our Bolsheviks and the problem is – how is Curzon to get the dear old Ruling Councillors & Dames of the Primrose League to swallow it.' Phillipps reported that he had seen Sir Henry Norman, a member of the Air Council and formerly a distinguished journalist, who 'was very full of the idea of a sudden dissolution by George during the first week in October – a few days after the completion of the Register – so as to prevent any meeting of Parliament until Ll.G. has been crowned as Arch-Bolshie with full powers to suppress all ill-conditioned fellows like you and me.'[1]

The signs, as Gardiner read them on 7 September, pointed clearly to an autumn election rather than one the following spring. Lloyd George, who held all the 'trump cards', could be expected to 'gather

1. Phillipps to Gardiner, 20 August 1918, G.P.

242

his political harvest while the sun shines, and not leave it out for the rigours and vicissitudes of an unknown winter'. Gardiner dreaded the prospect of 'Liberal and Labour candidates in open conflict, destroying each other in order to present a seat to the Unionist on a minority vote'. Even more, he dreaded the effect on the subsequent peace-making of a campaign that would inevitably whip up popular passions. The election, when it came, would decide 'the uses of victory . . ., whether the settlement of the world after the war will make for a permanent peace or a condition of economic strife which will not be peace but war smouldering'. He therefore hoped that the electors would be given adequate time to cast an informed vote.

Trying to divine Lloyd George's intentions, always a tricky business, was made more perilous by the fact that he seemed to revise his timetable from week to week. On 21 September, Gardiner cited welcome 'portents . . . that we are not to have a November election after all'. To his relief, the Prime Minister apparently realized that to plunge into electioneering would impede 'the political strategy of the war', as well as impair national 'solidarity'. By 26 October Gardiner was less confident of the Prime Minister's wisdom. His column that day, an impassioned condemnation of 'political thimble-rigging', put the case against an election that would 'turn on khaki'. The men who had defended the country deserved the courtesy of coming home to vote; and, besides, any result based 'on the existing registry', badly out-of-date, would 'be a travesty of the nation's judgment'.

Reluctant to go to battle without a London newspaper securely in his grasp, Lloyd George renewed efforts to acquire the *Daily Chronicle*. The speed with which he moved suggested that an election was imminent. He had had his eye on the *Chronicle* for more than a year, after several unsuccessful attempts to wrench the *Westminster Gazette* from Asquithian ownership. Early in 1917 he had intimated his willingness to pay as much as a million-and-a-half pounds for the property. The enterprise acquired new urgency as Robert Donald, once Lloyd George's golfing companion and a dependable ally, befriended the generals whom the Prime Minister was systematically denigrating. In May 1918 Donald went so far as to appoint as the *Chronicle*'s military correspondent the celebrated General Maurice. The red flag was hoisted, and the bull predictably responded. Beaverbrook, a specialist in transactions of this kind, was deputed to buy the *Chronicle* from Frank Lloyd, its proprietor. The 'deal didn't work', he told Arnold Bennett, and, as a result, 'Ll.G. was cross with him'.[1] But Lloyd George was persistent, and dispensed with an intermediary. He and F. E. ('Freddy') Guest, his chief whip, opened negotiations with Lloyd, who must have been surprised by their generosity. The bid was accepted, '& the secret so well kept', according to J. A. Spender, 'that Donald heard of it for the first time on Friday afternoon' (the 4th). 'No one believed that Lloyd's price (£1,600,000) could possibly be found,' Spender wrote in astonishment to Sir Donald Maclean,

& the names of the subscribers except Andrew Weir & James White are still in doubt. Grant Morden & some other of Beaverbrook's rascals are suspected, but I rather doubt if Ll.G. could have commanded them, unless he too has paid the price – which is total submission to Tories, tariff-reformers & grafters.[2]

Sir Henry Dalziel took charge of the *Chronicle* in Lloyd George's interest, and Donald was turned out of the editorship. The prompt dismissal of Maurice came as no surprise, and he and Harry Jones, the parliamentary correspondent, joined the *Daily News*. The *Chronicle* was to change hands twice again – in 1926 and 1928 – before its amalgamation with the *Daily News* in 1930. 'The first blow to its prestige was when it became the organ of Mr Lloyd George,' Donald recalled with unallayed bitterness when the paper eventually folded. 'This meant that its political news had to be shaped to suit his policy – in other words, that its political reports lacked the true perspective – and that its independence in opinion was sacrificed.'[3]

There were various attempts during wartime to tamper with the press, but few so blatant as this. Spender had his share of troubles, and came close to resigning as editor of the *Westminster Gazette* as a result of strong pressures brought to bear by 'hostile shareholders', who took dictation from Lloyd George.[4] Gardiner had a relatively

1. Entry for 5 October 1918, Arnold Bennett's Journal. It is not unlikely that Beaverbrook intended his disclosure as a smokescreen. For a more detailed account, see Taylor. *Beaverbrook*, pp. 157–8.
2. Spender to Maclean, 8 October 1918, Asquith Papers, cxlv, fols 48–9; see also H. A. Taylor, *Robert Donald*, pp. 175 ff.
3. *Daily Mail* interview, quoted in Herd, *March of Journalism*, p. 257.
4. See Spender's letter to Asquith, 4 October 1917, quoted in Wilson, *Downfall of the Liberal Party*, p. 116.

easier time of it, if only because he did not have to contend with a divided proprietorship. Yet the *Daily News* was penalized in more subtle ways for the critical attitude it adopted. A. P. Nicholson, its lobby correspondent, recalled how 'extraordinarily difficult' his assignment had been 'during the L.-G. Government's regime': no one, he insisted, 'will ever know . . . what craft I have had to exercise to get the real information, and keep our end up on news'.[1]

Gardiner was not at all surprised to suffer such treatment. What else, he may have been tempted to ask, could one expect from a Government that featured Lord Beaverbrook as Minister of Information? He thought it sadly typical of the new order that 'an obscure Canadian financier' with press connections should have been 'exalted from Sir Max Aitken into Lord Beaverbrook for arranging the dinners and breakfasts at which Mr George and Sir Edward Carson intrigued for the fall of the [Asquith] Coalition'.[2] Not that he particularly minded if Beaverbrook was rewarded for his service in honours, already a debased currency. What alarmed him was the political influence that Beaverbrook had come to wield. C. P. Scott, too, was concerned, and protested that men like Beaverbrook and Northcliffe, however much they knew about newspapers, were unsuited 'to direct propaganda' for the Government. The Prime Minister defended his choice:

> Beaverbrook was extremely clever & though he was described as a 'shady financier' he [Lloyd George] was not aware of any real foundation for the charge. As for Northcliffe he was safe as long as he was occupied & The Times hd. bn. quite reasonable during the 7 months he hd. bn. in America. It was necessary to find occupation for his abounding energies if they were not to run into mischief. Neither he nor Beaverbrook wd. allow their propaganda work to be determined by their personal political views – indeed he [Lloyd George] doubted if they had any considered views.[3]

This last point was well taken, and precisely the reason why Gardiner, all his life, so much distrusted Beaverbrook. He did not doubt that 'if

1. Nicholson to Gardiner, 17 October 1918, G.P.
2. 'A Letter to the Liberal Whip', *Daily News*, 9 February 1918. A.J.P.Taylor convincingly defends the merits of Beaverbrook's appointment, but acknowledges the bitter opposition to it in Tory as well as Liberal circles. *Beaverbrook*, pp. 137 ff.
3. Scott's Memorandum of 4 March 1918, Scott Papers, Add. MSS 50, 905, fol. 6.

the gifts of Lord Beaverbrook for manipulating men and events had been accompanied by any *considered view* of life or any moral purpose he would have been one of the most considerable figures of his time'. [1] But Beaverbrook, a far more complex personality than the two-dimensional Northcliffe, was perpetually driven by unknown furies. Even his acquisition of the *Daily Express* was shrouded in mystery, which his own statements helped to perpetuate. [2] Bennett and Masterman, who wrote columns for Beaverbrook, attested to his charm and generosity. 'There is something likeable – almost lovable about him,' Masterman told Gardiner, whom he attempted to recruit for the *Sunday Express* in 1921. [3] But Gardiner could not be persuaded. 'B. is an intriguer first, last & always,' he wrote to a friend many years later, '& he is the more dangerous because his intrigues are governed by no principle that I have ever been able to discover – always by personal aims & an insane passion to pull strings.' [4]

It was in the autumn of 1918 that the situation began to develop that brought Gardiner's editorship to a close a year later, and his services on to the open market in 1921. The previous March, his contract had been renewed on handsome terms. As 'a Consultative Director of the Company', he was 'to continue as heretofore to direct the editorial policy of the "Daily News"', and 'to act in an advisory capacity on other matters connected with the business of the Company as and when required to do so'. His annual salary was given at £2000, plus $2\frac{1}{2}$ per cent of the net profits up to the first £20,000 net profits made by the Company in any year. It was further stipulated that the agreement could be terminated only by 'twelve calendar months' notice in writing on either side'. [5]

At this time, Gardiner enjoyed especially cordial relations with

1. *Certain People of Importance*, p. 44 (italics added).
2. It was not until August 1917, more than half a year after the event, that Beaverbrook let on to Scott 'that he own[ed] a majority of the shares of the "Express," which is regarded as B[onar] L[aw]'s organ'. Scott's memorandum of 9–11 August 1917, Scott Papers. Add. MSS 50, 904, fol. 95. In certain respects the question was an academic one, as Beaverbrook exercised a dominant influence over the paper's editor, R. D. Blumenfeld, even before he acquired financial control.
3. Masterman to Gardiner, 26 March 1921, G.P.
4. Gardiner to Swinnerton, 11 May 1942, Swinnerton Papers.
5. Agreement of 21 March 1918 (copy), G.P.

the Cadburys, some of whom he naturally found more agreeable than others. He was then completing work on an official life of George Cadbury, originally intended for private circulation and eventually published commercially – with a subsidy from the family – in 1923, after its subject's death. He had devoted spare hours to the project ever since 1910, when he first agreed to undertake the commission. Cadbury was gratified by the finished product, and sent his biographer a flurry of letters, many of them lengthy appraisals of the world crisis. He concurred with the general outline of Gardiner's editorial policy, and was pleased to see that the paper now and then found a kind word to say for Lloyd George: 'If we endorse any good sentiments that he expresses, severe criticism of any folly comes with better grace, and shows that it is not personal spite, but that our whole idea is to benefit the public.'[1] Edward Cadbury, too, wrote friendly letters from Birmingham, endorsing Gardiner's views and inviting him to visit.[2] But Henry Cadbury was more prickly, and he, as manager of the paper, was in daily attendance in Bouverie Street. There seem to have been problems between the two men all along. Gardiner's diary for 1910 – the only volume that survives – is punctuated with references to his wranglings with Henry Cadbury, with whom he had an 'angry talk' on the afternoon of 17 January, and whose 'niggling criticisms' rankled so much that he asked whether Cadbury would like to 'take charge of the paper himself'.[3] This was a preview of things to come.

George Cadbury, whose opinions weighed heavily on his sons, was devoted to three causes: the first was Lloyd George, whom he refused to find guilty except in so far as he had allowed himself to become 'a mere tool of Lord Northcliffe, who through the "Times" and "Daily Mail" largely rules England';[4] the second was social reform, which could best be served by effecting an alliance between the Liberal and Labour parties; and the third was President Wilson's blueprint for a League of Nations. As Gardiner saw it, these three commitments were incompatible: Lloyd George was, on the one hand, an impediment to Liberal–Labour unity, and, on the other, a devious anti-Wilsonian.

1. George Cadbury to Gardiner, 25 June 1918, G.P.
2. Edward Cadbury to Gardiner, 29 July 1918, G.P.
3. Diary entry for 17 January 1910, G.P.
4. George Cadbury to Gardiner, 10 June 1918, G.P.

With the approach of the general election, he found it impossible to restrain himself as his proprietor urged. Cadbury scolded him, and then apologized. 'I have never asked for nor received any favor [*sic*] from Lloyd George,' he assured Gardiner. 'I had a strong presentiment that if he adhered to his radical views it might save a revolution and would absolutely dish! the Tory papers. But your policy may have been right. You are on the spot.'[1]

Edward Cadbury advised Gardiner to keep calm. Any 'Parliament elected now,' he predicted, 'will not have a very long existence', and there would soon come a time to make amends.[2] Gardiner rightly disagreed. Always inclined to depict issues in terms of personality, he painted a broad canvas with

> Mr President, in his black coat of citizenship, grappling with the Supreme War Lord, in his shining armour and 'divine right,' forcing him to his knees and pressing him back inch by inch towards the abyss in which despotism, and all that it connotes, will disappear for ever.[3]

In his Saturday column on 12 November, he examined the reasons 'Why Germany lost.' And, four days later, he counselled the Allies not to relax but to 'act at once and generously if they are to prevent a universal drift into Bolshevism and anarchy'. His words were applauded by Gilbert Murray, who spoke for many Liberals when he declared that 'I owe you a very great debt for your writings during the war'.[4]

But how were Englishmen to join President Wilson in saving mankind if they were forced into a premature election, and one in which the President's parliamentary allies, usually denied the Coalition 'coupon', faced certain defeat? 'The nation is in the presence,' A.G.G. warned on the 23rd,

> not of an election, but of a conspiracy. If the conspiracy succeeds the greatest thing will have happened that has happened in our history since 1688. But whereas the revolution of 1688 established our liberty and the principles of Parliamentary government, the revolution of 1918 would destroy both. . . .

1. George Cadbury to Gardiner, 16 October 1918, G.P.
2. Edward Cadbury to Gardiner, 4 November 1918, G.P.
3. 'A square deal', *Daily News*, 26 October 1918.
4. Murray to Gardiner, 17 November [1918], G.P.

The first fact to seize is this, that though the revelation is sudden the plot is not sudden. It has governed the mysterious evolutions that have puzzled the country during the war. . . . Honest men were being removed, parties were being broken up, all the agonies of the war were being exploited for the advertisement of the coming political adventure. . . .

Mr Lloyd George's aim is as it had always been, personal dictatorship. He is one of those restless, disturbing, ill-regulated minds which have been the affliction of peoples in all times – shallow, but astonishingly agile, boundless in ambition, unscrupulous in method, ungoverned by principles. Like Kleon, he plays with democracy. But he is not a democrat; he is the antithesis of a democrat; he is a demagogue. . . . His method is to break up the organised forces of society and to create a mob opinion – fluid, fluctuating, blown about by every wind of doctrine, the sport of the most dexterous cunning and the most skilful intrigue. . . .

He wove around himself a new system of government every element of which depended upon his personal will and reacted on his personal power. No one who opposed his domination survived. He became the centre of a camarilla, with its tentacles reaching out in every direction. Around him he gathered the Press lords and the financial magnates, the placemen and the people hungry for titles, the men with interests to protect, and the men with ambitions that looked for fulfilment.

And having built up his system behind the barrage of the war he now comes forward with his naked proposal that Parliamentary government, as we have known it for centuries, should be destroyed, that the House of Commons should be packed with his nominees, that it should no longer be the clearing-house of the nation's ideas, but the automatic register of his will, that no opposition should be allowed and that the independent member should be excluded.

It is not necessary to share Gardiner's opinions to admire his skilled invective. Few could rival him in a war of words. At his most splenetic, he remained eloquent. At his most forlorn, he remained ebullient. Considerable allowance must be made, of course, for journalistic overstatement: undoubtedly he exaggerated the degree of delibera-tion behind the granting of the 'coupon', let alone Lloyd George's earlier manoeuvres. Yet he managed to articulate the sense of frustration that, so often during the ensuing campaign, simply reduced his fellow-Asquithians to speechlessness. The response to his diatribe was as predictable as the outcome of the polling three weeks later. 'Loulou' Harcourt thanked him for his 'admirable article. . . . I hope you are reprinting this by the 10,000's: it ought to go everywhere.'[1] To the supporters of the Coalition, however, Gardiner had merely given further proof of his blind fanaticism.

With Donald removed from the *Chronicle*, and the *Manchester Guardian* (notwithstanding Scott's objections to an early election) in Lloyd George's corner, the Asquithians could rely upon only the *Westminster Gazette* and the *Daily News*. 'All your Election stuff is excellent,' John Gulland, the party whip, told Gardiner, whom he nonetheless offered 'suggestions on several points'. He hoped that it might be possible to alert the public to the 'variety of ways the Government is giving bribes over the Election to different classes of the community'. Lloyd George had had the temerity to turn public ceremonies – 'the Freedom of Burghs', for example – into 'political meetings'. And, given the 'tremendous number of three-cornered fights', it might be useful to show 'the luke-warmness of the present Government towards Radical measures'.[2] It was a pleasure for Gardiner to comply; day after day, he railed against the Prime Minister's electoral strategy and disputed the 'legend' that Lloyd George had won the war.

Fearing the virtual obliteration of all opposition, Gardiner pleaded with Labourites and independent Liberals to band together before it was too late. He counted dozens of constituencies in which two non-couponed candidates threatened to siphon support from each other, to the distinct advantage of the Coalition man. In these cases, he urged the weaker candidate to withdraw in favour of the stronger, regardless of party affiliation: it would be worth the price to save the seat from Lloyd George's clutches. The *Daily News*'s insistence that 'there is no essential difference between Liberalism of its own type and that of the I.L.P.' was derided by the *Morning Post*, which absurdly accused it (30 November) of Bolshevik sympathies. Yet Gardiner, his Blackburn experience to guide him, knew the value of cooperating with a responsible Labour man. 'As the Liberal who supported you and voted for you in the Khaki election of 1900,' he began a letter to Philip Snowden,

I write to wish you success in your present campaign. I have not shared your views in regard to the war and have publicly criticised your attitude,

1. Harcourt to Gardiner, 26 November 1918, G.P.
2. Gulland to Gardiner, 5 December 1918, G.P.

but I have recognised throughout the fundamental passion for democracy that has governed you. . . . I have opposed you often in the past and I expect to have to oppose you often in the future, but at this moment you stand for the one thing that is the foundation of all things that I as a Liberal cherish – the principles of a free and independent Parliament. [1]

Snowden was deeply grateful for 'such valuable help', and expressed 'great admiration of the present stand of the D.N.' The Blackburn Liberals, he informed Gardiner, were deeply split, and Ritzema was among the many who had gone over to the Coalition side. But he was not discouraged. 'It is the 1900 campaign all over again, but with this difference – that our forces are organised.'[2] Arthur Henderson was equally appreciative. On behalf of Labour's executive committee, he sent Gardiner 'thanks for the sympathetic treatment and prominent display accorded the Labour Party policy and views. . . . The fair play and sympathetic consideration which the "Daily News" has shown towards the Labour cause have assisted us in no small measure in educating and enlightening public opinion.'[3]

Not everyone was so pleased with his magnanimity. It was one thing to perpetuate an opposition, and another to save the Liberal Party. Gilbert Murray took time off from electioneering in the Westbury division on behalf of Geoffrey Howard ('who is opposed by a Coalition Tory and a new Labour man'), to ask Gardiner to be 'rather less neutral & more definitely liberal' in selecting which candidate to endorse. 'I am all for the cooperation, or the union, of Liberalism and Labour,' he professed, '& have . . . canvassed for [Sidney] Webb for London University.' Yet, all things equal, he preferred 'to concentrate on the Liberal' in those 'cases where (1) the Liberal is the sitting member, (2) he is a "free" Liberal & a genuine Liberal, and (3) he is the only progressive & democratic candidate who has any chance of winning the seat.'[4] Murray's advice did not go unheeded, as evidenced by leaders in the *Daily News* on 11 and 12 December.

As Gardiner had dreaded, Coalition spokesmen appealed for votes by fanning the flames of chauvinism and Germanophobia. The Prime

1. Gardiner to Snowden, 5 December 1918 (draft copy), G.P.
2. Snowden to Gardiner, 10 December 1918, G.P. Four days later, Snowden was defeated by a wide margin.
3. Henderson to Gardiner, 3 January 1919, G.P.
4. Murray to Gardiner, 6 December 1918, G.P.

Minister, who entered the campaign purring like a Liberal, soon began to echo the most menacing Tory growls. Vowing to 'Hang the Kaiser' and to 'exact the last penny we can get out of Germany up to the limit of her capacity', he had come a long way since he sanely remonstrated that 'mixing business and revenge' was as foolish and probably 'as fatal as the intrusion of poetry into the multiplication table'.[1] Some of his ministerial colleagues were even more histrionic. On 7 December, A.G.G. reviewed F. E. Smith's platform performance at Liverpool, and cautioned that promises of revenge and reparations, aside from being unrealistic, were 'not the thing about which the nation should give its judgment next Saturday'. These were not genuine issues, but bogus ones, intended to hoodwink the electorate into providing the Coalition with a 'blank cheque'. Anticipating 'an avalanche of letters' denouncing him as a pro-German, Gardiner was surprised to receive a congratulatory message from General Sir Hubert Gough, one of the culprits of the Curragh episode, who likewise deplored the willingness of 'the Prime Minister & his adherents . . . to prostitute the souls of the Nation for their immediate advantage'.[2]

Polling began on Saturday, the 14th. That morning, the *Daily News* carried its editor's 'Letter to a voter':

> Has Mr Lloyd George come to you and told you honestly what he means on any of the great questions on which he claims your mandate? Rhetoric you have had in abundance; but out of the jumble of vague and incoherent policies, the studied evasions, the half assertions, half denials, can you find what he means on any question? Do you know where he stands about Ireland, about Protection, about Russia, about India, about the League of Nations, about militarism, about indemnities, about Conscription? He has half-asserted everything and half-denied everything. . . . He does not mean that you shall know what he intends. For he does not want your mandate. He wants your blank cheque. . . .
>
> Do not give the blank cheque. Send back to Parliament men who are free, not men pledged to support Mr George no matter what he afterwards

1. Quoted approvingly by Gardiner in 'After the War: how to make a better job of the world', *Daily News*, 25 March 1916.
2. Gough to Gardiner, 12 December 1918, G.P. Gough, the commander of the Fifth Army, had a score to settle with Lloyd George, who had made sharp reference to him when he introduced the last Military Service Bill. *Parliamentary Debates* (Commons), 5th ser., civ, cols. 1343–44 (9 April 1918).

discloses as his purpose. Do not give a Coalition man, no matter what he calls himself, your vote, if you have the choice of a free Liberal or Labour candidate to vote for. Every free Liberal or Labour man is safe. He represents the tradition of an English Parliament and not of a Prussian Parliament. . . . No Coalition man can be trusted. He has surrendered his freedom. He will not go to Parliament as your representative. He will go as Mr Lloyd George's nominee.

But the electorate was in no mood to listen. When all the ballots were counted, 526 Coalition candidates (the overwhelming number of them Unionists) had been returned, giving Lloyd George the 'reliable majority' for which he had asked. The independent Liberals in the new Parliament numbered a mere thirty-three. Expecting to suffer losses, they had not been prepared for the worst of the humiliations that befell them, the decimation of their front bench. Runciman, McKenna and Herbert Samuel were among the casualties. Asquith, who proudly boasted never to read what the press said about him, was annoyed to 'hear . . . that the London papers have been publishing a tissue of absurdities' to the effect that he was encountering strong opposition, particularly among newly enfranchised women, at East Fife. He assured Gardiner that he had 'never had such enthusiastic & crowded gatherings', and called on him to contradict these malicious reports.[1] On the 28th, he learned that he lost the seat that he had held since 1886.

Comparatively speaking, Asquith was among the fortunate: early in 1920 a safe seat opened at Paisley, allowing him to resume his parliamentary career. Some of his best known supporters, evicted from the Commons in 1918, were never again to return. 'Confidence in an election like this is not permissible,' McKenna, fighting desperately to hold North Monmouthshire, wrote on the 19th, 'but I am hopeful.'[2] Adversity did not lessen his appreciation of all Gardiner had done:

Almost single-handed in the London press you have kept our flag flying, and now that we have to face disaster you have still to maintain a public fight and day by day to put heart into a defeated and broken party. You are entitled to all the help every Liberal can give and I am afraid you haven't received any.

1. Asquith to Gardiner, 16 December 1918, G.P.
2. McKenna to Gardiner, 19 December 1918, G.P.

Declining an invitation to publish a statement in the *Daily News* ('the less a beaten candidate says about the Election, the better'), he ventured a 'personal opinion' on the situation:

I think there are two outstanding reasons for the Liberal defeat, apart from the losses caused by three-cornered fights. Long years of political truce had let down the Liberal machine. Liberal voters were apathetic and even resentful. The small poll all over the country shows how dead was the interest in political issues. On the other hand anti-Germanism and the desire for revenge was strong amongst large numbers of people who voted for the Government in the belief that they would get all the indemnities Germany would pay and more. The Liberals are not thought as a party to be sufficiently venomous while the Ministers outbid each other in the number of thousands of millions Germany would be made to pay. There was a motive in voting for the Coalition candidate expressible in cash; the Liberal or Labour candidate could make no such appeal.

What was now to become of the historic Liberal Party? McKenna hoped that its weakness in Parliament would not be permitted to obscure the fact that it remained 'really strong in the country'. It was necessary 'to make up for 4 years of neglect and get to spade work in the constituencies', and this could best be accomplished by finding 'a name, a formula and a man to unite Liberal and Labour. There is no difference in our immediate political programme.' Asquith, he thought, would be well advised to 'call an early meeting of the Executive of the National Liberal Federation', place his 'resignation in their hands', and 'ask for the appointment of a special emergency committee to consider the whole position'.[1] But that was too much to ask of his sixty-seven-year-old chief, who retained the nominal leadership while Sir Donald Maclean deputized for him in the House.

Surveying the wreckage, George Cadbury asked himself whether his proprietorship had been worth the investment of years and capital. Since the turn of the century, the fortunes of the Liberal Party and concurrently those of the *Daily News* seemed to come full circle. The paper had 'lost influence in the country', he decided, 'because it has never acknowledged the good work that Lloyd George has done'. Presumably, the Liberal Party was rejected at the polls for the same reason. 'Constant nagging at an individual', he rebuked his editor, 'very largely diminishes the influence of a paper – it makes it too one

1. McKenna to Gardiner, 29 December 1918, G.P.

sided.' The *Manchester Guardian* and *The Times* were 'too wide awake to fall into this error', and consequently were taken more seriously than the *Daily News*.[1] True to the loyalties of Boer War days, he found it difficult to understand Gardiner's relatively recent attachment to Asquith, whom he looked upon as a Liberal Imperialist with patrician airs and whiggish proclivities.

What was Gardiner to say? To engage in either 'defence or argument,' he told Cadbury, 'would worry you without I am sure convincing you.' Besides, it would be painful to quarrel with 'one whose love and esteem I respect so much'. Their differences, so far as he could tell, were not profound. 'We have the same spirit and the same objects: what we disagree about is the interpretation of events and the reading of men.' But he could not for a moment allow 'to remain on record uncha[llen]ged' the 'assertion . . . that the influence of the D.N. has enormously lessened'. To the contrary, he was confident 'that by any test that could be applied the influence of the D.N. would be found to be greater today than at any period in its history'. In any case, he had no choice but to act in accordance with his beliefs, regardless of personal cost. 'I value my position and the responsibility it entails,' he stated,

but I value them only so long as I can fill the position and exercise the responsibility with increased conviction. I have never consciously acted against that conviction in the past and I do not propose to begin now. The issues of the time are far too grave to permit me to barter [such] . . . public influence as I have for any personal consideration whatever. If I were prepared to do so I should deceive both the D.N. and myself.[2]

On the face of things, Gardiner overreacted rather strenuously to his proprietor's letter, which neither cast aspersions on his integrity nor implied any impending change in the editorship. Yet one could trust Henry Cadbury to have let him know that his services no longer gave satisfaction.

For the time being, the matter was allowed to drop. However much the Cadbury's took exception to Gardiner's view of Lloyd George, they shared his devotion to President Wilson, on whom attention now focused. Colonel House was already in Paris, making arrangements

1. George Cadbury to Gardiner, 30 December 1918, G.P.
2. Gardiner to George Cadbury, 2 January 1919 (copy), G.P.

for the peace conference. He sent Frank Cobb of the *New York World*, who served on his staff, to discuss with Gardiner (and presumably other British friends) 'the advisability of the President personally attending the Conference'. Gardiner offered the 'opinion . . . that the President would be in a stronger position if, as head of a state, he appeared by proxy as would be the case with other heads of state'. Or perhaps, he suggested to Cobb, 'the President should simply pay a flying visit to Europe and make speeches in London, Paris & Rome'.[1] He was heard respectfully, but his advice was not taken.

Not even the indignities of the khaki election could divert the *Daily News* from the task of preparing a proper reception for President Wilson and his doctrines. House was delighted to receive a copy of Jerome K. Jerome's column of 3 December, and had it cabled to America in its entirety, and extracts from it sent throughout the Americas and Asia. 'Unless people like you and Mr Jerome take positive measures to make known your views,' he wrote to Gardiner, 'I fear our task at the Peace Conference will become exceedingly difficult. I notice a certain apathy everywhere, due largely, I think, to the relief which the ending of war has brought. It is this state of mind that I fear.'[2] Gardiner was pleased, but 'not surprised' that House was 'impressed by the Jerome article. . . . I rejoice that use is being made of it,' he replied,

for we need all the forces on our side to be organised at the present time. There are plenty of other forces at work to defeat, perhaps not intentionally but none the less effectually, the issue which you and I and all people of good will in all countries desire. I hope very much that the democracy of England will have the opportunity, while the President is in London, of showing how intense is its devotion to the ideal he has set up and how entirely he may rely on its support.[3]

To Ray Stannard Baker, he sent another *Daily News* cutting. 'I know how grave things are,' he admitted, 'but I rely on the stiff jaw of one great man.'[4]

Thrilled by the prospect of a presidential visit, Gardiner was

1. Autobiographical memorandum [n.d.], G.P.
2. House to Gardiner, 7 December 1918, G.P.
3. Gardiner to House, 16 December 1918, House Papers.
4. Gardiner to Baker, 13 December 1918, Baker Papers (Manuscript Div., Library of Congress).

'deeply anxious that no opportunity should be missed of showing sympathy with his policy and of paying him honour during his stay'. If the President would 'find it convenient to speak publicly', Gardiner promised House that 'the League of Nations Union, the Labour movement and all the Liberal elements in society, I think, would combine to provide an occasion. . . . Another idea which occurs to me and to others,' he continued, 'is that a welcome by the Press would give a most excellent opportunity for a powerful appeal to the world through the most powerful influence of all.' He put himself at the President's disposal. 'A wire to me here would enable me to set anything in train that might be regarded as fitting and useful.'[1] For reasons that should have been obvious to him, he was not called on. The President, whatever his private sentiments, could not appear under the auspices of the Prime Minister's most trenchant critic.

On Saturday morning, 28 December, President Wilson received the Freedom of London at the Guildhall. Gardiner portrayed the City's honoured guest to his readers as

the sort of man you would like to have at your back in a row. His face is a certificate, as Stevenson said of his companion on the immortal 'Voyage.' It is masterful and decisive, but clear, unambiguous and direct. The spacious smile, neither the cultivated smile of the courtier nor the furtive smile of the adventurer. It exhales good humour like a benediction. But it is good humour which has its limits. There is hard, uncompromising stuff behind the smile – as we might expect from one who unites the blood of Scotland and Ulster and has his roots in a Presbyterian manse.

These formalities completed, the President left London without contacting his most enthusiastic supporter. It was not until two days later, when he was en route from Manchester, that a member of his entourage wrote to say that the President 'would have been delighted to meet' Gardiner in London, but, as that had not proved possible, he 'will be glad if he can do so later in Paris'. Admiral Grayson, through whom the message was remitted, added that he had spent 'many a pleasant hour hearing the President read aloud from "Prophets, Priests and Kings" and "Pillars of Society"'.[2]

1. Gardiner to House, 17 December 1918, House Papers.
2. Frederick W. Wile to Gardiner, 30 December 1918, G.P.; also Mildred Acheson to Gardiner, 1 January 1919, G.P.

It was an opportunity that Gardiner would not have missed for the world. He had been weighing an invitation from the French authorities to tour the devastated areas, but probably would not have crossed the Channel without the inducement of a meeting with the President. He reached Paris on 19 January having thoughtfully delayed until Wilson had returned from Italy and settled in. Within an hour of his arrival, he was writing obliquely to Colonel House: 'I shall only stay here so long as is necessary to provide the occasion for which I have come & which you kindly promised to facilitate.'[1] The next morning, he brought General Maurice to breakfast with General Smuts, who had recently sent him an advance copy of his pamphlet on the League of Nations.[2] 'You see what is happening in America,' said Smuts, who observed that Wilson was losing touch with his people. 'I hope you will impress on the President as I have already done that if America goes out of the Peace the League is doomed. It will mean that the whole burden of carrying it will fall on the British Empire & the British Empire cannot carry the burden alone.'[3]

That evening Gardiner dined with the President. In the course of their conversation, which spanned a wide range of issues, he 'mentioned Smuts' anxiety & Wilson said he understood and shared it'. Without underestimating the growing isolationism among his countrymen, the President trusted 'that when I go back & am able to put the case for the League and the Covenant before them I shall carry them with me against the opposition'. Fortified by these reassurances, Gardiner left Paris much relieved, his ears ringing with Wilson's farewell remark: 'I hope you will be in America before I am out of office so that we can continue our talk in Washington.'[4] No one could have been more elated, except perhaps George Cadbury, who invited Gardiner to join him and Mrs Cadbury at Birmingham, and assumed it a duty to

1. Gardiner to House, 19 January 1919, House Papers; also Gardiner to House, 31 December 1918 and 14 January 1919, House Papers.
2. Smuts considered it 'very necessary that the idea of the League be brought down from the clouds and that a great volume of public opinion should be formed in support of it', and he wrote his pamphlet 'with that end in view': Smuts to Gardiner, 28 December 1918, G.P.
3. Autobiographical memorandum [n.d.], G.P.
4. Autobiographical memorandum [n.d.], G.P.; see also Gardiner's recollections of 'My interview with Mr Wilson', in the *Nation*, 2 April 1921.

get back the circulation of the 'Daily News' to a million; our support would then be worth having, and nothing short of this will give very much influence against the ten million copies of Sunday papers and the daily papers of large circulation that are only lukewarm in his support. [1]

Gardiner was fully alert to the problems that confronted the President. He received frequent letters from Ellery Sedgwick, who paid an autumn visit to London, and from P. W. Wilson, whom he sent to America as *Daily News* correspondent and who enjoyed the experience so much that he decided to remain in New York. At the Paris conference, the paper was represented successively by A. P. Nicholson, General Maurice, A. F. Whyte, and Wilson Harris. Maurice replaced Nicholson after the initial weeks, but 'never intended to stay in Paris long'. [2] Lord Robert Cecil, who granted him an interview there, thought he looked 'rather unhappy' as a journalist: 'It is a great waste of material that he should be doing such work.' [3] But Maurice took to the assignment with enthusiasm. His dispatches may have lacked the polish of those which J. L. Hammond wrote for the *Guardian*, but they tended to be more spirited and less morose.

Wherever he went, Maurice found 'people . . . very willing to talk', and he exploited his contacts with British military leaders as well as with diplomats. For Gardiner's benefit, he often accompanied his articles with 'a more intimate appreciation of the position', not intended for publication. He described in detail the 'political bargaining' that was going on in France, which he found 'absolutely disgusting' and all too reminiscent of the situation that prevailed in London. 'Nevertheless,' he assured Gardiner on 27 January, 'the League of Nations is steadily gaining ground, and I hope it is now certain to win through. But the French at this moment are rather like a hysterical woman who is recovering from an illness, and it is impossible to foresee what form their next tantrum will take.' The intractibility of the French was exceeded only by that of the Dominions, whose 'policy . . . is, to put it mildly, decidedly crude'. [4] In the best tradition of the *Daily News*, he was not content merely to report

1. George Cadbury to Gardiner, 14 January 1919, G.P.
2. Harris, *Life So Far*, pp. 114 ff.
3. Diary entry for 20 January 1919 (copy), Cecil of Chelwood Papers (British Museum).
4. Maurice to Gardiner, 27 January 1919, G.P.

events, but tried to shape them. 'I have been working hard among the Americans to get them to accept with more enthusiasm the idea of America's taking a practicle [*sic*] share in the responsibilities of the League,' he advised Gardiner on the 29th. It was his observation that American press opinion was slowly 'moving in the right direction'. The pace might be accelerated, however, if Lord Grey could be persuaded to address American correspondents. Maurice 'sounded Spender on the subject', and Spender agreed 'to put the proposal to Grey, who, he thinks, will accept it provided we get a message from Wilson to say he would like it'. Meanwhile, Maurice engaged in 'a good deal of talk with the Americans about Freedom of the Seas and the question of the size of their fleet', and he generously gave himself credit for having 'put both these problems to them in a light which they say is new and acceptable'. [1]

For all Maurice's valiant effort behind the scenes, the negotiators at Paris found it difficult to appreciate one another's fears and aspirations. 'While everyone wants a League of Nations in the abstract,' Gardiner complained in his column on 1 February, 'no one seems to want it to interfere with his own particular interests.' Bernard Shaw, who shared his friend's disappointment, prepared for publication a series of 'Peace Conference Hints', which he unabashedly described to Gardiner as 'magnificent and after your own heart, cribbed from you extensively, in fact.' He jested that he had considered sending the manuscript 'with a demand for publication in the D.N. But as you were doing the job much less temperately every Saturday, I spared you. Do not be ungrateful.' [2]

Soon after Gardiner's return from Paris, the President sent him a draft copy of the League Covenant, to which he appended an invitation for frank comment. 'I value your letter of February first and thank you for it most sincerely,' Wilson replied, after considering the points that Gardiner had raised:

The suggestion you make about the inspection of armament factories is one which we have just been discussing with a good deal of anxiety. Our present judgment is that it would not be wise to put a detail of that sort into the 'Covenant' itself, but that it would be wiser to leave matters of that

1. Maurice to Gardiner, 29 January 1919, G.P.
2. Shaw to Gardiner, 4 February 1919 (copy), G.P.

sort to be worked out by the League itself in insisting upon its right to know what armaments are being accumulated.

I have the same feeling about your suggestion with regard to Article VI and the detention of vessels which may be found in the harbors of contracting parties. I have very little doubt that such action will be insisted upon by the League as part of the means of enforcing the non-intercourse which is to constitute one of the chief penal instruments to be used against covenant-breaking states.

With regard to the suggestion in connection with Article XIII that it might be well to 'provide, not merely that no power shall enter into engagements inconsistent with the terms of the Covenant, but that all agreements of international character . . . shall be submitted for approval', I think we will perhaps be able to meet that by the requirements for publication which we have in contemplation. . . .

Your suggestion that many of the supplementary provisions might well be incorporated in the main body of the Covenant I agree with, and we are going to act upon it.

You have evidently given the document I gave you a very careful reading, and I am grateful to you for the suggestions you make. As a matter of fact, in our conferences we are working, not on the American draft, but on a condensed draft prepared by an American and an English lawyer, in which we are trying to boil down the contents to its essential substance – with more or less success.

It was a great pleasure to meet and know you, and I hope that our meetings will be frequent. It was delightful to have an evening with you. [1]

According to Admiral Grayson, the President spent his evenings in Paris 'reading a few chapters aloud to Mrs Wilson and myself' from Gardiner's books. 'The evening that you spent here with us', he told the flattered author, 'is often spoken of as a most delightful and interesting occasion.' [2]

Perceiving a direct link between domestic stability and international peace, Gardiner did not ignore the immense task of social reconstruction. Not that he feared that Bolshevism would rear its head in Britain, but he was committed to principles of justice and equality. Like many, he was irritated to find Liberalism so strangely deficient in ideas and energy. 'At this moment, which is a very vital moment,' Sir A. H. D. Acland wrote to him on 4 February, 'it seems

1. Wilson to Gardiner, 7 February 1919, G.P.
2. Grayson to Gardiner, 12 February 1919, G.P.

to me that unless the Free Liberal Party or shall I say the real Liberalism of the future makes a clean cut from some of its traditional methods it will have no future worth having.'[1] Gardiner said much the same thing in his 15 March column, where he argued that if the party was to show itself 'capable of taking its share with Labour in making this country the standard-bearer of the world's Liberalism', it would have to 'shape its social policy boldly and fearlessly according to the light of the present and the demands of the future'. Sidney Webb, requiring an ally to publicize the Sankey Report proposals for coal nationalization, knew that he could count upon Gardiner.[2] The Cadburys did not mind in the least: George 'rejoice[d] that there is an awakening among the working men', who had too long deferred to 'friends of capital', and he was 'glad to see' that Gardiner 'gave a benediction on the new Labour paper', which he welcomed to the news-stands;[3] Edward, though he declined to endorse 'a levy on capital', went on to express the hope that 'we shall have some more Sankey Commissions'.[4]

Gardiner would have remained in the Cadburys' good graces had he only refrained from his diatribes against Lloyd George. But these, by now, were second nature to him. His proprietors had risked unpopularity and sustained financial loss to defend a just cause. What they were not prepared to accept was contemptuous disregard. The Prime Minister made it known that he needed 'never heed' the *Daily News* or the *Nation* 'because I know that in their eyes I never can do right. I know beforehand what they're going to say.'[5] He was having a difficult time, and reportedly suffered a falling out with Northcliffe, who had aspired to a seat at the Paris conference. John Burns jubilantly inscribed in his diary that 'L.G. [was] getting frightened and his old supporters are nervous as to his ability to hold his own as agst. the Reactionaries who used him against Asquith and are wearying of his chiefmanship'.[6] The movement reached its climax in early

1. Acland to Gardiner, 4 February 1919, G.P.
2. Entry for 20 March 1919, Beatrice Webb, *Diaries*, ii, 155–6.
3. George Cadbury to Gardiner, 10 February and 1 April 1919, G.P.
4. Edward Cadbury to Gardiner, 1 April 1919, G.P.
5. Scott's memorandum of 21–22 February 1919, Scott Papers, Add. MSS 50, 905, fol. 184.
6. Entry of 4 March 1919, Burns Papers, Add. MSS 46, 341, fol. 57. A week later, Burns 'lunched like Lucullus at Romanos' with Gardiner and James

April: on the 8th, some 370 MPs (allegedly at Northcliffe's insti-
gation) telegraphed the Prime Minister at Paris for assurances that
he would fulfil his election pledges; three days later, the Government's
candidate was badly beaten in a by-election at Hull.

It was not easy to feel sympathy for the Prime Minister, who had
no one but himself to blame for the backbenchers who hounded at
his heels and the colleagues who pressed at his elbow. The worst of
Lloyd George's blunders, in Gardiner's opinion, was the appointment
to the War Office of 'Generalissimo' Churchill, a 'crude militarist, . . .
whom the world tragedy of the past five years has taught nothing'.
While President Wilson was 'holding up the banner of hope in the
world', Churchill was announcing plans for a renewal of conscription
and hefty army appropriations. [1] And Churchill was among the members of the Government most eager to intervene in the Russian civil
war. Although George Cadbury presumed that Gardiner would 'be
delighted with the action that Lloyd George is taking, fighting the
battle of the poor Russians with President Wilson against the French
financiers', [2] Gardiner wondered how long the Prime Minister could
resist the stout pressure of those who preached the Bolshevik menace.
'I am not a supporter of the Bolsheviks,' he averred on 5 April:

> I believe their ideas are wrong and their conduct only slightly less
> detestable than that of the Tsardom. But the way to defeat Bolshevism is to
> let Russia settle its own forms of government. . . . The threat of interven-
> tion makes [the Russian people] supporters of the Bolsheviks despite them-
> selves.

A week later, he cited 'welcome evidence of late that Mr Lloyd George
has been working in complete accord with President Wilson'. But he
did not expect the alliance to continue, given the fact that the Prime
Minister was 'hampered by the reckless promises with which he
baited his hook last December'. Those promises had yielded him his
parliamentary majority, but one that was 'more divorced from the
better mind of the country than any Parliament in living memory'. As
Wickham Steed recalled no less indignantly, Horatio Bottomley, a

---

Douglas, 'and a good 2 hours we had discussing Labour, the people, what the
large number of soldiers meant in London': *ibid.*, fol. 60.

1. 'Policy and events', and 'What it means', *Daily News*, 8 March and 12 April
1919.

2. George Cadbury to Gardiner, 1 April 1919, G.P.

scoundrel and a swindler, 'had been returned to that Parliament by a majority of 10,000 while Mr Asquith had been rejected by a majority of 2000'.[1]

Gardiner's final verdict on Lloyd George waited on the publication of the terms of the treaty with Germany. As late as 8 May, 'Alpha of the Plough' had not yet 'settled the full details of my private celebration of the peace', but he proclaimed in the *Star* that he was

clear about one item. I am going to have a good debauch of cricket. I am going through the turnstile at Lord's in good time on the first day of the Gentlemen and Players match and make for a nice seat in the front row to the left of the pavilion, and there I am going to sit in the sunshine until the last ball is bowled and the stumps are drawn.

It is more than unlikely that either 'Alpha' or his alter ego enjoyed the sunshine at Lord's that weekend. The Treaty of Versailles, as it was promulgated, signalled to Gardiner the triumph of *revanche* over reason. In his 10 May column, he translated its territorial provisions 'into English counties' to show his readers how their own homeland would be mutilated and drained of resources if it were made to bear the penalties now inflicted upon Germany. The analogy, although effective journalism, was not the least fair: as opposed to the economic terms of the settlement (which were, in fact, never fully implemented), the territorial terms were not unduly harsh. Again, Gardiner took an oversimplified view of international questions, which, except for the period of the Second World War, were never the clearcut struggle between good and evil that he tended to presume.

In the settlement of one war, Gardiner saw the seeds of another. 'If the Peace Terms are the last word we have to say to Germany,' he gravely intoned, 'let us make up our minds for the inevitable consequences. Let us decently bury the Covenant and prepare for the next war in whatever quarter it may break.' Among his private papers, he kept a cutting of this column, which, for more than one reason, had been an especially painful one for him to write. Across the top, he inscribed in a firm hand: 'This is the article wh. led to my resignation of the editorship of the Daily News.'

It is now generally conceded that, whatever the merits of the treaty, Lloyd George conscientiously pursued a more moderate

1. *Through Thirty Years*, ii, 322.

policy at the Paris negotiations than his critics believed or, for that matter, his public statements often suggested. Indeed, that he failed to receive due credit was much his own fault. 'In his anxiety to diddle the Right,' A. J. P. Taylor has explained, 'he overreached himself and failed to diddle the Left.'[1] Gardiner, who remained among the most stubbornly undiddled, was not inclined to give him the benefit of any doubt. He found the terms of the treaty shockingly reminiscent of the 'coupon' in the recent general election: they made a mockery of democratic procedures, subsidized the interests of reaction, pronounced 'a sentence of death on liberalism', and worked to 'intensify and embitter the old spirit' between nations. 'We cannot have both the Covenant and the Treaty in its present shape,' he declaimed in the *Daily News* on 7 June, 'and since the Covenant is only an abstraction, a pious aspiration, and the Treaty is a thing of hard facts, the Covenant will go under.' Yet, unlike many who had hoped in vain for a more idealistic settlement, he could not bring himself to repudiate the President, whom he urged Liberals everywhere to continue to support. Wilson had done his best, Gardiner concluded, but the forces arrayed against him were overwhelming. In the first place, it had been a 'fatal mistake' to hold the inter-allied conference at Paris, where Clemenceau held sway. But the cardinal error, he reckoned on the 14th, had been to schedule that 'disastrous election in England last December. It sacrificed the most priceless six weeks in history to a political gamble. It made us the supporter of France in the peace instead of the supporter of America. It debased the national mind and filled it with ideas of plunder.'

These columns gave no hint of the changes afoot in Bouverie Street. On 29 May, Gardiner had a long talk with Henry Cadbury who stiffly remonstrated that it was one thing for a contributor to lambaste the Prime Minister occasionally, and another for the editor to do so week after week. Edward Cadbury, informed of the 'interview' by his brother, was 'extremely sorry that I have not been able to avoid the difficulties that I foresaw were coming. I think I have from time to time fully explained my position to you,' he reminded Gardiner,

and while we agree entirely on essential principles, our differences have been on methods of expressing them. I suggest the following proposals to you:—

1. *English History, 1914–1945*, p. 137.

That while resigning actual Editorship and Executive Control of the policy of the 'Daily News' you should continue your present weekly articles in the 'Daily News' and the 'Star' and we should on our part be glad to carry out the terms of the 3 years Agreement, and pay you £2,500 per year salary and 1 % of the profits of the business. We hope that you will have a good holiday at our expense when your resignation of Editorship takes effect.

I think you understand my personal feelings towards yourself which remain unchanged, and if you can see your way to continue with us without quite such a heavy burden as you have had hitherto, we should only feel that this is in some measure meeting the debt which we owe to you, particularly in the early days of our connection. [1]

The terms were generous: Gardiner's two weekly articles fetched him a fee that averaged out well above the usual market rate, and there was no restriction on the views he expressed. It was further stipulated that he enjoyed the right to contribute to any other publication that did not compete directly with the *Daily News* or the *Star*; and because these deliberations preceded the appointment of his successor, he was assured that his opinion would 'have weight' so that the next editor would not be someone who 'would make the fulfilment of the conditions difficult'. [2]

In short, the Cadburys made every effort to accommodate Gardiner, for whom they felt a genuine concern. There can be no doubt that, for his own sake, the release came none too soon. His morale was at a low ebb, and he could have continued only at great physical cost to himself. Excitable by nature, he was now dangerously overwrought. His anxiety over world events was compounded by continual pro-prietorial interference. Not that his tug-of-war with the Cadburys was anything new: S. L. Hughes, 'chucked off' the staff during war-time, advised Arnold Bennett 'that neither Gardiner nor Parke had any influence at [the] Daily News & that the Cadburys ran every-

1. Edward Cadbury to Gardiner, 2 June 1919, G.P.
2. Henry Cadbury to Gardiner, 9 September 1919, G.P. According to the revised 'articles of association' that Edward Cadbury forwarded to Gardiner on 15 September, it was 'agreed that the publication of any article or articles written by the said Alfred George Gardiner under this agreement for publication in the "Daily News" or the "Star" should be at the discretion of the respective Editors of those newspapers, it being understood that the editorial authority, while em-powered to withhold publication or delete a given passage, shall not extend to alteration of phrase or meaning': G.P.

thing'.[1] Such a situation had been tolerable so long as there had existed a common approach to problems. But George Cadbury's abiding devotion to Lloyd George –a man, like himself, 'easily moved at the sight of human suffering' – and his insistence that 'no one but Mr Lloyd George . . . could take the lead in the great progressive movements of the peace',[2] rendered Gardiner's position an untenable one. Still, Gardiner did not exaggerate when he maintained that, after his professional relations with the Cadburys had been 'interrupted on what seemed to both of us a vital question, . . . the incident . . . made no difference to our private relations'.[3] Henry Cadbury did not allow the public announcement to be made without letting Gardiner

know that now onwards the chafings & difficulties of the past have gone by the board & only the real mutual esteem & the fine & noble side of a fearless soul con[tinue] to find place in my remembrance. I want to think of you always with that sunny smile which I have learned to know & I want us often to meet as men with a common object. 'The best is yet to be' – for we need faith & hope in large measure.[4]

On the morning of 10 September the *Daily News* confirmed that its editor for nearly eighteen years had relinquished his post, but that he had accepted appointment as a director and would continue to write his widely read Saturday column. It was anyone's guess exactly what this meant. Was it that the Cadburys lacked the courage to retain him in his full editorial capacity? Or were they afraid, or ashamed, to drop him altogether? The new arrangement could not be expected to last long. Massingham, looking back upon a 'long experience of editorial resignations', his own among them, was hard pressed to think of 'a more obfuscating announcement than that of Mr Gardiner's', which paid 'a glowing and not at all excessive tribute' to a man who was obviously being kicked upstairs. 'The trouble cannot be in Mr Gardiner's writing,' he reasoned in the *Nation* three days later, 'for the most conspicuous example of it remains.' Nor, apparently, had Gardiner been faulted for 'his conduct of the policy of the

1. Entry for 7 December 1915, Bennett's Journal.
2. George Cadbury to Henry Cadbury [November 1918?], quoted in Gardiner, *Life of George Cadbury*, p. 280.
3. *Ibid.*
4. Henry Cadbury to Gardiner, 9 September 1919, G.P.

paper, for', with a seat on the board of directors, 'he will have an important part in determining it in future. Then what is it?' Massingham asked rhetorically. 'Is it that Mr Gardiner was too fond of liberty and not fond enough of Mr Lloyd George?' Unable to solve the 'riddle', at least not in print, he 'merely . . . express[ed] the hope that whatever Mr Gardiner's resignation means, it does not signify that London has got a fresh recruit for the journalism of the tame cat'.

The search for a successor to Gardiner had begun in July. So far as one can tell, Henry Cadbury's first choice was J. L. Hammond. 'Personal circumstances however put the thing out of the question for me,' Hammond notified Gardiner, to whom he hastened

to say how profoundly I regret that your long & distinguished editorship is to come to an end. I hope the admiration of your friends is some measure of the satisfaction with which you look back on your work. I think all journalists – whether they agree or disagree with all your views – take pride in the courage, independence & character that have marked your tenure of office.[1]

The next to receive an offer ('if it can be called an offer') was Arthur Greenwood, who, at Leo Amery's injunction, was to speak for England on the eve of the Second World War. On this occasion, however, he declined to be anyone's mouthpiece. 'In the first place I'm merely an amateur & it would be presumptuous for me to pretend to follow you,' he told Gardiner:

Secondly, I think I should find that the work would tie me up too much. My third reason affects you more particularly. It is largely surmise but I feel uneasy about it. George has had his knife into Donald & Spender & I know you've got across him. Old Cadbury I believe is a 'Georgeite'. People don't give up the Editorship of a daily paper, or proprietors get rid of Editors for nothing. I suspect, therefore, the 'hidden hand'. I may, of course, be wrong in all this but if there's any truth in it I wouldn't touch the D.N. with a long stick.[2]

Clifford Sharp, the editor of the *New Statesman*, was also said to have refused a bid.

Only two days before the announcement of Gardiner's translation,

1. Hammond to Gardiner, 25 July 1919, G.P.
2. Greenwood to Gardiner, 4 August 1919, G.P.

Henry Cadbury journeyed to Manchester in hot pursuit of W. P. Crozier, the versatile news editor of the *Guardian*. He first sought the good offices of C. P. Scott, as did his father before him. Scott agreed that he would not stand in Crozier's way, although he confided to L. T. Hobhouse, his candidate the last time around, that 'If C. goes we shall be jolly well up a tree'. Personally, he very much doubted whether the position was worth Crozier's while: Gardiner had been 'only a "political" editor and that is what Cadbury wants. Crozier wouldn't take that', and would demand nothing less than 'a full editorship with general control.' The danger, as Scott saw it, was that Henry Cadbury, in his desperation, would 'promise anything without necessarily meaning strictly to perform. He's a weak and wobbly man and very hard up.' Scott placed far greater stock in Edward Cadbury, 'who is a real person', but who, unfortunately, was not 'on the spot' in Bouverie Street: 'Henry is a weak and rather shuffling person and would be a broken reed', incapable of sustaining an editor in a contest 'with the (extremely unsatisfactory) Board of Directors'. After weeks of haggling with the Cadburys, Crozier decided to remain at Manchester. Scott, greatly relieved, rewarded him with a directorship.[1]

The formal announcement of Gardiner's resignation brought him a flood of letters, too numerous and too repetitious to catalogue, testifying to his influence and esteem within the profession. Typical was a message from Robert Lynd, whom A.G.G. had brought to the *Daily News* for five guineas a week:

You have made all of us who worked under you feel your friends. You have given us a sense of freedom and ease as well as the great pleasure of good company. You have also given us the sense of being led by one who was fighting for good causes in a way that no other living journalist was doing or could do.[2]

Few of Gardiner's friends and colleagues had had any inkling of the situation. 'It came as a great surprise to me,' exclaimed Hirst, who prided himself in his Fleet Street contacts, and who trusted that Gardiner would 'be able to dedicate for a time to letters what you

1. Scott to Hobhouse, 9 and 27 September and 14 October 1919 (copies), *Guardian* Archives.
2. Lynd to Gardiner, 9 September 1919, G.P.

have hitherto devoted to party'. [1] Bennett, who signed his letter 'Your ex-contributor & admirer (not ex)', jocularly concurred. Languishing in Liverpool, where he was rehearsing a new play ('*I* hate the theatre'), he expected his friend 'to break out in a new place in the article way. See to't.' [2] Masterman, however, thought it was high time that Gardiner should 'go into Parliament. It's only a question of hammering away at your voice to make yourself an effective speaker,' he counselled, 'the *matter* is there all right. Why not become a high officer of State in an honest Administration! Only don't control food!' [3]

There was the inevitable – but groundless – suspicion that the Prime Minister had somehow pulled strings to rid himself of an enemy. T. P. O'Connor expressed the 'hope it wasn't [?] compulsory & under influences *d'en haut*'; [4] G. P. Gooch and others wrote in the same vein. But even if Lloyd George was not responsible, he was sure to take comfort. That, to his opponents, was sufficiently galling. 'Does this mean the hand of L. George?' wondered Austin Harrison, son of the Positivist leader and himself editor of the *English Review*. Already he had begun 'to sense a change in the policy of the D.N.', which seemed to him to be 'becoming woolly & anti-Labour. The next big change', he prophesied, 'will be . . . the Manchester Guardian, for Scott is ageing and there is a distinct want of direction on that paper. So one of the last individual editors is to go,' he concluded disbelievingly. 'The process of "nationalisation" is moving – whither?' [5]

The more prominent of Gardiner's sympathizers resisted the temptation to leap to conclusions. Instead, they paid tribute to his service to journalism and to the Liberal Party. Those who knew him best tried to buck him up. John Burns sent assurances that 'a cup of tea on Sundays' would always be waiting at Battersea. 'Where is that promised book on cricket?' he demanded to know. [6] Others could not suppress their own uneasiness. Gilbert Murray 'deliberately put off writing . . . till the storm of . . . letters should have abated', but

1. Hirst to Gardiner [n.d.], G.P.
2. Bennett to Gardiner, 10 September 1919, G.P.
3. Masterman to Gardiner, 10 September 1919, G.P.
4. O'Connor to Gardiner, 15 September 1919, G.P.
5. Harrison to Gardiner, 10 September 1919, G.P.
6. Burns to Gardiner, 10 September 1919, G.P.

nonetheless remained 'terribly anxious about the future. I have scanned the horizon anxiously, and I don't see anyone who can begin to take your place.'[1] His disquiet was shared by Asquith, who knew all too well what it was like to be turned out to pasture. Writing from Venice, the former premier declared that he was 'very sorry, though not wholly unprepared, to see the official announcement', which he regarded 'as a national calamity'. It was, he told Gardiner, 'a relatively small compensation to know that you will still have your weekly pulpit'.[2]

Newspapermen, understandably, saw the unshipping of Gardiner more as a professional than a personal misfortune. An unidentified correspondent in the *New Statesman* considered the 'extraordinary succession of changes in the Press' during the previous two decades: 'The single omnipotent editor has barely survived. He was always a much rarer being than people have imagined': Garvin was only 'a Sunday editor'; Spender was not master in his own house; and Scott exercised his authority in another capacity. 'Since the dominant tendency of the Press in our epoch is towards trust-ownership', it stood to reason that 'the greater number of the prize editorial posts' would go to 'men who are executive officers rather than publicists'. After all, 'no power on earth . . . can secure the continuous services of a thoughtful and independent editor to a newspaper which is the organ of a purely financial or party syndicate'. The *Nation*, published the same day, concentrated upon the political implications of the move: 'Certain things must happen now that the most animated and forcible diurnal assailant of the Georgian rule no longer sets the tone of the great popular organ of Liberalism in London and the North. The morning attack will lose its personal note; its afternoon repercussion in the "Star" may be something less resonant.' Such a prospect could hardly have dismayed the editors of the *British Weekly*, soon to identify themselves 'as ardent supporters of the Coalition, and especially of its illustrious head' (25 March 1920); yet, on 11 September, they too expressed 'sincere regret' at the loss to journalism, and satisfaction that Gardiner intended to continue his 'interesting Saturday articles', and presumably 'his delightful causeries as "Alpha of the Plough" . . . in the *Star*'.

1. Murray to Gardiner, 24 September 1919, G.P.
2. Asquith to Gardiner, 16 September 1919, G.P.

'Alpha's' admirers need not have feared. His was the voice with which Gardiner bade farewell to Fleet Street. 'Today I am among the demobilised,' he exulted on the 18th, virtually giving away the open secret of his identity:

I have put off the harness of a lifetime and am a person at large. For me, Fleet Street is a tale that is told, a rumour on the wind, a memory of far off things and battles long ago. At this hour I fancy it is getting into its nightly paroxysm. . . . I hear the murmur of it all from afar as a disembodied spirit might hear the murmurs of the life it has left behind.

An enterprising journal . . . wants my 'mellow reflections' on my experiences in Fleet Street. I am hardly in the mood yet for 'mellow reflections'. I am still overcome by the novelty of what in Lancashire they call 'shaking a loose leg'.

. . .

No more shall I ring in vain for that messenger who had always 'gone out to supper, sir,' or been called to the news room or sent on an errand. No more shall I cower nightly before that tyrannous clock that ticked so much faster than I wrote. . . . Time, that has lorded it over me so long, is henceforth my slave, and the future stretches before me like an infinite green pasture in which I can wander until the sun sets.

. . .

And if, perchance, as I sit under a tree with an old book, or in the chimney corner before a chessboard, there comes to me one from the great noisy world, inviting me to return to Fleet Street, I shall tell him a tale. One day (I shall say) Wang Ho, the wise Chinese, was in his orchard when there came to him from the distant capital two envoys, bearing an urgent prayer that he would return and take his old place in the Government. He ushered them into his house and listened gravely to their plea. Then, without a word, he turned, went to a basin of water, took a sponge *and washed out his ears.*[1]

A.G.G.'s admirers, not content to allow the genial 'Alpha' the last word, tendered a dinner in his honour at the National Liberal Club on 14 October. Originally intended as 'a modest gathering of personal friends', it grew in size and significance. Asquith took the chair, and Spender delivered a rousing speech on the virtue of political independence in journalism. Gardiner, 'flattered by such a conspicuous

1. 'Fleet Street no more', the *Star*, 18 September 1919; reprinted in *Windfalls*, pp. 203–8.

kindness', added 'a word or two' about 'the relation of the Press to Government', which he saw as the burning issue of the day. 'I am devoted to my calling,' he said. 'I believe it fulfils or ought to fulfil one of the highest functions of society. But it is not the function of government. Its business is to inform the public, and the function of government belongs to Parliament.' To the shame and misfortune of the nation, those functions had lately been confused: 'politicians have more and more relied on governing through the Press, on creating momentary impulses in the mob and serving their ends by riding on those waves of passion.' Take, for example, the industrial crisis of recent weeks, a subject on which he – in collaboration with Spender, Mrs Fawcett, and several clergymen – had written a letter to *The Times* on 3 October. Denounced by members of the Government as an 'Anarchist conspiracy', it was, more accurately, 'a wages dispute'. Nonetheless, 'it threatened the country with civil war. Yet Parliament was never called together. The Press was continually consulted; the Mayors were called together; the volunteer police were called out, but Parliament was treated as though it had no rights . . . and no duties to be performed.' Sounding more like a prospective candidate than an ousted editor, he pleaded for the reassertion of parliamentary supremacy and the rehabilitation of parties. 'If Parliament loses its authority,' he warned,

your Government will be a thing of intrigues and personal ambitions, of deals and bargains, and there will be no escape from the challenge of force on the one side and of direct action on the other.

If we are to get back from the dangerous courses into which we have drifted we must restore the authority and the principles of Parliament in place of personal rule through the Press. . . . We must have political leaders . . . whose principles are not fine weather principles, but are made to weather the storm as well as promenade in the sunshine. You cannot believe in Free Trade, for example, at odd moments. . . . You cannot be tremendously keen about liberty in Czecho-Slovakia and Jugo-Slavia and then fill Ireland with soldiers and machine guns. By what right has this country been warring for 18 months against the Russian Revolution?

Not since Charles James Fox had waged 'the indomitable struggle of Liberalism . . . with a following not much more formidable than that of Sir Donald Maclean today', had there been 'a time when the government of principle was more necessary in public affairs, and

273

when the spirit of liberalism had a greater task to perform'. The nations of the world had to be made to embark

on a new way of life, in which we shall all underwrite the freedom and security of each, establish a co-operative purpose in human society and banish the spectre of war by organising . . . for peace. The battle for the League of Nations is the battle of liberalism. That great idea can only be accomplished by the victory of the liberal idea. [1]

When the last toast was drunk and the guests had dispersed, Wilson Harris hurried back to Bouverie Street, where the next day's issue of the *Daily News* was being put to bed. 'That night', for some reason, 'there was a great dearth of leader subjects', and he suggested to Stuart Hodgson, 'who was *in loco editoris*', that a piece should be written along the lines of Spender's remarks. Hodgson 'at once agreed', and Harris set to work. 'It needed a certain delicacy of treatment,' he recalled, 'since the relationship between editor and proprietors obviously entered into it. . . .' He brought the first proof 'upstairs to H. W. Smith, the Night Editor, a man of the soundest judgment, and asked him whether he saw anything in it to which our own proprietors could take exception'. Smith read it through, and replied 'that, on the contrary, he thought it suffered from undue restraint'. Hodgson, too, 'read and passed it', and Harris went home to nurse the hope that he might be invited to succeed Gardiner. Two days later, however, 'Henry Cadbury came to my room and told me he had not trusted himself to speak till he had had time to govern his feelings. He then expressed himself' on the subject of the 15 October leader 'in terms' that left Harris no doubt that he 'could as well aspire to the Archbishopric of Canterbury as to the editorship of the *Daily News*'. [2]

Gardiner was well relieved of such a burden.

1. Gardiner committed 'the substance of the speech' to paper, G.P.; see also *The Times*, 15 October 1919, which carried the text of Asquith's tribute to Gardiner.
2. Harris, *Life So Far*, pp. 198–9.

11. At liberty

Strictly speaking, A. G. Gardiner's professional life – the subject of this book – ended in the autumn of 1919. The days had passed when a London editor could, seemingly overnight, exchange one desk for another. [1] The surviving newspapers were too few, and either Gardiner (with his literary bent) did not suit their requirements, or, more usually, they his politics. It was just as well. He had had his fill of editorial responsibilities, and preferred to keep his own principles and his own hours. Fortunately, he could count upon a pension from the Cadburys that relieved him of financial anxiety. Added to the remuneration he received from other sources, and to the return on his modest investments, he netted a better livelihood than he had ever enjoyed as an editor.

For the next quarter century, he busied himself as a weekly columnist, first for the *Daily News*, then for a succession of journals. He spent four-day weekends with his family, now permanently relocated at Whiteleaf, and the middle days of the week in London, where he discharged his professional and social obligations. The two halves of his week, like the two aspects of his life, were kept quite separate until age and the next war conspired to restrict his movements. He communicated with his editors by post, and rarely saw Fleet Street except from the window of the bus that took him from the Reform Club, where he spent most afternoons, to Toynbee Hall, where (after 1921) he kept midweek lodgings with the Mallons. It took time to adjust to the new situation, but, looking back, he was certain that 'the best years of my life have been from 60 onwards'. [2]

Yet however satisfying these later decades may have been, they

1. 'What can an ex-editor do? The range of opportunities is limited', Colin Seymour-Ure has written in his study of *The Press, Politics and the Public*. He provides a list of recent editors who, after being deposed, went into other fields (pp. 123–4).
2. Gardiner to Swinnerton, 12 August 1938, Swinnerton Papers.

were, by any standard, anticlimactic. Like his party, he drifted farther and farther from the locus of power, and his journalism suffered in consequence. No longer so well placed for information, he depended heavily on conversations at the Reform Club, and, to an extent that neither could have realized, on the experiences of his two sons-in-law, Mallon and Lionel (later Lord) Robbins. Often he did not disguise the fact that he relied, too, on what he gleaned from other journalists. Still capable of providing a pungent assessment of personality and an astute commentary on the issues of the day, his columns came to reflect rather than to guide opinion. The few politicians with whom he kept active contact were driven from their seats in the House of Commons as he was driven from his chair in Bouverie Street: there was indeed a correlation between the fate of the Liberal Party and the decline of its press.

Before embarking upon his 'second career' as a columnist, he at last realized his ambition to visit America. He had applied for his passport in July, and booked a two-month lecture tour. Accompanied by S. K. Ratcliffe, a veteran of many crossings, he sailed on the *Caronia* on 22 October. Twelve days later, he disembarked at New York.[1] Impressed by the city, he was immediately struck by 'the fierce conflict between capital & labour (much more volcanic and demented than our own), the conflict between black and white & so on. The impact of these great issues on the mind is overwhelming', he wrote at the close of his first day in the new world. 'It gives the feeling that big as our own problems are they are trivial compared with those with which America is faced. And so far as I can judge the spirit of the American is much fiercer and more explosive than our own.'

The days that followed only confirmed his initial reactions. '"Hell is a city much like London," said Shelley, but he didn't know New York', Gardiner wrote to his wife. He had walked along Fifth Avenue (which seemed to him a cross between Bond Street and Park Lane), and had ventured as far west as Riverside Drive, where he was rewarded with a spectacular view of the Palisades across the Hudson River. More excitingly, he had taken a lift to the top of the Woolworth

1. For the information of his wife, Gardiner 'put down from day to day a few notes about anything & everything that comes along . . ., without order and without considering whether it is worth putting down or not'. It is on these notes that the present account is based.

Building, a structure 'twice as high as St Paul's' in London. But it was not the visual aspects of the city that fascinated him most:

The speed of life here is unlike anything I have seen on earth. It isn't that people move faster or do more work – I think they probably move slower & perhaps do less – but the machine of life is so much more [finished?] & immense that the individual is lost in it & is whirred round in its complicated intricacies.

He did not mean to suggest

that the people are less civilised than ours. In mere externals, they are more civilised, more cordial, more responsive, more good natured. Their hospitality is extraordinary. . . . There is civility here, but no servility.

He was amazed by the assurance and self-respect of taxi-drivers, doormen, and chambermaids, who performed their services all the better for the pride they took in themselves and their work. Yet, at the same time, racial, religious, and 'social antagonisms' were 'fierce and naked'.

A full week after his arrival, the New York press featured an interview he gave at the City Club on his first evening. To American reporters, he looked

the typical Englishman. With his ruddy, smooth complexion and the carefully careless way he wears his clothes, his nationality would be known in any crowd. The tact of a diplomat is mingled with the greatest courtesy and amiability. He is of middle age, with bushy hair and a cropped mustache, the hair slightly gray. Slightly under medium height, he is rather thin, with sharp features and a firm mouth. From behind gold-rimmed glasses, keen blue eyes peer with an expression of unceasing intellectual activity. Despite his reputation as a ruthless critic, he has a kindly, engaging smile, illuminated by his eyes while framed by his lips.

Above all else he came across as a man of pronounced views. On the Treaty:

We could have been cheered in November last by a serious consideration of an American peace, had the opportunity not slipped through the fingers of the politicians. What did we get instead? A peace which was French, or near what the French wanted.

On the League:

People say that the League will guarantee an unjust peace. I do not take it that way. If we can't get the League of Nations, then it is all up with civilization; there will be a new balance of power, a new and more disastrous arming of nations, the conquest of science over the spirit.

On Anglo-American relations:

If it is based on American interest and British interest, instead of on something broader and something more spiritual, it is no friendship at all and is bound to result in eventual conflict.

Conceding the possibility of 'serious trouble in Ireland', he faulted Lloyd George's handling of the situation, but asserted that there was 'still time for reason and wisdom to prevail'. Dominion status made more sense, he argued, than the proclamation of an Irish republic. He derided Lloyd George's statement that the recent British railway strike had been the work of a 'conspiracy': Bolshevism posed no threat in Britain. On British politics: 'Liberalism has been badly stricken as a result of the war, and labor is not in a position at present to form a government, having neither the administrative power nor leadership.' It would not surprise him if, at the next general election, Lloyd George made a 'plunge from the right to the left. . . . So great is the obscurity that always surrounds him, he might be the leader either of the reactionaries or the revolutionaries.'[1]

From New York Gardiner went to Washington, where he hoped to renew his acquaintance with the President. He lunched at the White House with Mrs Wilson, Admiral Grayson, and the President's daughter, who brought word that her father was too ill to join them. After lunch, Mrs Wilson and Grayson led him along the corridor outside the President's bedroom. 'Do you think I might look in and see if the President is awake?' Mrs Wilson asked Grayson, the President's physician. 'He might just like to shake hands with Mr Gardiner.' Grayson nodded his assent and Mrs Wilson 'tiptoed into the room' only to return in a few minutes to say that her husband was asleep. The incident acquires a special significance in view of the fact that Lord Grey, on whom Gardiner called at the British Embassy that afternoon, was never given the chance to present his credentials to the President. The official explanation was that Wilson was physically incapacitated, but Gardiner suspected otherwise. 'If it [would have been] possible for the President to see me,' he deduced, 'it was evident that he was capable of seeing much more important people'. After

1. *New York Times* and *New York World*, 9 November 1919.

further investigation, he learned that the President's refusal to receive Grey was due to the presence on Grey's staff of an underling known to have made offensive remarks about Mrs Wilson. It was all terribly petty. Looking back, Gardiner believed that Grey, as 'ambassador on special mission', might somehow have prevailed upon Wilson to yield certain non-essentials to his congressional opponents in order to purchase their support for the League. [1]

In his travels from city to city, Gardiner often departed from his prepared text to comment upon the events of the day or the issues of greatest concern to his audience. At Boston, he spoke about the Irish problem; at Chicago, where he was introduced by the Governor of Illinois, about maritime controls. He seized every occasion to extol the President and to proselytize for the League. 'The doctrine of isolation', he preached, 'became for ever obsolete on that day that the United States entered the war, and the attempt to breathe new life into it is as futile as it would be for us to attempt to restore the Heptarchy.' He singled out for attack William Randolph Hearst, America's answer to Northcliffe, who ruthlessly exploited 'the powerful elements of anti-British sentiment in the American population'. Admittedly, Hearst had plenty to work with, especially among Irish Americans. A keen student of the press, Gardiner praised the job that was being done by the *New York Times*, the *New York World*, the *New York Evening Post*, the *Philadelphia Ledger*, the *Chicago Daily News*, and, among the weeklies, the *New Republic* and the *Nation*. But, 'outside this responsible class of journals, . . . there is a numerous and powerful body of newspapers which is definitely and actively anti-British', and capable of infinite harm. 'Of these the Hearst newspapers are by far the most formidable, though they by no means exhaust the list.' [2]

Clive, his elder son, kept him abreast of developments at home, and reminded him of his promise to return by Christmas. 'For the past

1. Autobiographical memorandum [n.d.], G.P. Many years later, Admiral Grayson told Lloyd George the same story about Grey's Washington mission. See entry for 17 September 1934, in Stevenson, *Lloyd George: a Diary*, p. 277.

2. Gardiner, *The Anglo-American Future*, pp. 10, 62. Gardiner later recalled that this 'little book' was written at the request of [Victor] Gollancz who was then with the Oxford University Press, '& it attracted much more comment in America than here': Gardiner to Swinnerton, 10 March 1941, Swinnerton Papers.

month or so', he wrote, 'the centre of gravity' in the Gardiner household in Finchley Road 'seems to have come unpinned in an extraordinary way, and there's something almost magical about the thought that somewhere around Christmastime the balance will be restored.' And, Clive was proud to report, 'these feelings aren't so local either. I honestly believe that people all over the place will be electrified when your first Saturday article appears again.' The political outlook remained bleak. 'Liberalism for the time being is stagnant if not dead.' Sir John Simon ('of all God forsaken dullards') had been adopted to stand in the Liberal interest in a by-election at Spen Valley, 'and I'm pretty sure it would be for the best if he got beaten. The Liberals have done very badly in recent bye elections,' Clive reminded his father, 'and will continue so to do until they get a bit of ginger into their bones instead of salt water and soap.'[1]

Gardiner barely managed to keep his promise to his family. The ship that brought him home came within sight of land early on the day before Christmas. The first 'precious' glimpse of the Scilly Isles, moved 'Alpha' to reflect upon Drake, who, 'sailing in from the Spanish main, saw these islands, and knew he was once more in his Devon Seas. I fancy I see him on the deck beside me with a wisp of hair, curled and questioning, on his baldish forehead, and I mark the shine in his eyes.'[2] Some of Gardiner's friends, eager to hear his impressions of America, entertained him at lunch on 4 February. The event was held at the Connaught Rooms, and tickets sold for 7s 6d. General Maurice presided, and the guests included Lord Beauchamp, Sir Donald Maclean, Walter Runciman, C. F. G. Masterman, and Robert Donald.[3]

What had become of the *Daily News* in the meantime? the mantle of editorship had fallen, more or less by default, on Hodgson. But he made no pretence to power. Gardiner's removal had occasioned neither a purge of the staff nor a voluntary exodus. Few journalists were in the enviable position of Arnold Bennett, who could spurn a handsome commission 'partly because now that Gardiner has gone my

1. Clive Gardiner to Gardiner, 28 November [1919], G. P. Simon was, in fact, rejected at Spen Valley.

2. 'On sighting land', the *Star*, 1 January 1920; reprinted in *Windfalls*, pp. 269–70.

3. *The Times*, 16 January 1920.

original distaste for the Cadburys has a free rein'.[1] Yet there were certain subtle changes that must have eluded all but the most attentive readers.

Determined to demonstrate to the novices in the Labour Party the mutual need for cooperation, the Liberal Party leaders undertook to fight Labour in a string of by-elections. The *Daily News* disapproved strongly of such a policy, but for reasons different from those in Gardiner's day. On 16 January, Henry Cadbury (regretting the unavoidable absence of his brother) went to see Maclean. He wished to make sure that Maclean and Asquith 'understood' exactly what was meant by his family's proclamation 'that the "Daily News", under their proprietorship, was an independent organ.' Maclean assured Cadbury that he and Asquith 'had never regarded the "Daily News" as a thick and thin supporter of the Party, in the sense that [they] might look upon the "Westminster Gazette"', in which the Party had invested substantial funds. Speaking for Asquith, as he was so often called upon to do, he acknowledged

that the wide circulation of the 'Daily News' throughout the provinces and in Scotland made it of exceptional power and influence, and it had been up till now, with all its independence, reckoned as the leading exponent of Liberalism in the London press, and one of the mainstays of the Liberal Party.

Cadbury emphasized that the paper had initiated a 'new policy which had been indicated lately in their columns'. Maclean, glad 'to clear the ground', thereupon asked whether 'it would be wise for us to assume that the "Daily News" was to be regarded in the future as a Labour organ'. Cadbury 'did not dissent . . . except in so far as to reiterate that they were an independent organ', which might support any party 'which would help in the propagation of its views'. It was 'the view of the Directors', he bluntly informed Maclean, 'that Labour should as early as possible be given responsibility'. Maclean considered this perfectly reasonable. Asquith, he revealed, looked forward to a coalition of Labourites and independent Liberals. But how was this to be accomplished if the latter held no seats? By 'endeavouring to crush out the Liberal Party at by-elections', the *Daily News* was frustrating its own purpose. The important thing, he

1. Bennett to Blumenfeld, 6 October 1919, *Letters of Arnold Bennett*, iii, 112.

told Cadbury, was not 'to get "rattled"'. Steadiness was more needed than any other quality – it had won through in 1900–1906 and would do so again.' Cadbury, however, 'was quite impervious'.[1]

Gardiner, to whom Maclean sent a transcript of his conversation with Henry Cadbury, was not the least surprised. The confrontation, he replied, 'illuminates the situation & shows what the Liberal party is face to face with in regard to the Press. . . . It seems to me to invite the question whether the party is to remain an effective organisation or to go under.'[2] For all the publicity that had been given his becoming a director, this was the first he had heard of the board's commitment to Labour. No matter. He had never really expected to have a say in policymaking.

Unlike the Cadburys, Gardiner was not prepared to admit publicly that the Liberal Party was moribund. The party's recovery, he predicted, would begin at Paisley, where Asquith was to attempt a comeback in a February by-election. Gardiner anticipated a Liberal victory not only in recognition of the candidate's superiority, but also as an expression of 'national resentment against that criminal hoax', the last general election, 'and all its disastrous consequences'. The result, when it was finally announced, could not have been more satisfactory. For a flickering moment, the Liberal renaissance seemed at hand. Gardiner warmly congratulated Asquith upon his

magnificent victory at Paisley. It is much more than a personal triumph, gratifying though that is to those who have felt the humiliation of past events: it is a welcome sign that the great political debauch is over & that Philip, who has been very drunk on very vile liquor, is becoming sober again. It was worth going through much bitterness to have such a resurrection & to know, as you know, that all that is best in the mind of the country is with you & looks to you to bring this nation, & not this nation only, back to clean paths & just & honourable purposes.[3]

He was among the many Londoners who lined the sidewalks to cheer Asquith on his way from Cavendish Square to Westminster.'Alpha' described the joyful scene in the *Star* (4 March), and brooded on the

1. Memorandum by Maclean of a conversation with Henry Cadbury, 16 January 1920, Asquith Papers, cxlviii, fols 92 ff.
2. Gardiner to Maclean, [18] January 1920, Asquith Papers, cxlviii, fol. 96.
3. Gardiner to Asquith, 26 February 1920, Asquith Papers, xxxiii, fols 238–9.

fickleness of public opinion, from which the best men always suffer most.

Asquith, back in the House, was notably more restrained than A.G.G., back in the *Daily News*. In reply to the Prime Minister, who had condemned as 'Bolshevism' proposals to nationalize the mines, Gardiner declared on 14 February that 'the Sankey decision stands as the only authoritative verdict on the subject'. Like 'Alpha', A.G.G. was exasperated by the man in the street, who did not yet seem to realize that

> when Mr Lloyd George is in a tight place, his invariable expedient is to shout 'Fire! Fire!' in order to divert the mind of the stupid public and send it stampeding in another direction. . . . The country has to be set in a blaze so that our nimble Premier may escape behind the smoke screen, and win new glory by coming up later and putting his own conflagration out.

But how was the situation to be saved if the Labour Party stubbornly insisted on going it alone? Gardiner, in his 21 February column, berated Labour for snubbing the Liberals at Spen Valley, and castigated Sidney Webb for his flippant suggestion that Labour was prepared, in the last resort, to 'buy Mr Lloyd George over the heads of the Tories'. Asquith, now attentive to press opinion, wrote that he had 'read the whole of your article with much admiration'.[1] With this encouragement, A.G.G. returned to the same theme one Saturday after another. Only a 'Liberal-Labour entente', he insisted on 6 March, 'would sweep the Coalition and all its works out of existence'. A week later, he explained that he favoured an interparty alliance, not 'a fusion. That is not possible even if it were desirable.' And on 17 April, he addressed 'A plain word to two parties', in which he enumerated the reasons why it was necessary 'to reverse the whole position at Westminster and get the country and the world out of the present hopeless rut':

> The revision of the Peace Treaty.
> The League of Nations.
> The abolition of militarism.
> Free Trade.
> Ireland.

1. Asquith to Gardiner, 21 February 1920, G.P.

Anglo-American relations.
Finance.
Social policy.

On each of these 'crucial issues', there was substantial agreement between Liberalism and Labour, and cooperation was facilitated by the fact that 'most of the Liberal reactionaries are now definitely in the Georgian camp and the Labour extremists are not a serious factor'. In point of fact, the 'Labour extremists' caused Gardiner considerable anxiety. It was his constant fear that they would make good their threat to call a general strike, and thereby play into the hands of Lloyd George. Ironically, the author of the People's Budget was now 'lead[ing] the dukes on a holy crusade against Bolshevism', or, as A.G.G. liked to put it, the Bolshevism opposed to his own. At his side was Winston Churchill, 'the Real Red Terror', who was dedicated to a 'policy of restoring a militarised world', and who especially outraged Gardiner by his innuendoes that the Labour Party, taking its orders from Moscow, was unfit to govern. Yet Gardiner had to admit that 'the daily avalanche of strikes' during the summer months gave credit to Churchill's pronouncements, and irresponsibly provided Lloyd George with 'a new lease of power to complete the work of devastation that he has carried so far'.[1]

Like many British publicists, John Maynard Keynes perhaps the most fiercely eloquent among them, Gardiner was a revisionist even before the Versailles Treaty was signed. It was more than fidelity to past principle that dictated his position. Along with General Smuts, whom he had long admired, he linked the recovery of British prosperity and world stability to 'the appeasement of Germany',[2] a phrase to which as yet no shame attached. Even Lloyd George, when it was at last safe to do so, said much the same thing.[3] 'The calamity that has befallen Europe since the Armistice,' Gardiner wrote in the *Daily News* on 10 April 1920, 'a calamity more grievous in some respects than the war itself, has been due to the fact that the spirit of revenge and not the spirit of appeasement has dictated the policy of the victors.'

1. *Daily News*, 13 and 20 March, 19 June, 3 and 31 July and 4 September 1920.
2. Statement to the press, 19 July 1919, quoted in Max Beloff, *Imperial Sunset*, i, 291.
3. See, for example, Lloyd George's pamphlet, *Is It Peace?* (London, 1923).

In August he went to see for himself German conditions, which he described in a series of midweek articles after his return. These were promptly reprinted as a shilling pamphlet, *What I Saw in Germany*, with a foreword by Lord Buckmaster. It was less his intention to plead for clemency than to allay British fears of a former enemy. His pilgrimage, which extended into Austria, took him to many of the so-called 'reactionary strongholds', where he was reassured to find 'no counter-movement, on any serious popular scale, to the overwhelming current of industrial Germany that represents the republican institution and the anti-militarist ideal'. The recent Kapp Putsch, an abortive attempt by right wing elements to seize control, gave welcome proof that 'larger tendencies' were opposed to a Hohenzollern restoration and the revival of a 'military autocracy'.

Gardiner resumed his regular column on 4 September with a tirade against 'the nimble-witted cleverness and charlatanry' of Lloyd George, whose 'skill in manipulating the political game is as conspicuous as his failure to understand the meaning of statesmanship'. It took Edward Cadbury three days to collect himself before he wrote to say how 'very glad' he was 'to see you back again in the "Daily News" on Saturday.' It was not 'the difficulties we are having to face', but concern for Gardiner's 'own influence in the country', that impelled him to take issue with one or two points:

> While I agree with your general distrust of the present Government and the opportunism of Lloyd George, we need a spirit of conciliation if the present tangled position is to be cleared. Hate and ill will are rife wherever one looks, and it seems to me essential that neither should find a place in the 'Daily News'.
>
> You say yourself if it comes to a fight Lloyd George will win – why stiffen his back and play into his hands?[1]

A week passed before Gardiner defended himself. Citing correspondence at the time of his resignation, he claimed a right to speak freely. The editor, after all, could always exercise his discretion. But perhaps, he wondered, it might be best for all concerned if he took his articles elsewhere. Edward Cadbury 'carefully considered' Gardiner's reply for a further six days, and assured him that 'a severance between you and the "Daily News" would be a real misfortune'. He sent along a

1. Edward Cadbury to Gardiner, 7 September 1920, G.P.

cutting of A.G.G.'s 4 September column, now long past, on which he indicated the particular phrases to which he took exception. 'The idea of the public that it is a personal question between yourself and Lloyd George is undoubtedly doing great damage to the "Daily News", and I am sure is also weakening your influence,' he again declared.[1] As Gardiner was no longer editor, he found it difficult to understand why his views as a columnist should reflect on the paper, which boasted a proud tradition as a forum for dissenting opinion.

Whatever the Cadburys may have thought, Gardiner had a loyal fan in Mrs Bernard Shaw, whose husband invited him to lunch in Adelphi Terrace with assurances that 'my wife – an ultra-Red who delights in your articles – would be enchanted to entertain you'.[2] G.B.S. himself must have been especially gratified by A.G.G.'s condemnation (2 October) of 'The war in Ireland', which likened the behaviour of the Black and Tans to the wartime atrocities of German troops in Belgium: 'In all our annals there has been nothing to parallel this record of organised and senseless savagery.'[3] The same policy of calculated inhumanity was pursued, on a larger scale, in Germany, and with more farreaching consequences. Gardiner devoted his next few columns to the subject, and, on the 19th, he was among those who addressed the second International Economic Conference at the Caxton Hall, Westminster. The theme of the two-day gathering, which drew a large contingent of German and Austrian delegates, was 'the restoration of Europe'. Lord Parmoor, a minister in the 1924 Labour Government, presided, and the other speakers included J. A. Hobson and Frau Schreiber Krieger, a member of the German Reichstag. Walther Rathenau, Germany's foreign secretary – he was soon to be assassinated as a 'November criminal' – had been invited to participate, but the British Foreign Office denied him permission to come to London. Gardiner protested the decision as 'an outrage'.

1. Edward Cadbury to Gardiner, 20 September 1920, G.P. Gardiner's letter of the 14th reportedly does not survive, but Edward Cadbury's reply makes clear its contents.

2. Shaw to Gardiner, 3 October 1920 (copy), G.P.

3. Gardiner's views on Ireland reflected the influence of Sir James O'Connor, the eminent Irish jurist, with whom he was meeting regularly, and who shared his antagonism to the Prime Minister: 'We ask for bread & L.G. offers us a stone, & offers it with malignity & contempt', O'Connor wrote to him on 13 October 1920: G.P.

Dr Rathenau, he said, 'was one of the most distinguished brains in Europe, and a great and enlightened capitalist. No one was more competent to discuss the European situation with more thoroughness and comprehension.'[1]

In his 30 October column, he gave the British public an idea of what they might have heard from Rathenau. It took the form of 'A letter to M. Poincaré', whose old-fashioned diplomacy he deplored. 'The Continent is strewn with your military alliances and swarms with your military missions,' A.G.G. scolded the President of the French Republic. He doubted, however, whether the French network of alliances would prove either 'enduring or trustworthy. It is the system of an hour, a jerry-built structure that will collapse at any blast of the realities of European life.' He reminded Poincaré that, a fortnight later, the Assembly of the League of Nations would convene for the first time at Geneva. 'We cannot have your policy and the policy of the League together. They are mutually destructive.' On 8 November, Poincaré replied to his critic on the front page of *Le Temps*. It was not often that a foreign journalist was paid such a compliment, but Gardiner did not take it as one. 'I do not think I shall misrepresent the reply,' he wrote testily on 13 November,

if I say that its main purpose is, not to deny the character I attributed to French policy, but to justify that policy. His second concern is to show that I do not represent British opinion, that I am inspired by Berlin if not by Lenin, and that behind my idealism is a base hunger for trade. . . . He recalls, a little unworthily, I think, and more than a little unwisely, the threadbare legend that I advocated neutrality in order that we might profit from the misfortunes of others.

He wished to make his position perfectly clear:

I am neither pro-German nor pro-French. I am pro-European. I want Germany to pay all that it ought to pay and all that it can pay to repair the wrong it has done. But it must be allowed to live and to labour freely and in peace in order to pay. It must be treated as a willing bankrupt and not as an immortal enemy. It must be brought into the European system on equal terms, and the deadly tyranny of the Supreme Council must give place to the League of Nations.

The new year brought a change of government at Paris, but not, so far as he could tell, any significant change of attitude. On 15 January

1. *The Times*, 20 October 1920.

he cautioned the French against abetting the secession movement in southern Germany. His admonition brought an indignant retort from the honorary secretary of the Anglo–French Society: 'Is it your aim to brand France as a villain [and] to cast odium upon her?' he asked the author of that morning's 'apparently one-sided and misinformed attack on France'. [1]

But Gardiner could not waste his ammunition on France with so many targets nearer at hand. In an address to the Federation of British Industries, Lloyd George spoke of the problems of 'down-trodden' Europe with a compassion that Gardiner refused to credit as sincere. 'No one would suppose from the tenor of that speech', he wrote on 4 December,

that Mr Lloyd George is the chief architect of the ruin he describes so picturesquely. . . . He has for four years exercised personal power un-exampled in this country since the days of the Tudors. The world is what he more than any other living man has made it. If it is in rags, the rags are of his manufacture.

It was too much to expect that the Prime Minister would be chastened by such familiar words from so predictable a source. What was needed was a demonstration of electoral opinion. An opportunity, in effect the first since Paisley, presented itself in late winter with the scheduling of three successive by-elections. Voters would be able to return a trio of prominent anti-Coalitionists – Llewelyn Williams, Ramsay MacDonald, and W. M. R. Pringle – to the Commons.

On 5 February, A.G.G. issued an appeal to the electors of Cardiganshire to reject the Coalition candidate and to vote instead for Williams, an independent Liberal who formerly sat for Carmarthen. [2] His column for the following Saturday, 'What is wrong with Parliament?', repeated his endorsement of Williams ('that able and independent Welshman'), and added commendations of MacDonald and Pringle: 'We shall not get either this country or the world into clear waters until the squalid tyranny that prevails at Westminster is bundled into oblivion.' Set up in type, this column was never published. The previous weekend, the Prime Minister, accompanied by

1. H.D.Davray to Gardiner, 15 January 1921, G.P.
2. The poll, a heavy one, was declared on the 19th, and Williams trailed his opponent – a Coalition Liberal – by nearly 3,600 votes.

his wife and daughter, had come to Birmingham to receive the freedom of the city and an honorary doctorate of law at the university. According to Gardiner, whose word cannot be corroborated, Mrs Lloyd George 'paid a visit to George Cadbury at the Manor House, Northfield', and the result was the letter that he received from Hodgson on the 13th, telling him that his column that day had been rejected.

Hodgson, an unassuming figure, deserves a measure of sympathy. He was 'empowered', according to the terms of Gardiner's contract with the Cadburys, 'to withhold publication or delete a given passage' at his discretion. His choice was either to offend his old chief or to defy his proprietors' instructions. 'It is clear that the position is impossible', he notified Gardiner.

I understand that the directors are determined that frontal attacks of this kind on L.G. are definitely to be discontinued. I have told H. T. Cadbury that I can't carry on between two fires. The agreement must be specifically varied

(1) either to cut out any alleged responsibility altogether, & to give you definitely carte blanche to write what you will, or

(2) you must come to some agreement with Birmingham on the general line of policy, or tactics, which is the real question. [1]

With this said, he left the next move to the principals.

There was a lull before the final storm. On 19 February, A.G.G. returned with an attack not on Lloyd George, but on the Labour Party, which had decided to oppose Pringle's candidacy at Penistone. On the 26th, he paid an unobjectionable tribute to Woodrow Wilson, who was due to leave the White House in a few days: It was easy 'to speak disparagingly of the failure of the President', but 'in the end the victory will be with him not by our virtues but by our necessities'. Fittingly, this was Gardiner's last regular column for the *Daily News*. For the following week he submitted an article entitled 'Coal and commonsense', which criticized the destruction of German industry and 'the policy of stripping Germany of coal'. It made no specific reference to Lloyd George. He was surprised, therefore, to have it returned with notice that publication was refused.

'I am very troubled about you & I know how you will feel the

1. J.S.H[odgson] to Gardiner [13 February 1921], G.P.

withholding of Sat[urday]'s article,' Henry Cadbury wrote to him on Sunday. At 'the risk of being misunderstood,' he suggested that 'for a few weeks it would be well to give up' the assignment:

> I am perfectly sure Edward wd. agree to indemnifying you under your agreement. So that financially you should in no way suffer.
>
> I know how strongly you feel the present political situation & I gather you would not be ready to write non-politically just now. As we are not in entire accord as to how the present situation should be tackled, is it not best to face that fact rather than that you should labour & the result not be used?
>
> Quite apart from this, I sincerely wish you could get a complete rest from all your activities for a while. I felt very unhappy about you when I saw you on Wednesday last.[1]

Gardiner did not know what to make of the suggestion. Why should the Cadburys wish him to write 'non-politically', when they employed 'Alpha' to do precisely that in the *Star*? Nor could he understand what was wrong with his 5 March column. Masterman, to whom he sent a proof copy, found it 'not only excellent in sentiment', but also in

> your very best style. It is not even emotional in tone or rhetorical. It is informative, containing facts which I never knew. You do not even rise to smite the Welsh Wizard.
>
> A Liberal paper that can reject this is *capable de tout*.[2]

Reluctant to see his 'long connection with the D.N. . . . peter out in a ragged edge of cross purposes & disagreements', Gardiner asked to be 'relieved altogether of the duty of writing articles wh. you do not want'. Any financial settlement was, of course, 'a matter for your own judgment'. He was willing to continue as a contributor to the *Star*, and, if desired, as a director. 'But I do hope that I may be relieved from the distress of the past few weeks,' he repeated. 'To cease my articles for some weeks, as you suggest, then to resume them with, I fear, a repetition of what has happened of late is a proposal that fills me with dismay.'[3] Henry Cadbury agreed. After an interview with Gardiner a few days later, he instructed the company

1. Henry Cadbury to Gardiner, 6 March [1921], G.P.
2. Masterman to Gardiner [March 1921], G.P.
3. Gardiner to Henry Cadbury, 7 March 1921 (copy), G.P.

secretary to confirm that a Saturday column was no longer required, 'but that the amount payable to you under the terms of this agreement for such contributions shall not be thereby affected and shall continue to be paid during the remainder of the currency of the agreement'.[1] This brought Gardiner £1000 a year, paid to him for the rest of his life and to his widow after he died.

A.G.G. vanished from the *Daily News* without a word of explanation. He returned later in the decade for a series of character sketches, but that was a different matter. By 26 March, Massingham, writing his 'London Diary' for the *Nation,* considered it safe to 'assume . . . that [Gardiner's] connection with that paper has ceased, and that its rather rueful pages will lack in future the one pen that seemed to have a definite political creed and force of conviction behind it'. Convinced that the 'mass of readers' of the *Daily News* did not 'want a thinner and feebler "Daily Mail"', he predicted that 'they will either go elsewhere for their accustomed diet, or will lose the services of a daily paper altogether'. That was no longer Gardiner's concern, although he remained a director for several weeks beyond his employment as a columnist.

Masterman sedulously carried word of his friend's predicament to Lord Beaverbrook, who, always glad to acquire a contributor on the rebound, offered Gardiner a place on the *Sunday Express.* Beaverbrook kept a stable of celebrated journalists, many of whom entertained political views antagonistic to his own. Despite encouragement from Masterman and Bennett, Gardiner had understandable misgivings about such an affiliation. The Cadburys, too, balked at the idea of his 'being a regular contributor of the "Sunday Express" and also remaining a Director of the "Daily News"'. Such an arrangement, they feared, 'would tend to identify the proprietary interest in the two papers in the public mind', and they did not choose to have any connection, however tenuous, with Beaverbrook.[2] Gardiner accordingly resigned his directorship and then, inexplicably, turned round and refused Beaverbrook's offer on the grounds 'that, while there is much agreement between us on the immediate situation, our attitude to affairs is so dissimilar that an enduring collaboration w[oul]d not be possible & in these circumstances, I think it is better in

1. T. G. Curtis to Gardiner, 15 March 1921, G.P.
2. Edward Cadbury to Gardiner, 18 April 1921, G.P.

your interest & mine that the experiment s[houl]d not be made'.[1] Finding himself without a journalistic platform, he grasped at any and every opportunity to proclaim his views. His vague plea in the correspondence columns of the *Nation* of 14 May for Labourites to join in 'A Radical revival', brought a swift rejoinder from Harold Laski, who demanded some 'proof that the change of heart which Mr Gardiner would indicate Liberalism has undergone is really true, and not simply the result of being out of office'. Along with letters to various editors, Gardiner churned out tiresome attacks on Lloyd George – some of them published anonymously – for journals as obscure as *Brain-Power*, the official publication of the Pelman Institute, which normally specialized in such features as 'How Lilian Gish learned to concentrate'. A two-part series, 'The case against Mr Lloyd George', that he wrote expressly for the *British Weekly* never appeared.[2] It must have pained him to realize how little he was accomplishing.

Nor was there any consolation in the pages of the *Daily News*, which he continued to peruse each morning. Asquith complained to a confidante that the paper gave 'more space and prominence to some remarks made in Welsh by Ll.G. to a lot of Calvinist parsons', than to his 15 June address to the Eighty Club.[3] A few weeks later C. P. Scott called at Bouverie Street in response to an invitation from Henry Cadbury to 'talk over the present position of Lib[eral]ism & its Leadership'. Scott, not the least to his surprise, found that Cadbury

really had nothing to say beyond reporting that his father thought ill of Asquith & wanted to know what I thought. I said I was entirely of his opinion & so was practically every Liberal whose opinion I had asked, but . . . it was extremely difficult to dispossess an ex-Prime Minister

1. Gardiner to Beaverbrook, 28 April 1921 (copy), G.P. Perhaps Gardiner's decision owed less to conscience than his letter to Beaverbrook would suggest. He subsequently complained to Bennett that, three weeks 'after settling preliminaries for his connection with the "Express",' Beaverbrook had yet to finalize arrangements. 'Gardiner said he had never been treated like that before in his life, & he wrote to Beaverbrook & called the whole thing off.' According to Bennett's account, 'Max replied that he was sorry as he was just fixing the thing up with the office staff': Arnold Bennett's journal, 5 May 1921.

2. I am grateful to Mr Denis Duncan, formerly editor of the *British Weekly*, for information on this point.

3. Letter of 16 June 1921, in *H.H.A.: Letters to a Friend*, i, 188.

from the leadership of a party except wi[th] his own good-will which at present appeared in A.'s case to be not forthcoming. [1]

Gardiner, however, continued to cling to Asquith. True, Asquith was less than inspiring on social issues, and sometimes a shade too grudging in his support of the League, [2] but Gardiner regarded his personal qualities as unrivalled. Whether Asquith returned his devotion is difficult to say. The previous autumn, he reported giving lunch at Bedford Square to 'the faithful Phillipps, the resourceful and devoted Pringle, and the rather resonant and polysyllabic A.G.G.', a threesome that had 'promised well, but was devastated and almost sterilized'. [3]

A.G.G. recovered something of his old spirit on 22 January 1922, when he made the first of several sporadic guest appearances in the *Sunday Express*. Again, his piece was only a recapitulation of earlier views: an assault on President Poincaré, 'the French Bismarck'. Elsewhere on the same page, a leader explained that the paper considered it its 'duty to print all the views as well as all the news', and that, having published Wells's controversial reports on America and the U.S.S.R., it was now pleased to present Gardiner's 'brilliant article' on France: 'Although to some extent it traverses our own views we do not on that account deem it right to deprive our readers of the privilege of studying Mr Gardiner's penetrating analysis and rhetorical swordsmanship.' The following Sunday, the space reverted to Lord Beaverbrook, who wrote on the art of merchandising.

1. Scott's memorandum of 12–15 July 1921, Scott Papers, Add. MSS 50, 906, fol. 53.

2. Asquith, Lord Robert Cecil complained to Scott, 'was mildly in favour of the League of Nations, but "not red hot" which was essential'. Scott's memorandum of 14–15 July 1920, Scott Papers Add. MSS 50, 906, fols 37–8.

3. *H.H.A: Letters to a Friend*, i, 155. When this letter (12 October 1920) was later published, Asquith's daughter wrote to assure Gardiner that *'honestly* the two adjectives he applies to you carry with them no *kind* of criticism – & might equally well (and with far greater justice perhaps!) have been applied to any one of us. . . . I think you will believe me when I tell you that my Father not merely trusted and relied upon you as a true & tested friend – but set the highest possible value on your judgement, the keen edge & fervour of your mind (these are his very words) & the unfailing delight he found in your society. This is the truth as I have heard it from him & knew it. The editing of these letters has been of course a blow to us & I fear to many others.' Lady Violet Bonham Carter (later Baroness Asquith of Yarnbury) to Gardiner, 4 December 1933, G.P.

There were rumours, which had no foundation in fact, that Gardiner intended to fight a spring by-election at Leicester.[1] His only excursion north was to Glasgow, where he had lectured the previous October on 'newspaper independence' to the local district of the Institute of Journalists.[2] He had further occasion to speak on the same subject at a dinner to commemorate J. A. Spender's departure, early in 1922, from the editorship of the *Westminster Gazette*.[3] Held at the National Liberal Club, with Lord Beauchamp presiding and Asquith giving the main address, the evening had a depressing quality of *déjà vu*.

With increasing frequency, he wrote freelance articles for the *Nation*, where, on 3 June, he celebrated the conviction for fraud of Horatio Bottomley, 'the symptom of a moral degeneracy which has spread like a palsy over our corporate life, and nowhere more disastrously than in the realm of public affairs'. On the same day, he made his debut in *John Bull*, now purged of its connections with Bottomley. W. Charles Pinney, the new editor, was determined to inaugurate 'a definitely new era in weekly journalism', and recruited such talents as Arnold Bennett, Hesketh Pearson, Lord Haig (who superintended 'a page for ex-service men of all ranks'), Harold Begbie, and Gardiner. In the 3 June number, which featured a report on Bottomley in Wormwood Scrubbs prison, A.G.G. wrote on 'Sport – and betting', and predictably came to the conclusion that 'gambling on sport poisons sport'. It was a feeble effort, which he did not take seriously. In truth, he was mildly embarrassed by the association with *John Bull*, which he did not expect to last long. But he continued his weekly column for twenty-three years, never once setting foot in the *John Bull* office and always requiring successive editors to consult with him at the Reform Club. His columns, which made no pretence either to influence or originality, do not warrant close scrutiny. Free to write on virtually any subject, only rarely did he lapse into discussions of whether husbands should assist with the

1. Charles A. McCurdy, Joint Parliamentary Secretary to the Treasury, to Lloyd George, 14 March 1922, Lloyd George Papers, F/35/1/32.

2. *Institute Journal* (January 1922), p. 16.

3. Spender explained that his resignation was 'entirely my own act'. Lord Cowdray, the proprietor, had unwisely converted the *Westminster* into a morning paper, and Spender declined to adjust to the new situation. Spender, *Life, Journalism and Politics*, ii, 133 ff.

cooking or change nappies. Such trifles were more typical of his contributions to *The Passing Show*, which began in 1925 and continued for the better part of a decade, and which were never more political than 'A note on noses' (27 November 1926), which evaluated the slope of Stanley Baldwin's nose.

He expressed himself more seriously in the 'weekly political dispatches' that were widely syndicated in America by the Consolidated Press Association. 'Gardiner's work is splendid', David Lawrence, the association's president, cabled his European agent.[1] Woodrow Wilson, now a private citizen, agreed. 'I often wish our too brief acquaintance might ripen into something much more intimate,' he told Gardiner. 'You may be sure that whether it does or not you have permanently won my admiration and friendship.'[2] Ellery Sedgwick, another trans-Atlantic friend, wondered if there was some 'British topic, social or political, that you may care to treat' in the pages of the *Atlantic Monthly*: 'We have printed nothing better on British politics than your keen and acidulated articles, and if your retirement from active interest is not complete, I trust you will not forget us.'[3]

It was not by choice that Gardiner saved his best work for export. Seldom did English journals give him the opportunity to show himself to advantage. In April 1923 the *Nation* changed hands, with John Maynard Keynes becoming chairman of the board, and H. D. Henderson succeeding Massingham as editor.[4] Gardiner was invited to contribute a weekly column on topical issues, and Keynes was delighted with the result: 'May I say how happy we are with your articles?' he wrote in July. 'They are a great success from our point of view, and we gather that our readers are much liking them.'[5] Early the following year, however, Gardiner was prevailed upon to do a feature on 'Life and politics' to replace Massingham's 'London Diary'. He was not suited to the assignment, which required him to cover disparate subjects in a succession of staccato-like paragraphs: his entries, which kept expanding into miniature columns, were increasingly devoted to obituaries and cricket scores. Although the

1. William Bird to Gardiner, 5 December 1922, G.P.
2. Wilson to Gardiner, 11 February 1923, G.P.
3. Sedgwick to Gardiner, 12 November 1923, G.P.
4. See Harrod, *The Life of John Maynard Keynes*, pp. 331 ff.
5. Keynes to Gardiner, 28 July 1923, G.P.

political side of the *Nation* was a good deal more sedate than its literary side, he was uncomfortable in the company of the priests and priestesses of Bloomsbury, who dominated each issue. In May 1925 he begged a second and final time for his release, apologizing for the quality of his recent performance. Henderson, who did 'not in the least share' his opinion, assured him 'that I am very grateful indeed for your past help & for giving us a feature which I know many of our readers find the best thing in the paper'. He hoped that Gardiner might 'be willing occasionally to write articles for us, when topics arise with which no one can deal as well as you'.[1]

Hitherto a specialist in brief character sketches, Gardiner in 1923 published the longest of his full-length biographies, a two-volume work on Sir William Harcourt. Writing in *John Bull* on 24 March, close to the date of publication, he lamented that the politicians of recent days fell so far short of those whose 'spiritual company' he had enjoyed for the past six years. He began research back in 1917, at the invitation of Lord Harcourt, Sir William's son, who had served his father as a private secretary and thereafter as the zealous guardian of his reputation. The financial terms were attractive: the author received periodic payments of £100 to defray expenses, and was assured of minimum royalties of £2000. But 'Loulou' Harcourt drove a hard bargain. He edited the documents he showed to Gardiner, most notably his own diary, and insisted upon retaining 'sole and absolute discretion as to the omission from or inclusion in the book of any matter, opinions, or phrase in which I may think it necessary to exercise such discretion'.[2] G. P. Gooch, to whom 'Loulou' had first offered the commission, declined out of doubt 'whether I should have the necessary independence with the most devoted of sons continually looking over my shoulder'.[3] It does not appear that Gardiner encountered any particular difficulties, probably because he (unlike Gooch) venerated Sir William, and possibly because he did not suspect the more subtle of 'Loulou's' manipulations. But T. P. O'Connor was not far from wrong when he described the life of Harcourt as

1. Henderson to Gardiner, 27 May [1925], G.P.
2. For Harcourt's efforts to withhold information from Gardiner and from posterity, see S. E. Koss, 'Morley in the middle', *English Historical Review*, lxxxii (1967), 553.
3. Gooch, *Under Six Reigns*, p. 261.

'prepared by his son, and written by the able pen of Mr A. G. Gardiner'.[1]

Despite its peculiar auspices, the Harcourt biography remains a classic of its genre: it is one of the few 'life and letters' treatments of a Victorian statesman to which scholars continue to pay respectful attention. Harcourt was a great 'House of Commons man', and Gardiner skilfully depicts the give and take of parliamentary management. The book is perhaps least satisfactory in its account of the post-Gladstonian leadership struggles, when Harcourt's irascibility got the better of him, and when the younger Harcourt was most directly involved in his father's career. 'You had a difficult subject to deal with,' Sir William's widow ('Loulou's' stepmother) wrote to Gardiner, whom she commended on a job well done.[2] The press was equally generous, with long reviews by Birrell in *The Times* and Hammond in the *Manchester Guardian*. Morley, the last of Harcourt's generation, congratulated Gardiner in a shaky hand for capturing the spirit of the man and his times.[3] Later that year, Gardiner published, with less fanfare, his *Life of George Cadbury*. Henry Cadbury, another gratified son, thought the book a 'splendid tribute . . . to Father', and 'an inspiration to do all one can to further the work which he had begun'.[4]

Gardiner produced one other biography in hard covers, also commissioned as an act of filial piety. Published early in 1925, *John Benn and the Progressive Movement* was not a success, except perhaps as a tract for municipal reform. The Benn family was more than satisfied, and John Burns pronounced it 'excellent', but they were devoted to the subject.[5] With greater justice, a reviewer in *The Times* (6 February) observed that the book focused on 'two subjects which are indeed closely associated, but not so closely that they can be satisfactorily treated as one'. As biography, it was unremittingly dull; as administrative history, it was perfunctory. Yet the work eloquently testifies to its author's belief in Lib–Lab cooperation.

1. O'Connor, *Memoirs of an Old Parliamentarian*, i, 251.
2. Lady Harcourt to Gardiner, 17 March 1923, G.P.
3. Morley to Gardiner, 10 March 1923, G.P.
4. Henry Cadbury to Gardiner, 11 June 1923, G.P.
5. Ernest Benn to Gardiner, 19 December 1923; also Burns to Gardiner, 25 February 1925, G.P.

There was also a further volume of character sketches, *Certain People of Importance*, published in 1926.[1] These pieces first ran in the *Daily News*, under a special arrangement that paid the author twenty guineas apiece, a handsome fee at a time when the usual rate for weekly columns was between five and ten guineas. The preface took note of the fact that 'the place that was filled in the previous volumes by Kings and Emperors is taken by the dictators', who had 'emerged to power from the welter of the war and the peace'. Cultural figures appeared abundantly: Sybil Thorndike ('It is as the St Joan of the British stage that she leads her battalions to Leicester Square'), Charlie Chaplin (who 'had that sensitiveness to impressions of life' that characterized the artistry of Wells or Dickens), and Shaw ('He may quite well become one of his own Ancients and live to see himself in stained glass windows as the St Bernard of a new dispensation'). Dean Inge, with his 'genius for controversy', reminded Gardiner of Shaw, although 'Shaw is, of course, much nearer the accepted Christian ethic'. Lady Astor won praise for the way she stood up to Horatio Bottomley, to the brewers, and for the League of Nations. And he thought that Keynes, with 'a little patience and a little of that detestable but necessary thing called tact', might qualify as 'the Moses to lead Liberalism out of the wilderness'. The Socialists were well represented: MacDonald ('He is a bourgeois Radical, as far removed from the thought of Clydeside as Lord Oxford [as Asquith had become] or Mr Baldwin, and much more of an orthodox constitutionalist than Mr Lloyd George'); 'Jim' Thomas ('Though he will sing the "Red Flag" as heartily as anyone, he has a warm corner in his affections for the Union Jack'); and the young Ernest Bevin, who was briefly mentioned in an essay on John Wheatley as 'one of the most responsible of trade unionist leaders'. The Tories included L. S. Amery, Sir William Joynson-Hicks, Austen Chamberlain ('His contribution to public life is that of a conscientious and painstaking rectitude, but he belongs to the past, and has no vision of the future'), Baldwin ('There are times when he seems to be the

1. An American edition was published the same year with the title *Portraits and Portents*. Among those to whom it gave 'much pleasure' was Louis D. Brandeis, the Supreme Court justice, who wrote: 'The insight and skill of the painter, and the wealth of his subjects confirm the impression that Britain's greatest period is to come': Brandeis to Gardiner, 8 March 1927, G.P.

prophet coming with a message hot from Sinai, and there are times when he suggests that Alice has wandered, round-eyed and innocent, into the wonderland of Westminster'), and, inevitably, Churchill ('He is neither a demagogue nor a sycophant, and if he changes his party with the facility of partners at a dance, he has always been true to the only party he always believes in – that which is assembled under the hat of Mr Winston Churchill').

Among the *Certain People of Importance* whom he catalogued, by far the least attractive to him was Lord Rothermere, Northcliffe's brother and heir to his tradition. With a controlling interest in five newspaper companies, each with multiple properties, Rothermere operated as 'an irresponsible power working through the passions of the mob. . . . From this position', Gardiner wrote in 1923, 'Fascism is not a far cry.' As the years passed, he watched with growing apprehension the activities of this 'titled mischief-maker'.[1] On 27 July 1927, he proposed a toast at a luncheon for visiting American editors: 'Public policy', he reminded them, 'was the outcome of public opinion, and public opinion in the end was the creation of the press.'[2] That was why Rothermere was so dangerous. He appealed to the lowest common denominator in public taste, and was rewarded for his cynicism by huge circulations. 'The public', Gardiner predicted to an audience of aspiring journalists, would 'ultimately lose its respect for the press and return contempt for contempt.'[3] Meanwhile, however, Rothermere flourished and his competition lost ground. In 1930 there came 'the sudden and sensational' announcement that the *Daily Chronicle* had folded and was to be merged with the *Daily News* as the *News Chronicle*. 'The news that a third of the *Daily News* Staff were to be dismissed in order to make room for a corresponding number of the *Chronicle* men did little to dissipate the gloom of what one writer vividly described as "the blackest week in Fleet Street".'[4]

1. *Nation*, 15 September 1923; also *John Bull*, 31 July 1926.
2. *The Times*, 28 July 1927.
3. On 10 October 1928, Gardiner gave the first in a series of lectures to 'junior members of the profession' at the Institute of Journalists. Donald gave the second a fortnight later. *Institute Journal*, November, 1928.
4. *Newspaper Press Directory, 1931*, pp. 55–6. At the time of the amalgamation, Henry Cadbury retired as managing director of the *Daily News*, and Edward Cadbury as chairman of the board.

Conspicuously absent from the table of contents of Gardiner's 1926 volume was Lloyd George. Was Gardiner implicitly denying his status as a Person of Importance, or did he not trust himself to deal dispassionately with the subject? The Coalition had capsized four years earlier, when Lloyd George was cut adrift by Tory buccaneers. Although he was never again to hold office, he remained, as Gardiner well knew, a figure to be reckoned with. Unlike some Liberals, Gardiner was not prepared to receive the prodigal son with open arms and outstretched palms. Lloyd George, he sternly warned the readers of the *Nation* (30 June 1923), was 'the heaviest political liability that any party, especially any party that claims to rest on a moral basis, can assume'. But Lloyd George worked his way back into the fold, and Gardiner could not stop him.[1]

To an even greater extent than any previous volume of Gardiner's character sketches, *Certain People of Importance* was a *tour de force*. The artist had never met most of the people whose portraits he painted, and his supply of anecdotes was largely secondhand. Gardiner's estrangement from the nation's political leadership had more obvious and serious effects upon his weekly journalism. Despite his tender feelings towards Labour – in the early months of 1923 he was reported to be contemplating a conversion[2] – he could never bring himself to change parties. In 1924, he accepted the advent of the first Labour Government 'without alarm and with indifference to the screams and hysteria' of the Rothermere press, all the while affirming that, while he was 'not a Labour man', he wanted 'Labour to prove that it *can* govern'. He gave Ramsay MacDonald high marks for a foreign policy 'free from the tendency to reaction, on the one hand, or revolutionary dreams, on the other'.[3] But he could not forgive MacDonald's 'resentful and uncouth' attitude towards the Liberals, who sustained him in office. MacDonald's ultimate act of ingratitude,

---

1. For Gardiner's participation in the Liberal Council, an organization designed to resist Lloyd George's influence and financial control of the party: see Wilson, *Downfall of the Liberal Party*, pp. 337–9.

2. Lucy Masterman, *C.F.G.Masterman*, p. 328.

3. Gardiner's enthusiasm was shared by Colonel House, who reported that MacDonald's adherence to the League had had 'a wholesome effect' on America, now brought to realize the penalty of her exclusion from world councils: House to Gardiner, 2 January 1925 (copy), House Papers.

as Gardiner saw it, was to call a November election that 'laid the Liberals flat'. [1] Asquith lost Paisley, and Lloyd George was elected to replace him as party chairman. Gardiner tried to console himself that the arrangement was only a temporary one, 'pending the return of Mr Asquith whose early reappearance in the House is not improbable'. [2] He completely misjudged the situation. Asquith, seventy-two years of age, went gratefully to the House of Lords as the Earl of Oxford and Asquith. 'It is a hard wrench,' Margot, now a Countess, confessed to Gardiner: 'I have wept many times at leaving the H. of Commons but there is *no* safe Liberal seat & he must lead his shattered party from the Lords. The alternative was retirement from public life wh[ich] w[oul]d have killed him.' [3]

Still, Gardiner refused to accommodate himself to Lloyd George, whom he opposed obsessively, and sometimes irrationally. Although he agreed wholeheartedly with Lloyd George's indictment of Italian fascism, he peevishly questioned the propriety of such a denunciation by a former premier. [4] In return, Lloyd George wrongly ascribed to Gardiner anonymous attacks made by others. The editor of the *Nation* soothed him with assurances that 'Kappa', whose remarks had given offence, 'is not A. G. Gardiner as, I think, you suppose.' [5]

The social paroxysms of the interwar years gave a jolt to Gardiner's puritan sensibilities. At regular intervals, he fretted in the pages of *John Bull* about the declining birth rate, decried those 'nasty new morals', and poured scorn on the prose of Joyce and the poetry of Eliot. Politics seemed to him to reflect the moral bankruptcy of the age. The National Government, which he had applauded at its inception, was the source of bitter disappointments, none greater than the foreign secretaryship of Sir John Simon, whose handling of the Manchurian crisis 'reached a depth of ineptitude that seems wellnigh

1. *Nation*, 26 April, 14 June, and 11 October 1924. The *Manchester Guardian* had the same complaint. 'The Prime Minister', it observed on 3 October, 'who can be so sweet to the foreigner from whom he differs most widely, has nothing but unconcealed dislike and exaggerated suspicion for those who in this country stand nearest to him in politics.'

2. *Nation*, 8 November and 6 December 1924, and 17 January 1925.

3. Margot Asquith to Gardiner, 23 January 1925, G.P.

4. *Nation*, 10 January 1925.

5. Henderson to Lloyd George, 12 November 1925, Lloyd George Papers, C/10/2/4.

fathomless'.[1] More regretfully, Gardiner also disowned Walter Runciman, another self-styled Liberal National, who had gravitated towards the Conservatives and into the protectionist camp.

It was the international situation that gave him greatest anxiety. Since the early 'twenties, he had deprecated the intransigence of western statesmen, who 'destroyed the influence of the moderating forces in Germany by convincing the people that there was no hope for them outside the recovery of their power to act and strike for themselves'. He looked to MacDonald, a pacifist in the last war and a servant of the League, to initiate 'a revision of the Versailles Treaty, a drastic scaling down of the Young Plan, and a loosening of the factors that are driving Germany to revolution and cooperation with Moscow'. Delay was fatal. Early in 1933, Adolph Hitler ('a hot-head with a hot-head policy') became Chancellor of the Reich.[2] Initially, Gardiner saw the advent of National Socialism as further justification for doctrines of appeasement: if Germans could obtain restitution through peaceful means, they would presumably not resort to arms. Yet he did not persist in this delusion half so long as some. In 1934 Lionel Robbins arranged for him to meet Dr Heinrich Brüning, the former Chancellor and an exile from Hitler's Germany, who gave him second thoughts about the efficacy of appeasement. 'Hitler . . . does not want a collective peace system', A.G.G. wrote in *John Bull* on 6 April 1935: '. . . Any nation which . . . takes the law into its own hands must be regarded as the common enemy of all and resisted with the might of all.' His denunciation of 'Mad race hate' in Germany (21 September 1935) brought him a number of 'frenzied letters' from *John Bull* readers, 'all of them anonymous and all of them anti-semitic'. He was not surprised: 'That anti-Semitism prevails in this country, as in other countries, is public knowledge but it is not an organised movement, and so long as free Parliamentary institutions hold sway it will never be a political cry or a social menace.'

As best he could, he managed the tortuous feat of combining support of the League with a policy of rearmament. Churchill, too,

1. *John Bull*, 1 October 1932. 'Once you are on the warpath there is no stopping you,' Simon replied, 'and I take it all in good part': Simon to Gardiner, 30 September 1932, G.P.
2. *Nation*, 28 June 1924; also *John Bull*, 20 June 1931, 5 March, 18 June and 30 July 1932.

spoke of 'Arms and the Covenant', but Gardiner preferred to reverse the sequence. Gradually, with the unwitting assistance of Neville Chamberlain, Gardiner was transformed into an ardent Churchillian. Jimmy Mallon was a more positive influence, as were various Reform Club friends: Sir Arthur (later Baron) Salter, Wilson Harris, and Lord Rhayader (formerly Leif Jones). On 30 March 1938, after the German invasion of Austria, 'Alpha' wrote a piece in the *Star* urging Churchill's recall to the Government. Margot Asquith, who thought it an 'admirable article,' was nonetheless not persuaded. 'I may be wrong,' she tactfully conceded, but Churchill

is the *last* man I'd put in a responsible position today. He *loves* war, & wd. get us into endless trouble. I'm afraid I am not of agreement with Labour, & with Liberals to-day & think the P.M. has shown the 3 *most* important qualities in times of crisis, Patience, Courage, & *Honesty*. I know this is not the popular view, nevertheless I think Neville is right, & if he fails we shall be no worse off.[1]

September's Munich crisis, which further polarized opinion, left Gardiner 'almost like an invalid, incapable of writing, incapable of reading, & finding everything savourless & boring including myself & Neville Chamberlain', whom he heard speak to the Foreign Press Association on the evening of 13 December. The Prime Minister 'sounded . . . like a complacent dunce incapable of understanding the meaning of anything. But what an eloquent audience it was,' Gardiner exclaimed. 'I have never heard such significant cheering & such impressive silence in my life.'[2]

Gardiner represented a minority position in the pages of *John Bull* which were strongly pro-Chamberlain. On 29 April, he was pitted against Sir Norman Angell, who plaintively asked 'Must it be war?' There was the same clash of opinion in the Liberal Party. J. A.

1. Margot, Countess of Oxford and Asquith, to Gardiner, 31 March 1938, G.P.
2. Gardiner to Swinnerton, 14 December 1938, Swinnerton Papers. Sir Harold Nicolson shared Gardiner's impression of the evening: 'Chamberlain . . . catalogued his achievements. Treaty with Eire (slight applause); Treaty with the United States (loud applause); Treaty with Italy (sporadic clappings); Anglo-German Treaty (you could have heard a pin drop so icy was the silence); with France we had relations which transcended all legal instruments, since our interests were the same (a wild ovation lasting several minutes)': Harold Nicolson, *Diaries and Letters, 1930–1939*, p. 382.

Spender wrote to *The Times* to censure Sir Archibald Sinclair, chairman of the parliamentary party, for attacks upon the Prime Minister. Nine prominent Liberals rallied to Sinclair's defence, but the editor of *The Times* declined to print their letter. At this point, Gardiner joined the fray to protest this double standard. His letter, too, was refused, allegedly because it 'covered the same ground' as one from Lord Cecil.[1] Furious, he wrote instead to the *News Chronicle* and the *Manchester Guardian*, both of which proved more receptive. The correspondence columns of *The Times*, he maintained, 'are in the nature of a public trust which should be administered not in order to fortify the views expressed in the leader columns, but as a general clearing house of public opinion'. He took issue with Spender, who cited the events of August 1914 as proof that Liberal policy was traditionally one of 'appeasement'. Gardiner sharply disagreed:

Mr Spender does injustice to Lord Grey's memory in suggesting that his efforts for peace in 1914 were on the same plane of surrender as those of the present Government up to March 15 last. I do not think Lord Grey would have seen the tragic sequence of events from Manchuria and China, onwards to Abyssinia, Spain, Austria, and Czecho-Slovakia without realising that he was in the presence of a spirit of aggression that called for other methods than those which culminated at Munich and crashed at Prague.[2]

Sinclair thanked him for his 'generous and timely support' in the controversy. 'Of course,' he acknowledged, 'I know that you have been actuated by much more important motives than concern for my personal position, but I am none the less proud of and grateful for your advocacy.'[3]

The outbreak of war soon put an end to these recriminations. Besides, Gardiner and Spender had too much affection for each other to perpetuate their quarrel. 'You and I have had a pretty good inning in the heart of things,' Spender reminisced a year later, '& I have not much to complain of on looking back. But you have added the touch

1. Lady Violet Bonham Carter thought *The Times*'s excuse 'very thin': Lady Violet Bonham Carter to Gardiner, 18 July 1939, G.P.
2. Gardiner's letter, written to *The Times* on 13 July, was sent to the other papers on the 16th. It was published the next day.
3. Sinclair to Gardiner, 17 July 1939, G.P. There was a letter of appreciation, too, from Hilaire Belloc: 17 July 1939, G.P.

of genius which I lack & for lack of which I so often stumble & halt.'
Like Gardiner, he professed to have 'misgivings about writing past or
present', and to 'pray for a future life, if I have one, in which there
will be no more ink & I shall not have to argue or preach or try to
convert anybody to anything'. [1] Despite these musings, an indulgence
permitted to men in their late seventies, neither of them would have
sacrificed the opportunity to promulgate his views. Spender, who
died in May 1942, kept up almost until the end his work for the
Sunday Times, the B.B.C., the Ministry of Information, and various
American and provincial journals. Gardiner, who survived him by
almost four years, rarely missed a week in *John Bull*, and regularly
appeared in the *Star* under his own name and as 'Alpha of the
Plough'.

The editor of *John Bull*, more out of opportunism than repentance,
commended Gardiner as 'The rightest man I know'. The 9 September
issue featured a series of extracts from previous columns, going back
to 1933, to show that A.G.G., 'more than any other present-day
writer on international topics, can be truly described as "the man
who has always been right"'. Gardiner himself made no claim to
powers of prophecy. As often as not, events took him by surprise.
Take, for example, his response when Churchill, at the outbreak of
war, returned to the Government and to his old place at the Admiralty.
Margot Asquith admitted that his piece ('Churchill mounts the
bridge') in the *Star* of 4 September was 'beautifully written', but she
cunningly offered him a wager: Churchill, she bet, 'will *oust* the P.M.
from 10 Downing St. just as Ll.G. ousted us'. [2] Gardiner did not
contemplate such an eventuality. Always opposed to changing pilots
in the middle of a storm, he grudgingly reconciled himself to Chamberlain's continued leadership. His greatest fear was that the ambitious
Simon, 'seeing a vacancy next door approaching', might begin
'mobilising his forces to proclaim him as next in succession'. If
Chamberlain were to go, the obvious man to take his place was Lord
Halifax, 'with Churchill leading in the Commons'. [3] In April 1940 he
accompanied Mallon to a lunch at the Dorchester to hear Halifax,

---

1. Spender to Gardiner, 5 August 1940, G.P.
2. Margot, Countess of Oxford and Asquith, to Gardiner, 5 September 1939,
G.P.
3. Gardiner to Swinnerton, 18 February 1940, Swinnerton Papers.

and came away 'greatly strengthened in my impression that he is the noblest Roman of them all – a firm, serene mind & a firm soul'.[1] He did not suspect Halifax's attitude of self-abnegation – few did – nor did he think that Churchill could possibly carry his own party. Needless to say, he was not the least disappointed when Churchill ascended to the premiership a few weeks later. Here was a welcome guarantee that there would be no accommodation with Hitler, whatever the terms. The tables had turned: while the aged Lloyd George advocated a compromise settlement, Gardiner demanded nothing less than the 'knock-out blow'.

Pre-empting 'Alpha', A.G.G. published a sketch of Churchill, 'Man of Destiny', in the *Star* on 22 August. In tone and quality, it was a far cry from his earlier portraits of the man, substituting hackneyed adulation for astringent observation. But, coming from the same pen that had described Churchill at virtually every stage in his career, it rekindled old memories. Henry Cadbury congratulated Gardiner for his article on 'our great leader', and Lady Violet Bonham Carter 'read it with double appreciation', having just written a '*very inferior*' piece along the same lines for *John o'London's Weekly*.[2] At this point in his life, Gardiner would brook no criticism of Churchill, who seemed to him to embody the spirit of the British people, from whom he singlehandedly and unexpectedly elicited such a magnificent response. 'Taken by & large, we are still the only people on this earth worth a damn – that is, as *a people*,' Gardiner crowed in the dark days of October 1940. 'And this I agree is its "finest hour". The misery of being alive is set-off by the grandeur of being alive to weather such a storm or perish in it.'[3] Bombs hit the Reform Club, which reopened in December with its library and dining room out of commission. In April the club was 'again closed (all the windows out)', and, two months later, Toynbee Hall was reduced to 'an obscene rubbish heap'. All of the Mallons' belongings were destroyed, and A.G.G. lost his dress clothes, which he did not expect he would have to replace.[4]

1. Gardiner to Swinnerton, 11 April 1940, Swinnerton Papers.
2. Henry Cadbury to Gardiner, 23 August 1940; also Lady Violet Bonham Carter to Gardiner, 28 August 1940, G.P.
3. Gardiner to Swinnerton, 17 October 1940, Swinnerton Papers.
4. Gardiner to Swinnerton, 29 December 1940, and 22 April and 16 June 1941, Swinnerton Papers.

He looked for deliverance to President Roosevelt as he had once looked to President Wilson. This time, however, he was eager for more material assistance. But, most of all, he looked to Churchill. He returned from London on 25 September 1941 with 'the impression of a deep undercurrent of criticism on the P.M. – too much the dictator, too much a bottle-neck of power that should be delegated & so on. Much truth in all this', he supposed, but the man had to be taken 'in the lump & taken so he is irreplaceable.'[1] Early the next year, he waited anxiously 'for news of Churchill', who had crossed the Atlantic to confer with Roosevelt. 'It is now ten days since the last reference to him in America appeared and it is time the suspense was over.'[2] Churchill returned safely to face 'a critical House' on 27 January. 'The war debate has gone rather heavily against Churchill,' Gardiner acknowledged, 'but I anticipate that he will be on top of the landslide in the lobby. . . . The plain fact is that there is no alternative . . . & everybody knows it & taken in the large his achievement has been superb.'[3]

Churchill was not the only one whose health caused Gardiner grave anxiety. His wife suffered a series of heart attacks, and he lived in dread of her death. 'I have always hoped to go first,' he confided pathetically to Swinnerton, 'for she means so much more to the family than I do & would be much less lonely alone than I should be.'[4] On one occasion her illness prevented him from completing his *John Bull* column, and Harold Laski (whom he despised as a 'pestilent little exhibitionist'[5]) was brought in to fill the breach. Fortunately, she recovered, and, in fact, survived him by two years. While he kept his vigil at her bedside, he reread the autobiography of Benjamin Franklin: 'All that is good in America today has its seed in him & that seed could have come out of no race but the English.'[6]

With the D-Day landings in June 1944, his thoughts turned to

1. Gardiner to Swinnerton, 25 September 1941, Swinnerton Papers.
2. Gardiner to Swinnerton, 15 January 1942, Swinnerton Papers. Lord Moran, Churchill's physician, has revealed that the Prime Minister suffered a heart attack during his Washington visit: *Winston Churchill: the struggle for survival*, pp. 16 ff.
3. Gardiner to Swinnerton, 28 January 1942, Swinnerton Papers; also see Moran, pp. 24–5.
4. Gardiner to Swinnerton, 16 November 1941, Swinnerton Papers.
5. Gardiner to Swinnerton, 26 May 1942, Swinnerton Papers.
6. Gardiner to Swinnerton, 13 June 1942, Swinnerton Papers.

international reconstruction. 'This time,' he insisted in his 10 June column,

the defeat of Germany shall be unequivocal. . . . Germany must be permanently starved of the key commodities of war.

Revenge there will not be, but retribution there will be. Stern justice there will be. . . .

The criminals who have ordered these horrors and the barbarians who have executed them must be punished. . . . But the mass punishment of Germans is questionable on economic and political grounds. . . . Purged of her crimes, convinced that aggression does not pay, [Germany] must know that there is a place for her in the New World Order.

His mind reeled with questions: 'What will Stalin do? What America? What De Gaulle? We are going to have trouble with that gentleman', he privately predicted.[1] Much would depend upon the outcome of the November balloting in America. Although Roosevelt seemed assured of a fourth term, a campaign conducted under wartime conditions invariably had its drawbacks, and Gardiner feared the possible repercussions upon Anglo–American relations.

The editor of *John Bull* commissioned him to provide portraits of 'the men of mark in 1944'. The first of these, 'What F.D.R. means to us', appeared on November 25, and the following weeks brought articles on Churchill, Stalin, Bevin, Sir William Beveridge ('He has gone far to put the Liberal Party on the political map again'), Eden, and Herbert Morrison. They were not vintage Gardiner, as he well realized. He declined an offer to publish them as a volume, pleading that he stood too far from his subjects to observe them properly. Yet, in his own way, he took pride in the work he was doing. The following spring, an over-zealous sub-editor dared to tamper with his copy, and he immediately threatened his resignation. Reassured that he had 'a free platform in "John Bull"',[2] he continued until 15 September, when it was announced that: 'Our distinguished contributor, Mr A. G. Gardiner has entered hospital for an operation and is therefore unable to write his weekly article.' He never resumed.

He celebrated his eightieth birthday on 2 June. Shortly thereafter, he went reluctantly to see a surgeon, who recommended a prostate

1. Gardiner to Swinnerton, 26 August 1944, Swinnerton Papers.
2. Gardiner to John Dunbar, editorial director of Odham's Press, 27 May 1945 (copy), G.P.; also Dunbar to Gardiner, 30 May 1945, G.P.

operation. 'Said it might add ten years to my life,' he told Swinnerton, 'but I replied that I was not a candidate for the long distance stakes. Well, he said, it will make the rest of the journey more comfortable. So that's that.'[1] The general election took his mind from his own discomfort, not that it lifted his spirits. Labour's phenomenal success left him feeling 'bruised all over, physically battered, mentally numbed'. Was there, he wondered, 'any parallel in history to the drama of Churchill? He saves the world & the world throws him on the rubbish heap like a bundle of rags.'[2] Curiously enough, he assigned no blame to his hero for going to the country before Japan was defeated and passions were spent. For weeks he continued to 'boil within over the ingratitude to Churchill', and especially over 'the universal silence of the press on the subject'.[3] He tried to remedy the situation with a letter to *The Times*, suggesting some testimonial ('Perhaps it might be a Churchill Fund, dedicated by him to any public purpose he might choose') to a man who was supposedly rejected not for himself, but as the leader of a party 'which had incurred the wrath of the nation for the "appeasement" policy of which he had been the fiercest assailant'.[4] That his letter was refused was perhaps as much a kindness to him as to Clement Attlee, Churchill's successor, whom Gardiner simply could not abide. He awoke at seven o'clock on the morning of 15 August to hear the 'great news' of military victory announced

in the sheeplike Ba-a-a of the guileless Attlee. God! said I. Hamlet with Sir Andrew Aguecheek in the role of the Prince of Denmark. Would that some newspaper had the wit to print, without comment, in Big Type, just half a stanza of 'O Captain, My Captain! Rise up and hear the bells'.[5]

Still brooding, he went for his operation in early September. Until he arrived at the hospital, he had had 'no notion it was a Roman Catholic institution, run by nuns & all the servants of which are Irish of the deepest dye, with a brogue as thick as Tewkesbury mustard. If I'm here a month,' he wrote cheerfully to his wife,

1. Gardiner to Swinnerton, 28 June 1945, Swinnerton Papers.
2. Gardiner to Swinnerton, 28 July 1945, Swinnerton Papers.
3. Gardiner to Swinnerton, 13 August 1945, Swinnerton Papers.
4. Letter to the editor of *The Times*, 7 August 1945 (draft copy), G.P.
5. Gardiner to Swinnerton, 15 August 1945, Swinnerton Papers.

'begorra I shouldn't wonder if I talk like a Dublin jarvey.'[1] The operation was more of an ordeal than he had anticipated, but he was soon home, unaware that a malignancy had been found. It was the world's ills, and not his own, that gave him the most complaint. 'Yes, what a world indeed,' he soon wrote to Swinnerton:

I'm quite prepared to close my a/c with it, but I'm sad to think of the commitments I leave behind. Horace Walpole refused to worry about . . . posterity, but he had no children. All the same, he was right of course. It is folly . . . to get in a stew about things that will certainly not happen as you imagine they will happen & which in any case you cannot influence one way or the other. My wife has the sensible philosophy. She counters all the miseries to which she is subject by dwelling on the happiness she has had in the past. I'm different. I'm a born grouser & now that I have really something to grouse about I am, as it were, having the time of my life.[2]

Professionally, however, he found himself 'at a dead end. My brain is made of mud & shies at every fence, falling down in a kind of dis-spirited helplessness. I haven't written since August last & begin to feel that the spark within has gone out finally.'[3] On 20 January the *News Chronicle* held a centenary dinner, and he was invited to attend. Laurence Cadbury 'tried to tempt him to come up promising to arrange sleeping accommodation on the spot for him'.[4] But, at the last moment, the doctors forbade the journey. That evening, as he 'look[ed] out on the fog & snow', it occurred to him 'that age & infirmity have their blessings. Did you by any chance listen to the Centenary show on the radio?' he asked Swinnerton.

I was astonished that the lime-light was turned on your humble servant. A[rnold] B[ennett] used to accuse me of vanity, but if he had known what a fraud I feel when the butter is laid on too thick (as last night when I was seen flagrantly out of perspective in the landscape of the D.N.) he would have withdrawn his accusation or at all events qualified it.[5]

Gardiner died at Whiteleaf on 3 March 1946. His neighbours paid him fond tribute as a J.P., a vice-chairman of the magistrates court,

1. Gardiner to his wife, 4 September 1945 (postmark), G.P.
2. Gardiner to Swinnerton, 29 September 1945, Swinnerton Papers.
3. Gardiner to Swinnerton, 4 December 1945, Swinnerton Papers.
4. Laurence Cadbury to Mrs Gardiner, 4 March 1946, G.P.
5. Gardiner to Swinnerton, 20 January 1946, Swinnerton Papers.

and a patriarch of the local golf club. At a meeting of the executive committee of the Liberal Party, Lady Violet Bonham Carter extolled his political services. Frank Swinnerton, writing in *The Times* on the 11th, recalled him as 'the perfect clubman, . . . unfailing in mirth, kindness, wisdom, and badinage (which was a mixture of all the rest)'. The next day, a memorial service was held at St Dunstan-in-the-West, Fleet Street. Wilson Harris gave the address, 'a compact summary of the rich career of editorial direction and political activity, of authorship and friendship'.[1] A second service was held that week-end at Princes Risborough. It was appropriate that there should be two ceremonies: one in town for A.G.G.; the other in the country for 'Alpha'.

By the time that Gardiner died, the *Daily News* was remembered with the same nostalgia that has more recently attached to the *News Chronicle*, which followed it to the grave (taking the *Star* in tow) in 1960. His editorship, like Dickens's, was already regarded as an episode in the history of British journalism and a chapter in the closed book of Liberal politics. In the previous year's general election, the party had fielded candidates in fewer than half the constituencies, and only a dozen MPs were returned. How different things had been when Gardiner sat in Bouverie Street, presiding over a paper that gave daily expression to the hope and purpose of Liberalism.

He was mourned not only for himself, but as one of the last of the 'great editors'.[2] The demise of the most individualistic of parties presaged, among other things, a decline in what had been the most individualistic of professions. The last of the breed was Garvin, who now became senior past president of the Institute of Journalists, and who, in that capacity, wrote a moving farewell to Gardiner:

The street of ink and typewriters has sometimes been called the street of ultimate oblivion. Even for most of those who are familiar and conspicuous while they do the day's work in its day and the night's work in its hours. But the name of A. G. Gardiner is one of those that cannot be forgotten in the history and memoirs of journalism. He has vanished from us at last full of years and honours. Those best honours that are paid by appreciation to achievement, by respect to character, and by affection to a

1. *Manchester Guardian*, 13 March 1946.
2. See, for example, 'Janus' in the *Spectator*, 8 March 1946, and Hamilton Fyfe in *John o'London's Weekly*, 22 March 1946.

kind and manly heart. In that he was worthy to admire, as he did, Samuel Johnson of Fleet Street.[1]

Did J.L.G. recall the biting sketch that A.G.G. had written about him in the old *Daily News* on 5 October 1912? If so, he carried no grudge: professional journalists seldom did against one another. Although he and Gardiner had usually fought on different sides, they were veterans of many of the same battles. Four years earlier, the Astors had relieved Garvin of his command at the *Observer*, and he, like Gardiner and Spender before him, embarked on a second and less spectacular career as a columnist. He died in January 1947. Since then, journalists have not been known by their initials.

1. *Institute Journal*, April 1946.

Bibliography

MANUSCRIPT COLLECTIONS

A. G. Gardiner Papers, courtesy of Patrick Gardiner, Wytham, Oxfordshire. Other items from various members of the Gardiner family, as acknowledged.

H. H. Asquith (Earl of Oxford and Asquith) Papers, Bodleian Library, Oxford.

Ray Stannard Baker Papers, Manuscript Division, Library of Congress, Washington.

Sir John Brunner Papers, courtesy of Sir Felix Brunner, Greys Court, near Henley-on-Thames, Oxfordshire.

John Burns Papers, British Museum.

Viscount Bryce Papers, Bodleian Library, Oxford.

Arnold Bennett's journals, Henry W. and Albert A. Berg Collection, The New York Public Library, Astor, Lenox and Tilden Foundations.

Sir Henry Campbell-Bannerman Papers, British Museum.

Viscount Cecil of Chelwood Papers, British Museum.

G. K. Chesterton Papers, selection courtesy of Miss D. Collins.

Baron Courtney of Penwith Papers, British Library of Political and Economic Science, London.

Sir Charles Dilke Papers, British Museum.

R. C. K. Ensor Papers, Corpus Christi College, Oxford.

Viscount Gladstone Papers, British Museum.

J. L. Hammond Papers, Bodleian Library, Oxford.

Viscount Harcourt Papers, courtesy of the 2nd Viscount Harcourt, Stanton Harcourt, Oxfordshire.

Colonel E. M. House Papers, Yale University Library.

R. C. Lehmann Papers, selection courtesy of John Lehmann, C.B.E., London.

David Lloyd George (Earl Lloyd-George of Dwyfor) Papers, Beaverbrook Library, London.

Reginald McKenna Papers, Churchill College, Cambridge.

Letters from C. E. Montague to Francis Dodd, British Museum.

Gilbert Murray Papers, Bodleian Library, Oxford.

H. W. Nevinson diaries, Bodleian Library, Oxford.

Bibliography

A. M. Pollen Papers, selection courtesy of J. A. Pollen, Sandwich, Kent.

Arthur Ponsonby (1st Baron Ponsonby of Shulbrede) Papers, courtesy of the 2nd Baron Ponsonby, Shulbrede Priory, Haslemere, Surrey.

Earl of Rosebery Papers, National Library of Scotland, Edinburgh.

Walter Runciman (1st Viscount Runciman of Doxford) Papers, the University Library, Newcastle upon Tyne.

C. P. Scott Papers, British Museum; also copies of materials in the *Guardian* archives, courtesy of David Ayerst.

Bernard Shaw Papers, British Museum.

J. A. Spender Papers, British Museum.

Frank Swinnerton Papers, the University of Arkansas.

H. G. Wells Papers, University of Illinois Library, Urbana-Champaign.

Woodrow Wilson Papers, Princeton University.

PUBLISHED SOURCES

Works by A. G. GARDINER

1. Books
   a. character sketches
      Certain People of Importance. London, Cape, 1926.
      Pillars of Society. London, Nisbet, 1913.
      Prophets, Priests and Kings. London, Alston Rivers, 1908.
      The War Lords. London, Dent, 1915.
   b. biographies
      John Benn and the Progressive Movement. London, E. Benn, 1925.
      Life of George Cadbury. London, Cassell, 1923.
      The Life of Sir William Harcourt. 2 vols. London, Constable, 1923.
   c. essays by 'Alpha of the Plough'
      Leaves in the Wind. London, Dent, 1919.
      Many Furrows. London, Dent, 1924.
      Pebbles on the Shore. London, Dent, 1916.
      Windfalls. London, Dent, 1920.
2. pamphlets (not including reprints of single articles)
      The Anglo-American Future. London, 1920.
      The 'Daily Mail' and the Liberal Press. London, 1914?
      The Duke Goes Canvassing. London, 1910?
      Ireland and British Misrule: Lloyd George's Insincerity. Washington, D.C., 1920.
      What I Saw in Germany. London, 1920?
3. speeches
      'The social policy', in *The Policy of Social Reform in England*. Brussels, Instituts Solway, 1913.

4. introductions

BLACK, CLEMENTIA. *Sweated Industry and the Minimum Wage.* London, Duckworth, 1907.

COPPING, ARTHUR E. *Pictures of Poverty.* London, Daily News, 1905?

C. F. G. MASTERMAN and others. *To Colonise England.* London, T. Fisher Unwin, 1907.

5. major articles (not including pieces in dailies or weeklies)

'Asquith', *The Nineteenth Century and After.* cxii (1932), 608–20.

'The British Admiralty', *Atlantic Monthly.* cxvi (1915), 540–9.

'The British Cabinet', *Atlantic Monthly.* cxv (1915), 672–82.

'British generalship', *Atlantic Monthly.* cxvi (1915), 99–108.

'The Editors' Tour in Germany', *Albany Review.* i (1907), 390–6.

'German generalship', *Atlantic Monthly.* cxvii (1916), 677–86.

'Lloyd George and the coup d'état', *Atlantic Monthly.* cxix (1917), 392–401 (published anonymously).

'Mr Henderson and the Labor Movement', *Atlantic Monthly.* cxxii (1918), 221–30.

'The Prime Minister', *Land and Water.* 8 June 1916, p. 15 (published anonymously).

'Reginald McKenna: an appreciation', *Pearson's Magazine.* xli (1916), 93–7.

'Sir John Jellicoe', *Pearson's Magazine.* xxxix (1915), 369–74.

'Two journalists: C. P. Scott and Northcliffe – a contrast', *Nineteenth Century and After.* cxi (1932), 247–56.

'Who will succeed Lloyd George?' *Century Magazine.* cii (1921), 813–19.

OTHER BOOKS AND ARTICLES

ADDISON, CHRISTOPHER. *Four and a Half Years.* 2 vols, London, Hutchinson, 1934. *Politics from Within.* 2 vols, London, Jenkins, 1924.

ASQUITH, MARGOT, Countess of Oxford and Asquith. *Autobiography.* 2 vols, London, Butterworth, 1920, 1922.

ASQUITH, H. H., Earl of Oxford and Asquith. *Fifty Years of Parliament.* 2 vols, Boston, Little, Brown, 1926. *H.H.A.: Letters of the Earl of Oxford and Asquith to a Friend* (ed. Desmond MacCarthy). 2 vols, London, Bles, 1933. *Memories and Reflections.* 2 vols, London, Cassell, 1928.

AYERST, DAVID. *Guardian: Biography of a Newspaper.* London, Collins, 1971.

BAKER, ELIZABETH B. and BAKER, P. J. NOEL. *J. Allen Baker, M.P., a memoir.* London, Swarthmore Press, 1927.

BARKER, DUDLEY. *Writer By Trade: a view of Arnold Bennett.* London, Allen and Unwin, 1966.

BARNETT, HENRIETTA O. *Canon Barnett, his life, work, and friends.* 2 vols, London, Murray, 1921.

BEALEY, F. and PELLING, H. *Labour and Politics, 1900–1906.* London, Macmillan, 1958.

BEAVERBROOK, LORD. *Politicians and the Press.* London, Hutchinson, 1925? *Politicians and the War.* 2 vols, London, Butterworth, 1928.

BELOFF, MAX. *Imperial Sunset.* Vol. i. New York, Knopf, 1970. *The Intellectual in Politics.* London, Weidenfeld & Nicolson, 1971.

BENNETT, ARNOLD. *Journals* (ed. Norman Flower). 3 vols, London, Cassell, 1932–3. *Letters* (ed. James Hepburn). 3 vols, London, Oxford University Press, 1968–70.

BENTLEY, E. C. *Those Days.* London, Constable, 1940.

BIRRELL, AUGUSTINE. *Things Past Redress.* London, Faber, 1937.

BLUMENFELD, R. D. *The Press in My Time.* London, Rich and Cowan, 1933. *R.D.B.'s Diary 1887–1914.* London, Heinemann, 1930. *R.D.B.'s Procession.* New York, Macmillan, 1935.

CHESTERTON, G. K. *Autobiography.* London, Hutchinson, 1937.

CLARKE, P. F. 'British Politics and Blackburn Politics, 1900–1910', *Historical Journal*, xii (1969), 302–27. *Lancashire and the New Liberalism.* Cambridge, Cambridge University Press, 1971.

COWLING, MAURICE. *The Impact of Labour, 1920–1924.* Cambridge, Cambridge University Press, 1971.

CROSS, COLIN. *Philip Snowden.* London, Barrie, 1966.

CUDLIPP, HUGH. *At Your Peril.* London, Weidenfeld & Nicolson, 1962. *Publish and Be Damned.* London, Dakers, 1953.

DEAN, JOSEPH. *Hatred, Ridicule or Contempt?* New York, Macmillan, 1954.

DOUGLAS, ROY. *A History of the Liberal Party, 1897–1970.* London, Sidgwick and Jackson, 1971.

ERVINE, ST JOHN. *Bernard Shaw.* New York, Morrow, 1956.

FORSTER, E. M. *Goldsworthy Lowes Dickinson.* London, Arnold, 1934.

FOWLER, W. B. *British American Relations, 1917–1918: The Role of Sir William Wiseman.* Princeton, Princeton University Press, 1969.

FYFE, HAMILTON. *Sixty Years of Fleet Street.* London, Allen, 1949.

GIBBS, PHILIP. *Adventures in Journalism.* New York, Harper, 1923.

GILBERT, BENTLEY B. *The Evolution of National Insurance in Great Britain.* London, M. Joseph, 1966.

GILBERT, MARTIN. *The Roots of Appeasement.* London, Weidenfeld & Nicolson, 1966.

GOLLIN, A. M. *The Observer and J. L. Garvin.* London, Oxford University Press, 1960. *Proconsul in Politics.* New York, Macmillan, 1964.

GOOCH, G. P. *Under Six Reigns.* London, Longmans, 1959.

GORDON, MICHAEL R. *Conflict and Consensus in Labour's Foreign Policy, 1914–1965.* Stanford, Stanford University Press, 1969.

GROSS, JOHN. *The Rise and Fall of the Man of Letters.* London, Weidenfeld & Nicolson, 1969.

HALE, JAMES ORON. *Publicity and Diplomacy.* Gloucester, Mass., 1964.

HALÉVY, ELIE. *Imperialism and the Rise of Labour, 1895–1905.* New York, P. Smith, 1961. *The Rule of Democracy, 1905–1914.* New York, P. Smith, 1961.

HAMMOND, J. L. *C. P. Scott of the Manchester Guardian.* London, Bell, 1934.

HARDY, G. H. *Bertrand Russell and Trinity,* Cambridge, Cambridge University Press, 1970.

HARRIS, H. WILSON. *The Daily Press.* Cambridge, Cambridge University Press, 1943. *J. A. Spender.* London, Cassell, 1946. *Life So Far.* London, Cape, 1954.

HARROD, R. F. *The Life of John Maynard Keynes.* New York, Harcourt, 1951.

HAZLEHURST, CAMERON. *Politicians at War.* New York, Knopf, 1971,

HERD, HAROLD. *The Making of Modern Journalism.* London, Allen & Unwin, 1927. *The March of Journalism.* London, Macmillan, 1952.

HIRST, F. W. *In the Golden Days.* London, Muller, 1947.

HOFSTADTER, R. *The Age of Reform: from Bryan to F.D.R.* New York, Knopf, 1955.

HOUGH, RICHARD. *First Sea Lord.* London, Allen, 1969.

HOUSE, E. M. *The Intimate Papers of Colonel House* (ed. Charles Seymour). 4 vols, Boston, Houghton Mifflin, 1926–8.

HUDSON, DEREK. *British Journalists and Newspapers.* London, Collins, 1945.

HYNES, SAMUEL. *The Edwardian Turn of Mind.* Princeton, Princeton University Press, 1968.

JAMES, ROBERT RHODES. *Rosebery.* London, Weidenfeld & Nicolson, 1963.

JENKINS, ROY. *Asquith.* London, Collins, 1964.

JONES, KENNEDY. *Fleet Street and Downing Street.* London, Hutchinson, 1919.

JONES, THOMAS. *Whitehall Diary* (ed. Keith Middlemas). Vol. i. London, Oxford University Press, 1969.

KELLEY, ROBERT. *The Transatlantic Persuasion.* New York, Knopf, 1969.

KENT, WILLIAM. *John Burns: Labour's Lost Leader*. London, Williams & Norgate, 1950.

KOSS, STEPHEN E. *John Morley at the India Office, 1905–1910*. New Haven, Yale University Press, 1969. *Lord Haldane: Scapegoat for Liberalism*. New York, Columbia University Press, 1969. *Sir John Brunner, Radical Plutocrat*. Cambridge, Cambridge University Press, 1970.

LINK, ARTHUR S. *Wilson: Campaigns for Progressivism and Peace, 1916–1917*. Princeton, Princeton University Press, 1965.

LLOYD GEORGE, DAVID. *War Memoirs*. 2 vols, London, Nicholson & Watson, 1934? *Is it Peace?*, pamphlet, London, 1923.

LUCAS, E. V. *Reading, Writing, and Remembering*. London, Methuen, 1932.

LYND, ROBERT. *Books and Writers*. London, Dent, 1952. *Essays on Life and Literature*. London, Dent, 1951.

LYONS, F. S. L. *John Dillon*. London, Routledge, 1958.

MC CARTHY, JUSTIN and ROBINSON, SIR JOHN R. *The 'Daily News' Jubilee*. London, Low, Marston, 1896.

MACCOBY, S. *English Radicalism, 1853–1886*. London, Allen & Unwin, 1938. *English Radicalism, 1886–1914*. London, Allen, 1953. *The English Radical Tradition, 1763–1914*. New York, New York University Press, 1957.

MANCHESTER PRESS CLUB. *Fifty Years of Us*. Manchester, 1922.

MARDER, ARTHUR J. *From the Dreadnought to Scapa Flow*. Vol. i. London, Oxford University Press, 1961.

MARSHALL, ARCHIBALD. *Out and About*. London, Murray, 1933.

MARTIN, L. W. *Peace Without Victory: Woodrow Wilson and the British Liberals*. New Haven, Yale University Press, 1958.

MARTIN, KINGSLEY. *Editor*. London, Hutchinson, 1968.

MASTERMAN, LUCY. *C. F. G. Masterman*. London, Cass, 1968.

MAY, ERNEST R. *The World War and American Isolation, 1914–1917*. Cambridge, Mass., Harvard University Press, 1959.

MAYER, ARNO. *Political Origins of the New Diplomacy, 1917–1918*. New Haven, Yale University Press, 1959. *Politics and Diplomacy of Peacemaking*. New York, Knopf, 1967.

MILLS, J. SAXON. *Sir Edward Cook, K.B.E.* London, Constable, 1921.

MONGER, GEORGE. *The End of Isolation*. London, Nelson, 1963.

MORAN, LORD. *Winston Churchill: The struggle for survival*. London, Constable, 1966.

MORLEY, JOHN, VISCOUNT. *Memorandum on Resignation*. New York, Macmillan, 1928. *Recollections*. 2 vols, New York, Macmillan, 1917.

MORRIS, A. J. ANTHONY. *Radicalism Against War, 1906–1914*. London, Longman, 1972.

NEVINSON, H. W. *Changes and Chances*. London, Nisbet, 1923. *Last*

Changes, Last Chances. New York, Harcourt, 1929. *More Changes, More Chances.* London, Nisbet, 1925.

NICOLSON, SIR HAROLD. *Diaries and Letters* (ed. N. Nicolson), Vol. i. London, Collins, 1966.

NOWELL-SMITH, SIMON, ed. *Edwardian England, 1901–1914.* London, Oxford University Press, 1964.

O'CONNOR, T. P. *Memoirs of an Old Parliamentarian.* 2 vols, London, Benn, 1929.

OSGOOD, R. E. *Ideals and Self-interest in America's Foreign Relations,* University of Chicago Press, 1953.

OWEN, FRANK. *Tempestuous Journey.* London, Hutchinson, 1954.

PELLING, HENRY. *Popular Politics and Society in Late Victorian Britain.* New York, St Martin's, 1968.

PHILLIPPS, VIVIAN. *My Days and Ways.* London, privately published, 1943?

PINSHAW, LEWIS. *Helps to the Study of 'Selected Essays' from 'Alpha of the Plough'.* Capetown and Johannesburg, Juta and Co., 1925.

POPE, WILSON, and others. *The Story of the 'Star', 1888–1938.* London, 1938.

PORTER, BERNARD. *Critics of Empire.* London, Macmillan, 1968.

POUND, REGINALD. *Arnold Bennett.* New York, Harcourt, 1953; and Geoffrey Harmsworth. *Northcliffe.* London, Cassell, 1959.

PRICE, R. G. G. *A History of Punch.* London, Collins, 1957.

RAE, JOHN. *Conscience and Politics.* Oxford, Oxford University Press, 1970.

RAPPAPORT, ARMIN. *The British Press and Wilsonian Neutrality.* Stanford, Stanford University Press, 1951.

RIDDELL, LORD. *Intimate Diary of the Peace Conference and After.* London, Gollancz, 1933. *Lord Riddell's War Diary.* London, Nicholson & Watson, 1933? *More Pages from My Diary.* London, Country Life, 1934.

ROBBINS, KEITH. *Sir Edward Grey.* London, Cassell, 1971.

ROBBINS, LORD. *Autobiography of an Economist.* London, Macmillan, 1971.

ROSKILL, STEPHEN. *Hankey, Man of Secrets.* Vol. i. London, Collins, 1970.

SCOTT, C. P. *Political Diaries, 1911–1928* (ed. Trevor Wilson). London, Collins, 1970.

SCOTT, J. W. ROBERTSON. *The Life and Death of a Newspaper.* London, Methuen, 1952.

SEYMOUR-URE, COLIN. *The Press, Politics and the Public.* London, Methuen, 1968.

Bibliography

SHARMA, DIWAN CHANDRA. 'A.G.G.: an appreciation', *Hindustan Review*, 1 (1926), 31–5.

SIMONIS, H. *Street of Ink*. London, Cassell, 1917.

SNOWDEN, PHILIP. *An Autobiography*. 2 vols, London, Nicholson & Watson, 1934.

SPEAIGHT, ROBERT. *The Life of Hilaire Belloc*. London, Hollis & Carter, 1957.

SPENDER, HAROLD. *The Fire of Life*. London, Hodder & Stoughton, 1926. *The Prime Minister*. New York, Doran, 1920.

SPENDER, J. A. *The Life of the Rt. Hon. Sir Henry Campbell-Bannerman*. 2 vols, London, Hodder & Stoughton, 1924. *Life, Journalism and Politics*. 2 vols, New York, Stokes, 1927. *The Public Life*. 2 vols, London, Cassell, 1925; and Cyril Asquith. *The Life of Lord Oxford and Asquith*. 2 vols, London, Hutchinson, 1932.

STANNARD, RUSSELL. *With the Dictators of Fleet Street*. London, Hutchinson, 1934.

STANSKY, PETER. *Ambitions and Strategies*. Oxford, Oxford University Press, 1964.

STEED, WICKHAM. *Journalism*. London, Benn, 1928. *The Press*. Harmondsworth, Penguin, 1938. *Through Thirty Years*. 2 vols, Garden City, N.Y., Doubleday, 1925.

STEVENSON, FRANCES. *Lloyd George: a Diary by Frances Stevenson* (ed. A. J. P. Taylor). London, Hutchinson, 1971.

STUTTERHEIM, KURT VON. *The Press in England*. London, Allen, 1934.

SWARTZ, MARVIN. *The Union of Democratic Control in British Politics during the First World War*. Oxford, Oxford University Press, 1971.

STEINER, ZARA K. *The Foreign Office and Foreign Policy, 1898–1914*. Cambridge, Cambridge University Press, 1969.

SWINNERTON, FRANK. *Background with Chorus*. London, Hutchinson, 1956. *Figures in the Foreground*. Garden City, N.Y., Doubleday, 1964. *The Georgian Literary Scene*. New York, Farrar & Rinehart, 1934. *Reflections from a Village*. London, Hutchinson, 1969. *Swinnerton: An Autobiography*. London, Hutchinson, 1937. *Tokefield Papers*. New York, Doran, 1927.

TAYLOR, A. J. P. *Beaverbrook*. London, Hamish Hamilton, 1972. *English History, 1914–1945*. Oxford, Oxford University Press, 1965. ed. *Lloyd George: Twelve Essays*. New York, Knopf, 1971. *Politics in Wartime*. London, Hamish Hamilton, 1964. *Struggle for the Mastery of Europe, 1848–1918*. Oxford, Clarendon Press, 1957. *The Troublemakers*. London, Hamish Hamilton, 1964.

TAYLOR, H. A. *Robert Donald*. London, Paul, 1934.

Bibliography

WARD, MAISIE. *Gilbert Keith Chesterton*. New York, Sheed & Ward, 1943.

WEBB, BEATRICE. *Diaries* (ed. Margaret Cole). 2 vols, London, Longmans, 1952, 1956. *Our Partnership*. London, Longmans, 1948.

WEBB, ROBERT. *Harriet Martineau*. London, Heinemann, 1960.

WEINROTH, HOWARD S. 'The British Radicals and balance of power, 1902–1914', *Historical Journal*, xiii (1970), 653–82.

WELLS, H. G. *Experiment in Autobiography*. New York, Macmillan, 1934.

WILLIAMS, WALTER. 'Organization of Journalists in Great Britain'. *University of Missouri Bulletin*. xxx (1929). Journalism Series No. 58.

WILLIS, IRENE COOPER. *How We Came Out of the War*. London, National Labour Press, 1921. *How We Got On with the War*. Manchester, National Labour Press, 1920. *How We Went Into the War*. Manchester, National Labour Press, 1919. (Three volumes reprinted as one, *England's Holy War*, with introduction by J. A. Hobson, New York, 1928).

WILSON, TREVOR. *The Downfall of the Liberal Party, 1914–1945*. London, Collins, 1966.

WINKLER, H. R. *The League of Nations Movement in Great Britain*. Methuen, N.J., Rutgers University Press, 1967.

SERIAL PUBLICATIONS

The British Weekly
The Daily Mail
The Daily News
John Bull
Journal of the Institute of Journalists (London)
Manchester Guardian
The Nation
The Northern Daily Telegraph and *Weekly Telegraph* (Blackburn)
The Passing Show
The Review of Reviews
The Star
Parliamentary Debates (Hansard)

Index

Index

dines, 124, 128, 131–2; applauds Gardiner, 163, 290; praises Beaverbrook, 246, 291; urges Gardiner to go into Parliament, 270; mentioned, 127, 280
Maurice Debate, 239
Maurice, Maj-Gen. Sir Frederick, 239, 240, 243, 244, 258, 259
Maxse, L. J., 9, 157, 216
McKenna, Reginald, Gardiner's dim view of, 95, 121; Gardiner's eventual ties to, 170, 175; as Chancellor of the Exchequer, 176, 179, 183, 188; loses seat, 253–4; mentioned, 68n, 230n
McNeill, Ronald (Baron Cushendun), 188
Meggy, Frederick Henry, 19
Melbourne, 2nd Viscount, 11
Methuen, A. M. M., 79
Mill, John Stuart, 69, 83
Mills, J. Saxon, 40, 41
Milne, A. A., 166
Milner, 1st Viscount (Sir Alfred Milner), praised by Cook, 32, 36; ignored by *DN*, 40; attacked by *DN*, 81, 138, 159, 180, 226–7, 229; mentioned, 80, 95, 178, 179, 236
Ministry of Munitions, 176
Mond, Sir Alfred (1st Baron Melchett), 136
Montagu, Edwin, 128
Montagu-Chelmsford Reforms, 241
Montague, C. E., 134
Morley, Arnold, 35, 37, 39
Morley, Dr E. S., 24
Morley, John (Viscount Morley of Blackburn), as a journalist, 11, 136; Gardiner reveres, 25, 28; connection with *DN*, 39, 40, 41, 42, 53, 90; as a Gladstonian, 80,

88; on the 1906 returns, 92–3; at the India Office, 95, 100, 128; and naval estimates, 122; at outbreak of war, 140, 151, 212; mentioned, 24, 297
Morley-Minto Reforms, 128
Morning Advertiser, 65
Morning Leader, 33, 65, 91, 165
Morning Post, 9, 63, 65, 94, 166–7, 171, 178, 200, 216, 221, 227, 231, 232, 233, 250
Morrell, Philip and Lady Ottoline, 168
Morrison, Herbert (Baron Morrison of Lambeth), 308
Murray, A. M., 239
Murray, Alexander, Master of Elibank (1st Baron Murray of Elibank), 129, 132
Murray, Gilbert, 150, 208, 241, 248, 251, 270–1

Nash, Vaughan, 32, 56, 57, 60, 97, 105, 127
Nation, founded, 33, 111; influence of, 107, 108; on Anglo-German relations, 121; on conscription, 178; its differences with Lloyd George, 199, 227, 231, 232, 236n, 262; on Gardiner's resignation and departure from *DN*, 267, 271, 291; Gardiner's letter to the editor, 292; Gardiner's weekly columns for, 5, 55, 294, 295–6, 300; changes hands, 295; mentioned, 9
Nation (New York), 279
National Anti-Sweating League, 77–8
National Committee for the Prevention of Destitution, 99
National Insurance, 130

Index